Integration Challenges for Analytics, Business Intelligence, and Data Mining

Ana Azevedo
CEOS.PP, ISCAP, Polytechnic of Porto, Portugal

Manuel Filipe Santos
Algoritmi Centre, University of Minho, Guimarães, Portugal

A volume in the Advances in Business Information
Systems and Analytics (ABISA) Book Series

Published in the United States of America by
IGI Global
Engineering Science Reference (an imprint of IGI Global)
701 E. Chocolate Avenue
Hershey PA, USA 17033
Tel: 717-533-8845
Fax: 717-533-8661
E-mail: cust@igi-global.com
Web site: http://www.igi-global.com

Library of Congress Cataloging-in-Publication Data

Names: Azevedo, Ana, editor. | Santos, Manuel Filipe, editor.
Title: Integration challenges for analytics, business intelligence, and
  data mining / Ana Azevedo and Manuel Filipe Santos, editors.
Description: Hershey : Engineering Science Reference, 2020. | Includes
  bibliographical references and index. | Summary: "This book provides
  insights concerning the integration of data mining in business
  intelligence and analytics systems, increasing the understanding of
  using data mining in the context of business intelligence and
  analytics"-- Provided by publisher.
Identifiers: LCCN 2020018689 (print) | LCCN 2020018690 (ebook) | ISBN
  9781799857815 (hardcover) | ISBN 9781799857822 (paperback) | ISBN
  9781799857839 (ebook)
Subjects: LCSH: Business enterprises--Data processing. | Business
  intelligence. | Data mining.
Classification: LCC HF5548.2 .I45368 2020 (print) | LCC HF5548.2 (ebook)
  | DDC 658.4/72--dc23
LC record available at https://lccn.loc.gov/2020018689
LC ebook record available at https://lccn.loc.gov/2020018690

This book is published in the IGI Global book series Advances in Business Information Systems and Analytics (ABISA)
(ISSN: 2327-3275; eISSN: 2327-3283)

British Cataloguing in Publication Data
A Cataloguing in Publication record for this book is available from the British Library.

All work contributed to this book is new, previously-unpublished material. The views expressed in this book are those of the
authors, but not necessarily of the publisher.

For electronic access to this publication, please contact: eresources@igi-global.com.

Advances in Business Information Systems and Analytics (ABISA) Book Series

Madjid Tavana
La Salle University, USA

ISSN:2327-3275
EISSN:2327-3283

MISSION

The successful development and management of information systems and business analytics is crucial to the success of an organization. New technological developments and methods for data analysis have allowed organizations to not only improve their processes and allow for greater productivity, but have also provided businesses with a venue through which to cut costs, plan for the future, and maintain competitive advantage in the information age.

The **Advances in Business Information Systems and Analytics (ABISA) Book Series** aims to present diverse and timely research in the development, deployment, and management of business information systems and business analytics for continued organizational development and improved business value.

COVERAGE

- Legal information systems
- Data Governance
- Big Data
- Statistics
- Decision Support Systems
- Business Decision Making
- Performance Metrics
- Management Information Systems
- Business Process Management
- Geo-BIS

IGI Global is currently accepting manuscripts for publication within this series. To submit a proposal for a volume in this series, please contact our Acquisition Editors at Acquisitions@igi-global.com or visit: http://www.igi-global.com/publish/.

Titles in this Series

For a list of additional titles in this series, please visit:
http://www.igi-global.com/book-series/advances-business-information-systems-analytics/37155

Managing Business in the Civil Construction Sector Through Information Communication Technologies
Bithal Das Mundhra (Simplex Infrastructures Ltd, India) and Rajesh Bose (Simplex Infrastructures Ltd, India)
Business Science Reference ● © 2021 ● 254pp ● H/C (ISBN: 9781799852919) ● US $195.00

Achieving Organizational Agility, Intelligence, and Resilience Through Information Systems
Hakikur Rahman (Institute of Computer Management and Science, Bangladesh)
Business Science Reference ● © 2021 ● 300pp ● H/C (ISBN: 9781799847991) ● US $195.00

Handbook of Research on User Experience in Web 2.0 Technologies and Its Impact on Universities and Businesses
Jean-Éric Pelet (ESCE International Business School, INSEEC U Research Center, Paris, France)
Business Science Reference ● © 2021 ● 426pp ● H/C (ISBN: 9781799837565) ● US $295.00

Empowering Businesses With Collaborative Enterprise Architecture Frameworks
Tiko Iyamu (Cape Peninsula University of Technology, South Africa)
Business Science Reference ● © 2021 ● 309pp ● H/C (ISBN: 9781522582298) ● US $195.00

Natural Language Processing for Global and Local Business
Fatih Pinarbasi (Istanbul Medipol University, Turkey) and M. Nurdan Taskiran (Istanbul Medipol University, Turkey)
Business Science Reference ● © 2021 ● 452pp ● H/C (ISBN: 9781799842408) ● US $225.00

Applications of Big Data and Business Analytics in Management
Sneha Kumari (Vaikunth Mehta National Institute of Cooperative Management, India) K. K. Tripathy (Vaikunth Mehta National Institute of Cooperative Management, India) and Vidya Kumbhar (Symbiosis International University (Deemed), India)
Business Science Reference ● © 2020 ● 300pp ● H/C (ISBN: 9781799832614) ● US $225.00

Handbook of Research on Integrating Industry 4.0 in Business and Manufacturing
Isak Karabegović (Academy of Sciences and Arts of Bosnia and Herzegovina, Bosnia and Herzegovina) Ahmed Kovačević (City, University London, UK) Lejla Banjanović-Mehmedović (University of Tuzla, Bosnia and Herzegovina) and Predrag Dašić (High Technical Mechanical School of Professional Studies in Trstenik, Serbia)
Business Science Reference ● © 2020 ● 661pp ● H/C (ISBN: 9781799827252) ● US $265.00

Internet of Things (IoT) Applications for Enterprise Productivity
Erdinç Koç (Bingol University, Turkey)
Business Science Reference ● © 2020 ● 357pp ● H/C (ISBN: 9781799831754) ● US $215.00

701 East Chocolate Avenue, Hershey, PA 17033, USA
Tel: 717-533-8845 x100 ● Fax: 717-533-8661
E-Mail: cust@igi-global.com ● www.igi-global.com

Table of Contents

Section 3
Modelling Issues

Section 4
Software and Security

Detailed Table of Contents

Section 1
Background and Literature Review

Ana Azevedo, CEOS.PP, ISCAP, Polytechnic of Porto, Portugal

From the middle of this second decade of the 21st century, analytics has become commonly associated with the topics business intelligence and data mining. Data mining (DM) is being applied with success in business intelligence (BI) environments and several examples of applications can be found. BI and DM have different roots and, as a consequence, have significantly different characteristics. DM came up from scientific environments; thus, it is not business oriented. DM tools still demand heavy work in order to obtain the intended results. On the contrary, BI is rooted in industry and business. As a result, BI tools are user-friendly. This chapter reflects on these differences from a historical perspective. Starting with a separated historical perspective of each one, analytics, BI, and DM, the author then discusses how they converged when DM is used and integrated in BI environments with success.

Atik Kulakli, American University of the Middle East, Kuwait

The purpose of this chapter is to analyze and explore the research studies for scholarly publication trends and patterns related to the integration of data mining in particular business intelligence in big data analytics domains published in the period of 2010-2019. Research patterns explore in highly prestigious sources that have high impact factors and citations counted in the ISI Web of Science Core Collection database (indexes included SCI-Exp and SSCI). Bibliometric analysis methods applied for this study under the research limitations. Research questions formed based on bibliometric principles concentrating fields such as descriptive of publication, author productivity, country-regions distribution, keyword analysis with contribution among researchers, citation analysis, co-citation patterns searched. Findings showed strong relations and patterns on these important research domains. Besides this chapter would useful for researchers to obtain an overview of publication trends on research domains to be concerned for further studies and shows the potential gaps in those fields.

Chapter 3

Boundaries between business intelligence (BI), big data (BD), and big data analytics (BDA) are often unclear and ambiguous for companies. BD is a new research challenge; it is becoming a subject of growing importance. Notably, BD was one of the big buzzwords during the last decade. BDA can help executive managers to plan an organization's short-term and long-term goals. Furthermore, BI is considered as a kind of decision support system (DSS) that can help organizations achieving their goals, creating corporate value and improving organizational performance. This chapter provides a comprehensive view about the interrelationships between BI, BD, and BDA. Moreover, the chapter highlights the power of analytics that make them considered as one of the highly impact's organizational capability. Additionally, the chapter can help executive managers to decide the way to integrate BD initiatives as a tool, or as an industry, or as a corporate strategy transformation.

Section 2
Big Data Issues

Chapter 4

Study of data quality for data mining application has always been a complex topic; in the recent years, this topic has gained further complexity with the advent of big data as the source for data mining and business intelligence (BI) applications. In a big data environment, data is consumed in various states and various forms serving as input for data mining, and this is the main source of added complexity. These new complexities and challenges arise from the underlying dimensions of big data (volume, variety, velocity, and value) together with the ability to consume data at various stages of transition from raw data to standardized datasets. These have created a need for expanding the traditional data quality (DQ) factors into BDQ (big data quality) factors besides the need for new BDQ assessment and measurement frameworks for data mining and BI applications. However, very limited advancement has been made in research and industry in the topic of BDQ and their relevance and criticality for data mining and BI applications. Data quality in data mining refers to the quality of the patterns or results of the models built using mining algorithms. DQ for data mining in business intelligence applications should be aligned with the objectives of the BI application. Objective measures, training/modeling approaches, and subjective measures are three major approaches that exist to measure DQ for data mining. However, there is no agreement yet on definitions or measurements or interpretations of DQ for data mining. Defining the factors of DQ for data mining and their measurement for a BI system has been one of the major challenges for researchers as well as practitioners. This chapter provides an overview of existing research in the area of BDQ definitions and measurement for data mining for BI, analyzes the gaps therein, and provides a direction for future research and practice in this area.

Chapter 5

Mohammad Daradkeh, Yarmouk University, Irbid, Jordan

The data lake has recently emerged as a scalable architecture for storing, integrating, and analyzing massive data volumes characterized by diverse data types, structures, and sources. While the data lake plays a key role in unifying business intelligence, analytics, and data mining in an enterprise, effective implementation of an enterprise-wide data lake for business intelligence and analytics integration is associated with a variety of practical challenges. In this chapter, concrete analytics projects of a globally industrial enterprise are used to identify existing practical challenges and drive requirements for enterprise data lakes. These requirements are compared with the extant literature on data lake technologies and management to identify research gaps in analytics practice. The comparison shows that there are five major research gaps: 1) unclear data modelling methods, 2) missing data lake reference architecture, 3) incomplete metadata management strategy, 4) incomplete data lake governance strategy, and 5) missing holistic implementation and integration strategy.

Section 3
Modelling Issues

Chapter 6

Roumiana Ilieva, Technical University of Sofia, Bulgaria
Malinka Ivanova, Technical University of Sofia, Bulgaria
Tzvetilina Peycheva, IBS, Bulgaria
Yoto Nikolov, Technical University of Sofia, Bulgaria

Modelling in support of decision making in business intelligence (BI) starts with exploring the BI systems, driven by artificial intelligence (AI). The purpose why AI will be the core of next-gen analytics and why BI will be empowered by it are determined. The role of AI and machine learning (ML) in business processes automation is analyzed. The benefits from AI integration in BI platforms are summarized. Then analysis goes through predictive modeling in the domain of e-commerce. The use of ML for predictive modeling is overviewed. Construction of predictive and clustering models is proposed. After that the importance of self-services in BI platforms is outlined. In this context the self-service BI is defined and what are the key steps to create successful self-service BI model are sketched. The effects of potential threads which are the results of the big data in the business world are examined and some suggestions for the future have been made. Lastly, game-changer trends in BI and future research directions are traced.

Chapter 7

Walisson Ferreira Carvalho, Centro Universitario Una, Brazil
Luis Zarate, Pontificia Universidade Catolica de Minas Gerais, Brazil

Feature selection is a process of the data preprocessing task in business intelligence (BI), analytics, and data mining that urges for new methods that can handle with high dimensionality. One alternative that have been researched to deal with the curse of dimensionality is causal feature selection. Causal feature selection is not based on correlation, but the causality relationship among variables. The main goal of this chapter is to present, based on the issues identified on other methods, a new strategy that considers attributes beyond those that compounds the Markov blanket of a node and calculate the causal effect to ensure the causality relationship.

Chapter 8

Abdelaziz Elbaghdadi, Abdelmalek Essaadi University, Morocco
Soufiane Mezroui, Abdelmalek Essaadi University, Morocco
Ahmed El Oualkadi, Abdelmalek Essaadi University, Morocco

The cryptocurrency is the first implementation of blockchain technology. This technology provides a set of tracks and innovation in scientific research, such as use of data either to detect anomalies either to predict price in the Bitcoin and the Ethereum. Furthermore, the blockchain technology provide a set of technique to automate the business process. This chapter presents a review of some research works related to cryptocurrency. A model with a KNN algorithm is proposed to detect illicit transaction. The proposed model uses both the elliptic dataset and KNN algorithm to detect illicit transaction. Furthermore, the elliptic dataset contains 203,769 nodes and 234,355 edges; it allows to classify the data into three classes: illicit, licit, or unknown. Each node has associated 166 features. The first 94 features represent local information about the transaction. The remaining 72 features are called aggregated features. The accuracy exceeded 90% with k=2 and k=4, the recall reaches 56% with k=3, and the precision reaches 78% with k=4.

Section 4
Software and Security

Chapter 9

Ângela Alpoim, University of Minho, Portugal
João Lopes, University of Minho, Portugal
Tiago Guimarães, University of Minho, Portugal
Carlos Filipe Portela, University of Minho, Portugal
Manuel Filipe Santos, University of Minho, Portugal

A huge growth in data and information needs has led organizations to search for the most appropriate data integration tools for different types of business. The management of a large dataset requires the exploitation of appropriate resources, new methods, as well as the possession of powerful technologies. That led the surge of numerous ideas, technologies, and tools offered by different suppliers. For this reason, it is important to understand the key factors that determine the need to invest in a big data project and then categorize these technologies to simplify the choice that best fits the context of their problem. The objective of this study is to create a model that will serve as a basis for evaluating the different alternatives and solutions capable of overcoming the major challenges of data integration. Finally, a brief analysis of three major data fabric solutions available on the market is also carried out, including Talend Data Fabric, IBM Infosphere, and Informatica Platform.

Chapter 10

    Sabyasachi Pramanik, Haldia Institute of Technology, India
    Ramkrishna Ghosh, Haldia Institute of Technology, India
    Mangesh M. Ghonge, Sandip Institute of Technology and Research Centre, India
    Vipul Narayan, MMM Collage, Gorakhpur, India
    Mudita Sinha, CHRIST University (Deemed), India
    Digvijay Pandey, Department of Technical Education, India & IET, India
    Debabrata Samanta, CHRIST University (Deemed), India

In the information technology community, communication is a vital issue. And image transfer creates a major role in the communication of data through various insecure channels. Security concerns may forestall the direct sharing of information and how these different gatherings cooperatively direct data mining without penetrating information security presents a challenge. Cryptography includes changing over a message text into an unintelligible figure and steganography inserts message into a spread media and shroud its reality. Both these plans are successfully actualized in images. To facilitate a safer transfer of image, many cryptosystems have been proposed for the image encryption scheme. This chapter proposes an innovative image encryption method that is quicker than the current researches. The secret key is encrypted using an asymmetric cryptographic algorithm and it is embedded in the ciphered image using the LSB technique. Statistical analysis of the proposed approach shows that the researcher's approach is faster and has optimal accuracy.

Preface

Nowadays the analysis of the data being held in the databases of the organizations and in eternal sources, plays a fundamental role in those organizations. Analytics, thus, arises as an issue of big importance for organizations. Davenport & Harris (2017 – pp 7) define Analytics as "the extensive use of data, statistical and quantitative analysis, explanatory and predictive models, and fact-based management to drive decision and actions." INFORMS defines analytics as the scientific process of transforming data into insights with the purpose of making better decisions. Usually, there can be considered three types of analytics, namely Descriptive, Predictive, and Prescriptive Analytics (Sharda, Delen & Turban, 2018). Descriptive Analytics refers to knowing what happened and what is happening in organizations and perceiving some underlying trends and the causes of such occurrences. Predictive analytics aims to determine what is likely to happen in the future. Prescriptive Analytics aims to recognize what is happening as well as the most likely predictions and make decisions to achieve the best performance. These three levels of Analytics are not exclusive, overlapping each other many times. From the middle of this second decade of the XXI century, Descriptive Analytics has become commonly associated with the topic Business Intelligence and prescriptive Analytics with the topic Data Mining. Davenport & Harris (2017) also consider another type of Analytics, namely autonomous analytics, which refers to the application of Artificial Intelligence to improve and learn from data.

Business Intelligence (BI) is one area of the Decision Support Systems (DSS) discipline and refers to information systems aimed at integrating structured and unstructured data in order to convert it into useful information and knowledge, upon which business managers can make more informed and consequently better decisions. Being rooted in the DSS discipline, BI has suffered a considerable evolution over the last years and is, nowadays, an area of DSS that attracts a great deal of interest from both the industry and researchers. A BI system is a particular type of system. One of the main aspects is that of user-friendly tools, that makes systems truly available to the final business user.

The term Knowledge Discovery in Databases (KDD) was coined in 1989 to refer to the broad process of finding knowledge in data, and to emphasize the "high-level" application of particular data mining (DM) methods (Fayyad, Piatetski-Shapiro & Smyth, 1996). The DM phase concerns, mainly, to the means by which patterns are extracted and enumerated from data. DM has several successful applications in many diversified fields.

DM is being implemented with success in BI and several examples of applications can be found. Despite that efforts are being made for the integration of DM in BI systems, DM has not yet reached to non-specialized users and thus it is not yet completely integrated with BI. Powerful analytical tools, such as DM, remain too complex and sophisticated for the average consumer of BI systems. McKnight supports that bringing DM to the front line business personnel will increase their potential to attaining

BI's high potential business value (McKnight, 2002). Another fundamental issue that is pointed out by McKnight is the capability of DM tools to be interactive, visual, and understandable, to work directly on the data, and to be used by frontline workers for intermediate and lasting business benefits. Currently, DM systems are functioning as separate isles, and hereby it is considered that only the full integration of the KDD process on BI can conduct to an effective usage of DM in BI (Azevedo & Santos, 2011). This book presents several interesting applications, for instance in healthcare systems, in finance as well as web and text mining applications.

Three main reasons can be pointed out for DM to be not completely integrated with BI, each one leading to a specific problem that constraints DM usage in BI. Firstly, the models/patterns obtained from DM are complex and there is the need of an analysis from a DM specialist. This fact can lead to a non-effective adoption of DM in BI, being that DM is not really integrated on most of the implemented BI systems, nowadays. Secondly, the problem with DM is that there is not a user-friendly tool that can be used by decision makers to analyze DM models. Usually, BI systems have user-friendly analytical tools that help decision makers in order to obtain insights on the available data and allow them to take better decisions. Examples of such tools are On-Line Analytical Processing (OLAP) tools, which are widely used. There are not equivalent tools for DM that allow business users to obtain insights in DM models. Finally, but extremely important, it has not been given sufficient emphasis to the development of solutions that allow the specification of DM problems through business oriented languages, and that are also oriented for BI activities. With the expansion that has occurred in the application of DM solutions in BI, this is, currently, of increasing importance. BI systems are, usually, built on top of relational databases and diverse types of languages are involved. As a consequence, DM integration with relational databases is an important issue to consider when studying DM integration with BI. Codd´s relational model for database systems (Codd, 1970; Codd, 1982) has been adopted long ago in organizations. One of the reasons for the great success of relational databases is related with the existence of a standard language – Structured Query Language (SQL). SQL allows business users to obtain quick answers to ad-hoc business questions, through queries on the data stored in databases. SQL is nowadays included in all the Relational Database Management Systems (RDBMS). SQL serves as the core above which are constructed the various Graphical User Interfaces (GUI) and user friendly languages, such as Query-By-Example (QBE), included in RDBMS. It is also necessary to define a standard language, which can operate likewise for DM. Several approaches have been proposed for the definition of DM languages. In the literature there can be found some language specifications, namely, DMQL (Han, Fu, Wang, Koperski & Zaiane, 1996), MINE RULE (Meo, Psaila & Ceri, 1998), MSQL (Imielinski & Virmani, 1999), SPQL (Bonchi, Giannotti, Lucchesse, Orlando, Perego & Trasarti, 2007), KDDML (Romei, Ruggieri & Turini, 2006), XDM (Meo & Psaila, 2006), RDM (De Raedt, 2002), QMBE (Azevedo & Santos, 2012), among others.

DM integration with BI systems can be tackled from different perspectives. On the one hand, it can be considered that the effective integration of DM with BI systems must involve final business users' access to DM models. This access is crucial in order to business users to develop an understanding of the models, to help them in decision making (Azevedo & Santos, 2012; Azevedo & Santos 2011). On the other hand, a different approach can be considered, through the outgrowth of new strategies that allow business users and DM specialists developing new communication strategies. Wang and Wang introduce a model that allows knowledge sharing among business insiders and DM specialists (Wang & Wang, 2008). It is argued that this model can make DM more relevant to BI. This book presents both perspectives.

Some efforts are being made seeking the establishment of standards in the DM area, both by academics, and by people in the industry field. Above all, the academic efforts towards a theory for DM and KDD follow closely the theory developed by Codd for the Relational Model. The main goal is to integrate DM with relational databases, thus allowing an easier application of DM to business systems, and making it more available to decision making. This also represents an important aspect to the integration of DM with BI systems. An important issue in this domain concerns DM languages, which were already discussed in this preface. Some of the efforts in the industrial field concern the definition of processes/methodologies that can guide the implementation of DM applications. For instance, SEMMA and CRISP-DM can be pointed out as such examples. Other efforts in the industrial field focus on the development of software suites for implementing some selected DM algorithms. There are also some efforts being made that intend to develop standards that will allow model representation to be platform independent. Nowadays, with the emergence of Big Data the focus starts to shift for, as can be seen in this book. The effective and efficient integration of Big Data in BI systems, and the analysis of Big Data with DM techniques are the big challenges for the future. Analytics is now accepted as the focus for researchers, and BI and DM can be seen as subfields of the field Analytics.

Despite new challenges are always to be find, we consider that the integration of DM in BI systems is a more mature field at the moment of the release of this publication, which includes both academic and industry perspectives.

The primary objective of this book is to provide insights concerning the topic of the integration of DM in business BI. This is a cutting-edge and important topic that deserves a significant approach, and this book is an excellent opportunity to do it. The book aims to provide the opportunity for a reflection on this important issue, increasing the understanding of using DM in the context of BI, providing relevant academic work, empirical research findings, and an overview of this relevant field of study. Professionals in the area of DM and BI, managers, researchers, academicians, practitioners, and graduate students, are the target of this book.

STRUCTURE OF THE BOOK

The book is constituted by 10 chapters divided into the four sections that together constitutes the book. Contributions come from several countries and from academics and people in the industry.

Section 1, "Background and Literature Review," includes three chapters. This first part aims to introduce some of the main aspects of the area approached in the book.

In Chapter 1, Ana Azevedo, presents a bibliometric comparative perspective of BI and DM. Starting from the analysis of the evolution of the number of scientific publications in DM, BI, and DM+BI, she defines historical generations that represent the evolution of the different paradigms for both fields, BI and DM.

In Chapter 2, Atik Kulakli, presents a research agenda, from 2010 to 2019, for the integration of DM and BI in Big Data Analytics. A bibliometric analysis is made and the author present the main profile of the publications, the main journals, the most relevant words, the most productive authors, institutions and countries, as well as a citation analysis.

Mouhib Alnoukari, in Chapter 3, presents an analysis of the relationship between BI, Big Data, and Big Data Analytics, emphasizing the power of analytics. It also reflects about the trends in Big Data adoption, which can help managers understanding the main issues to consider.

Section 2, "Big Data Issues," includes two chapters, that aim to reflect around the important aspects currently related to data, namely Big Data Quality, and Data Lakes.

In Chapter 4, Arun Thotapalli, presents a literature review of the important topic of Big Data Quality (BDQ) for DM in BI systems. The presentation of the main DQ measures that can be found in the literature, divided in three main categories (objective measures, subjective measures, and semantic measures), functions as the starting point to present the gaps that can be identified in this field of research. Following, the main approaches and frameworks for measuring DQ for DM are presented by the author and important research directions are recommended.

In Chapter 5, Mohammad Daradkeh, introduces the concept of Data Lakes. The main implementation approaches of Data Lakes implementation are developed, namely data modeling, Data Lake architecture, and metadata management. Next, practical challenges and research gaps are identified, and some recommendations are made.

Section 3, "Modelling Issues," includes three very interesting chapters about the modeling aspects.

Roumiana Ilieva, Malinka Ivanova, Tzvetilina Peycheva, and Yoto Nikolov, in Chapter 6, present the importance of data, and how to empower the self-service capabilities for the decision makers to analyze data and to find meaningful knowledge about their business, as well as how to model the data in such a way that the business users can embrace the opportunity to make data-driven decisions by themselves.

In Chapter 7, Walisson Ferreira Carvalho, and Luis Zarate, present their work which consisted in the merging of the two theories Theory of Causality, and Theory of Feature Selection to apply in the process of feature selection. This is an important step in the BI / DM / Analytics processes.

In Chapter 8, Abdelaziz Elbaghdadi, Soufiane Mezroui, and Ahmed El Oualkadi, introduce a model to detect illicit transactions in a blockchain environment. This can have several important applications in the context of BI and DM environments.

Section 4, "Software and Security," some issues related to software and security issues.

In Chapter 9 Ângela Alpoim, João Lopes, Tiago Guimarães, Carlos Filipe da Portela, and Manuel FIlipe Santos present a model for the evaluation of Big Data Integration Solutions, based on four types of metrics, namely, Ease of Integration and Implementation, Usability, Quality of Service and Support, and Costs. Case studies are introduced in order to show the use and relevance of the model for the process of choosing a big data fabric solution.

In Chapter 10, Sabyasachi Pramanik, Ramkrishna Ghosh, Mangesh M Ghonge, Vipul Narayan, Mudita Sinha, Digvijay Pandey, and Debabrata Samanta, describe a Novel Approach using Steganography and Cryptography to for image encryption. This represents a relevant issue, since expanding data assets are required to drive development in the business analysis and data mining.

CONCLUSION

This book presents a reflection about crucial issues concerning the integration of DM in BI systems. In this book, approaches, methodologies and applications are introduced, presenting important insights. Viewpoints from both the academic and the industry fields are included, which brings a deeper perceptiveness. All the papers included, represent important contributions to the development of the subject matter.

Nevertheless, we are aware that this work represents just the begging of a long path. Several research questions are still open to research, and several important business problems still remain to be resolved by the industry players. We consider that the research included in this book brings fundamental issues, which are very important to the development of the field, and can represent an impulse to this important area of research.

REFERENCES

Azevedo, A., & Santos, M. F. (2011). A Perspective on Data Mining Integration with Business Intelligence. In A. Kumar (Ed.), *Knowledge Discovery Practices and Emerging Applications of Data Mining: Trends and New Domains* (pp. 109–129). IGI Publishing. doi:10.4018/978-1-60960-067-9.ch006

Azevedo, A., & Santos, M. F. (2012). Closing the Gap between Data Mining and Business Users of Business Intelligence Systems: A Design Science Approach. *International Journal of Business Intelligence Research*, *3*(4), 14–53. doi:10.4018/jbir.2012100102

Bonchi, F., Giannotti, F., Lucchesse, C., Orlando, S., Perego, R., & Trasarti, R. (2007). On Interactive Pattern Mining from Relational Databases. In *Lecture Notes on Computer Science: Vol. 4747. Knowledge Discovery in Inductive Databases - 5th International Workshop, KDID 2006* (pp. 42-62). Berlin: Springer-Verlag. 10.1007/978-3-540-75549-4_4

Codd, E. F. (1970). A Relational Model of Data for Large Shared Data Banks. *Communications of the ACM*, *13*(6), 377–387. doi:10.1145/362384.362685

Codd, E. F. (1982). Relational Database: A Practical Foundation for Productivity. *Communications of the ACM*, *25*(2), 109–117. doi:10.1145/358396.358400

Davenport, T. H., & Harris, J. J. (2007). *Competing on analytics: the new science of winning*. Harvard Business Review Press.

De Raedt, L. (2002). Data Mining as Constraint Logic Programming. In Lecture Notes on Artificial Intelligence: Vol. 2408. Computational Logic: Logic Programming and Beyond - Essays in Honour of Robert A. kowalski - Part II (pp. 526-547). Berlin: Springer-Verlag. doi:10.1007/3-540-45632-5_20

Fayyad, U. M., Piatetski-Shapiro, G., & Smyth, P. (1996). From data mining to knowledge discovery: an overview. In U. M. Fayyad, G. Piatetski-Shapiro, P. Smyth, & R. Uthurusamy (Eds.), *Advances in knowledge discovery and data mining* (pp. 1–34). AAAI Press/The MIT Press.

Han, J., Fu, Y., Wang, W., Koperski, K., & Zaiane, O. (1996). DMQL: A Data Mining Query Language for Relational Databases. *Proceedings of the SIGMOD'96 Workshop on Research Issues on Data Mining and Knowledge Discovery (DMKD'96)*, 27-34.

Imielinski, T., & Virmani, A. (1999). MSQL: A Query Language for Database Mining. *Data Mining and Knowledge Discovery*, *3*(4), 373–408. doi:10.1023/A:1009816913055

McKnight, W. (2002). Bringing Data Mining to the Front Line, Part 1. *Information Management Magazine*. Retrieved on July, 16th 2009 at https://www.information-management.com/issues/20021101/5980-1.html

Meo, R., & Psaila, G. (2006). An XML-Based Database for Knowledge Discovery. In Lecture Notes in Computer Science: Vol. 4254. Current Trends in Database Technology - EDTB 2006 Workshops (pp. 814-828). Berlin: Springer-Verlag.

Meo, R., Psaila, G., & Ceri, S. (1998). An Extension to SQL for Mining Association Rules. *Data Mining and Knowledge Discovery*, 2(2), 195–224. doi:10.1023/A:1009774406717

Romei, A., Ruggieri, S., & Turini, F. (2006). KDDML: A Middleware Language and System for Knowledge Discovery in Databases. *Data & Knowledge Engineering*, 57(2), 179–220. doi:10.1016/j.datak.2005.04.007

Sharda, R., Delen, D., & Turban, E. (2018). *Business Intelligence, Analytics, and Data Science: a Managerial Perspective* (4th ed.). Pearson Education, Inc.

Wang, H., & Wang, S. (2008). A Knowledge Management Approach to Data Mining Process for Business Intelligence. *Industrial Management & Data Systems*, 108(5), 622–634. doi:10.1108/02635570810876750

Acknowledgment

To all the authors of the chapters, and to all the reviewers: we feel very much grateful with their collaboration with this project; without their work this could be not possible.

To all the members of the Publishing team at IGI: we are very much grateful for their help, expert support, and guidance.

Last but not the least, this book is dedicated to our respective families.

Section 1
Background and Literature Review

Chapter 1
Data Mining and Business Intelligence:
A Bibliometric Analysis

Ana Azevedo
https://orcid.org/0000-0003-0882-3426
CEOS.PP, ISCAP, Polytechnic of Porto, Portugal

ABSTRACT

From the middle of this second decade of the 21st century, analytics has become commonly associated with the topics business intelligence and data mining. Data mining (DM) is being applied with success in business intelligence (BI) environments and several examples of applications can be found. BI and DM have different roots and, as a consequence, have significantly different characteristics. DM came up from scientific environments; thus, it is not business oriented. DM tools still demand heavy work in order to obtain the intended results. On the contrary, BI is rooted in industry and business. As a result, BI tools are user-friendly. This chapter reflects on these differences from a historical perspective. Starting with a separated historical perspective of each one, analytics, BI, and DM, the author then discusses how they converged when DM is used and integrated in BI environments with success.

INTRODUCTION

Analytics represents a combination of computational technologies, scientific management techniques, and statistics to solve real-world problems, while considering that organizations have to analyze their data to understand what is happening, what will happen, and how to take the best option (Sharda, Delen & Turban, 2018). INFORMS defines analytics as the scientific process of transforming data into insights with the purpose of making better decisions. Usually, there can be considered three types of analytics, namely Descriptive, Predictive, and Prescriptive Analytics. Descriptive Analytics refers to knowing what happened and what is happening in organizations and perceiving some underlying trends and the causes of such occurrences. Predictive analytics aims to determine what is likely to happen in the future. Prescriptive Analytics aims to recognize what is happening as well as the most likely predictions

DOI: 10.4018/978-1-7998-5781-5.ch001

and make decisions to achieve the best performance. These three levels of Analytics are not exclusive, overlapping each other many times. From the middle of this second decade of the XXI century, Descriptive Analytics has become commonly associated with the topic Business Intelligence and prescriptive Analytics with the topic Data Mining.

BI is one area of the Decision Support Systems (DSS) discipline and refers to information systems aimed at integrating structured and unstructured data in order to convert it into useful information and knowledge, upon which business managers can make more informed and consequently better decisions. The term Business Intelligence (BI) was made popular by Gartner in 1989 (Power, 2007) (Zeller, 2007), but the first reference was made by Luhn in 1958 (Lunh, 1958), not necessarily with the same meaning. Being rooted in the DSS discipline, BI has suffered a considerable evolution over the last years and is, nowadays, an area of DSS that attracts a great deal of interest from both the industry and researchers (Azevedo & Santos, 2012).

The term Knowledge Discovery in Databases (KDD) was coined in 1989 (Wixon & Watson, 2010) to refer to the broad process of finding knowledge in data, and to emphasize the "high-level" application of particular data mining (DM) methods (Fayyad, Piatetski-Shapiro, & Smyth, 1996). The DM phase concerns, mainly, to the means by which patterns are extracted and enumerated from data. In recent years, DM has been applied with success to several diversified fields, such as bioinformatics, ecology and sustainability, finance, industry, marketing, scientific research, telecommunications, and several other applications, including BI.

DM is being applied with success in BI and several examples of applications can be found (Linoff, 2008) (Vercellis, 2009) (Hu & Cercone, 2004) (Cheung & Li, 2012) (Phan & Vogel, 2010). BI and DM have different roots and, as a consequence, have significantly different characteristics. DM came up from scientific environments, thus, in its roots, it is not business oriented (Kriegel, Borgwardt, Kröger, Pryakhin, Schubert, & Zimek, 2007) (Piatetsky-Shapiro, 2007). DM tools still demand heavy work in order to obtain the intended results, hence needing the knowledge of DM specialists to explore its full potencial value (Azevedo A., 2012). The main focus for DM researchers still is the improvement of algorithms and/or finding new algorithms that behaves better than others in some particular application, as can be recognized by a search in the main conferences and journal in the area of DM. On the contrary, BI is rooted in industry and business (Yermish, Miori, Yi, Malhotra, & Klimberg, 2010), thus it is business oriented. As a result, BI tools are user-friendly and can easily be accessed and manipulated by business users. The main focus for BI researchers is how to better use BI in organizations in order to improve decision making (Wixon & Watson, 2010).

Nevertheless, since the beginning of the second decade of the XXI century, DM and BI tend to converge. The gap existing between BI and DM is being filled (Azevedo & Santos, 2012) (Wang & Wang, 2008) (Hang & Fong, 2009). Researchers efforts are shifting towards the integration of DM in BI systens, and focusing on how DM can be used to improve decision making, and creating the possibility of DM tools being accessed and manipulated by business users at the same level as the other BI tools, thus making DM relevant to business. Analytics comes many times as a synonim of BI and both terms are used indistinguishably. At the beginning of the third decade of the XX1 century, we can see that the focus is now Big Data.

This papers presents DM and BI from a bibliometric comparative historical perspective. As far as our knowledge, there is no similar approach in the literature. The main contribution of this chapter is to provide a comparison between these different and yet convergent areas, from an historical perspective.

We consider that it is not possible to understand the present without knowing the past, thus this is an important issue to analyse.

The structure for the rest of the chapter is the following. Firstly Analytics is introduced. Following Business Intelligence is presented. Next, Data Mining is also presented. Finaly, Analytics, Data Mining and Business Inteligence are compared. The chapter ends with sections Future Research Directions and Conclusion.

Business Intelligence

The first reference to Business Intelligence was made by Luhn in 1958 (Lunh, 1958). In that article, Luhn describes a system whose main goal is to automately deliver the rigth documents, to the rigth "person" (which are named as "points of action"), at the right time. Since then, some articles can be found dealing with the topic but, like in the case of Lunh's article, not necessarily with the same meaning that is used nowadays. It is widely accepted that the current notion of Business Intelligence (BI) was coined by Howard Dresner, from Gartner, in 1989 (Power, 2007) (Zeller, 2007) (Wixon & Watson, 2010). From then on, BI gained popularity, firstly in business environments and latter in academia.

Figure 1 presents the evolution of the number of scientific publications with the topic Business Intelligence that can be found in the

"Web of Science – Core Collection"[1] between 1958 and 2019 (none can be found before that). As can be seen through the analysis of the graph, the number of scientific publications was insignificant until the year 2000, when the number of 20 annual publications was achieved, that is to say, more than one mensal publication. In 2007 the number of 121 annual publications was achieved and sustained after that. This is not much, mainly when compared with the more than one thousand annual publications in the area of DM achieved in 2002 and maintained after that (*Figure 2*). This reveals the low interest of the academic community in this topic of research.

The vast majority of the scientific publication in the topic BI is spread along several journals from computer science to information systems, business, and management. For instance, MIS Quarterly, which is recognized as one of the most influent journals in information systems, published an average of 9% BI publication between 1997 and 2006 (Jourdan, Rainer, & Marshall, 2008), which can be considered as an important rate. Even so, in 2013, there can be identified three journals containing "Business Intelligence" in the title, none of them indexed in the Web of science:

- Business Intelligence Journal [2], a journal published by TDWI; this journal was firstly released in March 2006 and has got a focus on industry and applications;
- International Journal of Business Intelligence and Data Mining[3], a journal published by Inderscience since 2006; this journal is focused on academic research and is indexed in Scopus[4] and is also indexed in DBLP[5];
- International journal of Business Intelligence Research[6], a journal published by IGI Global since 2010 and focused on academic research; this journal was indexed in DBLP.

At the moment of writing this chapter, these journals still maintain regular publications, and the International journal of Business Intelligence Research was able to achieve indexation in Scopus. Nevertheless, no significant advancements have occurred since 2013.

Figure 1. Evolution of the number of scientific publications with the topic "Business Intelligence" in ISI Web of Science – Core Collection, between 1958 and 2019

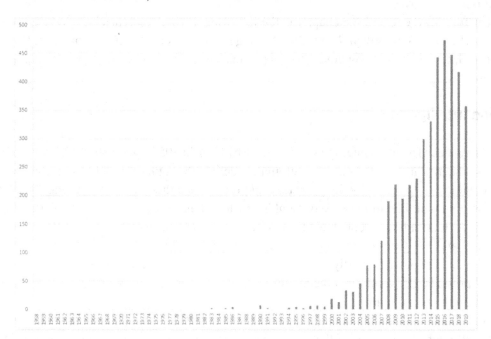

Concerning scientific conferences, at the moment of writing this chapter, there can already be found several conferences that include "Business Intelligence" in the title, being that some of them are indexed by Web of Science. Nevertheless, many other conferences include this topic in workshops, in special tracks/sessions, and in the conference topics. Actually, the vast majority of conferences and meetings having BI as the central topic have a focus on industry and applications.

From this analysis, it can be concluded that the interest of the scientific community in the topic BI is small, but is also slightly increasing. Jourdan, Rainer & Marshall (2008) conclude in their analysis that the types of research in the field of BI "indicate the beginnings of a body of research" (Jourdan, Rainer, & Marshall, 2008, p. 124). This growing interest from the scientific community in the topic and the construction of a body of research can certainly bring new useful insights that can help improving decision making in business environments.

Through the analysis of the literature, there can be considered that the evolution of BI along the time has got four distinct eras or historical generations, each one with specific characteristics, namely:

- **Pre-historical era** – The antecedents of BI systems are the Management Information Systems (MIS) from the 1970's, which were responsible for producing all the reports needed by an organization, and the Executive information systems of the 1980's and the 1980's, which were responsible for supporting senior managers of an organization in the decision making process (Turban, Sharda, & Delen, 2011).
- First generation – **The Technological era** – It can be considered that this era starts with the famous definition of Dresner, from Gartner, in 1989: "It describes a set of concepts and methods to improve business decision making by using fact-based support systems" (Power, 2007). Despite

the definition focus on concepts and methods, the major software houses emphasized the techno-logical issues, and it was then accepted that the simple introduction of the BI software will "magi-cally" resolve all the organization's problems.

- *Second generation* – **The Managers' era** – This era naturally emerged, in the begging of the 21st century, due to problems derived from the careless technological implementations done until then. As was clearly stated by Moss & Shaku (2003): "BI is neither a product nor a system". During this era the focus begin to change, and more attention was taken to management issues.
- *Third generation* – **The Intelligence era** – The Intelligence era emerged in the second half of 2000's, with the inclusion of artificial intelligence capabilities in BI systems. The concept of Adaptive Business Intelligence emerged. "Adaptive Business Intelligence systems include elements of data mining, predictive modeling, forecasting, optimization, and adaptability, and are used by business managers to make better decisions." (Michalewicz, Schmidt, Michalewicz, & Chiriac, 2007, p. 5)
- *Fourth generation* – **The Ubiquitous era** – We are living this era since the beginnings of the 2010's. It emerged with the widespread of mobile devices and of cloud computing, which allows us to be available everywhere, anytime – ubiquity. The large amounts of data consumed and gener-ated are also an important characteristic of this era – Big Data. This poses several important chal-lenges to BI, and certainly will conduct to a shift in the way organizations look at BI systems. We can say that they are an essential and established body of the organizations information systems.

DATA MINING

As stated above, DM came up from scientific environments. Figure 2 presents the evolution of the number of scientific publications that can be found in the "Web of Science – Core Collection)" between 1983 and 2019 having "Data Mining" as topic (none can be found before that). The first publication with this topic was in 1983, there were 2 publications in 1985, and just in 1992 there were 3 publications. After that, publications can be found yearly, but just after 1996 the number of publications experiments a significant increase, in our opinion due to the publication of the seminal work of Fayyad, Piatetski-Shapiro, Smyth, and Uthurusamy entitled "Advances in knowledge Discovery and Data Mining", surpassing 1000 in and after 2002, and reaching the maximum of 5882 in 2017. Despite we can observe some ups and downs, the interest of the scientific community in the topic still is relevant. DM can nowadays come out with the indication of different topics such as web mining, text mining, and others.

Despite the scientific publications in DM being spread along several important journals, one of the most important journals that can be found indexed in Web of science having "Data Mining" in the title is "Data Mining and Knowledge Discovery"7. This journal, at the moment of writing this chapter, which can be considered high, mainly if it is considered that DM is not a broad area of research. In addition, this journal is index as a Q1 journal in Scimago. Another relevant journal is "ACM Transactions on Knowledge Discovery from Data"8, which was founded in 2007, and presents a 5-year impact factor of 1.676 in 2013 and of 2.801 at the moment of writing this chapter, and is also Q1 in Scimago. Other DM journals can be founded in the main scientific indexes.

The first Workshop, IJCAI-89 Workshop on Knowledge Discovery in Databases, which took place at Detroit in 1989, led, in 1995, to the nowadays main annual conference in the area, ACM SIGKDD International Conference on Knowledge Discovery & Data Mining9. Many other important DM scientific

Figure 2. Evolution of the number of scientific publications with the topic "Data Mining" in ISI Web of Science – Core Collection, between 1958 and 2019

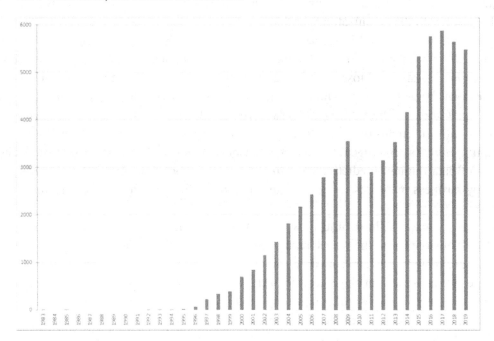

conferences occur yearly, and the topic "Data Mining" can be found in most of the conferences in the areas of computer science, information systems, and computer engineering. These figures are coherent with the graphic presented in Figure 2.

From this analysis, it can be concluded that the scientific community has got great interest in DM, that this is a "hot" research topic, and that DM can be considered as a consolidated research area.

Similarly to BI, through the analysis of the literature there can be considered that the evolution of DM along the time has got three distinct eras or historical generations, each one with specific characteristics, namely:

- **Pre-historical era** – DM emerges from the areas of statistics, artificial intelligence, and machine learning. In the begging, it was not positively regarded and several depreciative terms were used to name it, such as "Data Fishing" or "Data Dredging". Nevertheless, the positive results achieved conducted to important developments leading to the acceptance of the term Data Mining.
- *First generation* – **The Programmers' era** - KDD-1989, held in Chicago in August, 20th, can be recognized as the first important event in the area of DM, thus defining the beginning of this era. The creation of KDnuggets in 1993, and the Fayyad's et al. book "Advances in knowledge Discovery and Data Mining" published in 1996 are important landmarks in the establishment of the field. This era was focused on university, research, and in the development of better and better algorithms.
- *Second generation* – **The Suites era** – Doing DM by programming all the algorithms whenever needed represents a heavy task, thus DM suites, like WEKA10, R-Miner11, and other12, starts being developed. This era arose in the beginning of the 2000's. The suites present user-friendly

environments, when compared with those environments of the previous era, and represent an important step to bring near business users and DM.

- *Third generation* – **The Other Types of Data era** – Around the mid 2000's, DM mining started to be applied to unstructured data such as text, the web, social media, and others. This can be considered as the emergence of a new DM era, since these new types of data represent new challenges to data miners.
- *Fourth Generation* – **The Data Science Era** – Around the mid 2010's, the explosion of the interest for the so called big data can make us think of a new era. The paradigm is changing, from "improving data and algorithms" to "improving decision making", and we talk about data scientists, instead of data miners. From data scientists it is expected to have different types of skills, not just the technical skill related to data access and programming, but also management skills such as a strong domain knowledge, and problem definition, as well as soft skills. A stronger connection to BI can be verified.

Business Intelligence and Data Mining

Examining the primary journals and conferences in the DM field, mentioned in the previous section, it can be concluded that the main issues for DM research are related to improving data preparation for data mining, to developing better algorithms and methods for specific problems and applications, and to measuring the utility of the obtained models. Nevertheless, the interest in some specific DM applications is rising. DM applications in BI systems are one of them. *Figure 3* presents the evolution of the number of scientific publications that can be found in the "Web of Science – Core Collection" between 1998 and 2019 having both "Data Mining" and "Business Intelligence" as topic (none can be found before that). It can be verified that the number of publications is really very small, which is aligned with the low level of interest of the scientific community for BI, in general (Figure 1).

Nevertheless, several applications of DM in BI systems can be found in organizations and are reported by those organizations and software houses, even though, most of those applications are not analyzed from a scientific point of view. The "International Journal of Business Intelligence and Data Mining", already referred above, is the only journal that can be found with both "Data Mining" and "Business Intelligence" in the title.

In the opposite direction, the organizations also do not pay particular attention to DM, because most of the times they do not clearly understand the practical benefits of applying DM in their BI systems. To state it can be verified that, for instance, the TDWI "Journal of Business Intelligence" mentioned in section "Business Intelligence" have only got a few publications about DM applications.

Despite these figures, we believe that the interest of the scientific community for doing research in the area of DM applications in BI systems will grow, since there are many open issues for research (Jourdan, Rainer, & Marshall, 2008), and that the interest of the industry to increase the collaboration with the scientific community is also growing. This proximity will certainly bring many advantages for both the communities, and a better understanding of the main issues.

As stated above, the DM paradigm is changing, from "improving data and algorithms" to "improving decision making" guided by the interest in the so called big data. Also the interest of the BI community for the so called big data is growing. It can be said that big data can be the key element that will help closing the gap between the DM and the BI communities, thus bringing new insights and benefits for

Figure 3. Evolution of the number of scientific publications with the topic "Data Mining" AND "Business Intelligence" in ISI Web of Science – Core Collection, between 1958 and 2019

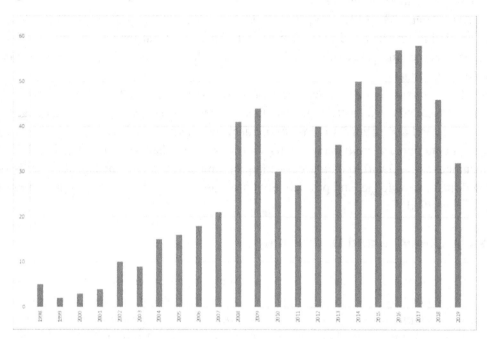

both of them. The new terminology used in the area with terms such as Analytics and Data Science, is also an important aspect to help stabilizing this area of research.

FUTURE RESEARCH DIRECTIONS

This chapter represents just a brief approach to some historical issues of the areas of DM and BI, starting from a bibliometric approach. Several research lines can be considered for future research. One research line, which is the focus of the book in which this chapter is included, is DM integration with BI systems. This is a promising research line whose main goal is to allow final business users to really access and be able to manipulate DM models in order to completely extract their inner value. Another connected research line concerns the definition of standards for DM. This is a very dynamic research line. The main goal from the academic point of view consists in defining a DM system similar to the Database Management Systems (DBMS) defined by Codd for the relational model for databases. The DBMS allow the user to easily access and manipulate data stored in databases and a similar system is desired for DM in order to allow the user to also access and manipulate de DM models. DM mining languages are being defined, similarly to languages defined for the relational DBMS, such as SQL and QBE. Some promising efforts were done, but there are some important drawbacks that need to be overcome. Just to present one example, the types of models that the referred languages can support are almost limited to rules. More recently, the emergence of Big Data presents some new challenging topics, namely on how to efficiently integrate Big Data into BI systems and analyze those data.

CONCLUSION

This chapter presented BI and DM from a comparative bibliometric perspective, showing that those areas are not running in parallel, but are instead converging. Considering both, DM and BI, over the years, distinct historical generations were identified for each one of them. Each of those areas represents different paradigms and the correspondent characteristics were briefly introduced. We can see that both areas are converging, since BI is adopting DM characteristics to help improving decision making, and DM, more connected with technological aspects, is approaching the business areas and incorporating BI in its reasoning.

This chapter represents a new approach since, as far as our knowledge, there are no similar approaches in the literature. As was referred in the introduction, that is not possible to understand the present without knowing the past, thus this is an important issue to analyze.

REFERENCES

Azevedo, A. (2012). *Data Mining Languages for Business Intelligence* (Doctoral Thesis). Retrieved from RepositoriUM: http://hdl.handle.net/1822/22892

Azevedo, A., & Santos, M. F. (2012). Closing the Gap between Data Mining and Business Users of Business Intelligence Systems: A Design Science Approach. *International Journal of Business Intelligence Research*, *3*(4), 14–53. doi:10.4018/jbir.2012100102

Cheung, C. F., & Li, F. L. (2012). A Quantitative Correlation Coefficient Mining Method for Business Intelligence in Small and Medium Enterprises of Trading Business. *Expert Systems with Applications*, *39*(7), 6279–6291. doi:10.1016/j.eswa.2011.10.021

Fayyad, U. M., Piatetski-Shapiro, G., & Smyth, P. (1996). From Data Mining to Knowledge Discovery: An Overview. In *Advances in Knowledge Discovery and Data Mining* (pp. 1–34). AAAI Press/The MIT Press.

Hang, Y., & Fong, S. (2009). A Framework of Business Intelligence-driven Data Mining for e-Business. In *Proceedings of the 2009 Fifth International Joint Conference on INC, IMS and IDC* (pp. 1964-1970). IEEE Computer Society. 10.1109/NCM.2009.403

Hu, X., & Cercone, N. (2004). A Data Warehouse/Online Analytic Processing Framework for Web Usage Mining and Business Intelligence Reporting. *International Journal of Intelligent Systems*, *19*(7), 585–606. doi:10.1002/int.20012

Jourdan, Z., Rainer, R. K., & Marshall, T. E. (2008). Business Intelligence: An Analysis of the Literature. *Information Systems Management*, *25*(2), 121–131. doi:10.1080/10580530801941512

Kriegel, H.-P., Borgwardt, K., Kröger, P., Pryakhin, A., Schubert, M., & Zimek, A. (2007). Future trends in data mining. *Data Mining and Knowledge Discovery*, *15*(1), 87–97. doi:10.100710618-007-0067-9

Linoff, G. S. (2008). Survival Data Mining Using Relational Databases. *Business Intelligence Journal*, *13*(3), 20–30.

Lunh, H. P. (1958). A Business Intelligence System. *IBM Journal of Research and Development*, 2(4), 314–319. doi:10.1147/rd.24.0314

Michalewicz, Z., Schmidt, M., Michalewicz, M., & Chiriac, C. (2007). *Adaptive Business Intelligence*. Springer-Verlag.

Moss, L. T., & Shaku, A. (2003). *Business Intelligence Roadmap: The Complete Project Lifecycle for Decision-Support Applications*. Pearson Education.

Phan, D. D., & Vogel, D. R. (2010). A Model of Customer Relationship Management and Business Intelligence Systems for Catalogue and Online Retailers. *Information & Management*, 47(2), 69–77. doi:10.1016/j.im.2009.09.001

Piatetsky-Shapiro, G. (2007). Data mining and knowledge discovery 1996 to 2005: Overcoming the hype and moving from "university" to "business" and "analytics". *Data Mining and Knowledge Discovery*, 15(1), 99–105. doi:10.100710618-006-0058-2

Power, D. J. (2007). *A Brief History of Decision Support Systems, Version 4.0*. Retrieved March 10, 2010, from DSSResources.com: http://dssresources.com/history/dsshistory.html

Sharda, R., Delen, D., & Turban, E. (2018). *Business Intelligence, Analytics, and Data Science: a Managerial Perspective* (4th ed.). Upper Saddle River, NJ: Pearson Education, Inc.

Vercellis, C. (2009). *Business Intelligence: Data Mining and Optimization for Decision Making*. West Sussex, UK: John Wiley and Sons.

Wang, H., & Wang, S. (2008). A Knowledge Management Approach to Data Mining Process for Business Intelligence. *Industrial Management & Data Systems*, 108(5), 622–634. doi:10.1108/02635570810876750

Wixon, B., & Watson, H. (2010). The BI-Based Organization. *International Journal of Business Intelligence Research*, 1(1), 13–28. doi:10.4018/jbir.2010071702

Yermish, I., Miori, V., Yi, J., Malhotra, R., & Klimberg, R. (2010). Business Plus intelligence Plus technology equals Business intelligence. *International Journal of Business Intelligence Research*, 1(1), 48–63. doi:10.4018/jbir.2010071704

Zeller, J. (2007, May 8). *Business Intelligence: The Chicken or the Egg*. Retrieved February 15, 2009, from BI Review magazine: https://www.information-management.com/bissues/20070601/2600340-1.html

ADDITIONAL READING

Azevedo, A., & Santos, M. F. (2008). KDD, SEMMA and CRISP-DM: a Parallel Overview. In *Proceedings of the IADIS European Conference on Data Mining, DM2008*, 182-185.

Azevedo, A., & Santos, M. F. (2009). Business Intelligence: State of the Art, Trends, and Open Issues. In Proceedings of the First International Conference on Knowledge Management and Information Sharing - KMIS 2009, 296-300.

Benoît, G. (2002). Data Mining. *Annual Review of Information Science & Technology*, *36*(1), 265–310. doi:10.1002/aris.1440360107

Berry, M. J. A., & Linoff, G. S. (2004). *Data Mining Techniques: For Marketing, Sales, and Customer Relationship Management*. John Wiley & Sons.

De Raedt, L. (2003). A perspective on Inductive Databases. *SIGKDD Explorations*, *4*(2), 6–77.

Imielinski, T., & Mannila, H. (1996). A Database Perspective on Knowledge discovery. *Communications of the ACM*, *39*(11), 58–64. doi:10.1145/240455.240472

Liao, S., Chu, P., & Hsiao, P. (2012). Data Mining Techniques and Applications – A Decade Review from 2000 to 2011. *Expert Systems with Applications*, *39*(12), 11303–11311. doi:10.1016/j.eswa.2012.02.063

KEY TERMS AND DEFINITIONS

Analytics: Analytics represents a combination of computational technologies, scientific management techniques, and statistics to solve real-world problems, while considering that organizations have to analyze their data to understand what is happening, what will happen, and how to take the best option.

Big Data: Big data is a buzz word that refers to collections of data that are big considering three Vs: volume, velocity, and variety. Some authors refer two more Vs: veracity and value.

Data Mining Suites: DM suites are software packages that provide several DM algorithms already implemented, generally having user-friendly environments.

Descriptive Analytics: Refers to knowing what happened and what is happening in organizations and perceiving some underlying trends and the causes of such occurrences.

Historical Periods for BI: Besides pre-historical era, four historical generations are considered, representing the different paradigms namely, Technological Era, Managers' Era, Intelligent Era, and Ubiquitous Era.

Historical Periods for DM: Besides pre-historical era, four historical generations are considered, representing the different paradigms namely, Programmers' Era, Suites Era, Other Types of Data Era, and Data Science Era.

Integration: Is the process by which a new element adapts to a system, thus allowing its inclusion.

Predictive Analytics: Aims to determine what is likely to happen in the future.

Prescriptive Analytics: Aims to recognize what is happening as well as the most likely predictions and make decisions to achieve the best performance.

ENDNOTES

[1]   http://apps.webofknowledge.com/, accessed 16/09/2020. Web of science is recognized as one of the most important scientific indexing resources.

[2]   https://tdwi.org/research/list/tdwi-business-intelligence-journal.aspx

[3]   http://www.inderscience.com/jhome.php?jcode=IJBIDM

[4]   https://www.scopus.com/, other important scientific indexing resource

5   http://www.dblp.org/, other important scientific indexing resource

6   https://www.igi-global.com/journal/international-journal-business-intelligence-research/1168

7   https://link.springer.com/journal/10618

8   https://tkdd.acm.org/

9   http://www.sigkdd.org/

10   https://www.cs.waikato.ac.nz/ml/weka/

11   https://rapidminer.com/

12   https://www.kdnuggets.com/software/suites.html

Chapter 2
Integration of Data Mining and Business Intelligence in Big Data Analytics:
A Research Agenda on Scholarly Publications

Atik Kulakli

ⓘD https://orcid.org/0000-0002-2368-3225

American University of the Middle East, Kuwait

ABSTRACT

The purpose of this chapter is to analyze and explore the research studies for scholarly publication trends and patterns related to the integration of data mining in particular business intelligence in big data analytics domains published in the period of 2010-2019. Research patterns explore in highly prestigious sources that have high impact factors and citations counted in the ISI Web of Science Core Collection database (indexes included SCI-Exp and SSCI). Bibliometric analysis methods applied for this study under the research limitations. Research questions formed based on bibliometric principles concentrating fields such as descriptive of publication, author productivity, country-regions distribution, keyword analysis with contribution among researchers, citation analysis, co-citation patterns searched. Findings showed strong relations and patterns on these important research domains. Besides this chapter would useful for researchers to obtain an overview of publication trends on research domains to be concerned for further studies and shows the potential gaps in those fields.

DOI: 10.4018/978-1-7998-5781-5.ch002

INTRODUCTION

Data management becomes the center of the decision-making process; Business Intelligence and Analytics (BI&A) has emerged as accessible (Buhl *et al.*, 2013) research area to be studied in academia and industry. With the movement of Big Data (BD) initiatives, these popular fields become more attractive for researchers (Maté *et al.*, 2015). Big data could be defined as the most unstructured and extremely massive data sets to be analyzed to reveal trends, associations, and patterns, related to human interactions (e.g., Social media data). In comparison, data mining is structured data in the databases to generate new information by mining the relations in data patterns. The data warehousing platforms should be established incorporation level with necessary data marts to analyze the large data sets. Moreover, big data analytics (as proper business decision tool); is a complex process of examining large and various data sets to uncover information in unstructured platforms with a variety of data sources and systems to discover hidden patterns, correlations, customer insights, and decisions as well as behaviors.

Data Mining (DM) with Big Data relations studied by Wu *et al.* (2014), it has outlined that Big Data concentrates large-volume, multiple sourced, complex, unstructured and autonomous (various) sources from the entire data platforms. In the research, the HACE theorem studied and proposed the Big Data processing model with mining techniques. While Big Data and traditional Business Intelligence discussed in different platforms, researchers studied the skill set and knowledge requirements for Big Data and Business Intelligence (Debortoli, Müller & vom Brocke, 2014) and conducted latent semantic analysis (LSA). According to findings, business knowledge is a crucial indicator of successful development and execution. Followed by Business Intelligence needs bigger than Big Data competencies, whereas Big Data is much more "human-capital-intensive" than Business Intelligence projects. Sun, Sun & Strang (2018) examined to use of Big Data Analytic services (service-oriented architecture-BASOA) to enhance Business Intelligence. Big Data ontology has three-layer analyses, such as descriptive, predictive, and prescriptive.

Since the number of academic publications has been increased and become very complex to follow, the trends would be a critical point for researchers and audiences. The impact of outcomes has resulted in directing research efforts to be concentrated on the most recent development fields in parallel. Scholars conduct different qualitative and quantitative studies to explore, discover, analyze, and organize the information to provide through wider scientific communities. Therefore, bibliometric methods as a usual proven approach provide systematic, transparent, process-based on the statistical measurement of science, and scientific activities (Aria & Cuccurullo, 2017).

This chapter aims to analyze and explore the research studies on big data, data mining in particular business intelligence, and big data analytics domains published in a recent research period (a decade). The study uses the Web of Science Core Collection database as a primary research platform and analysis the data for the period of 2010 to 2019. In this chapter, the author used a science mapping method with open-source Bibliometrix R-package that conducting bibliometric studies on scholarly high ranked sources. The chapter organized based on the IGI Global's structured template which devoted in seven main sections as Introduction, Background (literature review), Main focus (issues, controversies, problem statement, research methodology, bibliometric study definitions, and data collection strategy), Results and Discussions (analysis, findings, addressing the research questions), Solutions and Recommendations followed by Future research directions (Theoretical implications and research needs, Practical implications, and Limitations and future research), and Conclusion. The study also shows the research patterns and concentration areas in scholarly publications to find out the gap to highlight future research direction needs.

BACKGROUND (LITERATURE REVIEW)

In the information systems literature, data mining, business intelligence studied with different dimensions more than several decades. However, big data and its analytics related to business intelligence studies relatively less, and this study show recent research patterns. Business Intelligence (BI) related topics need the framework to identify the evolution, applications, emerging research areas (Chen, Chiang & Storey, 2012). In the study, the evolution highlighted as Business Intelligence and Analytics, BI&A 1.0 (DBMS-Based structured content), BI&A 2.0 (Web-based unstructured content), and BI&A 3.0 (Mobile and sensor-based content). In the highly cited paper, it was mentioned the emerging Analytics research areas such as "Big Data, Text, Web, Network, and Mobile" (Yu, 2017).

Kranjc *et al.* (2017)'s study provided a real-life platform with distributed computing in Big Data mining. The platform called ClowdFlows (cloud-based web) is to use for the workflow of components of mining, and development, whether batch or real-time processing modes in scientific publications. Similarly, some researches concentrated the forecasting and visualizing the energy consumption behavior with data mining modeling (Singh & Yassine, 2018; Zhu *et al.*, 2018; Kuo, Lin & Lee, 2018). Smart energy capabilities require complicated operational activities and procedures (Chongwatpol, 2016). Proposed Business Intelligent framework augments business analytics along with database management, and business performance approaches to manage the current system in the energy sector plant (Lin & Yang 2019; Liu *et al.*, 2018). An unsupervised data clustering analysis, energy time series data was used to forecast the energy usage with smart meter datasets. Zhu *et al.* (2018) systematically reviewed the scholarly publications on data preprocessing with component analysis. Robust techniques (Shuai *et al.*, 2018) discussed with various characteristics; therefore, Big Data has multi-dimensional, with various perspectives, give opportunities to the community. Wang & Yuan (2014) studied Big Data concerning spatial Data Mining. Geo-spatial data have been found a considerable amount in Big Data, so location-based data (Batran *et al.*, 2018) enormously used by individuals and organizations recently. It has roles and dimensions, such as social, economic, and environmental issues.

Gandomi *et al.* (2016) established a new algorithm of multi-objective genetic programming (MOGP) where addresses the problems by solving sophisticated civil engineering modeling. Big Data is used for model development along with various levels of structural properties. Another study showed that Big Data mining works well in parallel computing and cloud computing platforms (Zhang & Zhang, 2019) where parallel computing use the similar techniques as analytical methods offer, is to divide significant problems into small pieces and then the single processor would be carried out (Tsai *et al.*, 2016). There-fore, those methods used to solve Big Data problems. Parallel computing divides the dataset to work on it simultaneously with the different subsets while cloud-based platform used MapReduce based proce-dures. In other words, this composes the data on the map, therefore reduces the processes. Margolies *et al.* (2016) contributed to structured reporting and database development with data mining in the health sector. The research showed that breast imaging and diagnosing cancer detection, screening algorithm optimization are key success areas in highly complex datasets. A similar study conducted on Big Data mining on novel cancer cases and reanalyze the profiles of "Gene Expression Omnibus" to explore those "involved for DNS damage repair and genome instability" (Jiang & Liu, 2015).

Moreover, disease diagnosis and treatment have various schemes in classification by different departments and hospitals. These variations create problems such as inexperienced health staff, challenging to identify the symptoms and to apply proper treatment. In that research, the authors proposed a "Disease Diagnosis and Treatment Recommendation System (DDTRS)" to increase the utilization of advanced medical technology for the hospitals (Chen *et al.*, 2018). Similarly, the application and exploration of Big Data Mining studied by Zhang *et al.* (2016) in clinical medicine. The authors reviewed the theories and technologies of Big Data Mining and contributed that it has enormous potential to play a crucial role in the clinical medicine research area. Besides, medical Big Data mining processes have been developed by the support of IoT devices used in the medical services (Song, Jung& Chung, 2019).

Shadroo & Rahmani (2018) revealed the relation among Big Data, Data Mining (Lv *et al.*, 2018), and the Internet of Things (IoT). IoT has emerged in the last decade and can be seen in all devices such as wearable technological products, home appliances, vehicles, smartphones, air conditioning, heaters, natural gas meters, smart cities, and so on. Big Data and Data Mining work well together for efficient operations of IoT to transmit, analyze, and process data. The study was categorized into three clusters of the scholarly publications of 44 records, such as architecture and platform, framework, and application. Authors also outlined the opportunities (such as data aggregation, data analysis; new business models; and global visibility) and challenges (such as volume-variety-velocity-value (Huang *et al.,* 2017); visualization; knowledge extraction; and security-privacy) based on the published results. The furthermore mixed digital method used to combine qualitative and quantitative methods in Data Mining and visualize the data (Qi, Yang, & Wang, 2019) in a multilevel and contextual model for the texts (O'Hallorane *et al.,* 2018). Moreover, it has been contributed that Big Data, Data Mining, and Machine Learning (D'Alconzo *et al.*, 2016) approaches to utilize production, operations, sustainability, and management roles in precision animal agriculture. It helps to growth of complex data from different sources such as sensors, digital images, sound, and visual data used in highly technological platforms and computer systems (Morota *et al.,* 2018).

On the other hand, Xu *et al.* (2014) studied the threat and security issues for the private information of individuals (sensitive information, Xu *et al.*, 2016). It is called privacy-preserving data mining (PPDM), which concentrates data mining algorithms effectively-prepared based on security needs. It was identified four types of users' participated in data mining applications as "data provider, data collector, data miner, and decision-maker."

Mariani *et al.* (2018) outlined the academic developments of Business Intelligence and Big Data in Hospitality and Tourism Research (Li *et al.*, 2019) domains concentrated scholarly publications of 97 journal papers from WoS and Scopus databases. According to findings, although the applied analytical techniques in an upward movement, there is no clear framework of Business Intelligence and Big Data reflected in the literature yet (as of 2017). There is a missing link for the Big Data-driven knowledge development. Besides, more data has become available to use for different business problems to solve. Similarly, another study discovers the scientific publication patterns evolved concerning Business Intelligence and Big Data Analytics. Computer Science and Management Information Systems are dominant fields in the production of research studies. At the same time, "data mining," "social media," and "information systems" are highly common keywords all over the publications, however, "cloud computing," "data warehouse," and "knowledge management" recently evolved topics (Liang & Liu 2018). Unstructured data is available in various sources, and it emerges rapidly. Since the unstructured and complex data become very important for the companies' marketing strategies, Big Data supports the authentic decision-making process (Chow-White & Green, 2013; Liang & Liu 2018) with regarding of social, cultural, marketing campaigns, and consumer behaviors and expectations (Kim, 2014). Also, the cognitive network structure examined to understand the patterns of categorical mapping with Big Data Mining in social media (Sang *et al.*, 2016; Yang *et al.*, 2019) to represent the decision-making structure of consumers (Song *et al.*, 2014).

There is a wide range of studies on Big Data (Mining), Business Intelligence, Data Mining, and Analytics (Azevedo and Santos, 2009) field available in the literature. Big Data acquired in audiology (Mellor, Stone, & Keane, 2018), Privacy preserving big data mining (Zhang *et al*, 2018) for sensitive knowledge leakage, security (Afzali, & Mohammadi, 2017), big data in the food industry (Goti-Elordi *et al*, 2017), multimedia data mining-based smart transportation and telemedicine (Zhu, 2016) manufacturer's prediction of performance (Apgar, 2015), network architecture design with Big Data mining (Njah, Jamoussi & Mahdi, 2019), Agile Business Intelligence as responsive decision model (Chang, 2018), Intelligent SSD for big data mining (Bae *et al*, 2013), Big Data Mining based on high-performance applications (HPC) (Fu *et al*, 2012), "Cloud Computing and Big Data Mining based Intelligent Traffic Control System" (Shengdong, Zhengxian & Yixiang, 2019), "Big Data Mining for Public Distributed Computing" (Jurgelevičius & Sakalauskas, 2018), Stock Market Prediction with Big Data (Das *et al*, 2017), "Data Mining Technology in the Financial Management of Colleges and Universities" (Zhang & Zhang, 2019), Enterprise CRM based on Big Data Mining (Li & Feng, 2018).

MAIN FOCUS OF THE CHAPTER

Issues and Problem Statement

This chapter aims to analyze and explore the research studies on data mining in particular business intelligence and big data analytics domains published in the 2010-2019 period.

The study shows the research patterns and concentration areas in scholarly publications. Research patterns explore in highly prestigious sources that have high impact factors and citations counted in the ISI Web of Science Core Collection (Clarivate Analytics).

This work justifies its interest and importance in the field of Data Mining, Big Data, Business Intelligence, and related Analytics. Therefore, the focus of this study takes into account a variety of perspectives to support developments in the area. First, for authors (academics and researchers in the same fields), it can serve as a publication guideline along with mapping the related content, subject of interest, publication sources which provide detailed information about publishing their papers and in which sources are available to publish the research outcomes give the idea to apply in the publication process. Second, for readers or audiences from different parties, it is beneficial to have an overview of the research outcomes, source types, and subject interest to follow scientific progress to apply their practical sides or for academic fields. Third, for covering a broad community of science or industry experts or any other corporations, this study supports as useful and beneficial directions to show evolution and progress in the research domains. The trends and scientific mapping also aid in outlining the concepts and future research areas to be studied. Therefore the research concentrated those questions for analysis;

Research Concentration and Questions

To understand the patterns of research domains in "integration of big data, data mining in particular business intelligence and analytics"; the design of the research should be framed and structured based on research objective and scope. The study design consists of preparation for the research theme and patterns to explore data of research domains. Therefore, a bibliometric study which enables a researcher to gather all related publication data, and correctly analyze them to answer those questions below;

Q1 How many papers on "data mining, business intelligence, and big data analytics" have been published in 2010 and 2019?

Q2 In which journals/sources were the papers published most frequently, and which keywords used in those publications?

Q3 Who are the most productive authors/co-authors published in those periods?

Q4 What are the most productive institutions and countries?

Q5 What are the results of the citation for those authors and publications?

Although the research conducted in the ISI WoS platform, the consistency of a single data platform assures better citation analysis in highly ranked top publication sources to compare and find out the co-citation, coupling, and collaboration in the research domains. Moreover, for future research directions, the outcome of this study shows the opportunities and challenges to create new publication strategies and form the research ideas. It would also be helpful for journal editors, authors, publishers, readers, and broad audiences too.

Research Methodology

Bibliometric Study

Bibliometric is defined as the use of statistical methods to analyze the bibliometric publications data such as peer-reviewed journal articles, books, conference proceedings, periodicals, reviews, reports, and related documents. It has been widely used to present the relations of research domains with quantitative methods. It maps the patterns of existed knowledge areas in publications related to search criteria to highlight the research gap and direct the potential future studies. Researchers explore the emerging research fields to conduct descriptive analysis then follow with in-depth analysis according to search strategies obtained. After setting the research questions, the data collection stage applied to gather all related data from the database. To prepare data for analysis, filtering, ordering (sorting) should be conducted. Analysis of literature review with specific bibliometric tools further highlights the understandings of the topics in more details (Fahimnia et al., 2015; Kolle, 2016; Kolle et al., 2017; Yu et al., 2018; Oliveria et al., 2017; Kulakli and Valmira, 2020; Kulakli and Shubina 2020).

Data Collection Strategy

In this study, publication data (records) retrieved from the database with below search keyword strategy (Kolle, 2016; Kolle et al. 2017; Fahimnia et al., 2015; Kulakli and Valmira, 2020; Yu et al., 2018; Du et al., 2017, Kulakli and Shubina 2020). There are several search queries run on the database to gather better results. Unrelated documents were extracted, and search criteria filtered. The final search criteria and steps as follows below in Table 1; (in ISI Web of Science Core Collection database).

About Bibliometrix R-package

Table 1. Search criteria for the publication records

Search criteria	
TITLE	*("data mining*" OR "business intelligence*")*
TITLE	*("big data*" OR "data analytic*")*
Timespan	*2010 to 2019*
Database	*ISI WoS Core Collection*
Indexes	*SCI-EXPANDED and SSCI*
Search refining criteria	*Language: All*
	Document types: All

Results: 101 publications found (in all document types)

All 101 records downloaded as plain text and MS Excel spreadsheet file formats. Further, the analysis and data visualization conducted in R Studio (R Package) and MS Excel software. R is open-source software for programmers and users for specific analysis R Studio is an interface for who does not need or not experienced in programming.

Science mapping is sophisticated and complicated because it is multi-step and requires multiple software tools frequently. The Bibliometrix R-package is a tool for scientific and bibliometric quantitative analysis. Bibliometrix offers various routines for the import of bibliographical data from the science database such as Clarivate Analytics (Web of Science), Scopus, PubMed, and Cochrane; bibliometric analysis. (Aria et al., 2017). In this chapter, all figures, and tables prepared by using R Studio (Bibliometrix package), MS Excel, and MS Word programs.

Research Framework and Flow

Bibliometric studies widely used in library and information science and studies fields. Based on the research domains and objectives of the study, the authors conduct different analyses and tools to present the data set and findings of results. Data analysis and visualization tools such as Payek, BibExcel, Perish, R language, and R Studio (bibliometrix package), VOS viewer commonly use by researchers. The author has designed the research framework based on the literature (see in the Data collection strategy section above) and own experiences. The flow can be seen in Figure 1 below.

Figure 1. Research framework (flow)

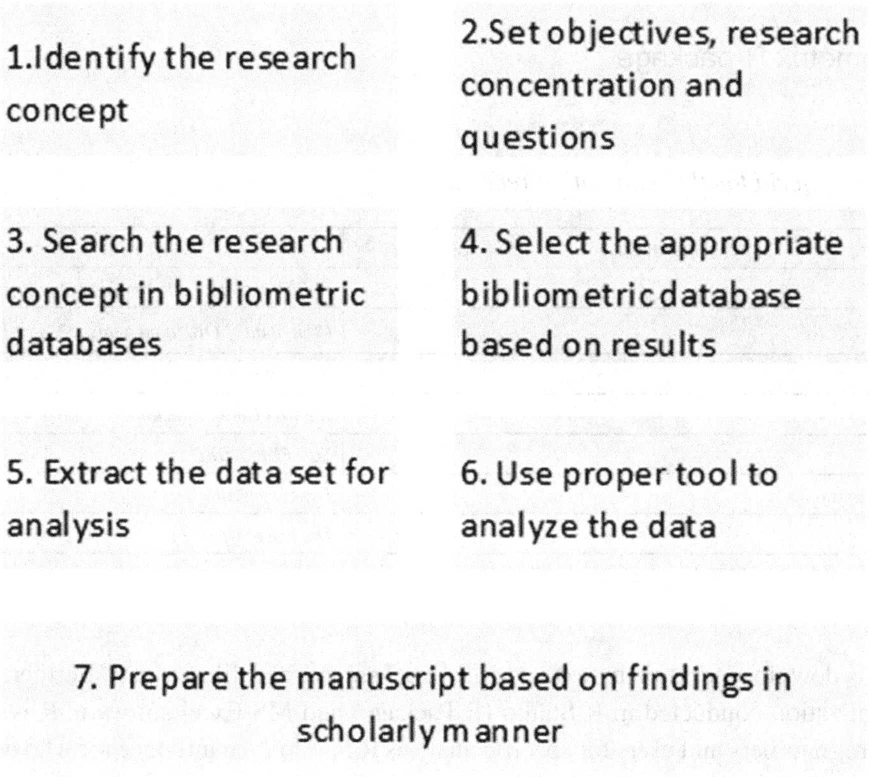

1.Identify the research concept	2.Set objectives, research concentration and questions
3. Search the research concept in bibliometric databases	4. Select the appropriate bibliometric database based on results
5. Extract the data set for analysis	6. Use proper tool to analyze the data

7. Prepare the manuscript based on findings in scholarly manner

RESULTS AND DISCUSSIONS

Publication Profile and Languages (Publication Structure)

Using the above-mentioned search strategy, a total of 101 publications were retrieved from the ISI WoS database related to research domains. The vast majority of the papers written in the English language (99 papers, 98.02%) whereas Chinese and Spanish languages (1 paper with 0.99% each). The descriptive information about the publications was given in Table 2 below. It shows the majority of the publications found in peer-reviewed journal articles with 70 papers (69.31%), editorial material 11 papers (10.89%),

Table 2. Distribution of publications by document types (2010-2019)

Document Types	Article	Editorial Material	Review	Meeting Abstract	Early Access	Book Review	Hardware Review	News Item	Proceedings Paper
records	70	11	9	8	2	1	1	1	1
% of 101	69.31%	10.89%	8.91%	7.92%	1.98%	0.99%	0.99%	0.99%	0.99%

Table 3. Top 33 WoS subject areas by publications (2010-2019)

WoS Subject Categories	Record	Percent (%)
Computer Science Information Systems	30	29.70
Computer Science Theory Methods	17	16.83
Engineering Electrical Electronic	14	13.86
Telecommunications	13	12.87
Computer Science Artificial Intelligence	8	7.92
Computer Science Software Engineering	8	7.92
Pharmacology Pharmacy	7	6.93
Computer Science Hardware Architecture	5	4.95
Management	5	4.95
Toxicology	5	4.95
Engineering Multidisciplinary	4	3.96
Genetics Heredity	4	3.96
Operations Research Management Science	4	3.96
Automation Control Systems	3	2.97
Chemistry Multidisciplinary	3	2.97
Computer Science Interdisciplinary Applications	3	2.97
Materials Science Multidisciplinary	3	2.97
Physics Applied	3	2.97
Biotechnology Applied Microbiology	2	1.98
Construction Building Technology	2	1.98
Energy Fuels	2	1.98
Engineering Chemical	2	1.98
Engineering Civil	2	1.98
Engineering Industrial	2	1.98
Environmental Sciences	2	1.98
Environmental Studies	2	1.98
Food Science Technology	2	1.98
Geography Physical	2	1.98
Green Sustainable Science Technology	2	1.98
Medicine General Internal	2	1.98
Multidisciplinary Sciences	2	1.98
Radiology Nuclear Medicine Medical Imaging	2	1.98
Remote Sensing	2	1.98

reviews nine papers (8.91%), and meeting abstract eight papers (7.92) rest of the publications in total with six papers in total (6%).

Table 4. Publication by years (2010-2019)

Publication by Years	2010	2011	2012	2013	2014	2015	2016	2017	2018	2019
records	0	0	2	2	8	4	15	12	34	24
% of 101	0.00	0.00	1.98	1.98	7.92	3.96	14.85	11.88	33.66	23.76

Web of Science-Core Collection subject category analysis shows the literature related research domains were categorized under the top 33 major subject areas and detailed the record count with percent of total publication count in Table 3 below;

The top ten WoS subject categories of publication structure have been found as *Computer Science Information Systems, Computer Science Theory Methods, Engineering Electrical Electronics, Telecommunications, Computer Science Artificial Intelligence, Computer Science Software Engineering, Pharmacology Pharmacy, Computer Science Hardware Architecture, Management,* and *Toxicology.* Therefore, the majority of the subject category records fall into various Computer Science (71) and Engineering (52) fields. Following that, the distribution also shows medical (24), science (13), and management (9) research domains.

Distribution of Publication by Years (2010-2019)

Table 4 shows the publications during the search period. At the beginning of the period, the years 2010 and 2011, there was not any publication. The publications started in 2012. The average journal articles

Figure 2. The linear trend line of publication count (2010-2019)

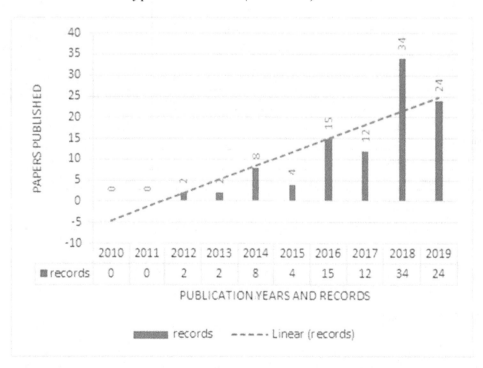

were published of this period (2012-2019) was 12.63 records. 2018 and 2019 are the most productive years found with above the average rate, and 2018 is the highest (peak) level with 34 records (33.66%).

Figure 2 shows the distribution of the number of publications per year (period of 2012-2019). The linear trend line shows an upward movement and illustrates the increased publication interest in the research domains. The increased number of publications in the period 2016 to 2019 showed that more than the average of total publications per year. In addition to this, 2018 is far more than the average publication records.

Journal Frequency and Keyword Analysis

Table 5 shows the publication frequency in the most relevant sources. However, there are no significant differences in publication history. The number of journals to some extend the top contributed journals (13 sources) as *Basic Clinical Pharmacology Toxicology, Cluster Comp. the J. of Networks Software Tools and Applications, IEEE Access* with a minimum of 4 papers above published between 2012 and 2019. The majority of the journals in the top publication sources category are *Computer, Engineering, and Information Science* categories. According to the findings, there are 81 single sources, and 101 total publication counts. Table 5 also shows the publication frequency of top sources, 13 journals have categorized as higher the number of publications in the field (more than two articles ranked in the records). Besides, there is 68 source listed as one publication for each in the data set. Although there is no significant number of articles published in one or a few journals, it seems that journals published a similar amount of the papers, respectively.

Table 5. Publication frequency by Journals (2010-2019)

Most Relevant-Top Publication Sources	Records	% of 101
Basic Clinical Pharmacology Toxicology	5	4.95
Cluster Comp. the J. of Networks Software Tools and Applications	4	3.96
IEEE Access	4	3.96
Agro Food Industry Hi-Tech	2	1.98
Applied Sciences Basel	2	1.98
Computer Networks	2	1.98
Concurrency and Computation Practice Experience	2	1.98
Expert Systems with Applications	2	1.98
Information Systems Frontiers	2	1.98
ISPRS International Journal of Geo-Information	2	1.98
KSII Transactions on Internet and Information Systems	2	1.98
Security and Communication Networks	2	1.98
Sustainability	2	1.98

Table 6. Most relevant keywords (Top 10)

	Author Keywords (DE)	Articles	Keywords-Plus (ID)	Articles
1	Big Data	45	Classification	7
2	Data Mining	25	Prediction	7
3	Big Data Mining	9	Systems	6
4	Business Intelligence	9	Analytics	4
5	Cloud Computing	5	Information	4
6	Big Data Analytics	4	Network	4
7	Deep Learning	4	Algorithm	3
8	Big Data Analysis	3	Algorithms	3
9	Machine Learning	3	Cloud	3
10	Business Analytics	2	Energy	3

Figure 3. Word Cloud of Keywords-Plus

Keyword/Year	2012	2013	2014	2015	2016	2017	2018	2019	
Classification	0	0	1	0	1	0	1	4	7
Prediction	0	0	0	0	4	0	1	2	7
Systems	1	0	0	0	0	1	4	0	6
Analytics	0	0	1	0	1	0	1	1	4
Information	0	0	1	0	0	1	1	1	4
Network	1	0	0	0	2	1	0	0	4
Algorithms	0	0	1	0	1	0	1	0	3
Cloud	0	0	0	0	0	1	1	1	3
Feature-Selection	0	0	0	0	1	0	1	1	3
Knowledge	0	0	1	0	0	0	2	0	3

Figure 4. Word growth of Keywords-Plus

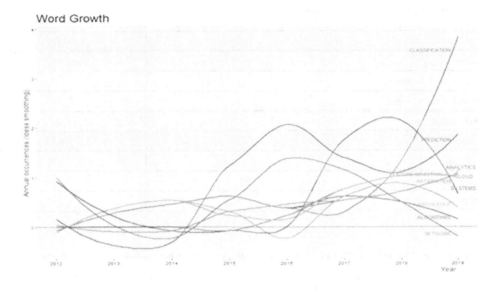

Table 6 highlights the most relevant keywords used in the articles. The first column represents author keywords (DE) which are *"Big Data"*, *"Data Mining"*, *"Big Data Mining"*, and *"Business Intelligence"* are the top keywords. The second column shows the keyword-Plus (ID), which are "Classification", "Prediction," and "Systems" are highly used keywords, among others. Author keyword (DE) analysis shows the frequency of the words in parallel with research titles and those matches.

Figure 5. Author's keywords

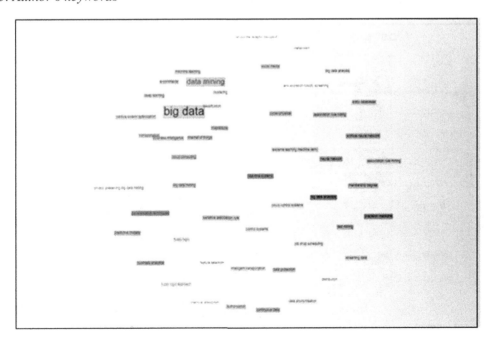

Table 7. Author and co-author descriptive results by documents (2010-2019)

Descriptive results	Records counted
Authors	315
Author Appearances	348
Authors of single-authored documents	15
Authors of multi-authored documents	300
Single-authored documents	15
Documents per Author	0.32
Authors per Document	3.12
Co-Authors per Documents	3.45
Collaboration Index	3.49

Figure 3 represents the Word Cloud of Keyword-Plus (ID). The cloud also highlights the weights and distribution of frequency of words yearly basis. Figure 4 shows the word growth of keyword-plus graphics with the same patterns compared to the word cloud. Besides, it represents the distribution of each Keyword-Plus frequency and appearance over the period decade. The "*Classification*", "*Prediction*", and "*Analytics*" have higher frequency and appearance.

Moreover, those first two keywords are in an upward movement in the graph. Also, Figure 5 illustrates the mapping of Author Keywords. The map shows the interrelation and the link of published paper's frequency about the author keywords such as "Big Data", "Data mining", and "Big Data Mining" are the highest keywords among all publications.

Figure 6. Most productive authors by publication volume

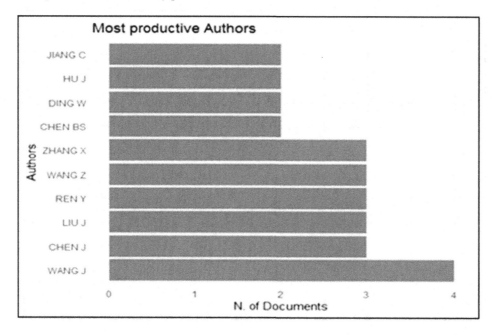

Most Productive Authors/Co-authors by Publication Count

Table 7 indicates the author and co-author detailed results by documents. Only 15 papers published as single-authored documents, while multi-authored documents stand as 300 documents, and 315 different authors with 348 appearances occur. Documents per author ratio are 0.32, while authors per document are 3.12.

Similar findings of publication frequency and the most productive authors can be seen in Figure 6 and their network in Figure 7. Although there is no significant difference among publication records by per author patterns, Wang J comparatively is on the top with four papers in total for the research period, it is followed by Chen J, Liu J, Ren Y, Wang Z, and Zhang X with three papers in total each. Furthermore, the rest of the list concluded Chen BS, Ding W, Hu J, and Jiang C with two papers each.

Analysis of the Most Productive Institutions and Countries

According to findings, the most productive and active institutions (Organizations Enhanced) on the research domains are Chinese Universities shown in Figure 8 are, Beijing Institute of Technology, Chinese

Figure 7. Most productive author's network

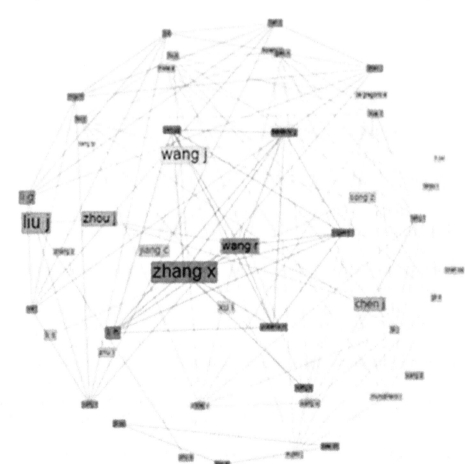

Academy of Sciences, Huazhong University of Science Technology, Tsinghua University, University of Electronic Science Technology of China, Chongqing University, Nanjing University of Science Technology, Nantong University, Southeast University China, Tianjin University, University of Chinese Academy of Sciences CAS, Zhejiang University. In contrast, Harvard University from USA, Nanyang Technological University and Nanyang Technological University National Institute of Education NIE from Singapore, and National Tsing Hua University from Taiwan are as followers stayed on top of the publications list.

Figure 8. Most productive organizations by publication count

Figure 8 illustrates the most productive institutions that contributed to research domains with more than two papers. The leading countries with institutions collaborated research in the field are Chinese institutions with 31 records (27.69%) on top of the list, followed by Singapore with four records (3.96%), and the USA with two papers (1.98%). The contributed institutions with only one paper counted are 194, whereas all institutions counted 210 in total with 233 country-region appearances in a total of 101 publications. In Figure 9, the most productive institutions network could be seen in parallel with Figure 8.

Figure 10 shows the most productive (top 10) countries regions that contributed to the research domain fields. The leading countries are China and the USA, followed by Taiwan, South Korea, Canada, India, Spain, the United Kingdom, Australia, and France. The figure shows two dimensions of collaboration patterns, such as Single Country Publications (SCP) and Multiple Country Publications (MCP).

Table 8 identifies the details of publication data with frequency, SCP, MCP, and MCP ratio of top countries. Therefore, China, with 40 articles in total (29 SCP and 11 MCP), is the leading country among the top 10 list. The USA has 11 articles (10 SCP, 1 MCP); Taiwan has seven articles (7 SCP, 0 MCP); South Korea has six articles (6 SCP, 0 MCP); Canada has four articles (2 SCP, 2MCP); India has three

Figure 9. Most productive institutions network

Figure 10. Most productive Country-Regions by SCP and MCP publication collaboration counts

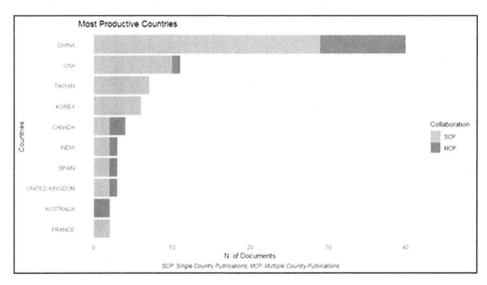

Table 8. Corresponding author's countries with frequency and ratios

	Country	Articles	Frequency	SCP	MCP	MCP Ratio
1	China	40	0.4211	29	11	0.2750
2	USA	11	0.1158	10	1	0.0909
3	Taiwan	7	0.0737	7	0	0.0000
4	South Korea	6	0.0632	6	0	0.0000
5	Canada	4	0.0421	2	2	0.5000
6	India	3	0.0316	2	1	0.3333
7	Spain	3	0.0316	2	1	0.3333
8	United Kingdom	3	0.0316	2	1	0.3333
9	Australia	2	0.0211	0	2	1.0000
10	France	2	0.0211	2	0	0.0000

SCP: Single Country Publications
MCP: Multiple Country Publications

articles (2 SCP, 1 MCP); Spain has three articles (2 SCP, 1 MCP); United Kingdom has three articles (2 SCP, 1 MCP); Australia has two articles (0 SCP, 2 MCP); and France has two articles (2 SCP, 0 MCP).

Figure 11. Publication network of most productive countries

Figure 12. Total citation counts per year (2010-2019)

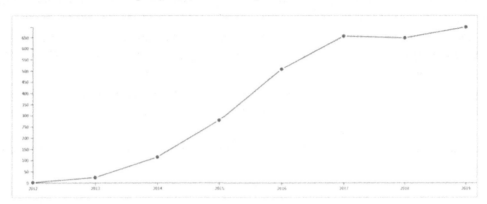

SCP and Country article distribution has similar characters in the data set. However, the USA relatively low in MCP with 1 article in comparison with the SCP ratio. It could also be said that authors from the USA prefer publication as a single author compares to China. Similar findings also can be said for Taiwan and South Korea. On the contrary, Australia shows the opposite pattern where multiple country publications were preferred. Figure 11 presents the publication network of most rich countries as parallel with Figure 10 and Table 8.

Citation Analysis of the Research Domains

Citation report for 101 publication results from Web of Science Core Collection between 2010 and 2019 show that the h-index is 14; average citations per item is 29.92; the sum of times cited 3022; without self-citations 3000; citing articles 2891; without self-citations 2874 counted. Figure 12 illustrates the total citation distribution from 2012 to 2019. Although the research period set as last decade (2010 to 2019), publications and citations started the year of 2012. The first two years (2012 to 2014) citation increased as regularly and reached just above 100 counts; then 2014 to 2017 it was sharply increased,

Table 9. Total citations per country (Top 10)

	Country	Total Citations	Average Article Citations
1	USA	1510	137.27
2	China	1239	30.98
3	Liechtenstein	47	47.00
4	Canada	43	10.75
5	Taiwan	39	5.57
6	Slovenia	35	35.00
7	South Korea	22	3.67
8	United Kingdom	20	6.67
9	Iran	17	8.50
10	Australia	13	6.50

citation count reached above 650. The term of 2017 to 2019 showed stability in citation figures as of 650 to 700 counts in the last two years.

Table 9 demonstrates total citations (Top 10) per country with author and co-author counts are combined. Although the USA has the highest total citations among the top 10 countries, followed by China, Liechtenstein, and Canada. However, Slovenia has a higher average of citations, even with the less total citations figures (35 counted). The data also shows that although China has second higher total citations. However, the average is relatively low. This means they produced more publications, and relatively the citation figures have not shown similar patterns.

Table 10 shows the most frequently cited articles during the literature review period. According to the findings, the most cited paper is related to research domains.

Table 10. Top ten articles' citation counts by publication years

	Author	Year	Source	TC	TC per Year
1	Chen H	2012	MIS Q	1421	157.89
2	Wu X	2014	IEEE Trans Knowl Data Eng	985	140.71
3	Xu L	2014	IEEE Access	132	18.86
4	Debortoli S	2014	Bus Inf Syst Eng	47	6.71
5	Kranjc J,	2017	Futur Gener Comp Syst	35	8.75
6	Singh S	2018	Energies	29	9.67
7	Zhu J	2018	Annu Rev Control	28	9.33
8	Gandomi AH	2016	Autom Constr	26	5.20
9	Tsai CF	2016	J Syst Softw	20	4.00
10	Margolies LR	2016	AM J Roentgenol	20	4.00

Figure 13. Co-citation of references network by authors

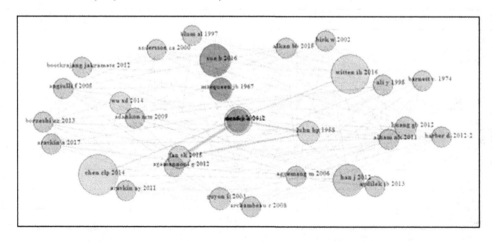

Figure 13 and Figure 14 illustrate the network analysis of the "Co-citation network by authors" and "Co-citation network by keywords". The network links for cited authors and related keywords show the connections and collaboration among published studies. The bigger the node size represents the impact and importance, the frequency in the network weights. (In Appendix 1A, 1B, 1C and 1D show the different level of the network sizes with nodes).

Figure 14. Co-citation of references network by keywords

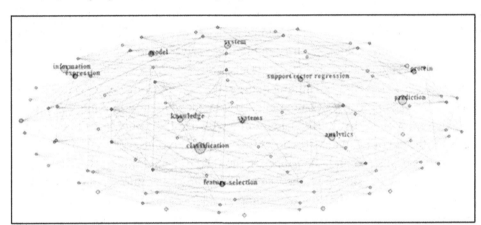

SOLUTIONS AND RECOMMENDATIONS

The aim of this research directed the iterative process of proven bibliometric methods to be conducted from beginning to end of the workflow. Exploring the relations among research domains reveals the publication patterns and answers to research questions formed based on the research strategy. The outcomes of this research have twofold. First, it has presented a descriptive structure of publication data to perform analysis on domains. Secondly, the distribution of institution, region, country, author collaboration, and productivity analyzed in-depth, further citation patterns indicated to show publication impacts and the country-author co-citations networks.

The evolution of the subjects and publication trends showed the concentration areas as "Big Data (in 45 paper)", "Data Mining (in 25 paper)", "Big Data Mining (in 9 paper)", "Business Intelligence/Analytics (in 11 paper)", "Big Data Analytics/Analysis (in 7 papers)" are top author keywords in recent studies of 101 publications. Similarly, "Classification", "Prediction", "Systems", "Analytics", "Algorithms", "Information", and "Network" are top terms in keyword-plus categories for the same publications.

Country-author collaboration is another crucial point of bibliometric study concerns. Most productive institutions and countries are China and the USA (in a total of 50.49%) (See Appendix 2). Followed by Taiwan, South Korea, Canada, India, Spain, the UK, Australia, and France. USA has shown as a leading country for single-authored publications, whereas China is a leading country all over the publications with a combination of single country publications (SCP) and multiple country publications (MCP).

In citation counts, although China is a leading country with publication counts, the USA shows the highest citations (1510 counts), above China (1239 counts). Following countries Liechtenstein, Canada, Taiwan, Slovenia, South Korea, UK, Iran, and Australia on top of the list. Comparing to previous data of publication productivity, Liechtenstein and Slovenia have higher citations than their productivity level. There is an exciting detail that also can be seen in productivity data, like India, Spain, and France appears in the top productive country; however, those do not appear in the top citied publication list. The impact of publication differs from the publication count. The ratio of USA 137.27 average article cited (1510 citations/11 paper=137.27), whereas China 30.98 average article cited (1239 citations/40 paper=30.98) in the period of research.

In light of those data and analysis, the significant developments of the research domains indicate that the impact of research does not depend on the publication quantity, it is more related to quality. Highest cited papers found in "Business Intelligence and analytics (Chen et al., 2012)", "Data mining and big data (Wu et al., 2014)", "Information security in big data: privacy and data mining (Xu et al., 2014)", "Comparison of business intelligence and big data (Debortoli et al., 2014)", "Online workflows in big data mining (Kranjc et al., 2017)", "Big data mining in the energy sector (Singh & Yassine, 2018)", "Review big data with data mining approaches (Zhu et al., 2018)", "Genetic programming for experimental big data mining (Gandomi et al., 2016)", "Big data mining with parallel computing (Tsai et al., 2016)", and "Breast imaging in the era of big data, structured reporting (Margolies et al., 2016)".

This work justifies its interest and importance in the field of Data Mining, Big Data, Business Intelligence, and related Analytics. Therefore, the focus of this study takes into account a variety of perspectives to support developments in the area for authors, readers or audiences from different parties and covering a broad community of science or industry experts or any other corporations.

FUTURE RESEARCH DIRECTIONS

Research domains have been found very popular, and growing interest shows in a parallel upward movement in the trend of publication records. According to results, the majority of the subject category records found in computer science and engineering. Following medical, science, and management subjects are also significant. Further research would be carried out with Big Data dominance to Data Mining, Analytics, and Business Intelligence related issues. More emerging topics such as "Smart Industry (manufacturing and service provision)", "Smart Technology, Smart Cities and Smart Devices", "Industry 4.0", "Cybersecurity", "Internet of Things (IoT)", "Blockchain Technology", "Cloud Computing", "Supply Chain Management", "New (sharing) economy and financial issues" and "Environmental (green) initiatives" should be studied both empirical, conceptual and systematic literature reviews along with in-detailed bibliometric studies too. More business and management case studies should also be conducted in parallel with Big Data emerged in various industries such as airlines, telecommunication, finance (bank, insurance, stock exchange), operations and logistics, tourism, internet services, e-commerce, information systems and services, security, contact centers, health, government and non-profit organizations (NPO).

Theoretical Implications and Research Needs

The originality and value of this chapter would found for researchers to obtain an overview of the publication trends on Big Data, Data Mining, Business Intelligence, and Analytics related areas to be interested in further studies and shows the potential gaps in those fields. The journal audiences in information studies area and the wider community such as academics, professionals, practitioners would also have benefits to extend their knowledge in the research, publication, and teaching purposes as well. The main theoretical contribution of this chapter could be said as systematically reviewed the records to analyze and present the findings of integrating Big Data (Mining), Data Mining, Business Intelligence, and Analytics. Therefore, in-depth literature review in all presented manuscripts showed a keen interest and contributions around the globe. The findings of the bibliometric study reveal several analysis parts as productivity of the publications (author, country, institution, type of publication), most important fields of studies and topics (with keywords, popular areas) supported with citations and co-citations, and mapping the scientific network.

Practical Implications

The purpose of this chapter was to bring together the existing research publications to analyze and represent the relation and gap for further practical research themes. Besides, theoretical concerns of this study more qualitative, quantitative, and inductive research would help to extend the current knowledge level with more practical studies. By introducing new practical ideas for any industry, sector, or country-specific studies would also support the continuation of research efforts. Moreover, it would help to stimulate further industry-specific researches such kind of empirical, conceptual, bibliometric analysis, and case studies. Those research outcomes would also provide comprehensive understandings of information in the specific fields and highlight the opportunities to launch new business projects. The awareness of information could also enlighten the professionals and practitioners' efforts for their successful business operations.

Limitations and Future Research

The paper has some limitations, likewise other scholarly research papers. The findings of the research are limited to the publications covered in the Web of Science Core Collection database (SCI-Exp and SSCI indexes) with the given keywords in the data collection strategy (TITLE and TOPIC search) of the methodology part. The study conducted and analyzed in January and February 2020 for the last decade. Although the publications retrieved from Web of Science Core Collection database, the value of the papers and impact factor of journals is not equivalent when the other papers published in lower impact factors. Besides, the journals ranked in four different quartiles (Q1 to Q4 ranking of ISI), which categorizes the journals within subject categories. The content analysis has not been applied for the study according to data set and structure. However, keyword frequency and analysis conducted and represented the trends in publications by years and highlight the contributions.

Identified research patterns and gaps direct new avenues on the business analytics field and also offer opportunities for researchers to contribute more in-depth researches by theoretical and empirical studies.

CONCLUSION

In this chapter, the author has attempted to explore and analyze the research stream in the literature of published papers related to "integration of big data, data mining in particular business intelligence and analytics", which indexed and ranked in ISI Web of Science Core Collection database between 2010 and 2019. A total of 101 were published on the research domains during the study period (2010-2019), with an average of 15.29 articles per year. However, publications related to the integration of those domains started in 2012. Exponential growth in publication count was observed for the period, in addition to citation patterns show similar growth as well. To understand and discover the research trends, collaboration, and networks around the globe, bibliometric methods were employed. According to the research objectives mentioned earlier, questions were formed, and the data collection stage completed with proper search strategies, the further analysis conducted to explore patterns and relations in more detail.

Publications started in 2012 (in 2010 and 2011, there is no publication). According to results, the study shows that the number of papers published in research topics has increased from 2016 to 2019 than average publication count (15.29 average number of articles per year). From 2012 to 2015 (4 years), 16 papers with 15.85%, on the contrary, between 2016 to 2019 (4 years) 85 paper with 84.15% published. The year in 2018 is the highest publication counted (34 papers with 33.66%).

Research outcome would clearly show that integration of Big Data, Data Mining, Business Intelligence, and related Analytics are popular topics and publication trend also validates the increase. Authors and researchers from different academic fields such as Engineering, Computer Science, Medical studies, and Science in general, as well as Management disciplines, have widely interested in publishing their research outcomes. Presented results also attempted to close the gap between theoretical and practical spheres in domains where Big Data, Data Mining, Business Intelligence, and Analytics plays a significant role. This chapter is relevant for researchers, academics, and practitioners in different disciplines as well as who works and contributes to the field of information studies, engineering, science, medical studies, management-business, and interdisciplinary-multidisciplinary studies.

ACKNOWLEDGMENT

This research received no specific grant from any funding agency in the public, commercial, or not-for-profit sectors.

REFERENCES

Afzali, G. A., & Mohammadi, S. (2017). Privacy preserving big data mining: Association rule hiding using fuzzy logic approach. *IET Information Security*, *12*(1), 15–24. doi:10.1049/iet-ifs.2015.0545

Apgar, D. (2015). The False Promise of Big Data: Can Data Mining Replace Hypothesis-Driven Learning in the Identification of Predictive Performance Metrics? *Systems Research and Behavioral Science*, *32*(1), 28–49. doi:10.1002res.2219

Aria, M., & Cuccurullo, C. (2017). bibliometrix: An R-tool for comprehensive science mapping analysis. *Journal of Informetrics*, *11*(4), 959–975. doi:10.1016/j.joi.2017.08.007

Azevedo, A. I. R. L., & Santos, M. F. (2009). An architecture for an effective usage of data mining in business intelligence systems. *Knowledge Management and Innovation in Advancing Economies: Analyses & Solutions*, 1319-1325.

Bae, D. H., Kim, J. H., Kim, S. W., Oh, H., & Park, C. (2013) Intelligent SSD: a turbo for big data mining. *Proceedings of the 22nd ACM international conference on Information & Knowledge Management*, 1573-1576. 10.1145/2505515.2507847

Batran, M., Mejia, M. G., Kanasugi, H., Sekimoto, Y., & Shibasaki, R. (2018). Inferencing human spatiotemporal mobility in greater Maputo via mobile phone big data mining. *ISPRS International Journal of Geo-Information*, *7*(7), 259. doi:10.3390/ijgi7070259

Buhl, H. U., Röglinger, M., Moser, F., & Heidemann, J. (2013). Big data. *Business & Information Systems Engineering*, *5*(2), 65–69. doi:10.100712599-013-0249-5

Chang, B. J. (2018). Agile Business Intelligence: Combining Big Data and Business Intelligence to Responsive Decision Model. *Journal of Internet Technology*, *19*(6), 1699–1706.

Chen, H., Chiang, R. H., & Storey, V. C. (2012). Business intelligence and analytics: From big data to big impact. *Management Information Systems Quarterly*, *36*(4), 1165–1188. doi:10.2307/41703503

Chen, J., Li, K., Rong, H., Bilal, K., Yang, N., & Li, K. (2018). A disease diagnosis and treatment recommendation system based on big data mining and cloud computing. *Information Sciences*, *435*, 124–149. doi:10.1016/j.ins.2018.01.001

Chongwatpol, J. (2016). Managing big data in coal-fired power plants: A business intelligence framework. *Industrial Management & Data Systems*, *116*(8), 1779–1799. doi:10.1108/IMDS-11-2015-0473

Chow-White, P. A., & Green, S. Jr. (2013). Data Mining Difference in the Age of Big Data: Communication and the social shaping of genome technologies from 1998 to 2007. *International Journal of Communication*, *7*, 28.

D'Alconzo, A., Barlet-Ros, P., Fukuda, K., & Choffnes, D. R. (2016). Machine learning, data mining and Big Data frameworks for network monitoring and troubleshooting. *Computer Networks*, *107*(1), 1–4. doi:10.1016/j.comnet.2016.06.031

Das, D., Sadiq, A. S., Ahmad, N. B., & Lloret, J. (2017). Stock Market Prediction with Big Data through Hybridization of Data Mining and Optimized Neural Network Techniques. *Multiple-Valued Logic and Soft Computing*, *29*(1-2), 157–181.

Debortoli, S., Müller, O., & vom Brocke, J. (2014). Comparing business intelligence and big data skills. *Business & Information Systems Engineering*, *6*(5), 289–300. doi:10.100712599-014-0344-2

Du, H. S., Ke, X., Chu, S. K. W., & Chan, L. T. (2017). A bibliometric analysis of emergency management using information systems (2000-2016). *Online Information Review*, *41*(4), 454–470. doi:10.1108/OIR-05-2017-0142

Fahimnia, B., Sarkis, J., & Davarzani, H. (2015). Green supply chain management: A review and bibliometric analysis. *International Journal of Production Economics*, *162*, 101–114. doi:10.1016/j.ijpe.2015.01.003

Fu, J., Chen, Z., Wang, J., He, M., & Wang, J. (2012). Distributed storage system big data mining based on HPC application-A solar photovoltaic forecasting system practice. International Information Institute (Tokyo) Information.

Gandomi, A. H., Sajedi, S., Kiani, B., & Huang, Q. (2016). Genetic programming for experimental big data mining: A case study on concrete creep formulation. *Automation in Construction*, *70*, 89–97. doi:10.1016/j.autcon.2016.06.010

Goti-Elordi, A., de-la-Calle-Vicente, A., Gil-Larrea, M. J., Errasti-Opakua, A., & Uradnicek, J. (2017). Application of a business intelligence tool within the context of big data in a food industry company. *Dyna (Bilbao)*, *92*(3), 347–353.

Huang, S. C., McIntosh, S., Sobolevsky, S., & Hung, P. C. (2017). Big data analytics and business intelligence in industry. *Information Systems Frontiers*, *19*(6), 1229–1232. doi:10.100710796-017-9804-9

Jiang, P., & Liu, X. S. (2015). Big data mining yields novel insights on cancer. *Nature Genetics*, *47*(2), 103–104. doi:10.1038/ng.3205 PMID:25627899

Jurgelevičius, A., & Sakalauskas, L. (2018). Big data mining using public distributed computing. *Information Technology and Control*, *47*(2), 236–248. doi:10.5755/j01.itc.47.2.19738

Kim, K. Y. (2014). Business Intelligence and Marketing Insights in an Era of Big Data: The Q-sorting Approach. *Transactions on Internet and Information Systems (Seoul)*, *8*(2).

Kolle, S., Vijayashree, M., & Shankarappa, T. (2017). Highly cited articles in maleria research: A bibliometric analysis. *Collection Building*, *36*(2), 1–12. doi:10.1108/CB-10-2016-0028

Kolle, S. R., & Thyavanahalli, S. H. (2016). Global research on air pollution between 2005 and 2014: A bibliometric study. *Collection Building*, *35*(3), 84–92. doi:10.1108/CB-05-2016-0008

Kranjc, J., Orač, R., Podpečan, V., Lavrač, N., & Robnik-Šikonja, M. (2017). ClowdFlows: Online workflows for distributed big data mining. *Future Generation Computer Systems*, *68*, 38–58. doi:10.1016/j.future.2016.07.018

Kulakli, A., & Osmanaj, V. (2020). Global research on big data in relation with artificial intelligence (A bibliometric study: 2008-2019). *International Journal of Online and Biomedical Engineering*, *16*(2), 31–46. doi:10.3991/ijoe.v16i02.12617

Kulakli, A., & Shubina, I. (2020). A bibliometric study on Mobile Applications for PTSD treatment: The period of 2010-2019. *Proceedings of 6th International Conference on Information Management*, 319-323.

Kuo, C. F. J., Lin, C. H., & Lee, M. H. (2018). Analyze the energy consumption characteristics and affecting factors of Taiwan's convenience stores-using the big data mining approach. *Energy and Building*, *168*, 120–136. doi:10.1016/j.enbuild.2018.03.021

Li, Q., Li, S., Zhang, S., Hu, J., & Hu, J. (2019). A Review of Text Corpus-Based Tourism Big Data Mining. *Applied Sciences (Basel, Switzerland)*, *9*(16), 3300. doi:10.3390/app9163300

Li, X. T., & Feng, F. (2018). Enterprise Customer Relationship Management Based On Big Data Mining. Latin American Applied Research-. *International Journal (Toronto, Ont.)*, *48*(3), 163–168.

Liang, T. P., & Liu, Y. H. (2018). Research landscape of business intelligence and big data analytics: A bibliometric study. *Expert Systems with Applications*, *111*, 2–10. doi:10.1016/j.eswa.2018.05.018

Lin, H. Y., & Yang, S. Y. (2019). A cloud-based energy data mining information agent system based on big data analysis technology. *Microelectronics and Reliability, 97*, 66–78. doi:10.1016/j.microrel.2019.03.010

Liu, B., Fu, Z., Wang, P., Liu, L., Gao, M., & Liu, J. (2018). Big-data-mining-based improved k-means algorithm for energy use analysis of coal-fired power plant units: A case study. *Entropy (Basel, Switzerland), 20*(9), 702. doi:10.3390/e20090702

Lv, S., Kim, H., Zheng, B., & Jin, H. (2018). A review of data mining with big data towards its applications in the electronics industry. *Applied Sciences (Basel, Switzerland), 8*(4), 582. doi:10.3390/app8040582

Margolies, L. R., Pandey, G., Horowitz, E. R., & Mendelson, D. S. (2016). Breast imaging in the era of big data: Structured reporting and data mining. *AJR. American Journal of Roentgenology, 206*(2), 259–264. doi:10.2214/AJR.15.15396 PMID:26587797

Mariani, M., Baggio, R., Fuchs, M., & Höepken, W. (2018). Business intelligence and big data in hospitality and tourism: A systematic literature review. *International Journal of Contemporary Hospitality Management, 30*(12), 3514–3554. doi:10.1108/IJCHM-07-2017-0461

Maté, A., Llorens, H., de Gregorio, E., Tardío, R., Gil, D., Munoz-Terol, R., & Trujillo, J. (2015). A novel multidimensional approach to integrate big data in business intelligence. *Journal of Database Management, 26*(2), 14–31. doi:10.4018/JDM.2015040102

Mellor, J. C., Stone, M. A., & Keane, J. (2018). Application of data mining to "big data" acquired in audiology: Principles and potential. *Trends in Hearing, 22*, 1–10. doi:10.1177/2331216518776817 PMID:29848183

Morota, G., Ventura, R. V., Silva, F. F., Koyama, M., & Fernando, S. C. (2018). Machine learning and data mining advance predictive big data analysis in precision animal agriculture. *Journal of Animal Science, 96*(4), 1540–1550. doi:10.1093/jasky014 PMID:29385611

Njah, H., Jamoussi, S., & Mahdi, W. (2019). Deep Bayesian network architecture for Big Data mining. *Concurrency and Computation, 31*(2), e4418. doi:10.1002/cpe.4418

O'Halloran, K. L., Tan, S., Pham, D. S., Bateman, J., & Vande Moere, A. (2018). A digital mixed methods research design: Integrating multimodal analysis with data mining and information visualization for big data analytics. *Journal of Mixed Methods Research, 12*(1), 11–30. doi:10.1177/1558689816651015

Oliveria, U., Espindola, L., & Marins, F. (2017). Analysis of supply chain risk management research. *Gestão & Produção, 25*(4).

Qi, E., Yang, X., & Wang, Z. (2019). Data mining and visualization of data-driven news in the era of big data. *Cluster Computing, 22*(4), 10333–10346. doi:10.100710586-017-1348-8

Sang, J., Gao, Y., Bao, B. K., Snoek, C., & Dai, Q. (2016). Recent advances in social multimedia big data mining and applications. *Multimedia Systems, 22*(1), 1-3.

Shadroo, S., & Rahmani, A. M. (2018). Systematic survey of big data and data mining in internet of things. *Computer Networks, 139*, 19–47. doi:10.1016/j.comnet.2018.04.001

Shengdong, M., Zhengxian, X., & Yixiang, T. (2019). Intelligent Traffic Control System Based on Cloud Computing and Big Data Mining. *IEEE Transactions on Industrial Informatics*, *15*(12), 6583–6592. doi:10.1109/TII.2019.2929060

Shuai, H., MingChao, L., QiuBing, R., & ChengZhao, L. (2018). Intelligent determination and data mining for tectonic settings of basalts based on big data methods. *Yanshi Xuebao*, *34*(11), 3207–3216.

Singh, S., & Yassine, A. (2018). Big data mining of energy time series for behavioral analytics and energy consumption forecasting. *Energies*, *11*(2), 452.

Song, C. W., Jung, H., & Chung, K. (2019). Development of a medical big-data mining process using topic modeling. *Cluster Computing*, *22*(1), 1949–1958. doi:10.100710586-017-0942-0

Song, G. Y., Cheon, Y., Lee, K., Park, K. M., & Rim, H. C. (2014). Inter-category Map: Building Cognition Network of General Customers through Big Data Mining. *Transactions on Internet and Information Systems (Seoul)*, *8*(2).

Sun, Z., Sun, L., & Strang, K. (2018). Big data analytics services for enhancing business intelligence. *Journal of Computer Information Systems*, *58*(2), 162–169. doi:10.1080/08874417.2016.1220239

Tsai, C. F., Lin, W. C., & Ke, S. W. (2016). Big data mining with parallel computing: A comparison of distributed and MapReduce methodologies. *Journal of Systems and Software*, *122*, 83–92. doi:10.1016/j.jss.2016.09.007

Wang, S., & Yuan, H. (2014). Spatial data mining: A perspective of big data. *International Journal of Data Warehousing and Mining*, *10*(4), 50–70. doi:10.4018/ijdwm.2014100103

Wu, X., Zhu, X., Wu, G. Q., & Ding, W. (2014). Data mining with big data. *IEEE Transactions on Knowledge and Data Engineering*, *26*(1), 97–107. doi:10.1109/TKDE.2013.109

Xu, L., Jiang, C., Chen, Y., Wang, J., & Ren, Y. (2016). A framework for categorizing and applying privacy-preservation techniques in big data mining. *Computer*, *49*(2), 54–62. doi:10.1109/MC.2016.43

Xu, L., Jiang, C., Wang, J., Yuan, J., & Ren, Y. (2014). Information security in big data: Privacy and data mining. *IEEE Access : Practical Innovations, Open Solutions*, *2*, 1149–1176.

Xu, L., Jiang, C., Wang, J., Yuan, J., & Ren, Y. (2014). Information security in big data: Privacy and data mining. *IEEE Access: Practical Innovations, Open Solutions*, *2*, 1149–1176. doi:10.1109/AC-CESS.2014.2362522

Yang, T., Xie, J., Li, G., Mou, N., Li, Z., Tian, C., & Zhao, J. (2019). Social Media Big Data Mining and Spatio-Temporal Analysis on Public Emotions for Disaster Mitigation. *ISPRS International Journal of Geo-Information*, *8*(1), 29. doi:10.3390/ijgi8010029

Yu, D., Xu, Z., & Wang, W. (2018). Bibliometric analysis of fuzzy theory research in China: A 30-year perspective. *Knowledge-Based Systems*, *141*, 188–199. doi:10.1016/j.knosys.2017.11.018

Yu, W. (2017). Challenges and Reflections of Big Data Mining Based on Mobile Internet Customers. *Agro Food Industry Hi-Tech*, *28*(1), 3221–3224.

Zhang, H., & Zhang, Z. (2019). Research on the Big Data Cloud Computing Based on the Network Data Mining. In Basic & Clinical Pharmacology & Toxicology (Vol. 124, pp. 150-151). Wiley.

Zhang, X., Jang-Jaccard, J., Qi, L., Bhuiyan, M. Z., & Liu, C. (2018). Privacy Issues in Big Data Mining Infrastructure, Platforms, and Applications. *Security and Communication Networks*, *2018*, 1–3. doi:10.1155/2018/6238607

Zhang, Y., Guo, S. L., Han, L. N., & Li, T. L. (2016). Application and exploration of big data mining in clinical medicine. *Chinese Medical Journal*, *129*(6), 731–738. doi:10.4103/0366-6999.178019 PMID:26960378

Zhang, Y. B. (2019). Application of the Data Mining Technology in the Financial Management of Colleges and Universities in the Age of the Big Data. *Basic & Clinical Pharmacology & Toxicology*, *124*(3), 143–143.

Zhu, D. (2016). Big data-based multimedia transcoding method and its application in multimedia data mining-based smart transportation and telemedicine. *Multimedia Tools and Applications*, *75*(24), 17647–17668. doi:10.100711042-016-3466-3

Zhu, J., Ge, Z., Song, Z., & Gao, F. (2018). Review and big data perspectives on robust data mining approaches for industrial process modeling with outliers and missing data. *Annual Reviews in Control*, *46*, 107–133. doi:10.1016/j.arcontrol.2018.09.003

Zhu, L., Li, M., Zhang, Z., Du, X., & Guizani, M. (2018). Big data mining of users' energy consumption patterns in the wireless smart grid. *IEEE Wireless Communications*, *25*(1), 84–89. doi:10.1109/MWC.2018.1700157

ADDITIONAL READING

Chang, B. J. (2018). Agile Business Intelligence: Combining Big Data and Business Intelligence to Responsive Decision Model. *Journal of Internet Technology*, *19*(6), 1699–1706.

Chen, H., Chiang, R. H., & Storey, V. C. (2012). Business intelligence and analytics: From big data to big impact. *Management Information Systems Quarterly*, *36*(4), 1165–1188. doi:10.2307/41703503

Debortoli, S., Müller, O., & vom Brocke, J. (2014). Comparing business intelligence and big data skills. *Business & Information Systems Engineering*, *6*(5), 289–300. doi:10.100712599-014-0344-2

Kulakli, A., & Osmanaj, V. (2020). Global research on big data in relation with artificial intelligence (A bibliometric study: 2008-2019). *International Journal of Online and Biomedical Engineering*, *16*(2), 31–46. doi:10.3991/ijoe.v16i02.12617

Liang, T. P., & Liu, Y. H. (2018). Research landscape of business intelligence and big data analytics: A bibliometric study. *Expert Systems with Applications*, *111*, 2–10. doi:10.1016/j.eswa.2018.05.018

Mariani, M., Baggio, R., Fuchs, M., & Höepken, W. (2018). Business intelligence and big data in hospitality and tourism: A systematic literature review. *International Journal of Contemporary Hospitality Management*, *30*(12), 3514–3554. doi:10.1108/IJCHM-07-2017-0461

Xu, L., Jiang, C., Wang, J., Yuan, J., & Ren, Y. (2014). Information security in big data: Privacy and data mining. *IEEE Access: Practical Innovations, Open Solutions*, *2*, 1149–1176. doi:10.1109/ACCESS.2014.2362522

KEY TERMS AND DEFINITIONS

Bibliometric Analysis: Bibliometric is defined as the use of statistical methods to analyze the bibliometric publications data such as peer-reviewed journal articles, books, conference proceedings, periodicals, reviews, reports, and related documents. It has been widely used to present the relations of research domains with quantitative methods.

Big Data: Is enormous data set (mostly unstructured data) that may be analyzed computationally to reveal patterns, trends, and associations, especially relating to interactions.

Big Data Analytics: Is the often complicated process of examining large and varied data sets, or big data, to uncover information—such as hidden patterns, unknown correlations, market trends, and customer preferences—that can help organizations make informed business decisions.

Business Intelligence: It is a collection of processes, architectures, and technologies that turn raw data into useful knowledge driving productive business behavior. To turn data into actionable knowledge it is a suite of tools and services.

Citation Analysis: Is a way of measuring the relative importance or impact of an author, an article, or a publication by counting the number of times that author, article, or other works have cited publication.

Co-Citation Analysis: Provides a forward-looking assessment on document similarity in contrast to Bibliographic Coupling, which is retrospective. The citations a paper receives in the future depend on the evolution of an academic field; thus, co-citation frequencies can still change.

Data Mining: Is the practice of examining large pre-existing (structured) databases in order to generate new information. The data warehousing platforms should be established incorporation level with necessary data marts to analyze the large data sets.

APPENDIX 1

A.   Co-citation of references level 1 (nod size n=20)
B.   Co-citation of references level 2 (nod size n=50)
C.   Co-citation of references level 3 (nod size n=100)
D.   Co-citation of references level 4 (nod size n=200)

APPENDIX 2

A.   Country Collaboration Map

Chapter 3
From Business Intelligence to Big Data:
The Power of Analytics

Mouhib Alnoukari
Syrian Private University, Syria

ABSTRACT

Boundaries between business intelligence (BI), big data (BD), and big data analytics (BDA) are often unclear and ambiguous for companies. BD is a new research challenge; it is becoming a subject of growing importance. Notably, BD was one of the big buzzwords during the last decade. BDA can help executive managers to plan an organization's short-term and long-term goals. Furthermore, BI is considered as a kind of decision support system (DSS) that can help organizations achieving their goals, creating corporate value and improving organizational performance. This chapter provides a comprehensive view about the interrelationships between BI, BD, and BDA. Moreover, the chapter highlights the power of analytics that make them considered as one of the highly impact's organizational capability. Additionally, the chapter can help executive managers to decide the way to integrate BD initiatives as a tool, or as an industry, or as a corporate strategy transformation.

INTRODUCTION

We are in the middle of data explosion. According to Statistica (2020), the size of the digital universe in 2013 was estimated at about 50 zetabytes, it is expected to reach 175 zetabytes by 2025. The global market for software, hardware, and services for storing and analyzing big data is estimated to triple in size in the next five years (Statistica, 2020).

According to Forbes report, "The Global State of Enterprise Analytics, 2020", Cloud Computing, IoT, and Artificial Intelligence/Machine Learning will have the greatest impact on enterprises' analytics initiatives over the next five years. Across all enterprise executives globally, Big Data, 5G, and Security/Privacy concerns are predicted to have the greatest impact (Columbus, 2019). Furthermore, advanced and predictive analytics are dominating enterprises' analytics initiatives today, improved efficiency and

DOI: 10.4018/978-1-7998-5781-5.ch003

productivity; achieving faster for more effective decision-making; and driving better financial performance are the top three benefits enterprises which are gaining from analytics (Columbus, 2019).

Going back to the 1990s, after the information warehousing quickly vanished, the BI era took over. This era introduced a way which is not only to reorganize data, but also to transform it into much cleaner and easier to follow. In this era, BI was pushed notably by the introduction of Data Warehousing (DW) and On-Line analytical Processing (OLAP) that provide a new category of data-driven DSS. OLAP tools provide users with the way to browse and summarize data in an efficient and dynamic way (Alnoukari, Alhawasli, Alnafea, & Zamreek, 2012). According to Ram, et al. (2016), BI is focusing mainly on structured and internal data. Therefore, many of valuable information embedded in the unstructured and external data remain hidden, which leads to an incomplete view and limited insights, thus biased decision-making.

Currently, the new technologies generate huge amount of data arriving from many sources including; computers, smartphones, tablets, sensors, social media, audios, videos, IoT, clickstreams, databases transactions, and so on (Walls & Barnard, 2020; Braganza, Brooks, Nepelski, Ali, & Moro, 2017; Fosso Wamba, Gunasekaran, Akter, Ren, Ji-fan, Dubey, & Childe, 2017). Wal-Mart generates about 2.5 petabytes per hour. Fiber optic cable, the most efficient media for data transfer, can transfer up to 100 gigabits per second. Wal-Mart, simply mean, produces more data than it could transfer to any another place (Brock & Khan, 2017).

Traditional tools are unable to store, manage and analyze such hug data. This situation leads to the creation of the new big data global phenomenon. In 1997, Michael Cox and David Ellsworth first used the word "Big Data" to explain data visualization and the challenges which would pose to computer systems (Wang, Kung and Byrd, 2018). BD moves away from traditional data management onto new methods focusing on data discovery, data integration and data exploitation within the context of "big" data. The word "big" does not only imply size, but rather the ability to produce insights, and manage complex types (Wang, Kung and Byrd, 2018). This leads to the adoption of famous BD three V's (Volume, Velocity, and Variety). The evolution of BD took place during the period from 2001 to 2008 when new tools and technologies were able to manage immense amount of data. 2009 was the year of the BD revolution where it was able to handle and manage unstructured data, in addition to the move from static environments into cloud-based environments (Wang, Kung and Byrd, 2018).

Another important challenge, BD technologies have to process BD in real-time (streaming processing). For example, the large hadrons collider (LHC) generates more raw data than the CERN computing grid can store; thus data has to be instantly analyzed, hence necessities the parallel and distributed computing (Brock & Khan, 2017).

Thus, in the light of this, the main goal of this study is to analyze recent literature of BD, and to find the relationship between BI, BD and BDA. Moreover, the study highlights the power of analytics that make them considered as one of the highly impact's organizational capability.

To achieve this goal, a conceptual literature review was adopted to find all the studies that relate BI with BD. Then, an analysis phase was required to find the interrelationship between both domains. Finally, the study helps managers to decide the way to adopt BD initiatives.

The remainder of this paper is organized as follows. The next section looks at the fundamentals of BI, BD, and BDA. Then a section discussing in details the relationships between BI, BD, and BDA. Thereafter, a section discusses big data analytics capability, and highlights the power of analysis in the current era. Then, the paper provides an overview about the current trends in BD initiatives adoption, with real examples and case studies. The final section ends this paper with some concluding remarks and future work.

BACKGROUND

Business Intelligence Overview

BI has received a widespread attention from scholars and professionals over the past three decades. BI has become an important technology to improve organizational performance (Alnoukari, Alhawasli, Alnafea, & Zamreek, 2012).

BI can be defined as a set of theories, methodologies, architectures, systems and technologies that support business decision making with valuable data, information and knowledge (Alnoukari, 2009; Sun, Zou, & Strang, 2015). Alnoukari et al. (2012) define BI as "The use of all organization's resources: data, applications, people and processes in order to increase its knowledge, implement and achieve its strategy, and adapt to the environment's dynamism". Jin & Kim (2018) consider BI as an information value chain gathering raw data that turned into useful information for better decision-making that in turn creates value and improves organizational performance.

BI main components include; tools for multidimensional data analysis (OLAP) and data mining, tools for data warehousing and DB management, tools for ETL, and tools for visualizations (Alnoukari, Alhawasli, Alnafea, & Zamreek, 2012; Sun, Zou, & Strang, 2015).

Arguably, BI can be seen as a DSS that includes the overall process of gathering huge data, extracting useful information, and providing analytical capabilities (Jin, & Kim, 2018). Other studies have been seen BI as an Information System to support decision-making (Sun, Zou, & Strang, 2015; Alnoukari, 2009), it consists of the following main steps; analysis, insight, action, and performance measurement (Sun, Zou, & Strang, 2015). Jin & Kim (2018) argue that the concept of BI has been growing according to the applications and technologies that support firm's to gather, store, analyze, and access data more effectively.

Self-service oriented BI architecture in an emergent BI approach that can empower casual users to perform custom analytics and to drive actionable information without having to involve BI specialist (Passlick, Lebek, & Breitner, 2017). Data lake implementation can be considered as a source for self-service BI (Llave, 2018).

Big Data Definition: From 3 V's To 7 V's

Literature refers to the three V's when trying to define BD. Many academics use this definition in the literature to date (e.g. Braganza, Brooks, Nepelski, Ali, & Moro, 2017). The three V's are volume, variety, and velocity. The main source of this exponentially increased data coming from the unstructured data of social networks, blogs, text messages, videos and audios (Braganza, Brooks, Nepelski, Ali, & Moro, 2017). Variety refers to the different types of data that can be manipulated using BD technologies (Faroukhi, El Alaoui, Gahi, & Amine, 2020). Structured, semi-structured, and unstructured data types are currently under BD process (Faroukhi, El Alaoui, Gahi, & Amine, 2020). Unstructured data is the challenge key that allows BD to overcome the main deficiencies of the traditional methods. Velocity refers to the speed at which data is generated and delivered (Faroukhi, El Alaoui, Gahi, & Amine, 2020).

Insights are close to the real time decision-making (Walls & Barnard, 2020). According to the three V's dimensions, BD was defined as; large volumes of extensively varied data that are generated, captured, and processed at high velocity (Walls & Barnard, 2020).

An additional two V's were embedded later to the set of BD definition. These are Value and Veracity. Value refers to the insights and benefits that can be gained from BD (Chen, Mao, & Liu, 2014; Erevelles, Fukawa, & Swayne, 2016; Faroukhi, El Alaoui, Gahi, & Amine, 2020). Veracity concerns to the anomalies and uncertainties in data, due to inconsistencies and incompleteness (Faroukhi, El Alaoui, Gahi, & Amine, 2020). The process of precluding bad data is therefore important to extract reliable insights (Faroukhi, El Alaoui, Gahi, & Amine, 2020). Based on the five V's definitions, Fosso Wamba et al. (2015) define BD as "a holistic approach to manage, process and analyze 5 V's (i.e., volume, variety, velocity, veracity and value) in order to create actionable insights for sustained value delivery, measuring performance and establishing competitive advantages.".

The five V's are lately extended to include Valence and Variability and became seven V's definition in order to provide the whole encompassing view of BD (Erevelles, Fukawa, & Swayne, 2016; Braganza, Brooks, Nepelski, Ali, & Moro, 2017). Valence refers to the connectedness of data collected, and Variability refers to constant and rapid changing of the data meaning (Braganza, Brooks, Nepelski, Ali, & Moro, 2017). With these all seven V's, BD is becoming a source of innovation and competitive advantage (Erevelles, Fukawa, & Swayne, 2016). Based on the seven V's definitions, we can update Fosso Wamba et al. (2015) BD definition as "a holistic approach to manage, process and analyze the 7 V's (i.e., volume, variety, velocity, veracity, value, valence, and variability) in order to create actionable insights for sustained value delivery, measuring performance, establishing competitive advantages, and becoming a source of innovation" (Figure 1).

Big Data Analytics Fundamentals

BDA is considered as a disruptive technology that will reshape BI (Fan, Lau, & Zhao, 2015). Sun et al. (2015) considered BDA as an emerging science and technology involving the multidisciplinary state-of-art information and communication technology, statistics, operations research, machine learning, and decision sciences for BD (Sun, Zou, & Strang, 2015). Hence, it encompasses a wide range of mathematical, statistical and modeling techniques. From strategic perspectives, BDA differs from traditional data analytics in the way that it offers the possibilities to discover new opportunities, to offer the customer a high-value and innovative products and services (Davenport, 2014).

According to Sun et al. (2015), BDA can be defined as the process of collecting, organizing and analyzing BD to discover patterns, knowledge, and intelligence as well as other information within the BD. Fan et al. (2015) define BDA as the domain that uses data analytics to gain business insights that will lead firms to improve decision-making. Jin & Kim (2018) define BDA as the overall process of applying advanced analytics to identify patterns, trends, correlations, and other useful techniques. Al-Qirim et al. (2019) argue that BDA is the process of uncovering actionable knowledge patterns from BD. Polese et al. (2019) argue that BDA can enhance the comprehension of business opportunity, and gain better insight into customer behavior, and services/products effectiveness. Insights provided by BDA can improve the efficiency of the organizations' whole operations, as well as the strategy (Walls & Barnard, 2020; Holmlund, Van Vaerenbergh, Ciuchita, Ravald, Sarantopoulos, Villarroel-Ordenes, & Zaki, 2020). Moreover, Sadovskyi et al. (2014) argue that BDA adds additional characteristics to the conventional data analysis including; innovated technologies and skills that enable organizations to own

Figure 1. Dimensions of Big Data

deep analytical capabilities, and integration of wide range of data types from a large number of relatively unreliable data source in order to provide a meaningful and reliable source of business information. Aligned with this viewpoint, Fosso Wamba et al. (2017) and Holmlund et al. (2020) consider BDA as an innovative approach to deliver sustained value, and enable competitive advantage (Mikalef, Pappas, Giannakos, Krogstie, Lekakos, 2016). BDA allows firms to manage and analyze strategy through data lens (Fosso Wamba, Gunasekaran, Akter, Ren, Ji-fan, Dubey, & Childe, 2017; Shams, & Solima, 2019).

BDA has four different levels of analysis (Figure 2): descriptive, inquisitive (or diagnostic), predictive, and prescriptive (Holmlund, Van Vaerenbergh, Ciuchita, Ravald, Sarantopoulos, Villarroel-Ordenes, & Zaki, 2020; Sun, Zou, & Strang, 2015). After generating BDA, organizations are able to generate different insights including market, behavioral and attitudinal insights. Descriptive BDA is related to "What happened?" question answers. This kind of analytics helps describing the situation further analysis (Holmlund, Van Vaerenbergh, Ciuchita, Ravald, Sarantopoulos, Villarroel-Ordenes, & Zaki, 2020). Typical examples include descriptive statistics using charts, cross tabulation, or clustering graphs. Inquisitive DBA is related to "Why did things happen?" question answers (Holmlund, Van Vaerenbergh, Ciuchita, Ravald, Sarantopoulos, Villarroel-Ordenes, & Zaki, 2020). This kind of analytics helps validating research hypotheses, determining causation, and identifying variables to achieve desired results. Typical examples include statistical inference techniques or factor analysis (Holmlund, Van Vaerenbergh, Ciuchita, Ravald, Sarantopoulos, Villarroel-Ordenes, & Zaki, 2020). Predictive BDA is related to "What could happen?" question answers. This kind of analytics helps predicting future trends. Typical examples include forecasting models, classification models, or neural networks (Holmlund, Van Vaerenbergh, Ciuchita, Ravald, Sarantopoulos, Villarroel-Ordenes, & Zaki, 2020. Prescriptive BDA is related to "What should happen?" question answers. This kind of analytics helps providing quantifiable answers when solving a problem (Holmlund, Van Vaerenbergh, Ciuchita, Ravald, Sarantopoulos, Villarroel-Ordenes, & Zaki, 2020). Typical examples include optimizations modeling, queuing modeling, or simulations. Building upon this tautology; BDA has been used successfully in many areas (Holmlund, Van Vaerenbergh, Ciuchita, Ravald, Sarantopoulos, Villarroel-Ordenes, & Zaki, 2020; Palem, 2014). Saidali et al. (2019) propose combining BDA and classical marketing analytics in order to gain valuable and real time insights, thus improve the marketing decision-making process. Different analytics have achieved great success including; usage based insurance, predictive maintenance, Epidemic outbreak detection, and sentiment analysis (Palem, 2014). Ram, et al. (2016) listed five main advantages when applying BDA; increasing data visibility, improving organizational performance, improving meeting customer's needs, revealing valuable insights, and revealing new business models, products and services. In their recent research, Faroukhi et al. (2020) propose a set of BDA tools that provide the ability to deal with various data status. DBA tools are categorized into three families; storage, processing, and visualization.

There is a strong relationship between BDA and strategic management (Şen, Körük, Serper, & Çalış Uslu, 2019; Mikalef, Pappas, Giannakos, Krogstie, Lekakos, 2016). BDA in the lens of strategic management are the capabilities required to gain organizational performance (Walls & Barnard, 2020). BDA provide the ability to show behavioral insights about customers (Suoniemi, Meyer-Waarden, & Munzel, 2017); these insights could be turned into strategic advantages (Şen, Körük, Serper, & Çalış Uslu, 2019). BDA can also improve the metrics used in decisional processes (Fosso Wamba, Gunasekaran, Akter, Ren, Ji-fan, Dubey, & Childe, 2017). Target Corporation is an example of how BDA can be used to track customers purchasing behaviors and predict future trends (Şen, Körük, Serper, & Çalış Uslu, 2019). A personalized purchasing recommendation program is another example (Şen, Körük, Serper, & Çalış Uslu, 2019). Furthermore, Şen et al. (2019) argue that BDA can be used in simulation modeling to gain insight knowledge about the simulated system, and determine the model parameters used in the simulation process.

The Relationship between Business Intelligence, Big Data and Big Data analytics

Scholars argue that there is a close relationship between BI, BD & BDA because BI provides the methodological and technological capabilities for data analysis (e.g. Llave, 2018; Sun, Zou, & Strang, 2015). BI supports firm's decision making with valuable data, information, and knowledge (Alnoukari & Hanano, 2017), hence BDA can be seen as a part of BI (Sun, Zou, & Strang, 2015). In addition, both BI and BDA share some common tools supporting decision-making process. Furthermore, BI and BDA are common in emphasizing valuable data, information, and knowledge. Moreover, BI and BDA involve interactive visualization for data exploration and discovery. Even more, BI is currently based on four cutting-age technology pillars of cloud, mobile, big data, and social technologies; they are also supported effectively by BDA as a service and technology (Passlick, Lebek, & Breitner, 2017; Sun, Zou, & Strang, 2015). Sun et al. (2015) further argue that BDA is an essential tool for developing BI from at least technological and data viewpoints. From technological viewpoint, BDA is data-driven and business oriented techniques, hence; facilitates firm's decision-making and then improves BI. From data viewpoint, knowledge dis-

Figure 2. Big Data Analytics Levels

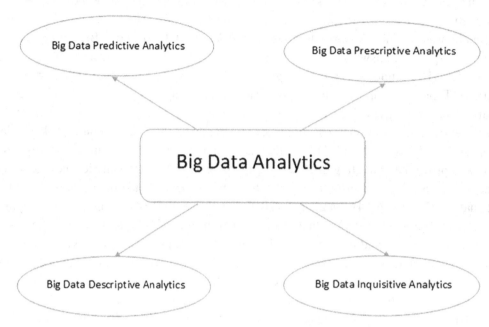

covery is the core of BDA & BI systems (Sun, Zou, & Strang, 2015). Jin & Kim (2018) consider that BI's "raw data" have been expanded into "Big Data" due to the advanced technology capability. Hence, it is logical to consider that BI/BD/BDA are not independent concepts. Consequently, it is beneficial to integrate all of them into an integrated DSS incorporating all processes from data gathering to data analytics and insights to decision making (Jin, & Kim, 2018). Fan et al. (2015) argue that BDA supports marketing intelligence by providing the ability to monitor customer opinions toward a product, service, or company using social media mining techniques. Fan et al. (2015) further argue that customer opinion mining is a key factor for strategic marketing decision that can be based on multiple data sources including; social media, transactions, surveys, and sensors, can be applied to discover marketing intelligence (Fan, Lau, & Zhao, 2015). Analytical models based on single data source may provide limited insights that consequently lead to biased business decisions. Using multiple and heterogeneous data sources can provide a holistic view of the business and result in better decision-making (Fan, Lau, & Zhao, 2015). Fan et Al. (2015) conclude that big data and its applications on BI have great potential in generating business impacts. In the same vein, Kimble & Milolidakis (2015) argue that BI generated from BD could be in immense value. Sun et al. (2015) argue that due to the dramatic development of BD technologies, BI is currently facing new challenges and opportunities; that is how to use BDA to enhance BI becoming a big issue for organizational performance (Sun, Zou, & Strang, 2015).

However, other scholars highlight many of BI drawbacks when comparing with BD/BDA (e.g. Llave, 2018; Ram, Zhang, & Koronios, 2016; Marín-Ortega, Dmitriyevb, Abilovb, & Gómezb, 2014). During the 2000s, BI was becoming a strategic direction that was adopted by business and technology leaders. BI was based on technology-driven data analytics that extracts usable information (Faroukhi, El Alaoui, Gahi, & Amine, 2020; Marín-Ortega, Dmitriyevb, Abilovb, & Gómezb, 2014). These tools provide the decision-makers with the ability to use the analytical results delivered by the reports, dashboards, and data visualizations. However, BI focuses primarily on structured and internal enterprise data, overlooking valuable information embedded in unstructured and external data (Marín-Ortega, Dmitriyevb, Abilovb, & Gómezb, 2014). This could result in an incomplete view of the reality, and biased enterprise's decision-making (Llave, 2018; Ram, Zhang, & Koronios, 2016; Marín-Ortega, Dmitriyevb, Abilovb, & Gómezb, 2014). Scholars highlight some of BI implementation drawbacks (e.g. Marín-Ortega, Dmitriyevb, Abilovb, & Gómezb, 2014) such as the inability to focus on individual needs, lack of business context information that forces users to understand the semantics of data by themselves, poor alignment between business and IT, and high costs related to model time for new BI implementation. BI classical data analytics are unable to acquire valuable business insights (Saidali, Rahich, Tabaa, & Medouri, 2019). BD insights close the knowledge and time gaps of the traditional methods (Walls & Barnard, 2020). According to Marín-Ortega et al. (2014), data management is the most critical and stressing stage during BI development due to its time consuming. Most of the BI solution providers are focusing on the technological part of data management stage rather than the availability of all the required information (structured and unstructured) to build a good solution. In their recent research, Faroukhi et al. (2020) listed some of the differences between BI and BD/BDA such as; BI is based on File-Based or Object-Based storage models; whereas BD is based on Block-Based storage model. Additionally, BI is based on traditional database data model such as SQL databases and data warehouses. However, traditional databases cannot meet BD challenges, mainly storing and processing hug amount of unstructured data; hence, distributed storage and NoSQL databases are mainly adopted for BD data model (Faroukhi, El Alaoui, Gahi, & Amine, 2020). In the same vein, the hardware storage infrastructure for BI is mainly based on storage devices; whereas, BD requires additional storage infrastructure such as storage network infrastructure and storage virtualization. Furthermore, BD requires distributed processing infrastructure in order to be able to share data, calculations, and processing on over several interconnected nodes. However, traditional BI does not require such distributed processing infrastructure (Faroukhi, El Alaoui, Gahi, & Amine, 2020). Finally, and from analytical viewpoint, descriptive and predictive analyses were mainly developed by BI traditional systems; whereas, BD provides the ability to effectively develop and use additional analytics capabilities such as prescriptive and diagnostic analysis (Faroukhi, El Alaoui, Gahi, & Amine, 2020).

One of the suggested approaches is to fix the ETL (Extract, Transform, and Load) stage bottleneck (Marín-Ortega, Dmitriyevb, Abilovb, & Gómezb, 2014). In typical BI infrastructure, ETL stage starts extracting raw data from Operational Data Sources (ODS), then transforming the raw data into a normalized form, before loading the processed data into the data warehouse. Processing raw data during the transformation phase is critical. A DW typically consolidates a multitude different ODS with multiple schemas; therefore, the raw data must be normalized. In addition, the ODS may contain corrupted, erroneous, or missing data; therefore, the process of cleansing and consolidating data is required (Alnoukari, Alhawasli, Alnafea, & Zamreek, 2012). According to Marín-Ortega et al. (2014), ETL technologies have not been improved in scalability and performance at the same level with the DW technologies. Consequently, most of the BI infrastructures are facing serious bottleneck; data cannot be easily transformed and loaded into the DW in an acceptable time, whereas, the decision makers are looking for real time information. One of the suggested approaches to tackle the ETL serious bottleneck is to throw the transformation phase to the end of the ETL after the loading phase. Hence, ETL is becoming ELT. The main advantage of this switch is that ELT allows firstly extracting and loading data, then applying on-demand transformations according to business needs. In addition, ELT allows to apply and to re-apply data transformation in accordance to the changes in the environment. This provides ELT the flexibility needed to respond to the market changes. As a result, ELT addresses the issue related to design BI solutions in shorter time, as well as, provides the BI with the flexibility to reflect environmental changes. Passlick et al. (2017) proposed BI/BDA architecture model that support both traditional BI analytical reports, and BDA. The proposed architecture model integrates BI components with the BD ones. The data processing layer uses the classic ETL process, extended by the possibility to perform the BD EL(T) process. In addition, in the storage and analysis infrastructure layer, data integration can be done using the classic DW, as well as other BD technologies such as in-memory databases, or Hadoop clusters (Passlick, Lebek, & Breitner, 2017).

Another suggested approach is to integrate the Data Lakes with BI (Llave, 2018). Llave (2018) argues that Data Lakes has made it possible for BI to acquire data without caring of its structure. It is a huge capability to store inexhaustible amounts of raw data without performing any data transformation. Data transformation is considered as a bottleneck when using ETL process between the data sources and DW. Hence, it is similar to ELT, where the transformation is performed in the last step (Llave, 2018).

Data monetization is one of the concepts that has seen notable evolution starting BI era, until the BD era (Faroukhi, El Alaoui, Gahi, & Amine, 2020). Data monetization is a new concept that relies on using the data from organization to generate profit. Explicit data monetization is selling the data directly for cache, or sharing the data, whereas, implicit data monetization is an indirect way relying on that data to create value by enhancing own data-based products (Faroukhi, El Alaoui, Gahi, & Amine, 2020). During the BI era, data monetization was generally implicit, delivered by descriptive analytics. Production data was generally used for internal purpose. Thereafter, data monetization gain popularity and critical evolution during the BD era. Data monetization is becoming attractive in the era of BD (Faroukhi, El Alaoui, Gahi, & Amine, 2020). Data is integrated from external and internal sources that results in advanced analytical capabilities based on data-driven products and services. This allows for explicit monetization by selling data and provides the agility required for creating and monetizing knowledge. Faroukhi et al. (2020) argue that monetizing BD can be articulated based on the following business models directions; extracting customers-based activities data (data extractors), collecting and selling data (data providers), aggregating services (data aggregators), and providing technical platforms that enable processing, consuming and sharing data (technical platform providers). Monetizing BD provides firms with the ability to unlock value, and maximize the data-driven capability (Faroukhi, El Alaoui, Gahi, & Amine, 2020).

Big Data Analytics Capability: The Analytics Power

The complexity nature of BD stems from the difficulties in dealing with huge data sources, dealing with the complexity nature of the data itself, and the data processing to generate data insights (Al-Qirim, Rouibah, Serhani, Tarhini, Khalil, Maqableh, & Gergely, 2019). Data and information cannot, themselves, provide insights. Data insights could be generated by data transformation through analysis and interpretation, values are gained through the ability to drive actions (Holmlund, Van Vaerenbergh, Ciuchita, Ravald, Sarantopoulos, Villarroel-Ordenes, & Zaki, 2020). BD is one of the organization's resources that are necessary but not sufficient to create a Big Data Analytics Capability (BDAC), since many other firms are able to collect huge data from different resources (Gupta, & George, 2016). BD initiatives and BDAC can lead to improved organizational performance through value creation, better strategic decision-making, gains in competitive advantage, efficiency gains, improved marketing and increased innovation (Walls & Barnard, 2020). The term BDAC has been referred to in literature as the "next big thing in innovation", "fourth paradigm of science", "next frontier for innovation, competition, and productivity", "new paradigm of knowledge assets" and "next management revolution" because of the universal adoption of BDA technologies (Fosso Wamba, Gunasekaran, Akter, Ren, Ji-fan, Dubey, & Childe, 2017). In their recent research, Walls & Barnard (2020) adopt BDAC definition as "the holistic approach to managing, processing and analyzing huge volumes of incongruent data to determine actionable ideas and reactions to the data for sustained value and competitive advantage". BDAC refers to the organizational capabilities that can enable firms to analyze their huge data with nontraditional methods using BD tools and techniques; hence, producing insights that enable data-driven decision-making process (Dubey, Gunasekaran, & Childe, 2018). In the same vein, Akter et al. (2016) define BDAC as the competence to provide business insights using data management, technology, and talent capability to transform business into a competitive advantage and gain business value. Therefore, BDAC can be seen as an integration of the following three intertwined capabilities; big data analytics management capability, big data analytics infrastructure capability, and big data analytics talent capability (Walls & Barnard, 2020; Fosso Wamba, Gunasekaran, Akter, Ren, Ji-fan, Dubey, & Childe, 2017). Gupta, & George (2016) refer them as; tangible, human and intangible resources. Big data analytical management capability ensures the proper decision-making. It can be enhanced by improving the quality of planning, investment, coordination, and control (Walls & Barnard, 2020; Fosso Wamba, Gunasekaran, Akter, Ren, Ji-fan, Dubey, & Childe, 2017; Akter, Fosso Wamba, Gunasekaran, Dubey, & Childe, 2016). Big data analytical technology capability refers to the BDA platform flexibility that effectively enables the developing, deploying and supporting firm's resources. It can be improved by enhancing the performance of the BDA platforms in terms of connectivity, compatibility, and modularity (Walls & Barnard, 2020; Fosso Wamba, Gunasekaran, Akter, Ren, Ji-fan, Dubey, & Childe, 2017; Akter, Fosso Wamba, Gunasekaran, Dubey, & Childe, 2016). Big data analytical talent capability refers to the ability of an analytics professional to perform assigned tasks in the BD environment. Akter et al. (2016) argue that analysts should be competent in four important skills, technical knowledge (e.g., database management); technology management knowledge (e.g., visualization tools, and techniques management and deployment); business knowledge (e.g., understanding of short-term and long-term goals); and relational knowledge (e.g., cross-functional collaboration using information). Nocker & Sena (2019) argue that most organizations treat talent analytics as a capability, not as a resource, in order to contribute to value creation. This is in line with the Dynamic Capability Theory where talent analytics capabilities may include; learning capability, as organizational learning should support the implementation of talent analytics across the organization, coordinating capability between different organization sections so that talent analytics can create value, and technical capability for processing HR data.

Wang et al. (2018) listed some of the BDAC in the health care such as; analytical capability for patterns of care, unstructured data analytical capability, decision support capability, predictive capability, and traceability. Holmlund et al. (2020) classified customer experience insights as attitudinal/ psychographic, behavioral, and market insights. Attitudinal/ psychographic insights provide knowledge about satisfaction, advocacy, and valuable efforts by organizations. Behavioral insights help organizations with the knowledge about the behavioral aspect and consequences of customer experience. Market insights are extremely valuable as they are related to the knowledge about organizational performance in terms of the customer experience in relation with the marketplace.

Cloud computing and BD are complementary approaches (Lněnička, & Komárková, 2015). The marriage between cloud computing and BD derived Big data Analytics as a Service (BAaaS). BAaaS is an emergent service that provides individual, or organization, or information system, with the ability to share a wide range of analytical tools that can be available on the web or used by the smartphones.

BAaaS is gaining popularity in recent years and many giant companies such as Microsoft, Amazon, and eBay adopted it (Sun, Zou, & Strang, 2015). Depeige & Doyencourt (2015) argue further that leveraging BDA to better manage and deliver knowledge services increases the benefits of Knowledge as a Service (KaaS) and its underlying processes offered in the cloud environment. KaaS can be considered as an on-demand knowledge store that has the ability to search, analyze and restructure its knowledge resources using cloud-computing environment (Depeige & Doyencourt, 2015). Furthermore, Depeige & Doyencourt (2015) argue on the close relationship between BI/BD/BDA and Knowledge Management (KM). Depeige & Doyencourt (2015) highlight the evolution of BI analytics towards contextualized Knowledge Analytics (K-Analytics) that improve the capability to gain business value from data insights based on descriptive and predictive methods. Depeige & Doyencourt (2015) introduced actionable KaaS concept to induce valuable results.

Trends in Big Data Adoption

Amazon, Facebook, Google, Netflix, Dell, eBay, LinkedIn, Procter and Gamble, Target, Tesco, UPS, Walmart, and Zara are examples of organizations that have been successful at sustaining BDAC and setting the example (Walls & Barnard, 2020). The majority of these companies have born digital; they had a head step by digitizing all their operations. They have already adopted data-driven process as the source of the corporate strategy (Walls & Barnard, 2020).

However, this is not the case of the majority of the current organizations that trying to adopt BDA, and sustainably utilize BD to its full potential and benefits. Scholars argued the surveys' results showing how it is difficult for organizations to understand how to leverage BD insights in order to create value (Erevelles, Fukawa, Swayne 2016; Walls & Barnard, 2020). Even though an organization may extract BD insights successfully, there is no guarantee that they are able to utilize these insights effectively (Erevelles, Fukawa, Swayne 2016; Walls & Barnard, 2020). Even more many organizations could not understand how BDAC will affect their business performance and competitive advantages, and this explains Erevelles et al. (2016) findings that more than 50% of big data initiatives do not achieve their targets.

Mazzei, & Noble (2017) presented a BD maturity framework that highlights how BD can be used as an evolutionary strategic management tool, not only an IT tool that can use data as a source for corporate strategies. The framework is based on three tiers: big data as a tool, as an industry, and as a strategic tool. Scholars used Mazzei, & Noble (2017) BD framework in their studies; e.g. Walls & Barnard (2020) utilized it to identify the success factors of BDAC on organizational performance. Our study will use this framework to differentiate between the organizations adopting BD initiatives, and highlight how deeply BD technologies are used by different companies and integrated in their internal processes (Figure 3).

Big Data as a Tool

Many organizations currently use BD initiatives to improve their core functions performance using its analytics technology (Mazzei, & Noble, 2017). For example, Volvo Cars Company implemented a new automatic fault monitoring system. Using the data collected from the sensors installed inside vehicles. This data, combined with the data collected from the maintenance workshops, and the customer analysis results obtained from the social media data analysis, this device is able to provide a high quality advisor for its customers (Sadovskyi, Engel, Heininger, Böhm, & Krcmar, 2014). Ford Cars Company constantly provides information regarding relevant car parameters in real time to the driver. Ford's engineers can use

Figure 3. Big Data Adoption Framework

Big Data as a Strategy

Big Data as an Industry

Big Data as a Tool

this data to continuously improve the product or provide additional services, like location service to the next charging station (Bischof, Gabriel, Rabel, & Wilfinger, 2016). Starbucks, the famous coffee giant is using BDA with crowd sourcing to determine the success of any new location. It uses the information about the location, traffic, area demographic, and customer behavior to assess the location before opening any new store. Such analytics provides Starbucks with accurate estimation of the success rate of the new location (Satish & Yusof, 2017). Target proactively utilizes consumer insights from BDA to predict consumer behavior. Target is able to estimate if a shopper woman is pregnant and her due date weeks before other competitors. The company is able due to predictive analysis to enhance adaptive capability to influence the customer's purchases towards baby items, and capturing sales before competitors (Erevelles, Fukawa, Swayne 2016). Southwest Airlines developed a BD application that extracts insights from customer's conversation records using a speech-analytics tool. Insights results are used to improve performance, and facilitate its dynamic capabilities (Erevelles, Fukawa, Swayne 2016). Los Angeles city is applying the demand-responsive pricing for parking application based on BDA. The goal is to reach a steadily high utilization of the parking spaces at all times, considering the data feed from parking sensors, the weather forecasts, holidays, etc. This BD based application helps them maximize parking utilization, with best pricing (El-Darwiche, Koch, Meer, Shehadi, & Tohme, 2014). United Healthcare, a large health insurance company, is using BD for its customer satisfaction application. The recorded voice files from customer calls to call center are transformed into text formats, and then analyzed to extract meaning from text using natural language processing. This analysis process is able to identify any customer's dissatisfaction (Davenport, 2014).

Big Data as an Industry

Organizations at this level are using BD for creating new ventures specialized in acquisition, storage and analysis of companies' huge data, construction of BD infrastructure, and development of all related software (Mazzei, & Noble, 2017). For example, Pivotal is using BD as an innovative industry. It provides "platform as a service" to allow clients to build their applications in its cloud (Mazzei, & Noble, 2020). Finning, a Caterpillar dealer, has transformed from a traditional repair service to a provider of support for customers' machines through predictive and prescriptive BDA. Customer experience insights enable Finning to track a machine's location, prevent premature failure, prolong service life, minimize downtime, increase operator efficiency, reduce the cost of repair, and recommend solutions (Holmlund, Van Vaerenbergh, Ciuchita, Ravald, Sarantopoulos, Villarroel-Ordenes, & Zaki, 2020). Netflix is a success story using BD sensing and seizing practices. Netflix created a new TV series, House of Cards, based on BDA that powerfully revealed viewers tastes such as favorites actors and actresses. This new innovative series brought Netflix millions as new revenues. This success showcase provides evidence supporting the relationship between market (customer) orientation and BD capability (Lin & Kunnathur, 2019; Akter, Fosso Wamba, Gunasekaran, Dubey, & Childe, 2016). Spotify, a streaming provider, created a personalized experience for each customer. Spotify capitalized on descriptive and predictive BDA to generate customer experience behavioral insights (i.e., knowledge on listening habits) and design highly personalized touchpoints. Spotify sent each customer a personalized email with information about their listening habits. These actions allowed Spotify to create personalized touchpoints in each customer's journey by generating custom playlists (Holmlund, Van Vaerenbergh, Ciuchita, Ravald, Sarantopoulos, Villarroel-Ordenes, & Zaki, 2020). Uber is the best showcase of the link between entrepreneurial orientation and BD capability. It is due to the entrepreneurial insights of Uber creators that helped them capturing the business value behind the real-time flow of digital data streams (Lin & Kunnathur, 2019).

Big Data as a Strategy

Organizations at this level reveal the new strategic thinking of using BD as a source of innovative business models of markets and products, and a driver of competitive strategy (Mazzei, & Noble, 2017). Inside these organizations, new leaders' innovative thinking concentrates on data flows rather than data stocks. They are able to create new ecosystems based on the data they accumulate and the increase of data flow. These learning organizations evolve dynamically; based on the uncovered trends in their data analysis. Organizations at this level have the ability to increase opportunities to diversify and expand into new markets (Walls & Barnard, 2020; Mazzei, & Noble, 2017; El-Darwiche, Koch, Meer, Shehadi, & Tohme, 2014). Amazon is an exceptional case where a company is using BD at all levels, as a tool, as an innovative industry, and as a corporate strategy (Mazzei, & Noble, 2020). Amazon is the best case showing a business model transformation based on Big-Data-Driven industry (Bischof, Gabriel, Rabel, & Wilfinger, 2016). Started as a traditional bookseller, it was evolved to one of the largest online traders.

The company's platform was opened to other traders providing them access to their customer database and logistics network. Amazon is currently transformed its business model into a full service provider based mainly on BD (Mazzei, & Noble, 2020; Bischof, Gabriel, Rabel, & Wilfinger, 2016). Amazon restructures its distribution strategy in order to gain greater value through radical innovation. Amazon is able to predict when a customer will make a purchase, and start shipping products to nearest hub before the customer submits the order (Erevelles, Fukawa, Swayne 2016). Currently, 35% of purchases are generated from personalized purchase recommendations to customers based on BDA (Fosso Wamba, Gunasekaran, Akter, Ren, Ji-fan, Dubey, & Childe, 2017). Additionally, 30% of sales were newly generated from the new predictive technique called 'collaborative filtering' that generate "you might also want" prompt for each product bought or visited based on customer data (Akter, Fosso Wamba, Gunasekaran, Dubey, & Childe, 2016). Apple is another best showcase of a company using big data as a strategy (Mazzei, & Noble, 2017). Starting initially from a personal computer manufacturer, the company expanded its ecosystem data flows by collecting data in digital music, videos, telecommunications and other markets. Using BD as their corporate strategy, Apple was able to tackle and expand to new markets, including wearable, automobiles and mobile payment services. All of which are strategically integrated to the core company's platform (Mazzei, & Noble, 2017). John Deere, Agricultural equipment manufacturer, capitalized on BDA and equipped its machines with sensors that allowed customers to access and analyze their machine data, benchmarking it against other machines and combining it with historical data in real time and for free. Thus, John Deere introduced new touchpoint design that changed its customers' entire journey. Currently, myJohnDeere.com platform is opened to suppliers, retailers, and software developers. John Deere transitioned from a manufacturing business model to a platform-centric model, thus achieved innovation and revolutionized the agriculture industry (Holmlund, Van Vaerenbergh, Ciuchita, Ravald, Sarantopoulos, Villarroel-Ordenes, & Zaki, 2020).

FUTURE RESEARCH DIRECTIONS

Although BDA is a new research challenge, it is becoming a subject of growing importance. However, BD research has a relatively short history, starting in 2011 from only 38 studies listed in the Science Citation Index Expanded (SCIE), Social Science Citation Index (SSCI), Arts & Humanities Citation Index (AHCI), and Emerging Sources Citation Index (ESCI). The number of studies was increased to 3890 studies in 2017 (Jin, & Kim, 2018).

This paper outlines some avenues for future researches in the arena of BD; integration of BD with strategic management is an important research direction. A fundamental question remains: To what extent strategic management theories can be adopted to provide organizations with the ability to best adapt with BD initiatives. Big Data Maturity Model is another search direction, although different models were suggested, there is still a room for improvement, especially from best practices viewpoint.

CONCLUSION

BI was characterized by flexibility and adaptability in which traditional applications are not able to deal with. Traditional process modeling requires a lot of documentation and reports and this makes traditional methodology unable to fulfill the dynamic requirements of changes of our high-speed, high-change environment. BI main drawbacks was mainly related to data management issues, especially when dealing with huge data amount, and unstructured data types.

Technological development in data storage and processing make it possible to handle exponential increases in data volume in different type format. Hence, it was the cornerstone behind BD revolution. BD has become a source for innovation and competitive advantage by transforming decision making and leading to new strategic models. Decision-making process was redefined to incorporate the new strategic effects of BD & BDA concepts.

Borderlines between BI, BD and BDA still unclear for many companies. This paper provided a comprehensive view about all these concepts, the interrelationship between them, the new created organizational capabilities, and the different levels of BD adoption. Companies already integrated BI in their internal processes can extend their technological infrastructure and skills, and restructure their processes to gain value from BI/BD/BDA integration, improve their competitive advantages, and enhance organizational performance.

This paper concludes that analytics capability is the core power of BI/BD/BDA. BD (including BDA) is an extension of BI. It is worth noting that BD is more than a technology, and to be fully effective, it should be incorporated into corporate strategy. Arguably, BD affects organizational culture; it converts firms to become data and evidence-based organizations. Most notably, BD enables organizations to create entirely new innovative products, and new business models.

REFERENCES

Al-Qirim, N., Rouibah, K., Serhani, M. A., Tarhini, A., Khalil, A., Maqableh, M., & Gergely, M. (2019). The Strategic Adoption of Big Data in Organizations. In Z. Sun (Ed.), *Managerial Perspectives on Intelligent Big Data Analytics* (pp. 43–54). IGI Global. doi:10.4018/978-1-5225-7277-0.ch003

Alnoukari, M. (2009). Using Business Intelligence Solutions for Achieving Organization's Strategy: Arab International University Case Study. *Internetworking Indonesia Journal*, *1*(2), 11–15.

Alnoukari, M., Alhawasli, H., Alnafea, H. A., & Zamreek, A. (2012). Business Intelligence: Body of Knowledge. In Business Intelligence and Agile Methodologies for Knowledge-Based Organizations: Cross-Disciplinary Applications (pp. 1-13). IGI Global.

Alnoukari, M., & Hanano, A. (2017). Integration of business intelligence with corporate strategic management. *Journal of Intelligence Studies in Business*, *7*(2), 5–16. doi:10.37380/jisib.v7i2.235

Bischof, C., Gabriel, M., Rabel, B., & Wilfinger, D. (2016). Strategic Implications of BIG DATA – A Comprehensive View. *Proceedings of the Management International Conference (MIC 2016)*, 143–160.

Braganza, A., Brooks, L., Nepelski, D., Ali, M., & Moro, R. (2017). Resource management in big data initiatives: Processes and dynamic capabilities. *Journal of Business Research*, *70*, 328–337. doi:10.1016/j.jbusres.2016.08.006

Brock, V., & Khan, H. U. (2017). Big data analytics: Does organizational factor matters impact technology acceptance? *Journal of Big Data*, *4*(21), 1–28. doi:10.118640537-017-0081-8

Chen, M., Mao, S., & Liu, Y. (2014). Big data: A survey. *Mobile Networks and Applications, 19*(2), 171–209. doi:10.100711036-013-0489-0

Columbus, L. (2019). *The Global State of Enterprise Analytics, 2020.* Retrieved May 9, 2020 from: https://www.forbes.com/sites/louiscolumbus/2019/10/21/the-global-state-of-enterprise-analytics-2020/#4966b9ba562d

Davenport, T. H. (2014). How strategists use 'big data' to support internal business decisions, discovery and production. *Strategy and Leadership, 42*(4), 45–50. doi:10.1108/SL-05-2014-0034

Depeige, A., & Doyencourt, D. (2015). Actionable Knowledge As A Service (AKAAS): Leveraging big data analytics in cloud computing environments. *Journal of Big Data, 2*(1), 12. doi:10.118640537-015-0023-2

Dubey, R., Gunasekaran, A., & Childe, S. J. (2018). *Big data analytics capability in supply chain agility: the moderating effect of organizational flexibility. In Management Decision.* Emerald. doi:10.1108/MD-01-2018-0119

El-Darwiche, B., Koch, V., Meer, D., Shehadi, R., & Tohme, W. (2014). *Big data maturity: An action plan for policymakers and executives.* Accessed April 25, 2020, https://www.strategyand.pwc.com/media/file/Strategyand_Big-data-maturity.pdf

Erevelles, S., Fukawa, N., & Swayne, L. (2016). Big Data consumer analytics and the transformation of marketing. *Journal of Business Research, 69,* 897-904.

Fan, S., Lau, R., & Zhao, J. A. (2015). Demystifying Big Data Analytics for Business Intelligence Through the Lens of Marketing Mix. *Big Data Research, 2*(1), 28–32. doi:10.1016/j.bdr.2015.02.006

Faroukhi, A. Z., El Alaoui, I., Gahi, Y., & Amine, A. (2020). Big data monetization throughout Big Data Value Chain: A comprehensive review. *Journal of Big Data, 7*(1), 3. doi:10.118640537-019-0281-5

Fosso Wamba, S., Akter, S., Edwards, A., Chopin, G., & Gnanzou, D. (2015). How 'big data' can make big impact: Findings from a systematic review and a longitudinal case study. *International Journal of Production Economics, 165,* 234–246. Advance online publication. doi:10.1016/j.ijpe.2014.12.031

Fosso Wamba, S., Gunasekaran, A., Akter, S., & Ren, S. (2017). Big data analytics and firm performance: Effects of dynamic capabilities. *Journal of Business Research, 70,* 356–365. doi:10.1016/j.jbusres.2016.08.009

Gupta, M., & George, J. F. (2016). Toward the development of a big data analytics capability. *Information & Management, 53,* 1049-1064.

Holmlund, M., Van Vaerenbergh, Y., Ciuchita, R., Ravald, A., Sarantopoulos, P., Villarroel-Ordenes, F., & Zaki, M. (2020). Customer Experience Management in the Age of Big Data Analytics: A Strategic Framework. *Journal of Business Research, 116,* 356–365. doi:10.1016/j.jbusres.2020.01.022

Jin, D. H., & Kim, H. J. (2018). Integrated Understanding of Big Data, Big Data Analysis, and Business Intelligence: A Case Study of Logistics. *Sustainability, 10*(10), 3778. doi:10.3390u10103778

Kimble, C., & Milolidakis, G. (2015). Big Data and Business Intelligence: Debunking the Myths. *Global Business and Organizational Excellence*, *35*(1), 23–34. doi:10.1002/joe.21642

Lin, C., & Kunnathur, A. (2019). Strategic orientations, developmental culture, and big data capability. *Journal of Business Research*, *105*, 49–60. doi:10.1016/j.jbusres.2019.07.016

Llave, M. R. (2018). Data lakes in business intelligence: Reporting from the trenches. *Procedia Computer Science*, *138*, 516–524. doi:10.1016/j.procs.2018.10.071

Lněnička, M., & Komárková, J. (2015). The Impact of Cloud Computing and Open (Big) Data on the Enterprise Architecture Framework. *Proceedings of the 26th International Business Information Management Association Conference*, 1679-1683.

Marín-Ortega, P. M., Dmitriyevb, V., Abilovb, M., & Gómezb, J. M. (2014). ELTA: New Approach in Designing Business Intelligence Solutions in Era of Big Data. *Procedia Technology*, *16*, 667–674. doi:10.1016/j.protcy.2014.10.015

Mazzei, M. J., & Noble, D. (2017). Big data dreams: A framework for corporate strategy. BUSHOR-1369. *ScienceDirect*. Elsevier.

Mazzei, M. J., & Noble, D. (2020). Big Data and Strategy: Theoretical Foundations and New Opportunities. In *Strategy and Behaviors in the Digital Economy*. IntechOpen. https://www.intechopen.com/books/strategy-and-behaviors-in-the-digital-economy/big-data-and-strategy-theoretical-foundations-and-new-opportunities

Mikalef, P., Pappas, O. I., Giannakos, N. M., Krogstie, J., & Lekakos, G. (2016). Big Data and Strategy: A Research Framework. *Tenth Mediterranean Conference on Information Systems (MCIS)*, 1-9.

Nocker, M., & Sena, V. (2019). Big Data and Human Resources Management: The Rise of Talent Analytics. *Social Sciences*, *8*(10), 273. doi:10.3390ocsci8100273

Palem, G. (2014). Formulating an Executive Strategy for Big Data Analytics. *Technology Innovation Management Review*, *4*(3), 25–34. doi:10.22215/timreview/773

Passlick, J., Lebek, B., & Breitner, M. H. (2017). A Self-Service Supporting Business Intelligence and Big Data Analytics Architecture. In J. M. Leimeister & W. Brenner (Eds.), Proceedings der 13. Internationalen Tagung Wirtschaftsinformatik (WI 2017) (pp. 1126–1140). Academic Press.

Polese, F., Troisi, O., Grimaldi, M., & Romeo, E. (2019). A Big Data-Oriented Approach to Decision-Making: A Systematic Literature Review. *22nd International Conference Proceedings*, 472-496.

Ram, J., Zhang, C., & Koronios, A. (2016). The implications of Big Data analytics on Business Intelligence: A qualitative study in China. *Procedia Computer Science*, *87*, 221–226. doi:10.1016/j.procs.2016.05.152

Sadovskyi, O., Engel, T., Heininger, R., Böhm, M., & Krcmar, H. (2014). Analysis of Big Data enabled Business Models using a Value Chain Perspective. Proceedings of Multikonferenz Wirtschaftsinformatik (MKWI 2014), 1127–1137.

Saidali, J., Rahich, H., Tabaa, Y., & Medouri, A. (2019). The combination between Big Data and Marketing Strategies to gain valuable Business Insights for better Production Success. *Procedia Manufacturing*, *32*, 1017–1023. doi:10.1016/j.promfg.2019.02.316

Satish, L., & Yusof, N. (2017). A Review: Big Data Analytics for enhanced Customer Experiences with Crowd Sourcing. *Procedia Computer Science*, *116*, 274–283. doi:10.1016/j.procs.2017.10.058

Şen, E., Körük, E., Serper, N., & Çalış Uslu, B. (2019). Big Data Analytics and Simulation for Better Strategic Management. *Journal of Current Research on Engineering. Science and Technology*, *5*(2), 1–12.

Shams, S., & Solima, L. (2019). Big data management: Implications of dynamic capabilities and data incubator. *Management Decision*, *57*(8), 2113–2123. doi:10.1108/MD-07-2018-0846

Statistica. (2020). Retrieved May 9, 2020 from: https://www.statista.com/statistics/871513/worldwide-data-created/#statisticContainer

Sun, Z., Zou, H., & Strang, K. (2015). Big Data Analytics as a Service for Business Intelligence. *14th Conference on e-Business, e-Services and e-Society (I3E)*, 200-211. 10.1007/978-3-319-25013-7_16

Suoniemi, S., Meyer-Waarden, L., & Munzel, A. (2017). Big Data Resources, Marketing Capabilities, and Firm Performance. In *2017 Winter AMA Conference*. American Marketing Association.

Walls, C., & Barnard, B. (2020). Success Factors of Big Data to Achieve Organisational Performance: Qualitative Research. *Expert Journal of Business and Management*, *8*(1), 17–56.

Wang, Y., Kung, L., & Byrd, T. A. (2018). Big data analytics: Understanding its capabilities and potential benefits for healthcare organizations. *Technological Forecasting and Social Change*, *126*, 3–13. doi:10.1016/j.techfore.2015.12.019

ADDITIONAL READING

Cecilia, A., Rusli, A., Rodziah, A., & Yusmadi, Y. J. (2016). Towards Developing Strategic Assessment Model for Big Data Implementation: A Systematic Literature Review. *Int. J. Advance Soft Compu. Appl*, *8*(3), 174–192.

Charles, V., & Gherman, T. (2013). Achieving Competitive Advantage Through Big Data. Strategic Implications. *Middle East Journal of Scientific Research*, *16*(8), 1069–1074.

Costa, J., Dantas, R., Santos, C., Medeiros, F., & Rebouças, S. (2018). The Impact of Big Data on SME's Strategic Management: A Study on a Small British Enterprise Specialized in Business Intelligence. *Journal of Management and Strategy*, *9*(4), 10–21. doi:10.5430/jms.v9n4p10

Court, D. (2015). *Getting big impact from big data*. McKinsey Global Institute. https://www.mckinsey.com/business-functions/business-technology/our-insights/getting-big-impact-from-big-data

Etzion, D., & Aragon-Correa, J. A. (2016). Big data, management, and sustainability: Strategic opportunities ahead. *Organization & Environment*, *29*(2), 3–10. doi:10.1177/1086026616650437

Zahra, S. A., & George, G. (2002). Absorptive capacity: A review, reconceptualization, and extension. *Academy of Management Review*, 27(2), 185–203. doi:10.5465/amr.2002.6587995

KEY TERMS AND DEFINITIONS

Big Data (BD): Is a holistic approach to manage process and analyze the 7 V's (i.e., volume, variety, velocity, veracity, value, valence, and variability) in order to create actionable insights for sustained value delivery, measuring performance, establishing competitive advantages, and becoming a source of innovation.

Big Data Analytics (BDA): Is the process of collecting, organizing, and analyzing big data to discover patterns, knowledge, and intelligence as well as other information within the big data.

Big Data Analytics Capability (BDAC): Is the organizational capabilities that can enable firms to analyze their huge data with nontraditional methods using big data tools and techniques; hence, producing insights that enable data-driven decision-making process.

Business Intelligence (BI): Is an umbrella term that combines architectures, tools, databases, applications, practices, and methodologies. It is the process of transforming various types of business data into meaningful information that can help, decision makers at all levels, getting deeper insight of business.

Cloud Computing (CC): Is the result of evolutions of distributed computing technologies, enabled by advances in fast and low-cost network, commoditized faster hardware, practical high performance virtualization technologies, and maturing interactive web technologies.

Data Mining (DM): Is the process of discovering interesting information from the hidden data that can either be used for future prediction and/or intelligently summarizing the details of the data.

Data Warehouse (DW): Is a physical repository where relational data are specially organized to provide enterprise-wide, and cleansed data in a standardized format.

Knowledge Management (KM): Is the acquisition, storage, retrieval, application, generation, and review of the knowledge assets of an organization in a controlled way.

Section 2
Big Data Issues

Chapter 4
Big Data Quality for Data Mining in Business Intelligence Applications:
Current State and Research Directions

Arun Thotapalli Sundararaman

Accenture, India

ABSTRACT

Study of data quality for data mining application has always been a complex topic; in the recent years, this topic has gained further complexity with the advent of big data as the source for data mining and business intelligence (BI) applications. In a big data environment, data is consumed in various states and various forms serving as input for data mining, and this is the main source of added complexity. These new complexities and challenges arise from the underlying dimensions of big data (volume, variety, velocity, and value) together with the ability to consume data at various stages of transition from raw data to standardized datasets. These have created a need for expanding the traditional data quality (DQ) factors into BDQ (big data quality) factors besides the need for new BDQ assessment and measurement frameworks for data mining and BI applications. However, very limited advancement has been made in research and industry in the topic of BDQ and their relevance and criticality for data mining and BI applications. Data quality in data mining refers to the quality of the patterns or results of the models built using mining algorithms. DQ for data mining in business intelligence applications should be aligned with the objectives of the BI application. Objective measures, training/modeling approaches, and subjective measures are three major approaches that exist to measure DQ for data mining. However, there is no agreement yet on definitions or measurements or interpretations of DQ for data mining. Defining the factors of DQ for data mining and their measurement for a BI system has been one of the major challenges for researchers as well as practitioners. This chapter provides an overview of existing research in the area of BDQ definitions and measurement for data mining for BI, analyzes the gaps therein, and provides a direction for future research and practice in this area.

DOI: 10.4018/978-1-7998-5781-5.ch004

INTRODUCTION

This Chapter is primarily focused on current challenges, research progress and directions in Data Quality (DQ) in Big Data environments where Big Data is used for Data Mining and consumed through Business Intelligence (BI) Applications, including Artificial Intelligence applications. We introduce a new term and concept, BDQ i.e. Big Data Quality to refer DQ issues related to use of Big Data. It is important to evaluate if the current knowledge of DQ concepts and definitions are all applicable to BDQ and if new concepts are added or if a new set of concepts are applicable for BDQ. This chapter seeks to address which of the below representations (Figure 1) holds good in the study of BDQ when applied to Data Mining for BI Applications.

Figure 1. BDQ Vs. DQ

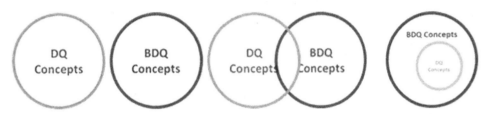

Let's start the discussions with a very brief definition of the 2 terms that are so extremely critical for this Chapter, namely Data Mining and DQ. A complete list of definitions of all other key terms is provided at the end of this Chapter. A frequently cited definition for Data Mining is given by Decker & Focardi (1995) as *"Data mining is a problem-solving methodology that finds a logical or mathematical description, eventually of a complex nature, of patterns and regularities in a set of data"*. According to Cios, Pedrycz, Swiniarski & Kurgan (2007), the goal (of Data Mining) is to efficiently and effectively extract information and knowledge from data that should make sense of the data, i.e., this knowledge should exhibit some essential attributes: *it should be understandable, valid, novel and useful*.

Many research publications have used the terms Data Quality and Information Quality (IQ) interchangeably, although certain differences exist between the two from the perspective of users of data / information. In the absence of a single definition of DQ or Information Quality or DQ as it pertains to Data Mining, we may resort to refer the standard global definition of quality that describes as "fit for use". DQ for Data Mining would encompass those factors that render the underlying data and the insights derived from Data Mining model to be appropriate for use in decision making process, enabled through a BI System. Thus, the factors or dimensions that constitute DQ for Data Mining in BI applications may be derived from these definitions as understandingness, validity, novelty, usefulness, actionability, etc. Extending this theory of knowledge to Big Data environments, new factors that influence quality of decisions and confidence of the consumers of data emerge. The essential characteristics of Big Data viz., Volume, Variety, Velocity, Veracity introduce these new DQ factors. Each of these characteristics changes the consumption paradigm which constitutes the need for new DQ factors.

The central theme of this Chapter revolves around DQ Measurement approaches for Data Mining. This Chapter is focused on presenting a comprehensive view of existing frameworks for measurement of DQ in Data Mining and analyzing them with a view to present the gaps in existing frameworks. The main contribution of this Chapter lies in proposing appropriate frameworks and specific directions for future research in the field of DQ for Data Mining, based on the proposed frameworks.

Traditional approaches of providing an enterprise wide single version of truth, from a monolithic enterprise data warehouse, after, several stages of transformation, isn't suitable to the changed paradigms of Big Data processing, where volume, variety and velocity necessitate new Data Architecture patterns and newer models of data consumption in an enterprise, including for Data Mining purposes. For Big Data analytics to be effective and meaningful, data needs to be processed efficiently and insights generated at a faster rate. In other words, as part of the emerging modern data architectures for Big Data processing, consumption of data is enabled at several layers such as raw zone, refined zone, enriched zone, user specific zone and many other variations of such data storage options. Enterprises may name their data storage layers differently (than the above zones indicated), but consumption is enabled at multiple layers. What these data storage layers also mean is that data is curated at different stages and attains different levels of maturity and/or standardization as the data passes through each of these layers. This Chapter addresses the resultant DQ challenges arising from such distributed data consumption layers within an Enterprise.

The objectives of this chapter are as follows:

- Identify new paradigm of data processing in Big Data leading to new for DQ issues using Big Data in Data Mining for BI
- Identify the factors that constitute BDQ and DQ measures for Data Mining
- Analyze existing DQ measurement frameworks in light of their applicability to BDQ as a means to Data Mining for BI.
- Review state of current research and future research directions in the study of measurement of BDQ for Data Mining in BI.

There has been a growing interest among researchers and industry practitioners in DQ, DQ measurement, DQ assessment and improvement, more so, with respect to Data Mining. DQ measure in Data Mining should be one that supports achieving the goal of Data Mining i.e. to build a model that most accurately predicts the desired target value for new data. Use of this measure in an incorrect form may lead to quality issues of the model. However, even the basic principles of DQ assessment in Data Mining and its improvement remain largely open.

Research interest in DQ remains an enduring subject, which is reiterated even by very recent literature. For example, Fehrenbacher & Helfert (2012) state that the importance of DQ is ever increasing and that research in this field focuses mainly on **2 aspects i.e. criteria and assessment**. This recent work observes that while researchers have developed a number of frameworks, criteria lists and approaches for assessing and measuring DQ, still research in this discipline indicates that assessing DQ remains to be challenging. This work argues that although DQ is subjective, most of the existing frameworks and assessment methodologies do not often consider the context in which the assessment is performed. Through empirical data research this cited work suggests that the perceived importance of DQ criteria has changed over the last decade.

Direct references to DQ in BI Systems in published literature are limited. The same may be explored through references to related types of Information Systems such as Datawarehouse, Decision Support System (DSS), Executive Information System (EIS) or Data Mining. Similarly, the terms DQ and IQ have been used interchangeably in literature and differentiation, if any, have been very thin. There has been no consensus about the distinction between DQ and IQ – DQ may be referred to technical issues or quality in sources or 'raw data' and IQ may be referred to non-technical issues or quality in processed data stores or insights presented from data for decision making. In this Chapter the term DQ refers to both these aspects.

In summary, past literature shows that despite the significance of both data quality and Data Mining research, each remains a largely distinct stream (Blake & Mangiameli, 2008). In Data Mining research, the concept of DQ is most closely matched to studies of the effects of noise and to studies of missing values. However, Data Mining research hasn't focused on DQ dimensions; DQ constructs have also not been explicitly explored in the study of DQ for Data Mining. The primary motivation for this Chapter arises from this gap as this Chapter attempts to cover how this large gap may be addressed in the study of DQ for Data Mining in BI applications.

This Chapter may not present detailed account of definitions or calculations of popularly known metrics (e.g. accuracy or sensitivity), because, this Chapter is intended for researchers with prior knowledge of Data Mining concepts or practitioners who are assumed to be familiar with such fundamental concepts. If any reader is not familiar with these basic concepts, they are encouraged to read through the references (Additional Reading section) that will be handy to get familiar with these basic concepts. This book is intended to cover 2 broad areas i.e. conceptual issues in DQ definition and measurement for Data Mining in BI and research issues and directions in the study of DQ for Data Mining.

This Chapter is organized into 4 sections. This section "Introduction" provides an overview of the subject of discussion, while the next chapter "Background" details the existing state of research in the study of DQ for Data Mining. The next section "Approaches and frameworks" introduces frameworks that exist today for DQ in Data Mining summarizes the gaps therein and provides a view of proposed frameworks to address the gaps, while covering in detail one of the recommended frameworks. The 4th section "Future research directions" details the emerging trends and directions in research of the subject of DQ for Data Mining.

BACKGROUND

As discussed in the previous section, there has been no consensus about the distinction between data quality and information quality. Specifically, in the context of measuring the quality of Data Mining model, this gap is even more glaring. In this chapter, the term DQ is used to refer those measures that are used to measure the quality of predictions from a Data Mining model.

Sources of DQ issues

Accordingly, DQ for Data Mining may be deemed as any Data Mining model that is fit for use in a select application; fit for use in this context would mean as that which would meet the objective of the BI application. For example, if the objective of a BI application is to identify patients that are likely to seek re-admission in the case of a hospital, the DQ of the Data Mining model built to identify potential re-admissions will be deemed 'fit for use' if the model is able to predict the same with the level of accuracy as expected by the application user, in this case the Doctors and/or Hospital administrators.

There are different methods for assessing DQ of a Data Mining model that may be broadly classified as below:

1)   Measure: Use measures to determine whether the Data Mining model performs to the expected quality levels i.e. whether or not the model produces the expected predictions. These measures may be statistical or mathematical, but, generally they are tested for statistical significance.

2)   Approach: Separate the data into training and testing sets to test the accuracy of predictions. Again, there are random or iterative approaches to conduct such tests. Again, these tests use measures of statistical significance to prove or disprove DQ levels of a Data Mining model.

3)   Judgment: In this approach business experts are involved to review the prediction results of the Data Mining model to determine whether the discovered patterns have meaning in the targeted business scenario (subjective measure)

As can be seen above the approaches are different and the DQ outlook are also different based on the approach i.e. DQ expectations are expressed as statistical measures or subjective attributes. Moreover, typically these techniques are used iteratively to define measure and improve DQ of Data Mining models to get them more robust to answer specific questions on predictions. The result of such a state has been that the academic world or the Industry practitioners haven't agreed on a common path either on definition or measurements or interpretations of DQ for Data Mining. Well, while that sounds like a huge problem statement, that also means a whole lot of opportunities for research and practice in formulating what can potentially be a common framework for Data Mining DQ.

Although a definition does not exist, it is possible to identify the potential sources of DQ issues, along the Data Mining process life cycle - more broadly Knowledge Discovery in Databases process (Maimon & Rokach, 2010). This is depicted in Figure 2 below (high level, non-exhaustive list of sources of DQ problems in Data Mining).

The above Figure 2 only lists the potential problems that are discussed in subsequent sections; however, a quick view of the possible solutions to address these DQ issues is given in Table 1. The objective of this Chapter is to focus not on the sources of and the solutions for DQ problems in Data Mining, but, on measurement of DQ for Data Mining.

While the above problems are relevant for most Data Mining applications for BI, the below (Table 2) additional challenges need to considered when the underlying data system happens to be Big Data.

DQ Measures for Data Mining

Study of Big Data Quality is still evolving and its study in the context of Data Mining applications is yet to take care in a meaning way. Researchers have found that "In addition to the importance, data quality has recently been taken into consideration by the big data community and there is not any comprehensive review conducted in this area".

Measures of DQ may be broadly classified into 3 categories i.e. objective measures, subjective measures and semantic measures (Geng & Hamilton (2006)). This section provides a view of existing body of knowledge in this area. Published literature summarizes these measures into 9 criteria list and categorizes them into 3 classifications, namely, objective, subjective and semantics-based. An objective measure is based only on the raw data and knowledge about the user or application is not required for such measures. A subjective measure takes into account both the data and the user of these data, for which, access to the user's domain or background knowledge about the data is required. A semantic measure considers the semantics and explanations of the patterns and some researchers consider them a special type of subjective measure.

Figure 2. Potential sources of DQ issues in Data Mining process

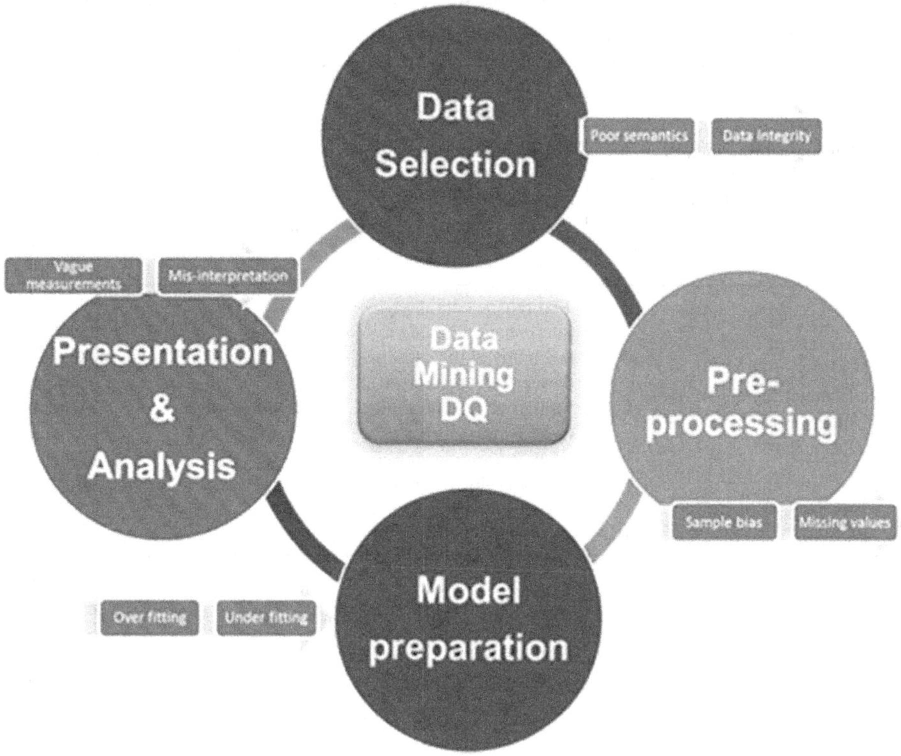

Table 1. Potential DQ problems and mitigation steps

S No	Phase	DQ Problems	Mitigation
1	Data Selection	· Poor semantics · Non-uniform sources · Data Integrity	· Information Catalogue · Data Profiling · Update Business Rules
2	Data Preparation or Pre-processing	· Sampling Bias · Missing Values	· Attribute selection · Representative sample · Best missing value approach · Imputation techniques · Duplicate detection · Object matching · Entity identification · Approximate string join
3	Model Training	· Over fitting · Under fitting	· Dimensionality reduction · Feature selection
4	Presentation & Analysis	· Incorrect interpretation · Vague measurements	· Update Business Rules · Statistical validation techniques · Re-train

Table 2. Potential BDQ problems from big data sources

Big Data Type	Characteristics	Data Mining applications	Insights from Data Mining	Examples
Variety Unstructured	High resolution images Terabytes/Petabytes of data, expensive to store and transmit	Pattern recognition Automated attribute extraction	Existence of a medical condition Damages to inventory Level of medical condition	Radiographic Images MRIs, CT Scans Ultrasound Pathology Camera Recordings, satellite images, images of properties or vehicles
Variety Un/Semi Structured text	Handwritten notes – more difficult to interpret Documents	Text requires curation, interpretation based on taxonomy of the chosen domain (e.g. healthcare formats or funds transfer message formats etc.) NLP, Pattern recognition Relationship analysis, Correlate with structured data	Enriching insights from structured data	Doctors Notes OMICS data Discharge summaries Pathology reports Continuous Care Document Customer complaints Service call records
Velocity Streaming	High velocity Highly structured data Need to filter noise, redundant versions, false positives	Real time alerts, Self-reported measures	Real-time insights	IoT data Weblogs Bedside, remote monitors Implants, Devices Wearables - Fitness bands Smart phones
Value Social Media	High volumes, Unstructured text, images	NLP Sentiment Analysis Level of Influence	Customer – Service Agent engagement Patient satisfaction	Facebook Whatsapp Twitter
Volume Structured Data from transaction systems	Large volume of data, structured; Disjointed data from disparate sources – MDM challenges	Traditional Analytics, BI; Correlate with big data to get real time insights	Business KPIs (Key Performance Indicators) Competitive Benchmarking	Sales, Marketing, Finance, Manufacturing data
Variety & Velocity Dark Data	High Velocity, Structured data, large volumes, but difficult to interpret	Pre-process data for patterns, correlate with Structured Data for better insights –	Impacted Business KPIs, due to Application outages	Server logs App error logs etc.

Objective Measures

Objective measures that evaluate the generality and reliability of Data Mining algorithm have been thoroughly studied by many researchers. They are usually functions of a 2×2 contingency table (Tan, Kumar & Srivastava, 2002; Lenca, Meyer, Vaillant & Lallich, 2004; Ohsaki, Kitaguchi, Okamoto, Yokoi & Yamaguchi, 2004). Traditionally, default measures that are used to quantify the quality of prediction (by a Data Mining model) were *accuracy* and *precision* and this was done based on the concept of true/ false positives and true/ false negatives, as depicted in the form of a matrix in Table 3.

From the above matrix, metrics defined in Table 4 were used by users of BI application to measure the quality of the underlying Data Mining model (Blake & Mangiameli 2008).

Table 3. Confusion matrix for traditional DQ measures

		Actual condition	
		Condition positive	Condition negative
Prediction result from Data Mining model	Positive	True positive (a)	False positive (c)
	Negative	False negative (b)	True negative (d)

Subjective Measures

Subjective measures are those that consider both the data or results and the users' knowledge or confidence or judgment in the results. Subject measures are essential to capture users' involvement in the DQ measurement process and also calibrate the measurement mechanism to cater to the knowledge of the users and their expectations from the mining model. The subject of subjective DQ factors has been widely studied and researched and several works have classified and consolidated subjective DQ factors as it relates to data used in decision context. Sundararaman (2012) lists 23 such DQ factors (e.g. objectivity, believability, reliability etc.). While these measures hold good for study of DQ in the context of underlying data itself (either for Transaction Processing Systems or Decision Support Systems or

Table 4. Traditional Data Mining Quality metrics

S. No	Metrics	Definition	Computation	Example / interpretation
1	Accuracy	Proportion of true results (both true positives and true negatives) in the population	$(a + d)/(a + b + c + d)$	Proportion of transactions that are known not to be fraudulent and not fraudulent and the model predicts correct 'positive' or 'negative' fraudulent indicator against each of them
2	Precision	Positive predictive value: proportion of the true positives against all the positive results	$a / (a + c)$	Proportion of actual fraudulent transactions over transactions that the model predicts as 'positive' fraudulent indicator
3	Sensitivity	True positive rate or the recall rate: proportion of actual positives which are correctly identified	$a / (a + b)$	Proportion of transactions that are known to be fraudulent and the model predicts 'positive' fraudulent indicator
4	Specificity	Measure of identification of negative results	$d / (d + c)$	Proportion of transactions that are known not to be fraudulent and the model predicts 'negative' fraudulent indicator
5	Receiver Operating Curves	2 dimensional graphs to visually depict the performance and non-performance trade-off of a model	True Positive Rate = $a / (a + b)$, False Positive Rate (or fall-out) = $c / (c + d)$	Visual representation and interpretation of performance of the model to spot optimal Vs. sub-optimal models.

Datawarehouse), these may not necessarily be relevant in the study of DQ for Data Mining in BI. Table 5 provides a summary of subjective measures consolidated from various research works and publications on this subject.

Table 5. Subjective DQ factors for Data Mining

S No	Factor Name	Description	Related criteria	Reference
1	Interestingness	Attribute to measure whether or not a knowledge or pattern discovered from Data Mining is interesting for the business user (published literature refers to 9 criteria to describe what constitutes interestingness)	Conciseness, Coverage, reliability, peculiarity, diversity, novelty, surprisingness, utility, actionability	Guillet (2007) Geng & Hamilton (2006)
2	Understandability	Attribute to measure the extent to which data are clear without ambiguity and easily comprehended	Comprehensibility, simplicity	Piltaver (2011)

While the above DQ factors have been in vogue for years, a newer set of factors driven by nature of Big Data dimensions are gaining significance in the study of DQ for Data Mining. These are termed as BDQ and are highlighted as below (Table 6).

Semantic Measures

Of the 3 categories, semantic measures seem to be the least explored in published literature and a good list of such measures does not exist in literature. Unlike subjective measures, where the domain knowledge expected from the users is about the data itself, in the case of semantic measures the domain

Table 6. Subjective BDQ factors for Data Mining

S No	Big Data characteristics	BDQ Factors (New)	BDQ Factor Explained
1	Volume	Class Imbalance Bias in feature selection	Ensure that the data is not skewed towards influencing outcomes of a particular outcome; e.g. 90% or data containing customers who have repayment defaults. Ensure that the data used to build and train the Data Mining model is devoid of any bias (class or gender or race or religion or language or other sensitive factors)
2	Variety	Interpretability	Ensure that data derived from unstructured content (i.e. data derived using MapReduce processes) are understandable and can be interpreted by data scientists and are compliant to standard definitions before they are used for Data Mining.
3	Velocity	Lineage Traceability	Data (categorical and ordinal) used in Data Mining models can be traced back to their source, establish connection to their derivations as the data flows through different layers of big data (i.e. from raw to refined or refined to enriched etc.)
4	Value	Credibility Reliability	Establish confidence level in the authenticity of the data elements, data values, data definitions and data semantics Although defined as single BDQ factor, this has potential to expand into multiple dimensions of credibility as listed above.

knowledge is represented in the form of utility functions that reflect the user's objectives in using the Data Mining model predictions. For example, in the case of a data clinical mining model, users who are Medical Professional might prefer association rules that relate to high-risk population subjects over those with higher statistical significance. In simple terms, sematic measures may be construed as those derived from combination of select objective and select subjective measures. As such, semantic measures are expected to consider not merely the statistical aspects of raw data, but the *utility* and *actionability* aspects of the Data Mining results as well. Because semantic measures consider the users' objectives, they may be more useful in real applications in decision-making problems i.e. BI applications involving Data Mining models. Table 7 provides a summary of subjective measures consolidated from various research works and publications on this subject.

Table 7. Semantic measures / approaches for Data Mining

S No	Measure Name	Description	Related criteria	Reference
1	Weighted Support	A simple method which assigns to each item a weight representing its importance	Support as a basic measure	Cai, Fu, Cheng & Kwong (1998)
2	Normalized Weighted Support	A variation of "Weighted Support" measure	Support as a basic measure	Lu, Hu, & Li (2001)
3	Vertical Weighted Support	A variation of "Normalized weighted support" measure	Support as a basic measure	Lu, Hu & Li (2001)
4	Objective-oriented utility-based association (OOA)	An approach whereby the users set objectives for the mining process by partitioning attributes into 2 groups - *target* and *non-target* attributes	Support as a basic measure	Shen, Zhang & Yang (2002)
5	Share-confidence framework	An approach based on weights on attribute-value	Confidence as a basic measure	Carter, C. L., Hamilton, H. J. & Cercone, N. (1997)
6	Fuzzy rules ranking	An approach where system matches discovered pattern against fuzzy rules (set by users for decision scenarios) and ranks them	Actionability	Liu, B., Hsu, W. & Chen, S. (1997)

Measures Focused on Quality of Outcome

In the discussions so far, it may be observed that either the objective or subjective measures help evaluating only the aspect of how good the model behaves. However, an emerging school of thought among the DQ research community focuses of using the quality of business outcome (i.e. extent of impact) as a measure of DQ. This school of thought is driven by the principle that DQ measurement in BI should be done to enable and support effective decision making. Traditional methods for evaluating DQ dimensions do so objectively without considering contextual factors such as the decision-task and the decision-maker's preferences. DQ Measurement is dependent on the purpose (task). The perceived quality of the data is influenced by the decision-task and that the same data may be viewed through two or more different quality lenses depending on the decision-maker and the decision-task it is used for. Shankaranarayanan & Cai (2006) have justified the need for incorporating contextual considerations in DQ measurement. This important issue has not been explicitly addressed by previous DQ research. Introducing a theoretical framework, the said work underlines the need for further research in the direction of implementation.

The key limitation of existing research is that it focuses merely on technical / architectural aspects of DQ. Addressing this limitation, Gustafsson, P., Lindström, Åsa., Jägerlind,C. & Tsoi, J. (2006) present a framework for assessing DQ focusing on how data supports the business. Research of DQ measurement has so far been focused on identifying a set of DQ factors or analyzing select set of DQ factors (e.g. timeliness or correctness). Even a recent study, Helfert, M. & Foley, O. (2009) reiterates this statement and emphasizes the need for comprehensive DQ measure considering all relevant DQ factors. Thus, the study of a comprehensive assessment framework, covering all appropriate DQ factors remains an open area of research in the study of DQ (Alkharboush, N & Li, Y. (2010)). Batini,C. & Scannapieco,M. (2006) emphasize the need for defining a comprehensive set of DQ measurement allowing objective assessment of the underlying DQ and appropriate assessment methods, while dealing with the problems associated with defining a reference set of data, quality dimensions and metrics.

Use of Data Mining techniques as a component of BI applications is becoming common with easier access to Data Mining software applications. Interestingly both BI Systems and Data Mining focus on advancement of knowledge discovery; the difference being that Data Mining tends to larger in application such as scientific, statistical, mathematical and other domains, beyond business problems. Researchers have expressed the need to integrate the approaches between Data Mining and business intelligence (Cody,W.F., Kreulen, J.T., V Krishna, V & Spangler, W.S. (2002)). This topic continues to be of evolving and even recently researchers have been exploring new approaches and methods for such integration. For instance, Yang & Simon (2009) propose a Data Mining methodology called "Business Intelligence-driven Data Mining" (BIdDM) which combines knowledge-driven Data Mining and method-driven Data Mining, and fills the gap between business intelligence knowledge and existent various Data Mining methods.

The relevance of Big Data characteristics on data quality for Data Mining is captured as below (Table 8).

Given the limited research advances in definition of DQ metrics or DQ measurement for BI, it will be valuable to focus on research based on DQ metrics requirements framework. As it applies to any other measurement, it is important to identify and summarize the requirements for DQ measurement. This view is supported in the works of Heinrich & Klier (2009). Such a focus is expected to guide the principles of DQ metrics definition and/or measurement – either for individual DQ dimensions or comprehensive (i.e. covering all DQ dimensions) DQ metrics such as overall DQ score (Sundararaman, 2012).

In summary, past literature confirms that poor quality of data in BI adversely impacts the usability of the System and managing DQ in BI is very important (Shankaranarayanan 2005). The needs of DQ definition and measurement approach for Data Mining in BI Systems are unique and different. However, most of the research works have approached with mathematics or statistical techniques that have associated practical problems in implementation and have not focused on implementation aspects of the framework. Important directions in the study of DQ measurement for BI are as below:

1. DQ measurement framework focused on practical implementation aspects (Gustafsson, Lindström, Åsa, Jägerlind & Tsoi, 2006)
2. Measure DQ with specific business context (Even & Shankaranarayanan, 2007)

Table 8. Influence of big data charactersitics on Data Mining

S No	Big Data characteristics	Influence on consumption	Relevance for Data Mining and BI / AI Applications
1	Volume	Higher levels of "completeness"	Sample size Training data sets
2	Variety	Ability to identify large number of variables, derived data elements, presenting new challenges for feature selection processes	Additional data process engineering steps before data is presented to Data Mining e.g. imposing or deriving structure from unstructured or semi-structured data rendering it fit for consumption.
3	Velocity	Improves "availability", "timeliness" factors	As the pace of inflow of data increases, the need for real-time and dynamic profiling of data to validate for ranges, anomalies, outliers etc. increases. This need increases the complexity of data profiling techniques. This complexity introduces the need for machine learning techniques as part of data processing pipelines itself, even before data is made ready for consumption by Data Scientists for Data Mining
4	Value	Improves "availability", "timeliness", "accuracy", "consistency" factors	Highly positive impact on the ability to generate higher levels of accuracy and relevance. Significantly increases the relevance of Data Mining, insights and BI applications. Adds new complexity in terms of higher thresholds of accuracy levels

APPROACHES AND FRAMEWORKS

Issues – Gaps in Literature Related to DQ Measurement for Data Mining for BI

Based on the discussions in the previous section, gaps in published literature related to DQ measurement for Data Mining for BI are presented below.

Gap 1: BDQ Factors relevant for Data Mining: Most of the past research work lead to a set of DQ factors that are largely related to underlying data itself and not on the quality of the Data Mining model or the quality of outcome from the BI application that uses the Data Mining model. In other words, DQ measures for measuring the quality of predictions or model outcomes are very limited. The impact of Big Data quality characteristics (volume, variety, velocity, value) on Data Mining applications have not been studied.

Gap 2: Data quality issues from data pre-processing: In a big data environment, data is replicated across layers and stored in different formats, different levels of aggregation and different levels of curation across layers (raw, refined, standard, enriched, user-defined and many other layers). DQ requirements and measurements for each of these layers vary based on how and the extent to which such data is consumed by Data Mining applications. Current DQ practices do not cater to multiple DQ assessment and/or measurement frameworks based on consumption points as discussed in above.

Gap 3: Lack of context for use: Past research has not captured the context (i.e. how the model predictions are used and its related business outcome) while studying DQ measurement for Data Mining. For example, *accuracy* as a measure (objective measure derived from the confusion matrix – please refer Table 3) of quality of Data Mining model may need differentiated approach when used in the case of clinical predictions Vs. customer relationship predictions. In such cases, almost every component of the DQ measure i.e. the definition of the measure, computation formulae and the tolerance levels etc., may need to be tailored to suit the sensitivities of the specific domain and experiences of the business. Data is intended to be used for different business decisions and as such any measure of DQ should be sensitive to this context of business decisions for which the data is being used and the quality of business outcomes based on such decisions.

Gap 4: Relative importance of DQ factor: In a set of different DQ factors not every factor impacts the overall DQ in the same extent. The degree of impact varies again based on the decision task for which the data is consumed – e.g. the impact of accuracy as a DQ factor on tactical decisions is different than that on airline safety decisions. Past research on DQ does not recognize this varying degree of impact. Moreover, the current approaches to DQ for Data Mining are highly skewed towards objective measures (e.g. accuracy or sensitivity), whereas an effective DQ measure should be derived with due consider for combination of applicable objective and subjective measures. For example, DQ of a Data Mining model for real-time identification of fraudulent transactions in a stock exchange application may have higher weightage for combination of factors such as *accuracy, understandability* and *novelty*. Existing research is far from suggesting such a framework that is sensitive to the decision task on hand.

Published literature call out some/all of these gaps specifically and provide a direction for further research. For example, Knight (2011) opines that systems information quality (DQ) investigative frameworks, thus far, lack a widely accepted model with which researchers can conceptualize the context of their study, and identify the important DQ characteristics to be examined and empirically tested. The result is a widely varied body of literature lacking a coherent and consistent approach to identifying and measuring systems DQ. Similarly, Gibson (2010) observes that DQ research to date has approached the subject independent from actual users although the interdependency between the two is obvious.

To summarize, existing approaches to measure DQ for Data Mining have resulted in 3 major gaps:

- DQ factors relevant to Data Mining BI are not studied in detail
- Lack of context in measurement of DQ for Data Mining
- Relative importance of DQ factors not considered ("how" a factor impacts DQ and "extent" to which it impacts are not considered)

Solutions: Existing Methods

As discussed in the previous section, evaluating the performance of Data Mining based on the outcome and context of application domain (e.g. high degree of accuracy expected in case of medical predictions vs. not-so-high level of accuracy expected in case of campaign management application) is fundamental to managing DQ of Data Mining model. The evaluation and measurement of such DQ of mining model is important for refining the model variables in an iterative process or selecting the most applicable algorithm for the predictive model. Several criteria may be considered for such evaluation and these differ based on the application domain or computational complexity or comprehensibility of the model and other parameters. The most widely used methods are listed in Table 9. From the table it can be observed that most of these methods are applicable for selective Data Mining model, whereas, the research need is for a model that may be tailored and adopted for any of the selected models. The evaluation model needs to focus on measuring DQ and offer flexibility for its adoption without being constrained by the Data Mining approach itself. It is based on this need that last 2 methods have evolved in the recent times in the study of DQ measurement for Data Mining.

Table 9. Methods for evaluation of performance of Data Mining model

S No	Name of the Methodology	Brief description	Applicability
1	Cross validation	Technique for estimating the generalization performance of predictive model – an alternative to random subsampling	Classification
2	Hold out method	Simple validation based on single split of data.	Classification
3	Random sub-sampling	An approach where hold out method is repeated several times to improve the estimation of a classifier's performance	Classification
4	k-fold cross validation	Improvement over hold out method, where the data is sub-dived (as training and validation sets) into *k* sub-sets.	Classification
5	MDL principle	A mathematical theory that works on the principle of best compression of hypothesis	Clustering
6	Statistical test	The modified Hubert statistic, Dunn family of indices, The Davies-Bouldin (DB) index & others	Clustering
67	Coverage	Proportion of cases in the data that have attribute values or items specified on the left hand side of the rule. A rule with coverage value close to 1 can be considered as interesting	Association
8	Support	Proportion of all cases in the dataset that satisfy a rule	Association
9	Comprehensive methodology for Data Quality Management	A Theoretical / conceptual framework for definition and measurement of DQ – may be tailored for adoption to measure DQ for Data Mining	Generic – across techniques
10	"Decision Categories Framework"	A contextual framework for comprehensive and context-aware measurement of DQ - may be tailored for adoption to measure DQ for Data Mining	Generic – across techniques

It is worthwhile considering the reasons behind DQ problems in Data Mining applications. A good understanding of the root causes is expected to improve to a large extent the quality of solutions that may be designed to address DQ issues.

1. Study of Data Mining typically makes assumptions such as unrestricted availability of data, data that is well organized and labeled and error free data. Reality is far from this assumption where in Data Mining implementations multiple complications arise such as non-availability of data (to train the model), data quality, poorly profiled data etc.

2. New business scenarios keep emerging and this causes prediction errors. Because of the nature of the complexity of businesses, the actual predictor scenarios keep emerging caused by newer

permutations and combinations of attributes, besides, introduction of ad-hoc exceptions. It is often the case that the predictive model isn't trained with such combinations in the training data set. This phenomenon leads to significant DQ issues in the BI application Data Mining predictions. Yang, Q & Wu, X (2006) argue that an important issue is that the learned models should incorporate time because data is not static and is constantly changing in many domains.

3. Algorithm applied without business context. Often times, algorithms that have found successful for any selected scenario is applied "as is" on the assumption and hope that the algorithm helps addresses different problem scenario. Well, if that happens so, it is most probably a case of chance only. HÄubscher, R., Puntambekar, S & Nye, A. (2007) suggest the need to consider domain specific aspects and issues all through the Data Mining process to increase the chance of finding meaningful patterns and they propose extending the mining process with the domain and problem specific representations and the support of pattern detection expertise of qualified users. Business experts (SMEs) carry the experience and expertise to interpret data, results and analysis beyond statistical measures. This forms as the foundation for a robust Data Mining model. Similarly, businesses Subject Matter Experts are the best to interpret the model results beyond mere statistical definitions and interpretations.

The solution to the above gaps (or problems) in measurement of DQ for BI lies in developing a context based, comprehensive DQ measurement framework. Such a framework may be evolved by adopting appropriate DQ measurement methodology from published literature and is depicted in Figure 3.

Table 10 below provides a summary view of approaches published in literature that help improve the quality of Data Mining model.

The Solution proposed by the Author, depicted in FIGURE 3 introduces a step for "learning" and "feedback" mechanism into the process of knowledge discovery. This iterative step comprises 2 components that are related to enhancing the training data and continuously refining the mining model variables (either adding new variables or dropping variable which are not found to be yielding statistically significant results). It is also interesting to observe that this new step, feeds both the predecessor and successor steps. Enhancing the training data is a function that feeds inputs to "Pre-processing" step, while, "refine model variables" provides inputs to "Model Preparation" step. There is no uniform guidance on how frequent or how long or how often or how many times this iterative step should be applied. Answers to these questions are based on the extent and significance of DQ problem in the specific context.

FUTURE RESEARCH DIRECTIONS

Researchers are inquisitive on the relevance of Data Mining in BI context and the research work continues to explore answers to the basic questions, a few of which are listed below (very partial list):

- How good is the quality of knowledge discovered by the mining model?
- Does the same method always produce the same results?
- Are different approaches and customization techniques required for different application domains?
- What factors affect performance of the Data Mining model?
- What are the new DQ factors as they related to big data sources?
- How do the weightage for these BDQ factors change based on the point of consumption?

Table 10. Existing approaches to improve DQ in Data Mining

S No	Name of the Approach	Brief overview	Phase applied	Reference
1	Feature selection	The main idea of feature selection is to choose a subset of input variables by eliminating features with little or no predictive information in order to significantly improve the comprehensibility of the model results.	Pre-processing	Kim., Y (2006)
2	Dimensionality reduction	An approach to lower the number of attributes in the data with a view to eliminate irrelevant features and reduce noise.	Pre-processing	Fodor, I. K (2002)
3	Outlier detection	Discovery of data that deviate a lot from other data patterns	Pre-processing	Mansur, M & Noor, M (2005)
4	Retraining	The process of reapplying Data Mining on a new or more complete dataset in order to either increase or refine model intelligence. This process is expected to derive more accurate patterns.	Verification	Symeonidis, A., Athanasiadis, I.N. & Mitkas, P.A. (2007)

- What BDQ measurement frameworks are required capture influence of credibility and bias in Data Mining models?

Emphasis on Accuracy of Prediction

Use of Data mining in BI applications continues to be primarily focused on predicting business outcomes in different domains e.g. credit card fraud detection or predict probable fraudulent insurance claims or predict probable tax evasion transactions and such. Also, on the computing perspective, a good chunk of research activities is focused on improving the underlying algorithms with a view to improve the accuracy of predictions. At a macro level it may be concluded that the accuracy of prediction from Data Mining application (thus the DQ of Data Mining in BI) is dependent on a combination of 2 factors i.e. 1) Computing aspects of underlying algorithm as implemented in the Data Mining tool and 2) the application aspect or the implementation aspect of the chosen algorithm represented through variables selection, data quality and such. The following section discusses importance of these core research and applied research areas and directions for future research.

Figure 3. Proposed solutions with "closed loop" approach for improving Data Mining DQ measure

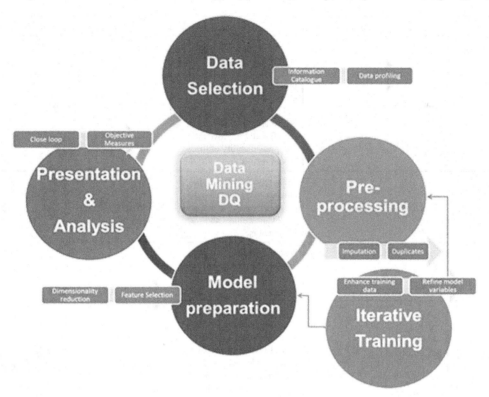

Focus on Implementation

Implementation of Data Mining in BI for different Industries or functions involves varied challenges and issues for deriving best DQ from the Data Mining models. These issues and challenges by themselves constitute huge scope and potential for future research in application of Data Mining in BI for specific industries or function. This section provides few examples of emerging research areas where domain based DQ considerations are important, while, this is not necessarily an exhaustive list of such industries or applications.

In a recently published work Amooee, Bidgoli & Dehnavi (2011) conducted experiments to use different Data Mining algorithms for fault detection in industrial equipment. Based on the results from their work in industrial equipment domain, while they acknowledge that research provides several approaches to measure DQ in Data Mining and many case studies constantly illustrate the difficulties in identifying the appropriate Data Mining algorithm that improves the quality of prediction, they recommend use of Data Mining in other industries such as food industry to measure products quality..

Adaptivity, one of the normative requirements, emphasizes that DQ is to be quantified in a goal-oriented way and that DQ metrics need to be adaptable to the context of a particular application. In the specific context of DQ for BI, this may be interpreted as the need for DQ to be measured in the context of decision tasks and quality of business outcomes. The field of BI is witnessing several technology advances such as use of Data Mining techniques or predictive analytics models or visualization techniques for BI. A noticeable development in this regard is that such applications which were previously limited to highly trained specialists are now made accessible to a wide range of users expanding the user base of BI. DQ of any Data Mining models should be carefully measured and any findings should either be cleaned or used as an indicator for the confidence level of the resulting Data Mining model (Stang, Hartvigsen & Reitan (2010)).

When developing Prognostic and Health Management (PHM) applications data acquired frequently comes with issues which hinder further data analysis. However, there is neither a clear definition of the data quality nor evaluation methods to quantify if acquired data is suitable for these prognostic modeling tasks such as failures detection, diagnosis and prediction. Furthermore, most of the existing metrics, such as clustering tendency in statistics and cluster-ability in Data Mining, only individually evaluate data characteristics without considering prognostic modeling. Chen, Zhu & Lee (2013) propose a new method to evaluate and improve data quality for system health diagnosis modeling and suggests new areas that carry potential for future research work such as a visual assessment based outlier detection method to recognize outliers from the data, which is expected to better evaluate and improve DQ of Data Mining models.

Data mining for Human Resource Management is emerging as a new research field. Strohmeier & Piazza (2013) identified research contributions in this field and reviewed them against the background of a domain driven Data Mining. They conclude that in order to improve the DQ of Data Mining in HRM, future research in this area need to consider specific domain requirements, such as evaluating the domain success or complying with legal standard.

"Big Data" Mining

With the emergence of "Big Data" as a technology trend in storage and access of data, "Big Data Mining" i.e. mining from Big Data sources is emerging as a related research topic (Che, Safran & Peng 2013).

As new algorithms, tools and techniques evolve to handle the basic Vs of Big Data (volume, variety and velocity), future research in Big Data Mining is expected to be focused on deriving quality insights from Big Data getting into domain of 2 additional Vs i.e. variability and value. Research should focus on quality of mining models that addresses variability (changes in the structure of the data and how users want to interpret that data) and higher focus on value (business value to the organization providing a compelling advantage, due to the ability of making decisions based in answering questions that were previously considered beyond reach). Rapidly changing data may make previously discovered patterns invalid thus leading to Data Mining DQ problems. As discussed earlier, this requires a shift from the current methodologies and approaches of measuring Data Mining DQ purely based on statistical and/or mathematical models to more domain results focused weighted sum measures.

Availability of quality data and its impact on accuracy of Data Mining model has been a problem since Data Mining existed; however, adequate pre-processing approaches were defined and implemented to address these problems with reasonable degree of coverage. With the emergence of big data, the data sources are of many different origins, not all well-known, and not all verifiable. Therefore, the accuracy and trust of the source data becomes an issue, which further propagates to the mining results as well i.e. the Big Data as a source by itself lends to additional challenges on DQ for Data Mining. In the case of big data, research problem that is emerging significance relates to approaches for extraction of additional evidences for verifying accuracy and building trust on the selected data and the produced mining results. The vast volume of big data attributes additional characteristics – high dynamics and evolution. So an adequate system for big data management and analysis must allow dynamic changing and evolution of the hosted data items.

Data Mining Process as a Solution for DQ Problems

Several researchers are exploring ways and means to improve the Data Mining process itself (introduction of improved methodology or approaches) with a view to improving DQ of the Data Mining model and its prediction results. Yang, Q & Wu, X (2006) list "Data Mining Process-Related Problems" as a significant problem while listing Top 10 challenging problems in Data Mining research. Per their work, important topics for further research exist in improving data-mining tools and processes through automation, as suggested by several researchers. Specific issues include how to automate the composition of Data Mining operations and building a methodology into Data Mining systems to help users avoid many Data Mining mistakes. Another issue is how to combine visual interactive and automatic Data Mining techniques together, because, in many applications Data Mining goals and tasks cannot be fully specified, especially in exploratory data analysis. Visualization helps to learn more about the data and define/refine the Data Mining tasks.

Similarly, pre-processing steps need new approaches for Big Data Mining to address the challenges that emerge with complexity of big data. New challenges emerge with each of the preprocessing steps such as Data filtering, cleaning, reduction and transformation. For instance, with data filtering, a classic research problem for future work may be 'how do we make sure that the discarded data will not severely degrade the quality of the eventually mined results under the complexity of great heterogeneity of big data?'

Yang & Simon (2009) suggest a new methodology called BI&DM that contains two processes: a construction process of a four-layer framework and a Data Mining process. This methodology is aimed at integrating Data Mining and Business Intelligence. This area carries immense challenges and potential for interesting findings and as such promises to be a potential area for future research work.

Tremendous scope exists for research in evolving process models and measurement frameworks for semantic measures that consider appropriate weightage for both statistical measures (on raw data) and subjective measures from mined results. Experiments involving domain based Data Mining applications may be carried out to evolve such a framework. The "decision categories framework" of DQ measurement (Sundararaman, 2012) may be leveraged as a foundation for such experiment, with an objective to identify domain specific parameters and tailoring required for DQ measurement (semantic measures) of Data Mining models.

Other Research Trends

- Objective and subjective measures both have merits and limitations; combination of objective and subjective measures (in defining DQ for Data Mining) is a possible research direction (Guillet & Howard, 2007). It is widely accepted that no single measure is superior to all others or suitable for all applications.
- A potential area for future research is to use meta-learning to automatically select or combine appropriate measures, to reflect real human interest in definition of what is interesting in predictions from the Data Mining model.

- Future research may also be directed towards developing an interactive UI to assist the user in selecting appropriate measures to define DQ. This UI may be based on visual interpretation of data and/or the model predictions according to the selected measure.

- Extensive experiments comparing the results of interestingness measures with actual human interest could be used as another method of analysis. Since user interactions are indispensable in the determination of rule interestingness, it is desirable to develop new theories, methods, and tools to facilitate the user's involvement. (Geng & Hamilton 2006)

- Explore new techniques for dimensionality reduction, such as nonnegative matrix factorization (NMF), which can be applied for finding parts-based, linear representations of nonnegative data. (As data grow, implementations of feature selection and dimensionality reduction techniques for high-performance parallel and distributed computing environments become more and more important).

- Yang & Wu (2006) argue that integrating Data Mining and knowledge inference is an important topic of future research in Data Mining. In particular, one important area is to incorporate background knowledge into Data Mining. This aspect is significant from DQ perspective since knowledge inference with specific context to the business domain is what fundamentally defines Information Quality expectation. *"The biggest gap between what Data Mining systems can do today and what we'd like them to do is that they're unable to relate the results of mining to the real-world decisions they affect — all they can do is hand the results back to the user. Doing these inferences, and thus automating the whole Data Mining loop, requires representing and using world knowledge within the system"*.

- Data mining approaches in BI is rapidly changing – from mining mere structured data to varied forms of "data" such as unstructured data or information in content or video or audio etc. and to graph mining. BI includes advanced econometric, statistical analyses, machine learning, predictive analytics and other modern approaches including methods of graph theory. Graph mining is emerging to be a field of mining information offering unique abilities in areas such as fraud detection, anomaly detection, finding key influencers, suspicious transactions, security intervention, predictive analytics, etc. These approaches demand new thoughts and research orientation to measure different objective, subjective and semantic measures around the mining outcomes.

CONCLUSION

Introduction of Big Data has certainly advanced Data Mining and Business Intelligence applications. Advantages include generation timely insights, access to large datasets and a variety of data for Data Mining. However, these introduce new challenges from data quality perspectives and these new DQ factors may be categorized as BDQ an emerging field of study. Apart from introducing new DQ factors, there is also a new need for a combination of factors based on the point of consumption of data for Data Mining. Research and practice in this area of BDQ is at very nascent stages, but, holds huge potential and promise in the immediate future. As the research focus in this area of BDQ gains pace and momentum, it is expected that newer DQ factors (or BDQ factors) get introduced, defined and used and new BDQ Measurements frameworks get evolve over a period of time. It is expected that these newer sets of BDQ Factors and measurement frameworks focus on measuring quality of data around volume, variety, velocity and value dimensions of Big Data and also provide for custom definition and measurements at different points of consumption viz., big data in its raw form, after initial refinement, post enrichment and after its gets fit into custom consumption models. It is envisaged that a single or a limited number of measurement frameworks will not suffice this vastly dynamic subject and/or the frameworks are flexible enough to be tailored for the select application. This infers that Enterprises need to define multiple sets of DQ assessment frameworks, DQ measurements and tolerance levels for each of these layers.

Although several measures, factors and approaches exist, many published works point to 3 basic quality expectations of the Data Mining models, namely, accuracy, comprehensibility and interestingness (Freitas, 2002). Most of the existing research has been focused on objective measures which are by nature based on theories in probability, statistics or information theory. This Chapter has introduced some of the most frequently used objective measures. However, in theory several other objective measures to evaluate DQ of Data Mining may be used – Jaccard, certainty factor, Odds Ratio, Klosgen, Gini Index, J-measure, cosine, Loevinger etc. to name a few. However, the major issue with these measures is that while these are strongly based on statistical / mathematical models, they lack ease of implementation or adoption in real-world scenarios due to their poor interpretability. Therefore, the need is to focus research efforts on defining more practical objective measures to evaluate effectiveness of Data Mining models and their prediction results. Such research may also be integrated with the science of generic DQ measurement and assessment techniques, so that the advances that are already made may be effectively leveraged for study of DQ for Data Mining.

Several measures, factors and approaches exist to define and measure DQ in Data Mining application; many published works point to three basic quality expectations of the Data Mining models, namely, accuracy, comprehensibility and interestingness. This Chapter has introduced some of the most frequently used objective measures. However, in theory several other objective measures to evaluate DQ of Data Mining may be used. Therefore, the need is to focus research efforts on defining more practical objective measures to evaluate effectiveness of Data Mining models and their prediction results.

The importance of DQ for better decision making and thus for better business outcomes can never be over emphasized. Corporate success hinges on the quality of its executive decisions, which in turn depends, to a large extent, on the quality of data in their BI Systems. DQ issues in the decision making process may lead to poor-quality decisions adversely impacting company's future. A recently published book (English, 2011) quantifies the cost of poor DQ for organizations to be in the range of 20-35% of operating revenue.

In summary, there exist 2 primary problems with respect to measurement of DQ for Data Mining. These are:

1. Very limited, yet, only mathematical / statistical measures that are non-comprehendible and
2. Limited real life experiences to validate these measurements.

It is very relevant to highlight here that the research effort from Massachusetts Institute of Technology (MIT), Total Data Quality Management (TDQM) has set out for itself objectives that are largely aimed to address the above gaps. The objective of this program is to establish a solid theoretical foundation and devise practical methods for business and industry to improve DQ. The research scope of this program covers 3 areas i.e. 1) definition of DQ that addresses issues of data quality definition, measurement, and derivations; 2) Analysis of DQ Impact on Business that addresses the value chain relationship between DQ and business outcome and 3) improvement of DQ that addresses various methods for improving DQ.

Therefore, the focus needs to shift from discovery to implementation, towards which the following guidelines may serve as a reference checklist.

1. Define DQ metrics with fair balance of objective, subject and semantic measures.
2. Keep the Data Mining DQ measurement framework simple and effective for practicality of implementation and easy adoption.
3. Keep the DQ measurement process simple to comprehend and implement, yet, effective in the results.

To conclude, the topic of DQ measurement for BI has been extensively researched which has contributed to multiple frameworks and methodologies. The need of the hour is not necessarily to explore newer methodologies or framework, but, to focus on adoption, tailoring and implementation of these methodologies and frameworks, so that real industry experiences can be captured for further making advances in this topic of research. Looking ahead, research community has outlined that the key challenge in study of DQ relates to approaching DQ as a measure of enabling users of BI applications to make decisions with high degrees of confidence and towards this topmost priority would be to direct research efforts towards providing lightweight, scalable mechanisms frameworks for determining Data Mining DQ metrics.

REFERENCES

Acharjya, D.P. (2016). A Survey on Big Data Analytics: Challenges, Open Research Issues and Tools. *International Journal of Advanced Computer Science and Applications*, 7(2).

Alkharboush, N., & Li, Y. (2010). A decision rule method for data quality assessment. *Proceedings of the 15th International Conference on Information Quality*.

Amooee, G., Bidgoli, B., & Dehnavi, M. (2011). A Comparison Between Data Mining Prediction Algorithms for Fault Detection. *International Journal of Computer Science Issues*, 8(6), 425–431.

Baldi, P., Brunak, S., Chauvin, Y., Andersen, C., & Nielsen, H. (2000). Assessing the accuracy of prediction algorithms for classification: An overview. *Bioinformatics (Oxford, England)*, 16(5), 412–424. doi:10.1093/bioinformatics/16.5.412 PMID:10871264

Batini, C., & Scannapieco, M. (2006). *Data Quality. Concepts, Methodologies and Techniques* (1st ed.). Springer-Verlag.

Blake, R., & Mangiameli, P. (2008). The effects and interactions of data quality and problem complexity on Data Mining. *Proceedings of the 13th International Conference on Information Quality*, 160—175

Cai, C. H., Fu, A. W., Cheng, C. H., & Kwong, W. W. (1998). Mining association rules with weighted items. *Proceedings of the International Database Engineering and Applications Symposium*, 68–77. 10.1109/IDEAS.1998.694360

Cai, L., & Zhu, Y. (2015). The Challenges of Data Quality and Data Quality Assessment in the Big Data Era. *Data Science Journal*, 14(0), 2. doi:10.5334/dsj-2015-002

Carter, C. L., Hamilton, H. J., & Cercone, N. (1997). Share-Based measures for itemsets. In *Proceedings of the Ist European Symposium on Principles of Data Mining and Knowledge Discovery*. Springer-Verlag. 10.1007/3-540-63223-9_102

Chandra, P., & Gupta, M. K. (2018). Comprehensive survey on data warehousing research. *International Journal of Information Technology*, *10*(2), 217–224. doi:10.100741870-017-0067-y

Che, D., Safran, M., & Peng, Z. (2013). *From Big Data to Big Data Mining: Challenges, Issues, and Opportunities*. Proceedings of the 18ᵗʰ International conference Database Systems for Advanced Applications workshop. 10.1007/978-3-642-40270-8_1

Chen, Y., Zhu, F., & Lee, J. (2013). Data quality evaluation and improvement for prognostic modeling using visual assessment based data partitioning method. *Journal of Computers in Industry*, *64*(3), 214–225. doi:10.1016/j.compind.2012.10.005

Cios, K., Pedrycz, W., Swiniarski, R., & Kurgan, L. (2007). *Data Mining: A Knowledge Discovery Approach*. Springer-Verlag.

Cody, W. F., Kreulen, J. T. V., Krishna, V., & Spangler, W. S. (2002). The integration of business intelligence and knowledge management. *IBM Systems Journal*, *41*(4), 697–713. doi:10.1147j.414.0697

Davidson, I., Grover, A., Satyanarayana, A., & Tayi, G. (2004). *A General Approach to Incorporate Data Quality Matrices into Data Mining Algorithms*. Proceedings of the *10th ACM SIGKDD International Conference on Knowledge Discovery and Data Mining*. 10.1145/1014052.1016916

Decker, K. M., & Focardi, S. (1995). *Technology overview: A report on Data Mining. Technical Report*. Swiss Scientific Computing Center.

English, L. (2011). *Information Quality Applied: Best Practices for Improving Business Information Processes and Systems*. Wiley Publishing.

Espinosa, R., & Zubcoff, J. (2011). A set of experiments to consider data quality criteria in classification techniques for Data Mining. *Proceedings of the International Conference on Computational science and its applications*. 10.1007/978-3-642-21887-3_51

Even, A., & Shankaranarayanan, G. (2007). Utility-Driven assessment of data quality. *The Data Base for Advances in Information Systems*, *38*(2), 75–93. doi:10.1145/1240616.1240623

Fan, W., & Bifet, A. (2013). Mining Big Data: Current Status, and Forecast to the Future. *SIGKDD Explorations*, *14*(2), 1–5. doi:10.1145/2481244.2481246

Fehrenbacher, D., & Helfert, M. (2012). Contextual Factors Influencing Perceived Importance and Trade-offs of Information Quality. *Communications of the Association for Information Systems*, *30*(8), 111–126. doi:10.17705/1CAIS.03008

Fodor, I. K. (2002). *A survey of dimension reduction techniques*. LLNL Technical Report.

Freitas, A. (2002). *Data Mining and Knowledge Discovery with Evolutionary Algorithms*. Springer-Verlag. doi:10.1007/978-3-662-04923-5

Ge, M., Helfert, M., & Jannach, D. (2011). Information quality assessment: validating measurement dimensions and processes. *Proceedings of the 19th European Conference on Information Systems.*

Ge, M., Helfert, M., & Jannach, D. (2011). Information quality assessment: validating measurement dimensions and processes. *Proceedings of the 19th European Conference on Information Systems.*

Geng, L., & Hamilton, H. (2006). Interestingness measure for Data Mining: A survey. *ACM Computing Surveys, 38*(3), 9. doi:10.1145/1132960.1132963

Gibson, N. (2010). *Improving information products for System 2 Design Support* (Ph.D. Thesis). University of Arkansas.

Guillet, F., & Howard, J. (2007). *Quality Measures in Data Mining.* Springer-Verlag. doi:10.1007/978-3-540-44918-8

Gustafsson, P., Lindström, Å., Jägerlind, C., & Tsoi, J. (2006). A Framework for Assessing Data Quality – from a Business Perspective. *Software Engineering Research and Practice,* 1009-1015.

Häubscher, R., Puntambekar, S., & Nye, A (2007). Domain specific interactive Data Mining. *Proceedings of the 11th International Conference User Model. Workshop Data Mining User Model,* 81-90.

Heinrich, B., Kaiser, M., & Kier, M. (2009). A Procedure to Develop Metrics for Currency and its Application in CRM. *ACM Journal of Data and Information Quality, 1*(1), 1–28. doi:10.1145/1515693.1515697

Heinrich, B., Kaiser, M., & Klier, M. (2007). How to measure Data Quality? – A metrics based approach. *28th International Conference on Information Systems.*

Heinrich, B., Kaiser, M., & Klier, M. (2008). Does the EU insurance mediation directive help to improve data quality? – A metric-based analysis. *Proceedings of the 16th European Conference on Information Systems.*

Heinrich, B., & Klier, M. (2009). A novel data quality metric for timeliness Considering supplemental data. *Proceedings of the 17th European Conference on Information Systems,* 2701-2713.

Helfert, M., & Foley, O. (2009). *A Context Aware Information Quality Framework.* Paper presented at Fourth International Conference on Cooperation and Promotion of Information Resources in Science and Technology, Beijing, China.

Helfert, M., Foley, O., Ge, M., & Cappiello, C. (2009). Limitations of Weighted Sum Measures for Information Quality. *Proceedings of Americas Conference on Information Systems.*

Janecek, A. (2009). *Efficient feature reduction and classification methods* (Ph.D. Thesis). University of Vienna.

Kaiser, M. (2010). A conceptional approach to unify completeness, Consistency, and accuracy as quality dimensions of data values. *European and Mediterranean Conference on Information Systems.*

Keeton, K., Mehra, P., & Wilkes, J. (2010). Do you know your IQ? A research agenda for information quality in systems. *Performance Evaluation Review, 37*(3), 26–31. doi:10.1145/1710115.1710121

Kim, Y., & Gao, J. (2006). Unsupervised gene selection for high dimensional data. *Proceedings of IEEE Symposium of Bioinformatics and Bioengineering*, 227-232. 10.1109/BIBE.2006.253339

Knight, S. (2011). The combined conceptual life-cycle model of information quality: Part 1, an investigative framework. *International Journal of Information Quality.*, 2(3), 205–230. doi:10.1504/IJIQ.2011.040669

Lenca, P., Meyer, P., Vaillant, B., & Lallich, S. (2004). *A multicriteria decision aid for interestingness measure selection.* Technical Report LUSSI-TR-2004-01-EN, LUSSI Department, GET/ENST, Bretagne, France.

Liu, B., Hsu, W., & Chen, S. (1997). Using general impressions to analyze discovered classification rules. *Proceedings of the 3rd International Conference on Knowledge Discovery and Data Mining*, 31–36.

Lu, S., Hu, H., & Li, F. (2001). Mining weighted association rules. *Intelligent Data Analysis*, 5(3), 211–225. doi:10.3233/IDA-2001-5303

Maimon, O., & Rokach, L. (2010). *Data mining and knowledge discovery handbook.* Springer-Verlag. doi:10.1007/978-0-387-09823-4

Mansur, M., & Noor, M. (2005). *Outlier Detection Technique in Data Mining: A Research Perspective.* Postgraduate Annual Research Seminar 2005, Universiti Teknologi Malaysia.

Mazón, J., Jacobo, J., Garrigós, I., & Espinosa, R. (2012). Open Business Intelligence: on the importance of data quality awareness in user-friendly Data Mining. *Proceedings of the Joint EDBT/ICDT Workshops.* 10.1145/2320765.2320812

Mehta, N., & Pandit, A. (2018). Concurrence of big data analytics and healthcare: A systematic review. *International Journal of Medical Informatics, Elsevier*, *114*, 57–65. doi:10.1016/j.ijmedinf.2018.03.013 PMID:29673604

Mirzaie, M. (2019). *Big Data Quality: A systematic literature review and future research directions.* Cornell University.

Naumann, F., & Rolker, C. (2000), Assessment methods for Information Quality criteria. *Proceedings of the 14th International Conference on Information Quality*, 148-162.

Nelson, R., Todd, P. A., & Wixom, B. H. (2005). Antecedents of Information and System Quality: An Empirical Examination Within the Context of Data Warehousing. *Journal of Management Information Systems*, *21*(4), 199–235. doi:10.1080/07421222.2005.11045823

O'Dowd, E. (2018). *Unstructured Healthcare Data Needs Advanced Machine Learning Tools.* HIT Infrastructure.

Ohsaki, M., Kitaguchi, S., Okamoto, K., Yokoi, H., & Yamaguchi, T. (2004). Evaluation of rule interestingness measures with a clinical dataset on hepatitis. *Proceedings of the 8th European Conference on Principles of Data Mining and Knowledge Discovery*, 362–373. 10.1007/978-3-540-30116-5_34

Piltaver, R. (2011). *Constructing understandable and accurate classifiers using Data Mining algorithms.* Jožef Stefan International Postgraduate School.

Pipino, L., Lee, Y., & Wang, R. Y. (2002). Data quality assessment. *Communications of the ACM*, *45*(4), 211–218. doi:10.1145/505248.506010

Popovič, A., Coelho, P. S., & Jaklič, J. (2009). The Impact of Business Intelligence System Maturity on Information Quality. *Information Research*, *14*(4).

Prat, N., & Madnick, S. (2008). Measuring Data Believability: a Provenance Approach. *Proceedings of the 41st Hawaii International Conference on System Sciences*. 10.1109/HICSS.2008.243

Rodríguez, N., & Casanovas, J. (2010). A structural model of information system quality: an empirical research. *Proceedings of the Americas Conference on Information Systems*.

Shankaranarayanan, G. (2005). Towards implementing total data quality management in a datawarehouse. *Journal of Information Technology Management*, *16*(1), 21–30.

Shankaranarayanan, G., & Cai, Y. (2006). Supporting data quality management in decision-making. *Decision Support Systems*, *42*(1), 302–317. doi:10.1016/j.dss.2004.12.006

Shen, Y. D., Zhang, Z., & Yang, Q. (2002). Objective-Oriented utility-based association mining. *Proceedings of the IEEE International Conference on Data Mining*, 426–433.

Stang, J., Hartvigsen, T., & Reitan, J. (2010). The Effect of Data Quality on Data Mining – Improving Prediction Accuracy by Generic Data Cleansing. *Proceedings of the 2010 International Conference on Information Quality*.

Strohmeier, S., & Piazza, F. (2013). Domain driven Data Mining in human resource management: A review of current research. *Journal of Expert Systems with Applications*, *40*(7), 2410–2420. doi:10.1016/j.eswa.2012.10.059

Sundararaman, A. (2011.) A framework for linking Data Quality to business objectives in decision support systems. *3rd International Conference on Trendz in Information Sciences and Computing*, 177-181. 10.1109/TISC.2011.6169110

Sundararaman, A. (2012). *Information Quality Strategy - an Empirical Investigation of the Relationship Between Information Quality Improvements and Organizational Outcomes* (Unpublished Ph.D. Thesis). Birla Institute of Technology and Science, India.

Sundararaman, A. Kandasamy, P., & Raji, D. (2018). Data Science Techniques To Improve accuracy of Provider Network Directory. *IEEE 25th International Conference on High Performance Computing Workshops (HiPCW)*, 119-128

Symeonidis, A., Athanasiadis, I. N., & Mitkas, P. A. (2007). A retraining methodology for enhancing agent intelligence. *Journal of Knowledge-Based Systems*, *20*(4), 388–396. doi:10.1016/j.knosys.2006.06.003

Taleb, M. A. S., & Dssouli, R. (2018). Big Data Quality: A Survey. *2018 IEEE International Congress on Big Data (Big Data Congress)*, 166-173. 10.1109/BigDataCongress.2018.00029

Tan, P., Kumar, V., & Srivastava, J. (2002). Selecting the right interestingness measure for association patterns. *Proceedings of the 8th International Conference on Knowledge Discovery and Data Mining*, 32–41. 10.1145/775047.775053

Turban, E., Sharda, R., & Delen, D. (2011). *Decision support and Business Intelligence*. Pearson Education.

Wang, S., & Wang, H. (2011). *Mining data quality in completeness*. University of Massachusetts.

Woodall, P., & Parlikad, A. (2010). A hybrid approach to assessing data quality. *Proceedings of the 15th International Conference on Information Quality*.

Yang, H., & Simon, F. (2009). A Framework of Business Intelligence-Driven Data Mining for E-business. *Fifth International Joint Conference on INC, IMS and IDC*.

Yang, Q., & Wu, X. (2006). 10 challenging problems in Data Mining research. *International Journal of Information Technology & Decision Making, 5*(4), 597–604. doi:10.1142/S0219622006002258

Zhu, X., & Davidson, I. (2007). *Knowledge Discovery and Data Mining: Challenges and Realities*. IGI Global. doi:10.4018/978-1-59904-252-7

ADDITIONAL READING

AlMabhouh, A., & Ahmad, A. (2010), Identifying quality factors within data warehouse, *Second International Conference on Computer Research and Development*, 65-72. 10.1109/ICCRD.2010.18

Ballou, D., & Tayi, G. (1999). Enhancing data quality in datawarehouse environments. *Communications of the ACM, 42*(1), 73–78. doi:10.1145/291469.291471

Batini, C., Cappiello, C., Francalanci, C., & Maurino, A. (2009). Methodologies for Data Quality Assessment and Improvement. *ACM Computing Surveys, 41*(3), 1–52. doi:10.1145/1541880.1541883

Bogza, R. M. (2008). Business intelligence as a competitive differentiator, *IEEE International Conference on Automation, Quality and Testing. Robotics, 1*(1), 146–151.

Daniel, F., Casati, F., Palpanas, T., & Chayka, O. (2008). Managing Data Quality in Business Intelligence Applications, *Program Committee Workshop on Management of Uncertain Data*, 133.

Decker, K. & Focardi, S. (1995). Technology overview: a report on Data Mining. Technical Report, *Swiss Federal Institute of Technology (ETH Zurich) Technical Report CSCS TR*-95-02, 1995.

Helfert, M & Herrman, C. (2005). Introducing data quality management in data warehousing. *Information Quality, Advances in Management Information Systems*, 135-152.

Lönnqvista, A., & Pirttimäkib, V. (2006). The Measurement of Business Intelligence. *Information Systems Management, 23*(1), 32–40. doi:10.1201/1078.10580530/45769.23.1.20061201/91770.4

Madnick, S., Wang, R. Y., & Zhu, H. (2009). Overview and Framework for Data and Information Quality Research. *ACM Journal of Data and Information Quality, 1*(1), 1–22. doi:10.1145/1515693.1516680

Manfred, A. J., Christoph, Q., & Matthias, J. (1998). Design and analysis of quality information for data warehouses. *Lecture Notes in Computer Science, 1507*, 349–362. doi:10.1007/978-3-540-49524-6_28

Maydanchick, A. (2007). *Data Quality Assessment*. Technics Publications.

McGilvray, D. (2010). *Executing Data Quality projects – Ten steps to quality data and trusted information*. Morgan Kaufmann Publishers.

Sintchenko, V., Magrabi, F., & Tipper, S. (2007). Are we measuring the right end-points? Variables that affect the impact of computerised decision support on patient outcomes: A systematic review. *Medical Informatics and the Internet in Medicine, 32*(3), 225–240. doi:10.1080/14639230701447701 PMID:17701828

Stvilia, B., Gasser, L., Michael, B. T., & Linda, C. (2007). A framework for Information Quality Assessment. *Journal of the American Society for Information Science and Technology, 58*(12), 1720–1733. doi:10.1002/asi.20652

Sundararaman, A. T. (2015). Data Quality for Data mining in Business Intelligence Applications – current state and research directions. In A. Ana & M. F. Santos (Eds.), *Integration of Data Mining in Business Intelligence Systems*. IGI Inc. doi:10.4018/978-1-4666-6477-7.ch003

KEY TERMS AND DEFINITIONS

Actionability: Prediction result enables decision making about future decision scenarios in the select business domain.

BDQ: Big data quality; data quality arising from big data characteristics.

Comprehensibility: Prediction results or patterns from the data mining model can be meaningfully interpreted in the context of the select business domain.

Conciseness: Pattern or prediction from data mining model that is relatively easy to understand and remember.

Coverage: The prediction results cover a relatively large subset of population data.

Diversity: The elements of a pattern discovered from Data Mining differ significantly from each other.

DQ Dimension: An attribute or factor of the data that serves as a perspective for study of DQ, for example, correctness or timeliness or accuracy.

DSS: Decision Support Systems – a unified system that supports decision making process in an organization at different levels and in multiple business functions such as tactical or strategic or planning.

DW: Data warehouse – a data store or repository created by integrating data from disparate sources, used for reporting and data analysis.

EIS: Executive Information System – a specialized form of DSS to support decision making process of executive/senior management teams in an organization.

Novelty: Prediction results or patterns discovered from data mining model was not obviously known before the model prediction.

Peculiarity: The prediction/pattern generated by the data mining model is far away from the other discovered results/patterns according to a defined distance measure.

Reliability: The relationship predicted by the data mining model is observed in a high percentage of population data.

Surprisingness: The prediction/pattern from the data mining model contradicts existing knowledge or expected outcomes.

Utility: Prediction result is of use to the business user to achieve the goal behind the BI application.

Chapter 5

Enterprise Data Lake Management in Business Intelligence and Analytics:
Challenges and Research Gaps in Analytics Practices and Integration

Mohammad Daradkeh

Yarmouk University, Irbid, Jordan

ABSTRACT

The data lake has recently emerged as a scalable architecture for storing, integrating, and analyzing massive data volumes characterized by diverse data types, structures, and sources. While the data lake plays a key role in unifying business intelligence, analytics, and data mining in an enterprise, effective implementation of an enterprise-wide data lake for business intelligence and analytics integration is associated with a variety of practical challenges. In this chapter, concrete analytics projects of a globally industrial enterprise are used to identify existing practical challenges and drive requirements for enterprise data lakes. These requirements are compared with the extant literature on data lake technologies and management to identify research gaps in analytics practice. The comparison shows that there are five major research gaps: 1) unclear data modelling methods, 2) missing data lake reference architecture, 3) incomplete metadata management strategy, 4) incomplete data lake governance strategy, and 5) missing holistic implementation and integration strategy.

DOI: 10.4018/978-1-7998-5781-5.ch005

INTRODUCTION

The digital transformation towards capturing and analyzing big data opens up new ways for enterprises to optimize their processes and improve their productivity and competitive advantage. For example, the Internet of Things (IoT) applications enable the continuous collection of data directly from the production line, which in turn enable descriptive, predictive and prescriptive analytics of manufacturing and service operations (Beheshti, Benatallah, Sheng, & Schiliro, 2020; Ravat & Zhao, 2019). External data sources, such as data from mobile and social networks, can also be integrated and analyzed to gain insights that lead to a better understanding of customers' behavior, characteristics and problems. Advanced analytics approaches, such as data mining, text mining and machine learning, can generate new knowledge from a variety of sources. By applying both traditional business intelligence (BI) and data mining, collectively described as business analytics (Llave, 2018), enterprises can gain real-time insights into multidisciplinary business functions and improve overall decision making to ultimately achieve better business performance and competitive advantage (Miloslavskaya & Tolstoy, 2016).

Typically, the data used for BI and analytics applications in enterprises are heterogeneous, complex, and very large. Relevant data for BI and analytics applications can also be available in different structures and in internal and external data sources. It is not uncommon for enterprises to have multiple data silos that can only be dismantled with great effort; which poses significant challenges to traditional BI and analytics practices based on data warehouses. This is because data warehouses are traditionally not flexible enough to handle such a variety of data and usage scenarios (Beheshti et al., 2020; Inmon, 2016; Nargesian, Zhu, Miller, Pu, & Arocena, 2019). To bring all this data together and be able to extract valuable insights and knowledge from it, it can be integrated into an enterprise data lake; a scalable data repository and management platform for data exploration and analytical purposes (Gryncewicz, Sitarska-Buba, & Zygała, 2020; Llave, 2018).

In the enterprise data lake, diverse types of data, including structured, semi-structured and unstructured data, are captured, managed and analyzed using exploratory analysis and data mining without a predefined schema. For this purpose, huge amounts of data are collected from different sources (local or outside the organization) and directly ingested and stored into a data lake in its native and original state, with little or no cleansing, standardization, or transformation (Fang, 2015; Laurent, Laurent, & Madera, 2020; Llave, 2018). The native format of the data enables the transition from descriptive to predictive and prescriptive as the data management and structure can be imposed at the time of analysis, unlike traditional structured data storage where data must be mapped to a schema at ingest (Campbell, 2015; Fang, 2015). It also ensures that data analysts, data scientists, and other self-service business users have access to abundance of raw data that they can repurpose and integrate into a variety of analytics applications as needed (Fang, 2015; Larson & Chang, 2016; Llave, 2018; Tomcy & Pankaj, 2017).

While data lakes offer a variety of advantages to increase synergies and reduce the integration effort for analytics applications (Farid, Roatis, Ilyas, Hoffman, & Chu, 2016; Gorelik, 2019; Laurent et al., 2020; Llave, 2018), enterprises still encounter several challenges when building and leveraging data lakes in practice for data analysis and integration (Llave, 2018; Sitarska-Buba & Zygala, 2020). Existing literature on the concept and individual components of the enterprise data lake is vague and inconsistent. Furthermore, there are many approaches to implementing individual components of the data lake, such as data modeling and data lake governance (Farid et al., 2016; Giebler, Gröger, Hoos, Schwarz, & Mitschang, 2019; Giudice, Musarella, Sofo, & Ursino, 2019). There are also rules and concepts for roles, responsibilities, and processes in the data lake architecture, especially with regard to data security, privacy and quality. Nevertheless, it remains unclear whether and how these approaches can be brought together for the practical implementation of a data lake in BI and analytics practices and integration, whether they are generally sufficient or whether further concepts are required.

In addition to the technical challenges, proper organizational structure and capabilities are particularly important for the successful implementation of the data lake solution. Thus, the construction of a data lake should be driven by top management. The development of a data lake with a button-up approach is rarely successful, because the individual departments or business units usually lack the strategic view of the business value of the data. Ideally, therefore, as part of a digitization initiative, management is tasked with collecting, describing and ingesting the data relevant to the organizational units into the enterprise data lake (Laurent et al., 2020). Moreover, in the data lake architecture, it is important from the beginning to implement a reliable metadata management concept that provides a catalog of the available data, including their semantic modeling and description (Grossman, 2019; Gryncewicz et al., 2020; Hai, Geisler, & Quix, 2016; Halevy et al., 2016).

This chapter aims to extent the current knowledge on data lakes by investigating the practical and integration challenges associated with the implementation of data lakes for BI and analytics, taking into account concrete practical requirements, as illustrated by an example of a globally operating industrial company. Based on these requirements, the current state of art on enterprise data lakes is discussed and corresponding recommendations for action are presented. This chapter makes the following contributions to the literature on integration challenges for BI, analytics, and data mining. First, it explores several representative BI and analytics projects from an industrial company, in which a data lake is implemented in practice. Second, it identifies the different types of enterprise data used in these projects, including their data management requirements and the main requirements for building a data lake that meet their own needs. Third, it examines the literature on data lakes and compare it with practical requirements. Finally, it highlights research gaps and challenges related to the development and use of data lakes for BI and analytics practices and integration.

The rest of this chapter is structured as follows: the next section identifies the requirements for the enterprise data lake that arise in practice. For this purpose, a practical, representative example is presented, from which a classification of the data types relevant in the field of BI and analytics is derived. The resulting requirements form the basis for further discussion. In the following section, the existing literature on data lakes is discussed in general terms, while the following section considers concrete implementation approaches for individual aspects of data lakes and compares them with the practical requirements. Based on the findings and insights gained, the practical challenges and research gaps in the implementation of data lakes for BI and analytics integration are identified. The last section concludes this chapter with a summary of main findings and avenues for future research.

Practical Requirements for the Enterprise Data Lake

In order to analyze the current state of art on data lakes and identify challenges and research gaps, the necessary functions and characteristics of the data lake must first be identified. Without a clear picture of the central requirements for the data lake, it is not possible to comprehensively discuss the concrete approaches for implementing the individual components of the data lake. To derive such requirements, this section examines the example of a large, globally industrial enterprise. In several BI and analytics projects, different types of enterprise data are identified and categorized based on their data management requirements. The observations made in this example could also be applied to other large industrial enterprises. Based on the insights gained, three central requirements for data lakes are derived, which serve as a basis for further investigation of the current state of data lakes in BI and analytics practices and integration.

Practical Example

The application example used in this chapter is a global industrial company operating in Jordan called thyssenkrupp Elevator and Services (https://www.thyssenkrupp-elevator.com/jo/), which is part of the German-based thyssenkrupp AG. Thyssenkrupp's elevators carry more than one billion passengers worldwide each day (Thyssenkrupp Elevator, 2020). The operational and service reliability of elevators is therefore a competitive delimitation criterion for the company, as is the fast and efficient repair of damage in the event of technical failures. Thyssenkrupp uses a whole range of built-in sensors to collect extensive data on each of its elevators. These include door movements, cabin calls, travel times and error codes in case of malfunctions. The data collected from each individual elevator is compiled in a separate internal cloud. This extensive database allows the analysis and prediction of maintenance problems and the life cycle of elevator components. The goal of the underlying analytics is therefore to report and inductively predict operational failures based on real-time data from elevators before they actually occur. Consequently, predictive analytics and machine learning techniques utilizing Internet of Things (IoT) technologies are used to increase the availability and reliability of elevators by reducing out-of-service situations through real-time diagnosis and predictive maintenance. Thyssenkrupp translates the results of the analytics models directly into actions by providing service technicians with accurate and predictive diagnoses before the damage occurs.

Additionally, the operational IT landscape at Thyssenkrupp consists of a large number of systems from various functional areas of the organization, from computer-aided design (CAD) and product lifecycle management (PLM) systems to enterprise resource planning (ERP), manufacturing execution systems (MES) and customer relationship management (CRM) systems. To maintain and expand their competitiveness, the digital transformation towards Industry 4.0 and data-driven decision making are central aspects of industrial enterprises (Massaro, Contuzzi, & Galiano, 2020; Teixeira de Azevedo, Martins, & Kofuji, 2019). Generally speaking, Industry 4.0 aims at greater efficiency and flexibility through the application of IoT technologies, machine learning and data analytics across the entire industrial value chain (Căpușneanu, Topor, Maria (Oprea) Constantin, & Marin-Pantelescu, 2020; Štrukelj, Mulej, & Zabukovšek, 2020). The company under consideration focuses in particular on the massive use of IoT sensors in production, the collection of customer and product-related data from the web and the integration of all enterprise data across the entire value chain. To manage all this heterogeneous raw data from multiple sources, the company plans to leverage an enterprise-wide data lake to accelerate the development of analytics-driven applications and facilitate the integration of traditional BI and advanced analytics capabilities.

Throughout Thyssenkrupp, several BI and analysis projects were launched in various functional areas to exploit the potential value of both new big data and traditional enterprise data (left in Figure 1). The data generated in these projects is jointly managed in an enterprise-wide data lake and integrated as required. There is a great variety of projects because the projects cover different business areas, such as complaint management and product life cycle management. In the complaint management project, for example, data on customer orders from ERP and CRM systems are integrated with images and videos that customers have attached to their complaints. This facilitates the categorization of product complaints and the accurate detection of malfunctions. In the product life cycle management project, data on customers, processes and products sold to customers is constantly being collected, integrated and compared with simulation data from the product development life cycle. In this way, the performance of the product in which it is used can be better investigated and product development can be adjusted accordingly in future iterations. These exemplary projects show the variety of data that needs to be managed in an enterprise data lake (right in Figure 1). This diversity goes beyond the mere consideration of data structure (e.g. structured customer data and unstructured image files); data may be particularly sensitive and worthy of protection (e.g. personal customer data or product data), may be voluminous (e.g. sensor data) or may have other characteristics that must be taken into account when integrating and using them in analytics applications.

Figure 1. An overview of the practical example. Data analytics projects (left) and data characteristics (right) come together in an enterprise-wide data lake.

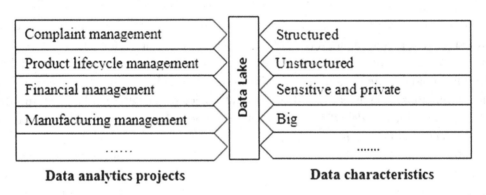

The example considered is representative of industrial enterprises, since it comprises a large number of data sources and thus different types and structures of data are available for analytical purposes (Ravat & Zhao, 2019; Tomcy & Pankaj, 2017). To determine exactly what requirements a data lake must meet, these different data types and their integration and management requirements must be taken into account. The following section identifies different types of data that are critical in industrial, analytics-intensive enterprises.

Types of Enterprise Data

Three important types of enterprise data that are used for analytical purposes can be derived from several BI and analytics projects of the industrial company: master data, transactional data and IoT data (see Table 1). This categorization does not claim to be complete. Depending on the domain and application, additional data types and other data properties may exist (Giudice et al., 2019). However, this categorization is sufficient to show the different data management requirements that are imposed on a data lake. The following paragraphs describe the identified data types in more detail and explain the corresponding requirements for data integration and management.

Table 1. Types of data available for analytical purposes in the practical example.

Master data	Transactional data	IoT data
Static	Associated with business transactions	Temporal, Short-lived nature
Structured	Structured, Semi-structured, Unstructured	Semi-structured, Unstructured
Sensitive	Big	Unknown quality
		big

Master data refer to statistical data about business objects that are central to business processes, such as customers, orders, employees, or products (Schäffer & Leyh, 2017). These data are typically structured, even in the case of the company under consideration, and are rather static in nature, i.e. the data rarely changes. By managing these data in an enterprise-wide data lake, can be linked to other data types. For example, product data can be directly linked to photos and videos of product defects and maintenance issues. Master data are of great value to companies and their accuracy is very important. They must therefore be classified as sensitive data and must be protected accordingly. In addition, high data quality must be established and maintained. Therefore, comprehensive governance is required to protect the data from unauthorized access, alteration and other attempts of fraud.

Transactional data are associated with the daily transactions and processes within the company (Borek, Parlikad, Webb, & Woodall, 2014). They are linked to an event at a specific point in time, such as the receipt of a customer complaint. Once they have been recorded, they are usually not changed. Transaction data can exist in a wide variety of structures, from structured to unstructured. Structured transaction data plays an important role in traditional data warehousing and BI applications. Thus, if they are properly managed in a data lake, traditional BI and analytics, such as reporting and analytical online processing (OLAP), must continue to be enabled on them, as is possible in a traditional data warehouse. Semi-structured and unstructured data associated with transactions, such as a PDF document with an invoice or a photo with a product complaint, are also considered transactional data. Regardless of their structure, they must be managed and integrated with other data to enable holistic data analysis and integration. They are also linked to master data, for example, customer and product data are central components of a complaint. Transactional data are generated by business processes in large quantities and are therefore voluminous.

IoT data are all the data collected in connection with IoT devices, such as sensor values or data from manufacturing and operating facilities. They are typically treated as a data stream. In contrast to transactional data, they have no direct reference to business transactions, processes or objects. Such a reference must first be established using integration steps, for example, by assigning sensor values to the device in which they were recorded using the sensor ID. IoT data are of temporal nature as they describe the current status, which can change immediately after capture. They can be both semi-structured and unstructured. Semi-structured IoT data are sensor values that are represented as key-value pairs, e.g. as a JSON object (Bouaziz, Nabli, & Gargouri, 2019). Unstructured IoT data, on the other hand, are images or videos recorded by the IoT device. IoT data are collected at periodic time intervals, resulting in large amounts of heterogeneous data. In most cases, the quality of these data is unknown. This can cause images to be blurred or sensor values to be affected. IoT data usually linked to master data or transactional data; for example, sensor values are assigned to a specific product. Therefore, all these data, regardless of their structure, must be integrated. Furthermore, due to their temporal nature, the history of IoT data must also be recorded and analyzed.

Main Requirements for Enterprise Data Lakes

Based on the insights from the previous sections, three main requirements can be derived for the effective implementation of an enterprise-wide data lake to support the development and integration of BI and analytics applications:

R1. *Management and integration of different data types.* All three data types described in the previous section must be integrated and organized in an enterprise-wide data lake. This means that data with different structures (structured, semi-structured, unstructured) comes together in an enterprise-wide data lake. It is important to integrate the data according to the context, regardless of their degree of structuredness. In the case of a product complaint, for example, unstructured photos and videos of the malfunction or damage can be analyzed to classify the maintenance problem, e.g. a material defect. By linking to the structured product data, the faulty material can be identified. The knowledge gained in this way can be used to prevent similar malfunctions. However, it is also important to consider other characteristics of the data, such as volume and diversity, when integrating and managing them.

R2. *Support the development and integration of diverse types of analytics.* The analytical applications that are implemented with the data in the data lake are as diverse as the data itself. As described in the previous section, some of the data are used for reporting and OLAP, such as the calculation of key performance indicators (KPIs). There are also advanced analytics, such as machine learning and text analytics, which can be used to gain new insights into processes, customers and other aspects. Both types of analytics are implemented based on the data from a data lake. The analytics range from descriptive to diagnostic and predictive to prescriptive analytics (Giudice et al., 2019). Furthermore, the integration of IoT data also requires the support of data stream processing in the data lake. At the same time, batch processing must be possible in order to analyze large amounts of data. An enterprise data lake must be able to support the development and integration of all these types of analytics applications (Gryncewicz et al., 2020; Hai et al., 2016; Halevy et al., 2016).

R3. *Governance of different data types.* The term data lake governance is used to summarize strategies and rules that contribute, for example, to data security, data quality or compliance with legal requirements in the data lake (Farid et al., 2016). Data lake governance ensures that data is accurate, reliable, and of high quality. As shown in the previous section, some of the data integrated and managed in the data lake, in particular master data, requires strict governance to protect them from unauthorized manipulation and to ensure high data quality (Malysiak-Mrozek, Stabla, & Mrozek, 2018; Miloslavskaya & Tolstoy, 2016; Nargesian et al., 2019). For other, less critical data, on the other hand, such extended governance represents a disproportionate burden that may hinder or even prevent flexible and exploratory analysis. It is therefore necessary to manage the different types of data with the appropriate policies and guidelines (Jovanovic, Nadal, Romero, Abelló, & Bilalli, 2020). A data lake must meet all governance requirements to support the development and integration efforts of various BI and analytics applications.

Data Lake in Business Intelligence and Analytics

The term data lake appeared for the first time in a blog post by Dixon (2010) as an alternative to data warehouses for storing and analyzing big data. Dixon defined a data lake as a centralized repository in which data are stored in their raw and original state without any predefined or strict scheme. In this way, it can be accessed and used by users for sampling, mining, or any other analytical purposes (see requirement R2), since no information is lost through transformations. As a result, a variety of analytical applications can be performed later on with the data that were not initially planned. According to Dixon (2010), a data lake contains large amounts of heterogeneous data (see requirement R1) that come from a single source. However, the idea of a data lake that is only fed from a single source was hardly accepted otherwise. More recent definitions consider a data lake as a repository for data from multiple sources (Laurent et al., 2020; Llave, 2018; Miloslavskaya & Tolstoy, 2016; Quix & Hai, 2018; Ravat & Zhao, 2019; Roh, Heo, & Whang, 2019). Even for the practical example under consideration, a data lake for a single data source is not sufficient, since data from a variety of sources must be integrated and analyzed according to requirement R1.

The storage of large, heterogeneous amounts of data (see requirement R1) also poses a financial challenge. Data lakes must therefore use a scalable and cost-effective infrastructure for data storage and processing (Fang, 2015). In many cases, the data lake concept is directly linked to Hadoop (http://hadoop.apache.org/) and the Hadoop Distributed File System (HDFS). Hadoop is just one of many ways to build and use a data lake. It is often suggested in the literature to build a data lake with a variety of storage systems such as Azure or IBM (Sawadogo, Scholly, et al., 2019) in order to have the most suitable storage system available for each analytics application (see requirement R2). For example, structured data can be managed in a relational database, while voluminous IoT data is stored in a highly scalable NoSQL data store (Bouaziz et al., 2019). A wide range of data storage systems such as MongoDB and Neo4J can be used in a data lake (Gallinucci, Golfarelli, & Rizzi, 2018; Halevy et al., 2016). The storage components of a data lake can also be located both on-premise and in the cloud. The selection of several suitable storage systems is also advantageous for the practical example presented in order to support a wide range of analytics applications as adequately as possible (see requirement R2). The use of several storage systems for different data types is also advantageous for the management of large, heterogeneous data volumes (see requirement R1).

Other characteristics of the data lake vary greatly according to the definition under consideration. There are also discrepancies between the definitions, especially with regard to the role of the data lake, user groups and the management of the data lake and metadata. In the literature, the role of the data lake ranges from pure data storage to a data management platform that manages and makes data available for various types of analytics applications—from visualizations and dashboards to real-time analytics, big data analytics and machine learning—to enable better and faster decision-making. In accordance with requirement R2, a data lake is understood to be the latter.

The user groups that access the data lake also vary greatly depending on the definition. In some data lake definitions, a wide variety of users interact with the data lake, whose expertise in the field of data analytics is different: from data analytics experts (data scientists) to self-service business users and analysts whose expertise tends to be in other fields, such as marketing, sales and financial planning. Other definitions, on the other hand, recognize data scientists who use different techniques and models to predict and prescribe what action to take as the sole users of a data lake (Llave, 2018). In particular, considering requirement R2 of the practical example, the data lake must support a wide range of analytical applications, from advanced analytics (typically performed by data scientists) to BI reporting, descriptive analytics, and OLAP applications (typically performed by less tech-savvy business users). For the practical example, several types of users must be supported.

In the area of data lake governance and metadata management, there has been a change in the literature over time. In early work, the data lake concept excludes any integration of governance and metadata management. In the more recent literature, however, these are aptly described as major components of data lakes (Nogueira, Romdhane, & Darmont, 2018; Quix, Hai, & Vatov, 2016; Terrizzano, Schwarz, Roth, & Colino, 2015; Tomcy & Pankaj, 2017). Appropriate data lake management and comprehensive metadata management ensure that the data in the data lake is understandable, reusable, and trustworthy (see requirement R3). Without governance and metadata management, the data lake runs the risk of turning into a so-called data swamp, i.e., a data management repository in which data can no longer be used for agile and value-added analytics, due, for example, to lack of data quality, comprehensibility, or clarity (Sawadogo, Kibata, & Darmont, 2019; Sawadogo, Scholly, et al., 2019; Suriarachchi & Plale, 2016).

Overall, it can be concluded that the literature is very divided when it comes to defining a data lake. Nevertheless, for all requirements of the practical example discussed in this chapter, suitable characteristics are found in the existing definitions. To meet all the requirements listed above and to support the development and integration of BI and analytics applications, a data lake must comply with the following proposed definition: A data lake is a scalable data management platform for data of any structure that is stored in their raw format to enable different types of analytics without a predefined schema. A data lake can also include pre-processed data to increase the efficiency and flexibility of data analysis and integration. Data from multiple sources is integrated into a data lake and accessed by different user groups. A data lake can span multiple types of storage systems. Data lake governance and metadata management are critical components of a data lake. However, this definition alone is not sufficient to implement a data lake in practice. Instead, different components should be addressed and integrated into an overarching data lake architecture. This requires implementation approaches for the individual components of the data lake. A number of these approaches are discussed in the following section.

Implementation Approaches for Data Lakes

In addition to general conceptual work on data lakes, there are various approaches for the implementation of individual components of data lakes. In order to meet the requirements listed above, the issues of data modeling, data lake architecture and metadata management shown in Figure 3 are of central importance. These are discussed in detail in the following subsections.

Figure 2. The main components of the data lake and different implementation approaches.

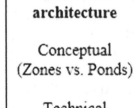

Data modelling	Data lake architecture	Metadata management
Data Droplet		Commercial tools
Data Vault	Conceptual (Zones vs. Ponds)	
3NF		Open source approaches
Head Version	Technical	
...	Data processing Data storage	

Data Modeling

The data modeling issue deals with requirement R1 (management and integration of different data types). In the context of data lakes the schema-on-read is often used in the literature (Sawadogo, Scholly, et al., 2019). This means that all data are initially stored in the data lake without a strict schema and data transformation and modeling are only implemented when the data are read according to the intended analytical application. This allows the data to be stored in the data lake with minimal effort. However, the complete postponement of any kind of data modeling until the data are used in the analysis leads to various problems, such as data quality, data comprehensibility and information integration (Llave, 2018; Nargesian et al., 2019). Without an underlying data model, it becomes very complex to consolidate data from different source systems. The storage of raw data already requires a data model to keep track of data over time. However, when modeling data in the data lake, care must be taken to maintain the flexibility of the data lake.

Initial implementation of data modeling methods specifically for data lakes already exist to support the integration of heterogeneous data (see requirement R1). One example is the Data Droplet method (Fang, 2015). With this modeling method, each item in the data lake, such as an entry in a table or document, is modeled as a Resource Description Framework (RDF) graphic. For example, the data for a single customer can be modeled as a droplet. If the customer files a complaint, this complaint is also modeled as a droplet with all associated data, and the two subgraphs are connected by edges. The integration of these smaller diagrams by adding edges creates a large, holistic data lake diagram that represents the relationships between the data. Another method of modeling data in the data lake is to represent the data fragments and their metadata as a quadruple, which is then linked to other data fragments as a diagram (Sawadogo, Kibata, et al., 2019). However, none of these methods have yet been evaluated or demonstrated effective.

An alternative approach is to apply existing data modeling methods to data lakes (Giebler et al., 2019; Sitarska-Buba & Zygala, 2020). For example, Giebler et al. (2019) proposed to use the Data Vault Model to model data in data lakes. Data Vault is originally a modeling method for structured data in data warehouses. Since Data Vault allows flexible and scalable modeling, it is well suited for structured data in data lakes (Puonti, Raitalaakso, Aho, & Mikkonen, 2017). In addition to Data Vault, there are other data modeling methods for structured data (such as third normal form (3NF) or head version tables) that can also be considered for data lakes (Giebler et al., 2019). There is also work on integrating semi-structured data into the Data Vault modeling method (Linstedt & Olschimke, 2016; Puonti et al., 2017). However, for unstructured data, as they have to be considered in data lakes, such approaches do not yet exist in Data Vault. There are approaches for linking structured and unstructured data from the data warehouse context, such as link-based integration, that can be used for this purpose (Bouaziz et al., 2019; Linstedt & Olschimke, 2016). However, no research has yet been conducted to assess their effectiveness in the context of data lakes.

In summary, neither the data modeling methods from the data lake context nor those from other areas have so far received a comprehensive assessment of their suitability for data modeling in data lakes. In particular, it remains unclear how well the different data modeling methods can handle heterogeneous amounts of data. Therefore, there are still several challenges that need to be addressed in data modeling of data lakes.

Data Lake Architecture

A variety of concepts can be summarized under the aspect of the data lake architecture, addressing requirement R1 (management and integration of different data types) and requirement R2 (support the development and integration of different types of analytics). The different perspectives can be divided into conceptual data lake architecture and technical data lake architecture.

Conceptual Data Lake Architecture

The conceptual data lake architecture describes how the data flows within the data lake and where it can be found by the user. It is located at a higher level of abstraction than data modeling and can itself define data modeling methods. The definition of the conceptual data lake architecture is intended to facilitate the use of data in a data lake, since it describes where data can be found and in what state. Possible states are raw, pre-processed or archived (Laurent et al., 2020). Raw data can be used flexibly for any type of analytics application, while pre-processed data can be avoided from certain transformation steps, making it more efficient to use. In particular, repetitive analytical applications can be supported, which contributes to fulfilling requirement R2.

In the literature on data lakes, there are two variants of conceptual data lake architectures, namely the data pond and the zone architectures (Inmon, 2016). In the data pond architecture (Inmon, 2016), the data is located in exactly one of five different data ponds at any given time (see Figure 4). When data are ingested in the data lake, they are first stored in the raw data pond. However, only data that is not used or does not fit in any of the other data ponds remains here. As soon as they are needed, all other data are forwarded to the Analog Data Pond, Application Data Pond or Textual Data Pond and deleted from the Raw Data Pond. The data pond to which the data are forwarded depends on the type of data; measurement data (e.g. log files or IoT data) migrate into the analog data pond, data from transactions and applications (e.g. data on a complaint process) migrate into the application data pond and text data (e.g. e-mails) migrate into the Textual Data Pond. Other data, such as videos or images, remains in the Raw Data Pond. If data are no longer needed, they leave the corresponding data pond and are moved to the Archival Data Pond. It can happen that data that are required for the same analytics application can be found in different data ponds. For example, data on complaints can be found in the Application Data Pond, while associated text can be found in the Textual Data Pond and images in the Raw Data Pond. The type of preparation and processing depends on the data pond to which the data are forwarded. For example, the Analog Data Pond removes outliers. This has the advantage that the data in the various data ponds are already pre-processed and thus can be analyzed more easily. An important drawback, however, is that the data are deleted from the Raw Data Pond, so that their raw form is lost. Thus, the data pond architecture contradicts the basic idea of the Data Lake.

The zone architecture is a structured approach that describes how data is conceptually organized and where they can be found within a data lake during the data analysis workflow (Ravat & Zhao, 2019). In the literature, there is no uniform concept for the zone architecture; instead, there are many alternatives that differ in several aspects, such as the number and purpose of the zones (Gorelik, 2019). One of the many zone architectures is shown in a simplified form in Figure 5. The idea behind this architecture, however, always remains the same: a zone determines the degree to which the data it contains is processed (Gorelik, 2019; Laurent et al., 2020). Each zone architecture initially stores the data in a raw zone, where the data are stored in its raw format. The data are then copied to other zones or views

Figure 3. The data pond architecture (Inmon, 2016). The data flows from the Raw Data Pond into the data pond, which contains the appropriate type of data (analog data, application data, and text data). If they are no longer needed, they flow into the Archival Data Pond.

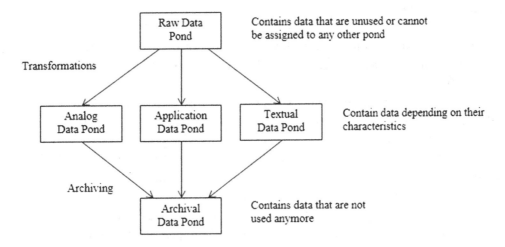

of the data are created and the data are further processed. For example, the data are cleaned up (e.g. in the Trusted Zone) or processed for specific analytics applications (e.g. in the Process Zone). The data are stored multiple times at different processing levels in different zones. However, the raw data always remains available in the Raw Zone.

Although the zone architecture is more commonly used than the data pond architecture in BI and analytics practice, there is no generally accepted scientific and practical evidence linking the zone architecture with the goal of promoting the appropriate application of data analytics (Laurent et al., 2020). To our knowledge, there are no evaluations or comparisons for the two different alternatives. While the zone

Figure 4. The zone architecture (Laurent et al., 2020). The data are simultaneously available in processing levels. The data are processed from zone to zone, but the raw data are retained in the Raw Zone.

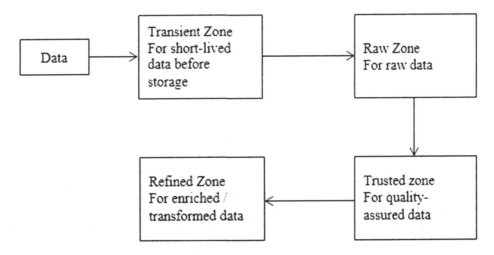

and data pond architectures always consider technical processing aspects, these are not the focus of these data lake architectures and are therefore considered separately in the technical data lake architecture.

Technical Data Lake Architecture

The technical data lake architecture describes the interaction of the technical components of the data lake. Here, two different challenges have to be addressed, namely data processing and data storage (Laurent et al., 2020).

Data processing deals with the different types of processing used in the data lake (e.g. stream or batch processing). It is therefore particularly important for requirement R2. In the literature, the Lambda architecture (Munshi & Mohamed, 2018; Tomcy & Pankaj, 2017) is proposed to process both data streams and large, static data sets. For example, field and IoT data collected as a data stream can be processed transiently in real time and stored permanently. The concept behind this architecture is shown in Figure 6. Data arriving as a data stream in the architecture are duplicated and forwarded to the two parallel branches. In the upper of the two branches, the data are stored permanently and processed as batches at regular intervals. On the other branch, the incoming data are processed as a data stream to provide real-time analysis results. In this way, both accurate (batch processing) and timely (stream processing) results can be delivered. In practice, the lambda architecture is often adapted to the analytics application (Tomcy & Pankaj, 2017). Examples of such adaptations are the BRAID architecture (Giebler, Stach, Schwarz, & Mitschang, 2018) and Bolster (Nadal et al., 2017). However, there are no evaluations of the different architectures, especially in the context of the data lake.

Figure 5. The Lambda architecture provides both batch and stream processing in parallel branches (Marz & Warren, 2015).

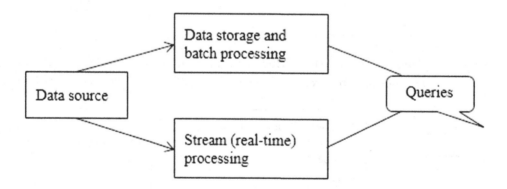

Data storage describes which systems and tools make up a data lake and how they interact with each other. However, apart from the use of HDFS and the recommendation of a heterogeneous system landscape, there is little evidence from the literature. Abstract concepts for a technical data lake architecture can only be found in a few cases (e.g., Mehmood et al., 2019; Miloslavskaya & Tolstoy, 2016). For the implementation of this sub-aspect, known and proven concepts from other contexts can also be used, such as the Polyglot Persistence (Khine & Wang, 2019). Polyglot Persistence, as proposed for the data lake, combines different data storage systems with different data sources to support the storage and integration requirements of different types of BI and analytics applications.

Overall, the definition and implementation of the data lake architecture is a major challenge, as there are hardly any evaluated and applied concepts. It remains unclear which architecture alternatives are well or less suitable for the development and integration of different types of analytics applications in enterprises. The literature on this aspect is rather abstract, so that the concrete implementation of different approaches is not possible without further preparatory work. Furthermore, neither the relationships between the two categories of the data lake architecture (i.e. conceptual and technical) nor between the data lake architecture and the other components are considered, although the data lake architecture affects both the data modelling and the metadata management.

Metadata Management

Metadata refers to the information that describes the syntax and semantics of the data itself, including its schema, semantics or data origin (Maccioni & Torlone, 2017). Metadata management describes how this data is managed in the data lake (Sawadogo, Kibata, et al., 2019). It helps to find, understand and describe data and thus enables the verification and control of compliance with rules. As with all data in the data lake, metadata management raises questions about appropriate data modeling and integration into the architecture of the data lake. However, since metadata management differs from normal data management in some concepts across these two aspects, it is considered as a separate aspect here.

Metadata in data lakes is crucial to the implementation of a governance approach (Alserafi, Abell´o, Romero, & Calders, 2016). Appropriate management of metadata thus contributes to meeting requirement R3 (governance for different types of data). For a comprehensive governance concept, both technical and organizational aspects such as user roles, assignment of rights, data classification and compliance with rules play a central role. Since these are not technically feasible approaches, they will not be discussed in detail in this chapter. There are some initial governance frameworks that attempt to detail these organizational aspects (Fang, 2015; Ravat & Zhao, 2019; Sawadogo, Kibata, et al., 2019; Sawadogo, Scholly, et al., 2019). However, they are very general and do not take into account the necessary flexibility of the data lake, different types of data that need to be managed, or different types of analytical applications that need to be developed and integrated.

The different existing approaches to metadata management can be divided into commercial tools and open source approaches from research. Commercial tools of metadata management can be divided into three categories: system-integrated data directories, data catalogs and data lake management platforms. However, none of the three categories offers all the functions required for holistic metadata management. For example, data catalogs lack certain types of metadata, such as metadata about IoT devices. As an alternative to commercial tools, there are open source approaches to metadata management in the literature (Ravat & Zhao, 2019; Sawadogo, Scholly, et al., 2019). Some data lake concepts already include extensive metadata management systems that allow storing and retrieving metadata. However, their closure creates the same problems as commercial tools.

Furthermore, there are approaches for the implementation of components of metadata management, particularly metadata extraction and metadata modeling (Nargesian et al., 2019; Sitarska-Buba & Zygala, 2020). Given the large amounts of data stored in the data lake, automatic metadata extraction is very important. Tools such as GEMMS can be used to enrich the metadata with semantic information and to enable queries on them (Quix et al., 2016). Schema profiling can also be used to extract schema information from schema-free data sources (Bouaziz et al., 2019; Gallinucci et al., 2018).

There are also different approaches to metadata modeling in the context of data lakes (Nogueira et al., 2018; Quix & Hai, 2018; Quix et al., 2016; Sawadogo, Kibata, et al., 2019; Sawadogo, Scholly, et al., 2019). However, many of these metadata models have a specific focus on individual analytical use cases, thus they lack the necessary generality and integration capability. There are also conceptual metadata models that have this generality. For example, the metadata model proposed by Quix et al. (2016) contains both information about the format and the semantic context of the data. The metadata model proposed by Sawadogo, Scholly, et al. (2019) defines other types of metadata (intra-object, inter-object and global metadata) and how they can be linked to the data. Due to their high generality, however, these metadata models are kept abstract; consequently, their technical implementation in practice remains difficult. For example, it is not clear how global metadata can be implemented in Sawadogo's model (Sawadogo, Scholly, et al., 2019). The high degree of abstraction also requires numerous adaptations to enable holistic metadata management. For example, abstract constructs, such as structural data in Quix and Hai (2018), must first be elaborated further before the model can be used in an implementation.

overall, it can be argued that although implementation approaches for metadata management already exist, commercial solutions do not yet offer the scope required in practice. Even the open source approaches from the literature still lack holistic concepts for metadata management, especially with regard to the modeling of metadata. As in the areas of data modeling and data lake architecture, a comprehensive evaluation of proposed and existing approaches is still missing.

Practical Challenges and Research Gaps

According to the above discussion, there are many different approaches for implementing individual components of data lakes (i.e., data modeling, data lake architecture, and metadata management). However, a holistic implementation strategy for an enterprise-wide data lake that is capable to support the development and integration of BI and analytics is still missing. In addition, an examination of current implementation approaches shows that further research is needed on data modeling, data lake architecture, metadata management, and data lake governance. As such, there are five key practical challenges

Figure 6. Key challenges and research gaps in the implementation of data lakes for the development and integration of enterprise BI and analytics.

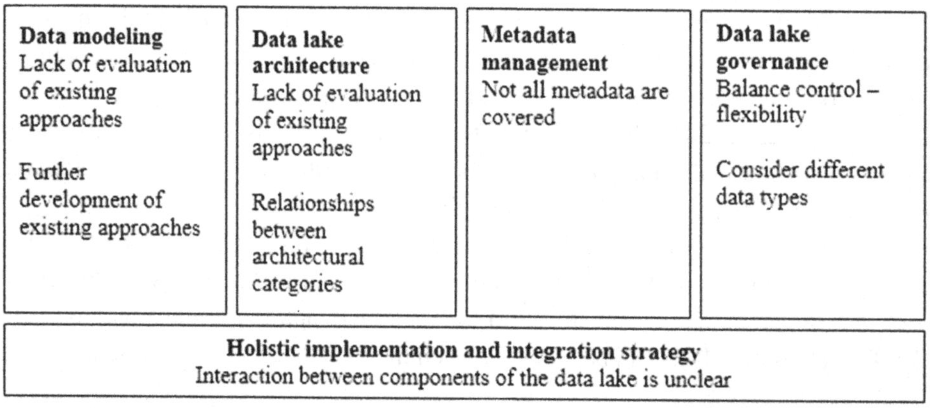

Data modeling Lack of evaluation of existing approaches Further development of existing approaches	**Data lake architecture** Lack of evaluation of existing approaches Relationships between architectural categories	**Metadata management** Not all metadata are covered	**Data lake governance** Balance control – flexibility Consider different data types
Holistic implementation and integration strategy Interaction between components of the data lake is unclear			

and research gaps that impact the successful implementation of data lakes for enterprise BI and analytics development and integration, as summarized in Figure 6.

1. **Unclear data modeling methods:** Although there are various data modeling methods both from the data lake context and from other areas, there are hardly any assessments or evaluations of these methods. It remains unclear which data modeling methods are appropriate for data lakes. Especially with data modeling methods from other areas there is also no possibility to integrate heterogeneous data. Accordingly, they must be expanded to be applicable in the context of data lakes.

2. **Missing data lake reference architecture:** The heterogeneity of available approaches poses a challenge with regard to the appropriate data lake architecture. There is neither a generally accepted architectural concept nor are proposed architectures evaluated. Some of the proposed architectures, such as the data pond architecture, are inconsistent with the fundamental characteristics of the data lake concept. In addition, details for deriving or implementing the concepts are often missing, which makes their application rather difficult. In this case, it is necessary to evaluate the existing work comparatively and to develop uniform architectural concepts that also take into account the interrelationships between the architectural categories (conceptual and technical).

3. **Incomplete metadata management concept:** Neither commercial software nor open source approaches from research to metadata management cover all the metadata required in the data lake. It is therefore necessary to adapt and extend existing approaches to enable comprehensive metadata management.

4. **Incomplete data lake governance concept:** Since data lakes are designed to provide a high degree of flexibility for the development and integration of different types of analytics applications, a governance approach is necessary that can also provide this flexibility. A balance between control and flexibility must also be achieved. In particular, the different types of data and their governance requirements for data lakes, such as different data quality requirements, must be taken into consideration. In order to close this research gap, it is necessary to develop a holistic approach to data lake governance that includes an appropriate organizational framework for the roles and processes in the data lake.

5. **Lack of holistic integration and implementation strategy:** In addition to the challenges associated with implementation of individual components of data lakes, a general and holistic strategy for the integration and implementation of a data lake is missing. Such a strategy should not only address specific characteristics of the data lake, but also consider the interactions between the different components that comprise the data lake. For example, the relationships between the data modeling and the architecture of the data lake should be considered. This creates a coherent, systematic and comprehensive data lake concept that provides guidance for practical implementation.

CONCLUSION AND FUTURE OUTLOOK

Due to the ever-increasing abundance of data, the traditional data warehouse approach has reached its limits, as it can no longer keep up with the integration and development requirements of BI and analytics applications in enterprises. A well-designed data lake provides a unified repository for capturing both new big data and traditional enterprise data in a governed and managed environment that supports both development and integration of different types of analytics, including descriptive, predictive, and prescriptive analytics that both technical and business users need.

This chapter provides valuable insights into the current status of data lakes in research and practice. Through several use cases and analytics projects from an industrial corporation, different types of enterprise data have been identified that are used for analytical purposes. Based on these analytics projects, the main requirements for the implementation of an enterprise-wide data lake were derived. By comparing these requirements with the literature on data lakes, it can generally be concluded that the existing approaches to implementing individual components of data lakes are often inconsistent and not sufficiently detailed and evaluated. In particular, in the areas of data modeling, data lake architecture, metadata management and data lake governance, there are a number of challenges and research gaps that need to be addressed. Furthermore, there is a lack of a holistic integration and implementation strategy for data lakes that takes into account the dependencies between different data lake components.

To realize a data lake that meets the practical and integration requirements of BI and analytics applications, it is necessary to close these challenges and research gaps. Only then can a holistic and enterprise-wide data lake concept be defined and realized in practice. Future work should therefore focus on addressing the challenges and research gaps identified and discussed in this chapter. Existing implementation approaches and concepts for data lakes need to be discussed and evaluated in more detail. Subsequently, the insights gained must be used to define a holistic strategy for data so that they can be used successfully and effectively for the development and integration of BI and analytics applications in enterprise.

REFERENCES

Alserafi, A., Abell'o, A., Romero, O., & Calders, T. (2016). *Towards information profiling: data lake content metadata management.* Paper presented at the IEEE 16th International Conference on Data Mining Workshops (ICDMW), Barcelona, Spain. 10.1109/ICDMW.2016.0033

Beheshti, A., Benatallah, B., Sheng, Q., & Schiliro, F. (2020). Intelligent Knowledge Lakes: The Age of Artificial Intelligence and Big Data. In U. Leong, J. Yang, Y. Cai, K. Karlapalem, A. Liu, & X. Huang (Eds.), *Web Information Systems Engineering. WISE 2020. Communications in Computer and Information Science* (Vol. 1155). Springer. doi:10.1007/978-981-15-3281-8_3

Borek, A., Parlikad, A., Webb, J., & Woodall, P. (2014). *Total Information Risk Management.* Morgan Kaufmann.

Bouaziz, S., Nabli, A., & Gargouri, F. (2019). Design a Data Warehouse Schema from Document-Oriented database. *Procedia Computer Science, 159*(1), 221–230. doi:10.1016/j.procs.2019.09.177

Campbell, C. (2015). *Top five differences between data lakes and data warehouses.* Retrieved 07 May, 2020, from https://www.blue-granite.com/blog/bid/402596/top-five-differencesbetween-data-lakes-and-data-warehouses

Căpușneanu, S., Topor, D., Constantin, D., & Marin-Pantelescu, A. (2020). Management Accounting in the Digital Economy: Evolution and Perspectives. In I. Oncioiu (Ed.), Improving Business Performance Through Innovation in the Digital Economy (pp. 156-176). Hershey, PA: IGI Global.

Dixon, J. (2010). *Pentaho, Hadoop, and data lakes.* Retrieved 07 May, 2020, from https://jamesdixon. wordpress.com/2010/10/14/pentaho-hadoop-and-data-lakes/

Fang, H. (2015, 8-12 June). *Managing data lakes in big data era: what's a data lake and why has it became popular in data management ecosystem.* Paper presented at the 2015 IEEE International Conference on Cyber Technology in Automation, Control, and Intelligent Systems (CYBER), Shenyang, China. 10.1109/CYBER.2015.7288049

Farid, M., Roatis, A., Ilyas, I., Hoffman, H., & Chu, X. (2016). *CLAMS: bringing quality to Data Lakes.* Paper presented at the International Conference on Management of Data (SIGMOD/PODS'16), San Francisco, CA.

Gallinucci, E., Golfarelli, M., & Rizzi, S. (2018). Schema profiling of document-oriented databases. *Information Systems, 75*(1), 13–25. doi:10.1016/j.is.2018.02.007

Giebler, C., Gröger, C., Hoos, E., Schwarz, H., & Mitschang, B. (2019). Modeling Data Lakes with Data Vault: Practical Experiences, Assessment, and Lessons Learned. In A. Laender, B. Pernici, E. Lim, & J. de Oliveira (Eds.), Lecture Notes in Computer Science: Vol. 11788. *Conceptual Modeling. ER 2019.* Springer. doi:10.1007/978-3-030-33223-5_7

Giebler, C., Stach, C., Schwarz, H., & Mitschang, B. (2018). *BRAID - a hybrid processing architecture for big data.* Paper presented at the 7th International Conference on Data Science, Technology and Applications (DATA) (2018), Porto, Portugal.

Giudice, P., Musarella, L., Sofo, G., & Ursino, D. (2019). An approach to extracting complex knowledge patterns among concepts belonging to structured, semi-structured and unstructured sources in a data lake. *Information Sciences, 478*(1), 606–626. doi:10.1016/j.ins.2018.11.052

Gorelik, A. (2019). *The Enterprise Big Data Lake: Delivering the Promise of Big Data and Data Science.* O'Reilly Media, Inc.

Grossman, R. (2019). Data Lakes, Clouds, and Commons: A Review of Platforms for Analyzing and Sharing Genomic Data. *Trends in Genetics, 35*(3), 223–234. doi:10.1016/j.tig.2018.12.006 PMID:30691868

Gryncewicz, W., Sitarska-Buba, M., & Zygała, R. (2020). Agile Approach to Develop Data Lake Based Systems. In M. Hernes, A. Rot, & D. Jelonek (Eds.), *Towards Industry 4.0 — Current Challenges in Information Systems. Studies in Computational Intelligence* (Vol. 887, pp. 201–216). Springer. doi:10.1007/978-3-030-40417-8_12

Hai, R., Geisler, S., & Quix, C. (2016). *Constance: An Intelligent Data Lake System.* Paper presented at the 2016 International Conference on Management of Data, San Francisco, CA. 10.1145/2882903.2899389

Halevy, A., Korn, F., Noy, N., Olston, C., Polyzotis, N., Roy, S., & Whang, S. (2016). Managing Google's data lake: An overview of the Goods system. *A Quarterly Bulletin of the Computer Society of the IEEE Technical Committee on Data Engineering, 39*(3), 5–14.

Inmon, B. (2016). *Data Lake Architecture: Designing the Data Lake and Avoiding the Garbage Dump.* Technics Publications.

Jovanovic, P., Nadal, S., Romero, O., Abelló, A., & Bilalli, B. (2020). Quarry: A User-centered Big Data Integration Platform. *Information Systems Frontiers*, *22*(2), 1–25.

Khine, P., & Wang, Z. (2019). A Review of Polyglot Persistence in the Big Data World. *Information*, *10*(4), 141–165. doi:10.3390/info10040141

Larson, D., & Chang, V. (2016). A review and future direction of agile, business intelligence, analytics and data science. *International Journal of Information Management*, *36*(5), 700–710. doi:10.1016/j.ijinfomgt.2016.04.013

Laurent, A., Laurent, D., & Madera, C. (2020). *Data Lakes* (Vol. 2). John Wiley & Sons. doi:10.1002/9781119720430

Linstedt, D., & Olschimke, M. (2016). Intermediate Data Vault Modeling. In D. Linstedt & M. Olschimke (Eds.), *Building a Scalable Data Warehouse with Data Vault 2.0* (pp. 123–150). Morgan Kaufmann.

Llave, M. (2018). Data lakes in business intelligence: Reporting from the trenches. *Procedia Computer Science*, *138*(1), 516–524. doi:10.1016/j.procs.2018.10.071

Maccioni, A., & Torlone, R. (2017). Crossing the finish line faster when paddling the data lake with KAYAK. *Proceedings of the VLDB Endowment International Conference on Very Large Data Bases*, *10*(12), 1853–1856. doi:10.14778/3137765.3137792

Malysiak-Mrozek, B., Stabla, M., & Mrozek, D. (2018). Soft and declarative fishing of information in Big Data Lake. *IEEE Transactions on Fuzzy Systems*, *26*(5), 2732–2747. doi:10.1109/TFUZZ.2018.2812157

Marz, N., & Warren, J. (2015). *Big Data: Principles and best practices of scalable real-time data systems*. Manning Publications Co.

Massaro, A., Contuzzi, N., & Galiano, A. (2020). Intelligent Processes in Automated Production Involving Industry 4.0 Technologies and Artificial Intelligence. In M. Habib (Ed.), *Advanced Robotics and Intelligent Automation in Manufacturing* (pp. 97–122). IGI Global. doi:10.4018/978-1-7998-1382-8.ch004

Mehmood, H., Gilman, E., Cortes, M., Kostakos, P., Byrne, A., Valta, K., . . . Riekki, J. (2019, 8-12 April 2019). *Implementing Big Data Lake for Heterogeneous Data Sources*. Paper presented at the 35th International Conference on Data Engineering Workshops (ICDEW), Macao, Macao.

Miloslavskaya, N., & Tolstoy, A. (2016). Big Data, Fast Data and Data Lake Concepts. *Procedia Computer Science*, *88*, 300–305. doi:10.1016/j.procs.2016.07.439

Munshi, A., & Mohamed, Y. (2018). Data Lake Lambda Architecture for Smart Grids Big Data Analytics. *IEEE Access: Practical Innovations, Open Solutions*, *6*(1), 40463–40471. doi:10.1109/ACCESS.2018.2858256

Nadal, S., Herrero, V., Romero, O., Abell, A., Franch, X., Vansummeren, S., & Valerio, D. (2017). A Software Reference Architecture for Semantic-Aware Big Data Systems. *Information and Software Technology*, *90*(1), 75–92. doi:10.1016/j.infsof.2017.06.001

Nargesian, F., Zhu, E., Miller, R., Pu, K., & Arocena, P. (2019). Data lake management: Challenges and opportunities. *Proceedings of the VLDB Endowment International Conference on Very Large Data Bases, 12*(12), 1986–1989. doi:10.14778/3352063.3352116

Nogueira, I., Romdhane, M., & Darmont, J. (2018). *Modeling Data Lake Metadata with a Data Vault.* Paper presented at the the 22nd International Database Engineering & Applications Symposium, Villa San Giovanni, Italy. 10.1145/3216122.3216130

Puonti, M., Raitalaakso, T., Aho, T., & Mikkonen, T. (2017). Automating Transformations in Data Vault Data Warehouse Loads. *Frontiers in Artificial Intelligence and Applications, 292*(1), 215–230. doi:10.3233/978-1-61499-720-7-215

Quix, C., & Hai, R. (2018). Data Lake. In S. Sakr & A. Zomaya (Eds.), *Encyclopedia of Big Data Technologies* (pp. 1–8). Springer International Publishing. doi:10.1007/978-3-319-63962-8_7-1

Quix, C., Hai, R., & Vatov, I. (2016). *Metadata Extraction and Management in Data Lakes With GEMMS Complex Systems. Informatics and Modeling Quarterly, 9*(9), 67–83.

Ravat, F., & Zhao, Y. (2019). Data Lakes: Trends and Perspectives. In S. Hartmann, J. Küng, S. Chakravarthy, G. Anderst-Kotsis, A. Tjoa, & I. Khalil (Eds.), Lecture Notes in Computer Science: Vol. 11706. *Database and Expert Systems Applications. DEXA 2019* (pp. 304–313). Springer. doi:10.1007/978-3-030-27615-7_23

Roh, Y., Heo, G., & Whang, S. (2019). A Survey on Data Collection for Machine Learning: A Big Data - AI Integration Perspective. *IEEE Transactions on Knowledge and Data Engineering, 31*(2), 99–112. doi:10.1109/TKDE.2019.2946162

Sawadogo, P., Kibata, T., & Darmont, J. (2019). *Metadata management for textual documents in data lakes.* Paper presented at the 21st International Conference on Enterprise Information Systems (ICEIS 2019), Heraklion, Greece. 10.5220/0007706300720083

Sawadogo, P., Scholly, É., Favre, C., Ferey, É., Loudcher, S., & Darmont, J. (2019). Metadata Systems for Data Lakes: Models and Features. In T. Welzer, J. Eder, V. Podgorelec, R. Wrembel, M. Ivanović, J. Gamper, M. Morzy, T. Tzouramanis, J. Darmont, & A. Latifić (Eds.), *New Trends in Databases and Information Systems. ADBIS 2019. Communications in Computer and Information Science* (Vol. 1064, pp. 440–451). Springer. doi:10.1007/978-3-030-30278-8_43

Schäffer, T., & Leyh, C. (2017). Master Data Quality in the Era of Digitization - Toward Inter-organizational Master Data Quality in Value Networks: A Problem Identification. In F. Piazolo, V. Geist, L. Brehm, & R. Schmidt (Eds.), *Innovations in Enterprise Information Systems Management and Engineering. ERP Future 2016. Lecture Notes in Business Information Processing* (Vol. 285, pp. 99–113). Springer. doi:10.1007/978-3-319-58801-8_9

Sitarska-Buba, M., & Zygala, R. (2020). Data lake: Strategic challenges for small and medium sized enterprises. In M. Hernes, A. Rot, & D. Jelonek (Eds.), *Towards Industry 4.0-current challenges in information systems. Lecture Notes in Computational Intelligence* (Vol. 887, pp. 183–200). Springer. doi:10.1007/978-3-030-40417-8_11

Štrukelj, T., Mulej, M., & Zabukovšek, S. (2020). Socially Responsible Culture and Personal Values as Organizational Competitiveness Factors. In Z. Nedelko & M. Brzozowski (Eds.), *Recent Advances in the Roles of Cultural and Personal Values in Organizational Behavior* (pp. 81–101). IGI Global. doi:10.4018/978-1-7998-1013-1.ch005

Suriarachchi, I., & Plale, B. (2016). *Crossing Analytics Systems: A Case for Integrated Provenance in Data Lakes.* Paper presented at the 12th International Conference on e-Science (e-Science), Baltimore, MD.

Teixeira de Azevedo, M., Martins, A. B., & Kofuji, S. T. (2019). Digital Transformation in the Utilities Industry: Industry 4.0 and the Smart Network Water. In L. Ferreira, N. Lopes, J. Silva, G. Putnik, M. Cruz-Cunha, & P. Ávila (Eds.), *Technological Developments in Industry 4.0 for Business Applications* (pp. 304–330). IGI Global. doi:10.4018/978-1-5225-4936-9.ch013

Terrizzano, I., Schwarz, P., Roth, M., & Colino, J. E. (2015). *Data Wrangling: The Challenging Yourney from the Wild to the Lake.* Paper presented at the 7th Biennial Conference on Innovative Data Systems Research (CIDR '15), Asilomar, CA.

Thyssenkrupp Elevator, A. (2020). *MAX: the game changer.* Retrieved 04 May, 2020, from https://www.thyssenkrupp-elevator.com/en/max/

Tomcy, J., & Pankaj, M. (2017). *Data Lake for Enterprises.* Packt Publishing Ltd.

ADDITIONAL READING

Azevedo, A. (2016). Data Mining and Business Intelligence: A Comparative, Historical Perspective. In M. Association (Ed.), *Business Intelligence: Concepts, Methodologies, Tools, and Applications* (pp. 1819–1829). IGI Global. doi:10.4018/978-1-4666-9562-7.ch090

Azevedo, A. (2019). Data Mining and Knowledge Discovery in Databases. In M. Khosrow-Pour (Ed.), *Advanced Methodologies and Technologies in Network Architecture, Mobile Computing, and Data Analytics* (pp. 502–514). IGI Global. doi:10.4018/978-1-5225-7598-6.ch037

Azevedo, A., & Santos, M. F. (2015). *Integration of Data Mining in Business Intelligence Systems.* IGI Global. doi:10.4018/978-1-4666-6477-7

Blokdyk, G. (2019). Data Lake Architecture Strategy A Complete Guide - 2020 Edition. Plano, TX, USA: 5STARCooks.

Gorelik, A. (2019). *The Enterprise Big Data Lake: Delivering the Promise of Big Data and Data Science.* O'Reilly Media, Inc.

Gryncewicz, W., Sitarska-Buba, M., & Zygała, R. (2020). Agile Approach to Develop Data Lake Based Systems. In M. Hernes, A. Rot, & D. Jelonek (Eds.), *Towards Industry 4.0 — Current Challenges in Information Systems. Studies in Computational Intelligence* (Vol. 887, pp. 201–216). Springer. doi:10.1007/978-3-030-40417-8_12

Gupta, S., & Giri, V. (2018). *Practical Enterprise Data Lake Insights: Handle Data-Driven Challenges in an Enterprise Big Data Lake.* Apress. doi:10.1007/978-1-4842-3522-5

Inmon, B. (2016). *Data Lake Architecture: Designing the Data Lake and Avoiding the Garbage Dump.* Technics Publications.

Laurent, A., Laurent, D., & Madera, C. (2020). *Data Lakes* (Vol. 2). John Wiley & Sons, Inc. doi:10.1002/9781119720430

Panwar, A., & Bhatnagar, V. (2020a). Data Lake Architecture: A New Repository for Data Engineer. [IJOCI]. *International Journal of Organizational and Collective Intelligence, 10*(1), 63–75. doi:10.4018/IJOCI.2020010104

Panwar, A., & Bhatnagar, V. (2020b). Scrutinize the Idea of Hadoop-Based Data Lake for Big Data Storage. In Johri P., Verma J. & P. S. (Eds.), Applications of Machine Learning. Algorithms for Intelligent Systems (pp. 365-391). Singapore: Springer.

KEY TERMS AND DEFINITIONS

Big Data: The high number and complexity of the data records that are processed and stored by electronic applications.

Business Analytics: The skills, technologies, applications, and practices to continuously iteratively examine past business performance to gain insight and drive business planning. Business Analytics focuses heavily on data and statistical analysis.

Data Governance: The management of data throughout its entire lifecycle in the company to ensure high data quality. Data Governance uses guidelines to determine which standards are applied in the company and which areas of responsibility should handle the tasks required to achieve high data quality.

Data Lake: A scalable data management platform for data of any structure, which is stored in its raw format to enable different types of analytics without predefined scheme.

Data Swamp: A data management platform in which the data can no longer be used for agile and value-added analytics, for example due to a lack of data quality, intelligibility, or comprehensibility.

Data Warehouse: A tool for integrating different data sources in a unified repository to support business intelligence and reporting.

Decision Support System: A tool that allows decision-makers to combine personal assessment and computer output in a human-machine interaction to provide rich information to support a decision process.

Data Mining: Techniques and processes are also used in big data analysis and business intelligence to provide summarized, targeted, and relevant information, knowledge for the user is autonomously generated from large amounts of data.

Industry 4.0: The fourth industrial revolution, which was initiated by the rapidly advancing digitalization and the use of artificial intelligence (AI) technologies and is already evident in many areas.

Section 3
Modelling Issues

Chapter 6
Modelling in Support of Decision Making in Business Intelligence

Roumiana Ilieva
Technical University of Sofia, Bulgaria

Malinka Ivanova
https://orcid.org/0000-0002-8474-6226
Technical University of Sofia, Bulgaria

Tzvetilina Peycheva
IBS, Bulgaria

Yoto Nikolov
Technical University of Sofia, Bulgaria

ABSTRACT

Modelling in support of decision making in business intelligence (BI) starts with exploring the BI systems, driven by artificial intelligence (AI). The purpose why AI will be the core of next-gen analytics and why BI will be empowered by it are determined. The role of AI and machine learning (ML) in business processes automation is analyzed. The benefits from AI integration in BI platforms are summarized. Then analysis goes through predictive modeling in the domain of e-commerce. The use of ML for predictive modeling is overviewed. Construction of predictive and clustering models is proposed. After that the importance of self-services in BI platforms is outlined. In this context the self-service BI is defined and what are the key steps to create successful self-service BI model are sketched. The effects of potential threads which are the results of the big data in the business world are examined and some suggestions for the future have been made. Lastly, game-changer trends in BI and future research directions are traced.

DOI: 10.4018/978-1-7998-5781-5.ch006

INTRODUCTION

Modeling is a process that includes several steps: identification of the real problem, data gathering from authentic sources, and applying data mining techniques for converting data into meaningful knowledge. Knowledge could be presented in the form of tables, graphics, charts, infographics and is used for supporting the business leaders, business consultants or business users to take the right decisions, to plan the correct strategy or to solve an emerging issue. A wide variety of models – analytical and predictive could be prepared through different statistical and Artificial Intelligence (AI) techniques that show the past situation, current problem state or future events.

This chapter discusses the importance of data for business improvement and how to empower the self-service capabilities for the decision makers to analyze data and to find meaningful knowledge about their business. The cycle of data preparation, transformation, analysis and presentation for advanced analytics or descriptive analytics are almost the same, but how to model the data in such a way that the business users can embrace the opportunity to make data-driven decisions by themselves. The knowledge about the business process in the organizations is in sales, accounting, marketing and inventory departments. So, what if they have a powerful Business Intelligence (BI) system in which they prepare complex analysis and data explorations and they gain meaningful new information by analyzing huge amounts of data. This can be accomplished when the BI tool has the right user interface and the development team of the BI system prepares data modules for self-service.

Furthermore, in this chapter the importance of self-service BI for business users is proved. In organizations, private or public, most of the decisions are based on domain knowledge, experience and available information in the systems. But this approach leads to ineffective decision making and nowadays with the rapid economic development of the world, organizations cannot rely on intuitive and subjective approaches. The decision making in progressive organizations must be based on analytical methodologies and mathematical models. The main purpose of BI systems is to provide capabilities that allow business users to make effective and timely decisions. And this can be accomplished by letting them do the real analytics jobs, to dig deep into trusted, organized data and extract meaningful information and then make data-driven decisions.

The aim of this chapter is to present several techniques and methods for models creation in the area of Business Intelligence through four case studies: (1) modeling in the context of Artificial Intelligence based Business Intelligence systems; (2) modeling the domain of e-commerce to predict the future events; (3) modeling with aim to afford business users at self-services usage in the Business Intelligence platforms; (4) tracing game-changer trends in BI.

BACKGROUND

Business Intelligence had become a thought leadership function through, among other factors, procuring highly skilled employees to research their respective industries, technologies and geographies and to inform executive decision makers. Many team members were working closely with their stakeholders, gaining a great deal of insights and efficiency in their function.

In order to better communicate their ideas and capabilities to their stakeholders, as well as continuously learn, BI decided to implement a knowledge management system that would make processes, methodologies, best practices and information sources easily accessible to all members of the organization. BI sought to create a unified standard data source and information management upon which a knowledge management system could be built. According to Rud (2009), Dedić and Stanier (2016) the following necessities were essential:

- Needs for information:
    - Team members needed quick and easy access to data as well as knowing where to get information.
    - Stakeholders also needed easy access to data – so they did not have to continuously email team members to forward along the data – as well as transparency as to the source and the structure of the data.
- Needs for knowledge:
    - Team members benefited from quick access to best practices, explanations and examples of methodologies, as well as finished projects and insights already gleaned.
    - Stakeholders benefited from an one-stop overview of BI capabilities, as well as easy access to market facts and knowledge about customers.

The goal here was to both document processes and methodologies and make the team's breadth of knowledge more visible. The team wanted to make results accessible to the wider organization and the learning curve for a specific role as easy as possible.

- Needs for ideas:

    - Team members wanted to be able to generate ideas in a timely manner to elevate their strategic importance to their stakeholders and the wider organization.
    - Stakeholders benefited from team members who had more time to concentrate on high value activities.

Ideas were integral to the team's ability to produce impacting insight and promote a data-based decision-making culture. Transforming information into ideas was not as efficient as it could be. The steps between gathering information and creating ideas and insight were mapped and the activities were categorized into non value add and value add. Inefficient steps were highlighted with the goal of trying to eliminate them.

MODELING IN BUSINESS INTELLIGENCE SYSTEMS, DRIVEN BY ARTIFICIAL INTELLIGENCE

The objective of the study is to combine the use of the two concepts BI and AI to explore the synergy between them. Business intelligence can be determined to the use of various technologies and tools to collect, analyze and transform raw data into meaningful and useful information, in order to build an effective strategy, as well as to create tactical and operational insights for decision-making faster than they otherwise could. On the other hand, Artificial Intelligence core principle is the use of computer systems or computer intelligence to mimic various tasks of human intelligence. For example, decision making, problem solving, learning and predicting different scenarios faster and without the need of human interference. Though in its technological infancy, businesses see potential in AI to eliminate simple tasks and deliver more time for meaningful work.

Why AI will be Essential for the Next Generation Analytics

Nowadays the development of Artificial Intelligence and Machine Learning techniques has become a key part of BI platforms. Nevertheless, as analytics boards have advanced, AI aids to BI still hasn't evolved to this extend where analytics techniques can actually release people from their routine, reiterating and simple duties related to data analysis, besides where data analysis is part of ordinary requests processes. Seeing how organizations are moving into an innovative epoch ruled by big data, evolution of AI as a crucial element that figures business processes and BI resolution constructing on a regular foundation is constantly growing. Companies from all sizes are influenced by AI to improve the proficiency of business processes and supply smarter, self-driven and more advanced customer experience (Analytics Insight, 2019).

Why AI Powered BI

The exponential growth of novel big data properties similar to social data from media platforms, machine data generated by industrial equipment, machinery sensors, and even web logs which track user behavior to transactional data, generated from online and offline tasks compel the companies to be no more overloaded by enormous volumes of fixed reports generated by BI software schemes. These require more exploitable visions. This guides to the need of AI driven BI system which can convert corporate data into modest, accurate, instantaneous statistics and reports. The following figure 1a and b shows the projected growth of structured and unstructured data in exabytes (1 exabyte=1 million terabytes) over the last 7 years as well as the prediction for the next 3 years. It can be seen that the unstructured data (data from VoIP and social media) growth is exponential and this tendency will continue in the future. The predictive models are created in GMDH Shell environment after applying deep learning on data taken from (IDC and EMC, 2012).

Data Overload Solution

The data growth is at unprecedented rate and can easily overcome company's business operations.

When a company has data blasting its BI platform from different sources, this is where AI powered BI tools come in to help analyzing the data and deliver insights. Investment in enhancing such technology to power up the analytical functions in Business Intelligence software will assist companies to break

Figure 1.Big Data growth: a) unstructured; b) structured

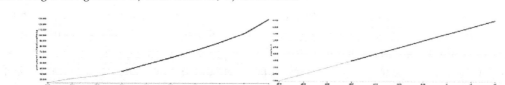

down data into manageable insights towards smart data. Figure 2 presents the benefits for companies at big data usage and analysis according to (statista.com, 2020).

Figure 2.Usage of Big Data and benefits for companies

64%	• improved efficiency and productivity
56%	• more effective decision making
51%	• better financial performance
46%	• new product creation and service revenue
46%	• improved customer acquisition and retention
44%	• improved cistomer experience
43%	• competitive advantage

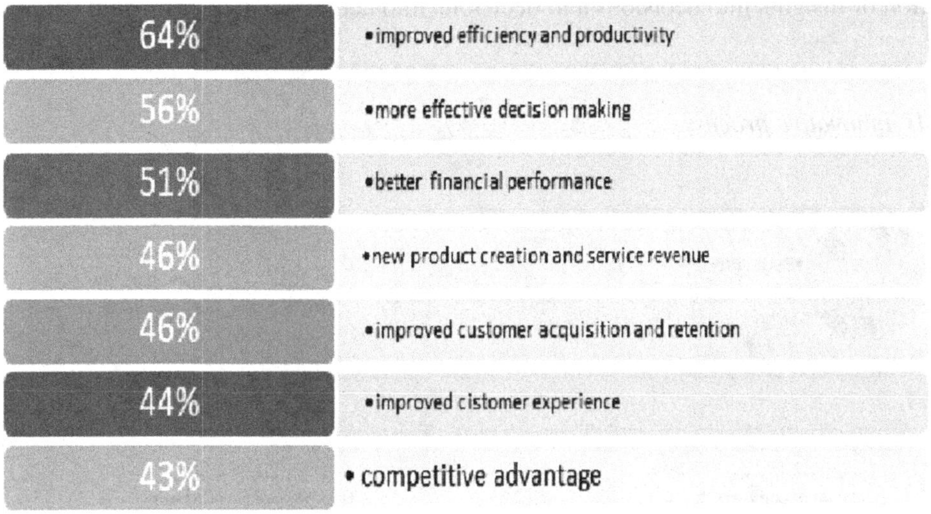

Providing Real Time Insights

Big data growth in the market is constantly slowing down strategic decisions. (Berntzen&Krumova, 2017) investigates big data from a business stand point. To bring real time insights the researchers will need a modern way, one that can ingest real-time data transfers and integrate with destinations that can receive data on the fly. Real time data sources as well as tools that analyze and provide insight. Lastly, you need capabilities that will allow you to take meaningful actions to create new segments, refresh information, retarget and much more and all this in real time. AI powered BI techniques will be the solution to offer dashboards that provide alerts and business insights to managers for vital decision making.

Team Scarcity Facilitation

There is a scarcity of specialists with data investigative talents. Implementing AI powered BI software can convey fabulous alterations in companies, retaining them viable in the innovations-driven corporate surroundings.

AI in Business Processes Modelling

One of the most important roles in AI integration is optimizing the process of decision making: gaining bigger variety and volume of data, better computational power collectively enabling AI technologies to analyze big data sets for delivering useful results eliminating the need of more storage and easing the company's databases. Speaking of databases, the people usually think of huge and complex data storages with tons of data, here AI and specifically its subset machine learning helps the extraction of meaning from this data in a way that the people's brains can't handle. Machine learning is so advanced nowadays that it has the power to make business decisions without human intervention. The authors believe that machine learning has the potential to identify the most significant growth opportunities no matter the business industry it is implemented. As almost all the people know, the good strategy is an evolution of transformation of insights into decisions and decisions into actions to deliver the real value (figure 3).

Figure 3. ML innovative process

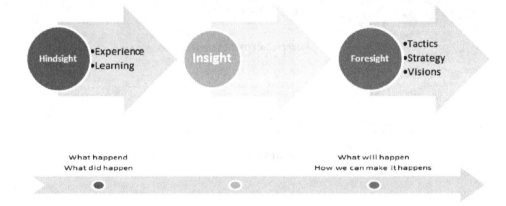

ML has the potential to give the business the most precise foresight intelligence, resulting in greater process automation, human free errors, significant productivity gains and much more. If it is implemented accordingly, ML has the power to elevate data analysis in a whole different level. Using this innovative process companies will be able to create forecasts and predict sales figures, optimal costs, planning of human resources, evaluate risk, segmentation and much more, well in advance of traditional methods. This transformational process can be observed in the following figure 4.

Recent trends suggest that companies are looking for innovative model to optimize their workflow. Hence one of the biggest setbacks emerge the decision-making process. No matter how prominent, well organized and designed workflow the organization has, it takes a vast amount of period in creating conclusions. Occasionally it is since the people in charge are engaged with plentiful extra responsibilities. Kopanakis, J.(2019) states that most of their time is occupied and they need to reschedule all activities to be able to make a reasonable decision, or for the reason that a particular endorsement stage in the business encompasses numerous decision makers. Here are how loopholes emerge, affecting cost-effectiveness and efficiency of business processes negatively. Various machine learning agendas are available for companies to integrate in their business models. They do not simply investigate data, but correspondingly define wide-ranging tendencies in the authorization of the processes, so that fine-established results could be done autonomously. For example, when there is a dilemma, ML appliances will be able to advice the decision maker what have been the foregoing solutions to such circumstances in the historical past situations. This particular methodology can deliver intelligence on decision making trends over given period of time, depending of the given training data. Once the mechanism acquires a

Figure 4. ML added transformational process from predictive towards optimization model

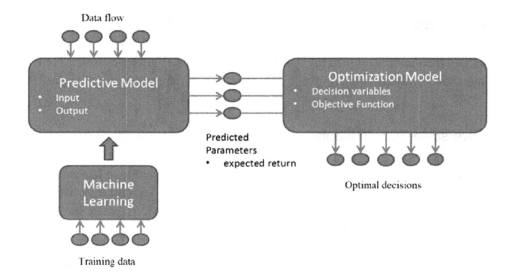

definite amount of accurate opportunities, it will be able to make forecasts on its own, lacking any kind of human involvement. There for fast decision making will optimize significant information flows and procedures through the whole organization and will help decision makers with pre-analyzed data and recommend the best outcome (figure 5).

Figure 5. Automated decision-making process

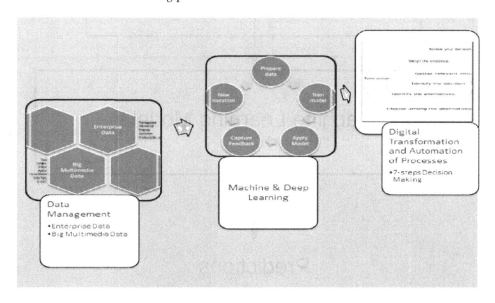

Summary of the BI Benefits from AI Integration

Optimization of Decision Making and Faster Response Rate

Making faster and precise decision-making will be the game changer in BI processes. For example, the help of AI integrated in dynamic pricing statistics may lead to the improvement of profit margins at least by 5%.

Handling Diversified Source Inputs

Feeding data models may differ or be very similar, human brain is not able to handle so many feature instantaneously, technologies and particularly ML is much more time and cost effective. Also is able to process countless data at the same time and make multifaceted conclusions, create foresights or recommend the best conceivable action (figure 6).

Reduced Fatigue

Another benefit is reduced fatigue. Duo to exhaustion, overload people often are obligated to make conclusions in a short frame, hence the excellence of those resolutions keeps decreasing. Conversely,

Figure 6.ML handling multiple diversified source inputs

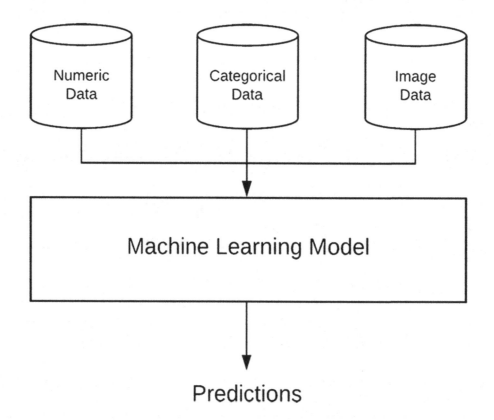

machines cannot be affected by working environment; they make correspondingly good conclusions at any occasion, avoiding wrong choices thanks to depletion.

PREDICTIVE MODELING IN THE DOMAIN OF E-COMMERCE

E-commerce and Predictive Analytics - Introduction

E-commerce utilizes Internet technologies to provide electronic services for online shopping and trading, for marketplaces organization and business management (Kutz, 2016). Its main functions are related to: online negotiation, establishment of business-to-business-to-customers communication, distribution of products and services, sales support, management of customer relationship, delivering of additional services. Planning the interaction strategy for successful e-commerce activities is in the focus on different business models. In practice, the following business approaches are realized (Nagaty, 2010; Rajarshi, 2019):

- Business-to-business (B2B) model that supports services, information and products exchange among different businesses like manufacturers, wholesalers, distributors, vendors, retailers.
- Business-to-customer (B2C) model that facilitates online goods purchases and services delivery from business providers and retailers to the end customers.
- Customer-to-customer (C2C) model that manages the transactions among customers through intermediation of a third party.
- Customer-to-business (C2B) model that assists customers when they perform sells of products or services to a given business, realize online transactions for paying bills, or when they propose freelance services.
- Business-to-government (B2G) model that describes the relationship between business service providers to government representatives and organizations.
- Customer-to-government (C2G) model that facilitates conductance of transactions for taxes and tuition paying by customers to government.

Despite of realized business model for e-commerce, huge arrays of data circulated in such interactions and they are used by businesses to improve customers' experience and to optimize their online activities as well as to improve decision making process and recommendation mechanisms. The term customer relationship management (CRM) appears to describe business management strategy that values the information regarding customer online behavior with aim to improve the relationships between companies and customers (Buttle and Maklan, 2019). This leads to building policy by companies for customer satisfaction, for customer growth in long term and for implementation of customer-centric processes. CRM relays on data analysis, performed not only with classical statistical techniques, but also with novelty methods like data mining and machine learning algorithms. The created analytical and predictive models have capacity with given accuracy to point out trending and challenging issues as well as to describe typical patterns and anomalies. These analytical conclusions are used by different e-commerce participants like manufactures, service providers, distributors and customers for better understating given events and processes, for facilitating problem solving and for accelerating the decision making. For example, Airbnb company uses more than 100 machine learning models to study online customers' behaviour and to propose personalized recommendations and advices (Harvard Business

Review, 2019). Sequential customers interactions are tracked as well as all possible their combinations to create models for optimization the customer experiences. Supervised machine learning methods learn examples through input and output data to predict events and processes or to classify items and issues. Unsupervised machine learning algorithms learn input data with aim to identify clusters within this data through discovering patterns and regularities (Management Solutions, 2018).

Predictive analytics facilitates e-commerce giving possibility for deeper understanding the customers' behavior and their requirements, for predicting the products prices and sales, for minimizing the wrong activities with aim to avoid frauds, for supporting critical businesses to make the right decision faster (IQLECT, 2018).

Machine Learning for Predictive Modeling – Literature Review

With aim the domain of e-commerce to be outlined a bibliometric approach is applied (Grosseck, 2019) that includes construction of a bibliometric network after extracting the bibliographic data for the term *e-commerce* from Scopus scientific database for the last three years. The bibliometric network presents the connections between the term *e-commerce* and other terms that are part of keywords, title and abstract of published papers as well as the frequencies of terms occurrences. Such approach allows the created factual picture to give visual notion about the most common use and combination of the term *e-commerce* with other terms. The produced inferences suggest the areas and context of the term *e-commerce* utilization. Such bibliometric network is created in the environment of VOSviewer that is software for analyzing and visualizing the bibliographic data. It can be seen on Figure 8 that the term *e-commerce* has strong relationship with the terms: *machine learning (and concrete machine learning algorithms such as: neural networks, support vector machines, random forest, logistic regression, fuzzy logic, clustering techniques, etc.), decision making (risk analysis, fraud detection, purchase decision and intention),* and *prediction (forecasting).* It means that the explored scientific papers, indexed in Scopus, often contain in the title, abstract and keywords these terms and the publications discuss topics related to *machine learning, decision making,* and *prediction.*

The detailed examination of some papers shows that the machine learning techniques are well accepted approach in the field of e-commerce to model and to give solutions for a wide variety of real-world problems.

For instance, Gupta and Pathak (2014) propose a framework for predicting the online purchases by customers based on concepts for dynamic prices. They apply data mining, statistical and machine learning methods to predict better price for customers who are grouped in four clusters. For this purpose, firstly the customer segments are determined, and they are classified in four clusters through usage of kMeans machining learning algorithm. Secondly, the appropriate price range for customers from different clusters are predicted through statistical and regression techniques and thirty, to predict whether the customer will make purchase or not at this price range through logistic regression algorithm. In another paper, presented by Stubseid and Arandjelovic (2018), the factors that reflect on customers' decision making regarding the purchases are explored and on this base the prediction regarding their behavior and decisions to be conducted. Two classification algorithms Naïve Bayes and RandomForest are applied on dataset and they are compared according to performance parameter. The superiority is given to the RandomForest classifier. Kamthania et al. (2018) introduce a Business Intelligence tool based on principal component analysis and clustering algorithm for analysis the click user behavior on e-commerce web sites and geographical information with aim a map with market segmentation to be created. Authors conclude that the architecture of the proposed tool facilitates small businesses and startups to formulate their business strategies. De Souza et al. (2018) propose an approach for automatically generation the labels about product information on e-commerce web sites through usage of stack decoder search algorithm and for predicting the quality of generated labels through applying neural network supervised machine learning technique.

The created factual picture through bibliometric approach and the performed short overview of scientific papers prove that the data-driven science and machine learning methods have huge impact for outlining bottlenecks, benefits and trending issues in the area of e-commerce.

Figure 7. The constructed bibliometric network related to the term e-commerce

Construction of Predictive and Clustering Models

Machine learning relies on suitable datasets to learn and to construct different analytical and predictive models. Free data is collected by several organizations and they are available for exploration and analysis by researchers. Free datasets related to e-commerce issues are proposed by Eurostat on EU Open Data Portal. The datasets concerning e-commerce purchases (2020), e-commerce sales (2020) and e-commerce, CRM and secure transactions (2020) are used for further exploration and analysis. The machine learning algorithms for time series prediction and kMeans clustering method is applied to discover patterns and trends in e-commerce purchases, sales and CRM at national (Bulgarian) and European level. Figure 8a, figure 8b and figure 8c present respectively, the tendency of all enterprises, small and medium enterprises in Bulgaria (without financial) to realize purchases via computer mediated networks for the next three years. The predictive models are created on the dataset that includes e-commerce purchases, published on the Eurostat web site and data training is performed through data series prediction algorithm in GMDH Shell environment. The constructed curves show that in the next

Figure 8. Predicting the percentage of the enterprises in Bulgaria that have purchases via computer mediated networks

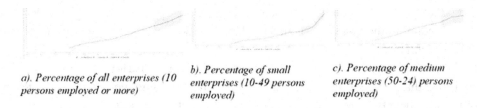

a). *Percentage of all enterprises (10 persons employed or more)*

b). *Percentage of small enterprises (10-49 persons employed)*

c). *Percentage of medium enterprises (50-24) persons employed)*

three years the percentage of enterprises in Bulgaria which will use computer mediated networks to support online purchases will increase a little bit.

The countries are grouped in five clusters according to the percentage of enterprises which give possibilities for purchases via computer mediated networks (without financial) and this is depicted on figure 9. kMeans clustering algorithm is applied for data training in GMDH Shell environment. The first cluster (red dots) includes countries with the smallest percentage of e-commerce purchases for 2017 and 2018 year. The second cluster (yellow dots) consists of courtiers with higher percentage of e-commerce purchases in comparison to countries from the first cluster. The third cluster (green dots) takes the countries with average percentage of e-commerce purchases and the fourth and fifth clusters (respectively blue and purple dots) present countries with high and very high percentage of e-commerce purchases. It can be said that with the smallest percentage of enterprises which have experience with computer mediated purchases are Bulgaria, Romania and Greece and with the highest percentage are Ireland, Sweden and Netherland.

The prognosis for the next three years about the percentage of all, small and medium e-commerce enterprises in Bulgaria (without financial) selling online (at least 1% turnover) are show on Figure 10a, Figure 10b and Figure 10c and it can be concluded that this percentage will not be changed.

Figure 9. Formed countries clusters regarding the percentage of enterprises that perform e-commerce purchases

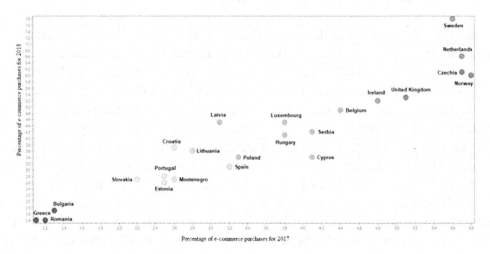

Figure 10. Percentage of enterprises in Bulgaria selling online (at least 1% turnover)

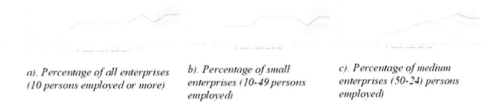

a). Percentage of all enterprises (10 persons employed or more)

b). Percentage of small enterprises (10-49 persons employed)

c). Percentage of medium enterprises (50-24) persons employed)

Clustering model concerning the percentage of enterprises that realize online sales (without financial) by countries is shown on Figure 11 and the countries are grouped in five clusters. The first and the second cluster includes countries with very small and small percentage of enterprises that propose e-commerce sales (respectively, red dot and yellow dots), the third, the forth and the fifth clusters (respectively, green dots, lilac dots and blue dots) consists of countries with average, high and very high percentage of enterprises, selling online. With the smallest percentage of enterprises that perform online selling is Bulgaria and with the highest percentage are Sweden, Denmark and Ireland.

Figure 11. Formed clusters with countries concerning the percentage of enterprises selling online

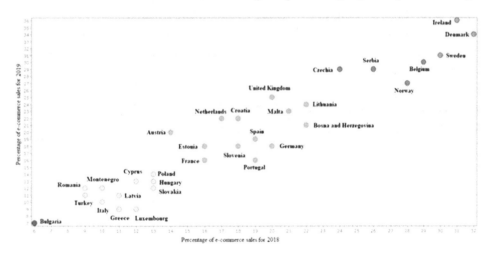

Predictive model about the trend in percentage of all enterprises (without financial) which relay on CRM and secure transactions in Bulgaria is presented in figure 12. The prediction is depicted through irregular curve and it can be seen that this percentage will not be changed in the next three years.

Figure 13 outlines clusters with countries which enterprises implement the strategy about CRM and secure transactions in the area of e-commerce (without financial). The formed clusters are five: the first cluster includes countries with very small percentage of enterprises that use the strategy about CRM and secure transactions in e-commerce (red dots), the next clusters comprise countries with small percentage of enterprises adopting CRM strategy (lilac dots), average percentage (green dots), high percentage (yellow dots) and very high percentage (blue dots). Bulgaria, Romania, Greece and Turkey are countries

Figure 12. Trend in percentage of all enterprises which relay on CRM and secure transactions in Bulgaria

with smallest percentage of enterprises that grasp the strategy about CRM and secure transactions and with the highest percentage are Belgium, Sweden, Denmark and Ireland.

The constructed models with datasets from Eurostat give clear picture regarding the current state and future development of e-commerce in Bulgaria and European countries. It can be concluded that the situation regarding e-commerce evolvement in Bulgaria in the next three years will not be changed or will be changed a little bit. With smaller percentage of enterprises that are involved in e-commerce (without financial organizations) are Bulgaria, Romania, Greece and Turkey and with highest percentage are Ireland, Denmark and Sweden.

Figure 13. Clusters of countries regarding the percentage of all enterprises which use the strategy about customer relation management and secure transactions in e-commerce

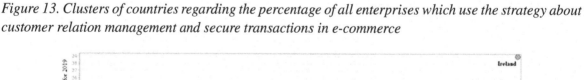
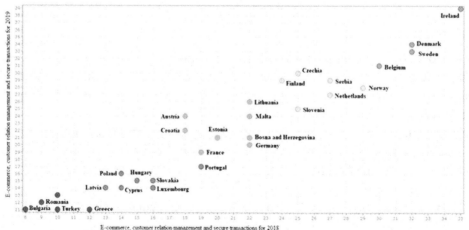

From the machine learning perspective it can be said that the algorithms for predictions and for clustering give huge possibilities for performing analysis in support of improvement the customer experience, for enhancement the business-to-customer relationship and to accelerate the decision making process of enterprises and customers.

THE IMPORTANCE OF SELF-SERVICES IN BUSINESS INTELLIGENCE PLATFORMS

What Is Self-Service BI?

Self-service Business Intelligence is to give power to business users to create their reports and to analyze within an approved and predefined data model in analytics platform without involving the organization's BI and IT teams. In this section the importance of self-service BI for business users is discussed.

In organizations, private or public, most of the decisions are based on domain knowledge, experience and available information in the systems. The decision-making process is based on validated data sets extracted manually from source systems that are only verified for a specific department needs. A common problem is when an organization is reporting on the same metrics but presented by different departments, there is a discrepancy in results. A typical example of such a discrepancy can be given with the financial statements for a specific month of the organization and the sales and revenue reports of the sales'department. The main reason for this type of discrepancy lies in the way the data is extracted, transformed and filtered by the different departments or the different data access that they have. The finance department uses the order revenue data to subtract the cost of delivery, transportation, and other internal costs for the organization to calculate profit for a month. On the other hand, the sales department reports revenue results only on the basis of completed orders and subtracted delivery costs. But this approach leads to ineffective decision making and nowadays with the rapid economic development of the world, organizations cannot rely on intuitive and subjective approaches. The decision making in progressive organizations must be based on analytical methodologies and mathematical models. The main purpose of BI systems is to provide capabilities that allow business users to make effective and timely decisions. And this can be accomplished by letting them do the real analytics jobs, to dig deep into trusted, organized data and extract meaningful information and then make data-driven decisions and one of the ways to do it is to have a data model for self-service BI. One of the main advantages of the self-service model is that it provides the so-called single point of truth for the data because the data is collected from different sources then is transformed and filtered by common rules and loaded in one repository called Data Warehouse from where all the business units can have access and prepare reports with verified trusted data in the BI platform (Kimball and Ross, 2013).

What are the key Steps to Create Successful Self-Service BI Model?

Step 1: Gathering business requirements and identifying the need of data analytics

This is the first step of data modelling and analytics process. Before launching a modern BI platform with self-service capabilities, the Business Intelligence development team (BI team) should understand the needs of the business, as well as the source data. The BI team should setup meeting sessions with business people divided by subject areas like Accounting, Sales, Marketing, Finance and start asking interview questions. These interview sessions are really important, first of all, when you prepare data

Figure 14. Star Schema Model

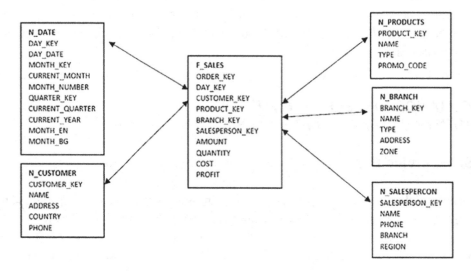

model you should know the main purpose and need of it and second when the team knows how the business understands the data, they will easily prepare useful data model for self-service. The team must understand the business users, their job responsibilities, tasks and goals. Determine the decisions that the users want to make with the help of the BI system. They should ask questions about the source systems and the business process. When the BI team gathers all the information, they must prepare the documentation for data requirements and then proceed to step 2.

Step 2:   Analyze the source data

After the BI Team understands the business requirements in different departments, they should analyze data in the source systems and prepare the data model. This could be accomplished with the Subject Oriented Approach. In this approach, the developers should divide the analysis into Subject areas and model the data in that way. The subject area is a logical grouping of tables related to a particular subject or application context. This approach is similar to the interview sessions approach, when the developers, should understand the different business areas and departments' needs before starting to analyze the data. In step 2 they should follow the same logic: For example, when BI Team analyzing the Subject Area Sales, they should analyze: Sales tables in the source system, this could be Orders table in database, where they will find detailed data about particular order, after that they should analyze the products in this order and the customer who was placed the order, the salesperson, the branch or online store and other meaningful information.

Step 3:   Prepare the data model

There are different data modelling techniques when BI Team considers the right one, they must think about the self-service capabilities, performance of the platform and database. This chapter will present the ***dimensional modelling technique***, more popularly known as the ***Star Schema approach***. Popularized by Ralph Kimball (Kimball and Ross, 2013), the Star Schema modelling is now widely accepted as the optimal method to organize information for analytics consumption. In this model, the data is collected in two types of tables: Dimensions and Facts. In fact, tables are stored measures and dimension keys. In the dimension tables are stored the descriptions of the facts. Now following the example of Sales analysis in the previous step, in Figure 14 is illustrated a Star Schema model for Sales analysis.

Dimensional modeling is making database design simple and easily understandable by business users, this is why the authors recommend the Star Schema approach for self-service data modeling. There are two important requirements that this model fulfill:

• Delivered data that is understandable to the business users

The data model is subject-oriented, and all the tables are labeled with meaningful business names. All the aggregations and extract-transform-load (ETL) transformation are documented, and the business users can read them and understand the metrics in the fact tables. Information in the model must be consistent and this is making it more reliable and trustful to the users.

• Delivered fast query performance

The organization of the tables in the model accelerates the query performance. All join statements are written with indexed data number keys. The SQL statements are much simpler then complex SQL statements for extracting data from multiple tables in operational systems. Another advantage is that the query execution process is placed in the Datawarehouse database, so if there is a need for more complex queries, they won't affect the performance of the operational systems.

Step 4:   Empower the self-service capabilities in the data module

In the previous step the BI Team should prepare the Star Schema model and deploy it in the database (Datawarehouse) and after that BI developer must prepare meta data model and business view in the BI tool with all data marts organized in subject oriented folders in the BI platform with defined join conditions between tables. They need to do this, because this is the best way business users to get familiar with the data sets and start using them, by themselves. In business data marts the names of the fact tables and

Figure 15. Business view for the Star Schema data model

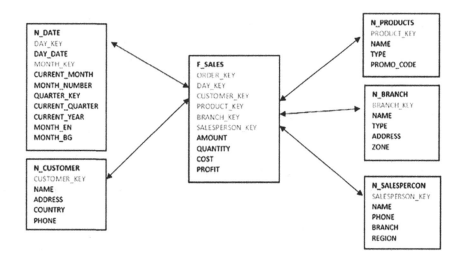

dimensions must be meaningful to the business users. They must recognize the labels of the columns and tables. This is the essential requirements for the success of the self-service BI. For example, if in the Datawarehouse the Sales subject area is designed like in Figure 14, now in Figure 15 is presented how the business view for the Star Schema data model should look like:

All the Grey labels in figure 15 must be hidden from data model business view because they don't bring any meaningful information and they may confuse the business users. The grey table columns are with number data inside and these surrogate keys (system-generated key) are made to handle the data consistency and query performance in the model. This technique can be accomplished in the BI platform by using functions to hide unnecessary table fields or by creating custom SQL query and don't selecting these columns from the tables in the database if the BI platform doesn't support data modeling.

These were the main steps to prepare self-service BI model. The education time for business users is less than half working day, and after that when they trust the data and understand the data entities easily, they will start to explore the information, to do data mining and to analyze the hidden patterns of the data without the need of SQL knowledge or programming skills. This modelling technique will support the user to make fast, trustful and competitive decisions based on reliable data. And this is the only way to start working in a data-driven organization instead of the slowly operated reporting organization.

GAME-CHANGER TRENDS IN BI

In the near future, the exact nature and value of data will emerge, and companies will be able to tune their businesses according to that value. Data will flexibly adjust and manage processes and operations through business analytics and BI. Teams shaped around the data paradigm will evolve towards the creation of clearly defined and effective data to stimulate achieving profitable solutions. Analysts and business users will receive rigorously synchronized results from complex data queries that will create the preconditions for an increasingly successful business (Durcevic, 2019).

The vision for building the future gives an idea of what the data scenery will look like over the next few years. From Graph Analytics, helping in fraud detection, through Natural Language Processing, empowering all the staff to perform complex data analysis, to Continuous Intelligence, Explainable AI and In-Memory Computing can provide super-fast performance and real-time insights. The 'Datafication of Everything' through fascinating Data Storytelling will inspire a Data-Driven Culture for Agile BI Integration which as a whole can result in an exciting Customer Experience.

Business Intelligence has been revolutionized. Flow of raw data is increasing. Business units want to use available information and extrapolate possible future results. Therefore, the demand for BI tools also increases. There are so many BI trends.

This statement is based on reports on hot Business Intelligence trends. It is focused on research which include Data Quality Management (DQM), Data Discovery, Artificial Intelligence, Predictive analytics tools, Collaborative Business Intelligence, Data-driven Culture etc. All these trends are implemented by some well-known companies which have been examining them. Today, large amounts of data can be analyzed, and this is making huge changes in the lives of people, companies, states, and researchers. Because of the growing Big Data, the companies are looking for useful information concerning all the data that appears.

In figure 16 the significance of BI trends is ranked by the BI-Survey report (2019). According to it Data Quality/Master Data Management, Data Discovery/Visualization and Data-Driven Culture are the uppermost three topics BI experts recognize as the most essential trends in their activities.

Figure 16. Ranks of BI Trends Significance (BI-Survey, 2019)

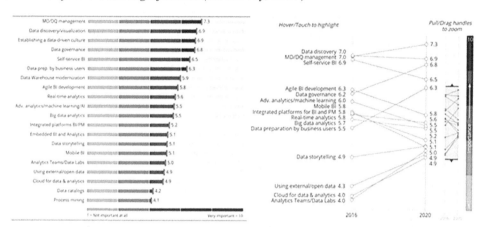

This part of the chapter explores and summarizes some of the hottest BI trends in 2020 that are impacting the industries:

Data Quality Management

A research conducted by the Business Application Research Center (BI-Survey, 2019) stated the Data Quality Management as the most important trend in 2020. It is not only important to gather as much information as possible, but the quality and the context in which data is being used and interpreted serves as the main thing for the future of BI. That is why it is the first and one of the most important general sense and critical, but very difficult to achieve. It continues to be among the major challenges facing data analysts around the globe. Good data quality is critical for deriving the right insights from the available data and taking the right decisions. Among the most promising trends in BI, DQM is crucial for avoiding the pitfalls for poor data quality and leveraging any company's investments in BI technologies. DQM-related processes ensure that the business acquires compliance with data quality standards and regulations across the globe. According to the Oracle® Warehouse Builder User's Guide (2009)a model of the main phases of DQM to provide high quality information to the business users is visually presented in the following figure 17.

Data Discovery and Visualization for Actionable Analytics Everywhere

Another leading trend is the use of BI for sales and marketing teams across companies. Thanks to the use of BI dashboards, sales and marketing professionals can access the latest sales and purchasing trends among their customers without relying on any technical IT expert or business analyst. Through the adop-

Figure 17. Main phases elaborated in providing DQM

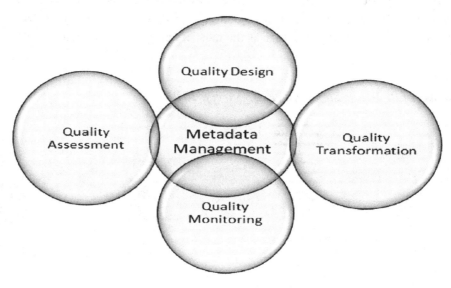

tion of the right BI tools for sales and marketing, companies can benefit from higher revenues (due to product cross-selling and up-selling) and ensure higher customer satisfaction. Also referred to as data analysis for business users, data discovery is among the leading BI trends in 2020. For a business user, data discovery is a business process aimed to detect patterns and deriving insights in data through data analytics tools. It requires understanding the relationship between data in the form of data preparation, visual analysis and guided advanced analytics. Thanks to the visualization tools, business users are able to discover business trends and even anomalies easier and take immediate and appropriate actions. Data visualization issues provided by Microsoft Power BI can be observed in the next figure 19.

Figure 18. Data Visualization. (Microsoft Power BI, 2020)

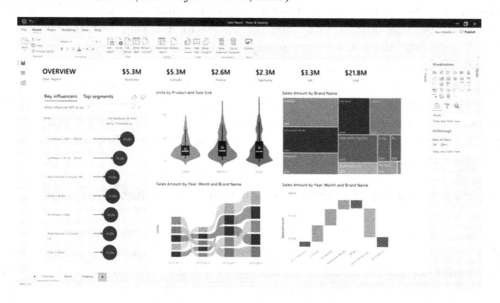

Data-Driven Culture

Making a decision without relying on data could lead to potential damages that will be hard to recover from, but implementing the data culture across departments can prove to be beneficial across the board: the mentality of employees will change, data will be stored on the cloud where is easily accessible, accurate market segmentation will become a standard, and the costs will significantly decrease. All organizations have the capacity to create a data culture, no matter how big or small, or data understanding or not, they are. By adopting a data-driven culture, an organization is better equipped to find and address the waste in care processes, while making quality improvement interventions more effective. In a data-driven culture, staff seeks out data to help achieve goals, and data takes a more active role in measuring quality and success. The following compilation showed in figure 19 gives any suggestion for the complicated processes driven in such organizations.

Figure 19. Data Driven Culture

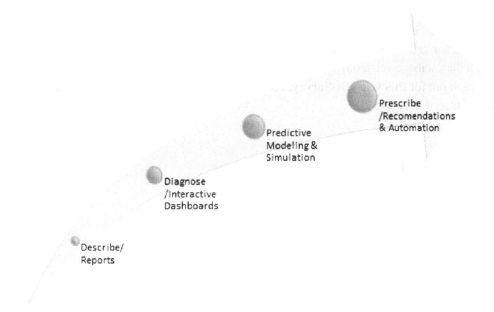

The most important features of the following next two trends, selected among the 20 in BI-survey, have been analyzed above in details.

The Indispensable Role of Artificial Intelligence in BI Platforms

The foremost step trending selected by Gartner in 2020 Strategic Technology Trends report (Gartner, 2019), chains AI with autonomous equipment and hyper automation focused level of security in which AI risks of emerging vulnerable points of attacks (Durcevic, 2019). AI is the science intending to force engines to perform as the complex human intelligence is capable.

The AI robotic assistants like Alexa or Siri are tools developing AI feature that lets users to communicate with the software plain language. The user just has to type a question or request and the best possible answer will be generated. Doing it via Chatbots or data-driven customized services, 97% of manufacturing professionals appreciate a foremost role for tools of AI&ML in marketing (Countants, 2020). At the same time, AI and ML can also be deployed in business strategies related to BI and analytics. Among the latest trends identified in the 2020 Gartner report, AI and ML technologies are useful for detecting any anomalies or unexpected patterns in data analytics. For example, through advanced neural systems, AI algorithms can analyze historical data and accurately detect anomalies or unexpected events. How the application of new AI tools makes BI smarter and more useful is analyzed in (Korolov, 2018).

Self-service BI Evolution Towards Smart BI

Another trend in BI is related with self-service BI. Traditional BI tools are structured around a central data warehouse and data stores. However, this centralized infrastructure is insufficient for today's business enterprise that needs to have data access anytime and by any user. This has led to the emergence of the self-service BI model that provides BI users with more flexibility and independence when it comes to accessing data. That is why data automation cannot be skipped. Also referred to as hyper-automation, data automation is rated among the most disruptive technologies for the year 2020. Gartner predicts that 40% of all data science-related tasks will be automated by this year, thus making data automation a BI trend to watch out for this year (BI-Survey, 2019). The transition towards Smart Analytics and their features can be traced in figure 20.

Figure 20. Te transition towards Smart Analytics

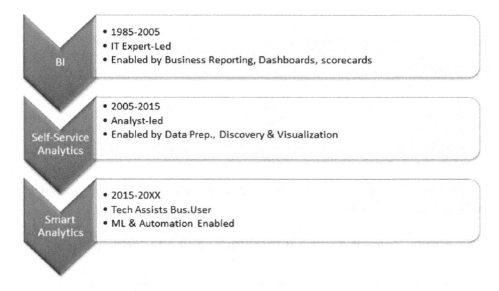

136

Augmented Analytics

The augmented stuffs have crossed the threshold into the analytics world in recent years and further the technologies will be even more concentrated on alterations in this direction. Associated with the trend in building a data-driven culture to be able to make better decisions, according to Gartner (Cheng et al., 2020), augmented analytics takes the first place for data analytics trends in 2020. According to Durcevic (2019), automating findings and optimizing decision-making will definitely influence companies of all scopes. Some visual interpretations of Gartner's insights for the augmented analytics as the next big disruptor can be seen in figure 21.

Figure 21. Augmented analytics as the next big disruptor (Uphindia Ind., 2019)

The focal concept of augmented analytics is that uses ML automation and AI methods to augment (expand) human acquaintance and contextual intelligence. It drives less subjective conclusions and more mindfulness across the business, and it will cause another flood of analytics disruption in 2020. That doesn't imply that the abilities of an information researcher or progressed investigative capacities will totally disappear. They will be enlarged to the point that investigation could be utilized by everybody in an organization without the need to consider complex maths or software engineering but utilizing them with the assistance of contemporary software. It will provide even the normal business clients with the ability to construct examination models and exploit complex equations in an increasingly straightforward and congenial manner.

With everything taken into account, according to (BI-Survey, 2019), these top trends indicate the basis for companies to deal with their own data and utilize it. Moreover, it exhibits that the companies know about the significance of high-quality data and its viable use. These patterns represent fundamental structures being changed: Companies need to go beyond the collection of as much data as could reasonably be expected and effectively use this information to improve their business choices. This is likewise upheld by data warehouse reconstruction, which is once more in seventh rank this year.

A few trends have marginally expanded in significance since a year ago (e.g., real-time analytics and integrated platforms for BI and PM) (Huez, 2020). Notwithstanding, they all climbed only one position except of establishing a data-driven culture, which leaped two places spots. In this manner, no enormous move can be seen as far as upward patterns.

BUSINESS PROCESS TRANSFORMATION TRENDS

To remain on pinnacle of customer demands business companies mature to be more and more agile. That is why Business Process Management (BPM) persists to incorporate technological innovation in the following directions:

Robotic Process Automation (RPA) via Bots

Monotonous repetitive processes driven by rules are automation friendly. Capable of replicating human activity bots via AI can do these responsibilities error-free.

Adaptive Case Management (ACM) Increasing the Efficiency of Predictable Tasks

Nowadays most of the personnel cope with duties where the result is well-known, but the pathway to it may vary due to unpredictable work patterns. The appropriate decision is to respond ad-hoc to every unscheduled event including the ability to deal with adaptive cases.

A Hype in Demand for Low-Code Systems

More and more companies intend ready-to-wear solutions that can be personalized in a matter of days. Requests for entirely working automated processes are more popular these days. Suppliers will start release updated products with process-focused low-code platforms, following products that already offer this low-code ability.

Enhanced Collaboration in the Workforce

Chat in data shared environments are considered vital for effectively operating a business today, and these are exceptionally valuable to BPM solutions. Pairing a chatbot service with a BPM solution like digital twins eliminates the boring conversations to determine consumer requirements.

These trends point to a significant shift forward in BPM. While the first wave of technology made BPM a reality, bots, low-code, adaptive automation, and many other tools are deliberately replicating in the second wave. Actually, even these technologies are seeing their replacements in their rear-view mirror: low code is slowly being overtaken by its successor, no-code platforms (Kissflow, 2020).

FUTURE BI TRENDS DIRECTIONS

The future is bright for every sector that dares to develop itself. According to (Conrad, 2019) some of the future divisions in BI trends are in the following areas:

- Collaboration – BI tools will become more collaborative, simplifying teamwork, a lot of new options for sharing and ease of use.
- Integration – Third party systems will be increasingly entangled with BI, streamlining data processing and responding to actionable perceptions.
- Machine Learning – AI investigates historical data to provide insights and forecasting.
- Data Proactivity – Proactivity–motivated landscapes will reply inevitably to investigations and convey appropriate data to users.
- Network Advancements – Technology infrastructure will grow to store huge volumes of data and better support BI systems.
- Data-Driven Culture – Implementing a data-driven culture encompasses giving all personnel the resources to integrate BI into daily processes.

CONCLUSION

Business Intelligence is a subject of a great importance and comprises new future opportunities which will practically allow running a company. That is why all companies in the corporate world are well informed. In the near future, AI and BI fusion tools will go beyond surfacing insights. They will propose ways to address or fix issues, run simulation tasks to optimize processes, make new performance targets based on predictions, and take action governed by complex AI-engine. All these actions helping processes to be analyzed and preprocessed data are delivering better insights and are easing management decision makers.

Even as data analytics is aging, not enough businesses have been able to adopt this technology to its maximum potential in their operations. With the available tools, nowadays everyone can easily get and analyze his competitors' data even if he is on a bootstrapped budget. A lot of companies use data-driven approaches for their email marketing campaigns, their SEO strategy and more but this is just the beginning. The future of Business Intelligence is likely to be much more automated and aggressively utilized, with fewer bottlenecks in terms of interface limitations and the free flow of data. Future BI trends are all part of a quickly evolving model that is essential to the progression of modern businesses.

Nowadays, companies are under increasing pressure to make better decisions faster. These examples are only a few of the hot BI trends that are used by companies and people working in them, so that they can use big data faster and more usefully each day. By the examples given in this chapter it is shown that BI has been revolutionized the past few years and the more data has been collected, the many new examples and trends are coming out.

ACKNOWLEDGMENT

This research received no specific grant from any funding agency in the public, commercial, or not-for-profit sectors. The first author expresses a deep gratitude to her MSc students from ELFE at the Technical University of Sofia for their enthusiastic state-of-the–art investigations and contribution in tasks and discussions related to the hot BI trends. The research of the last author, described in this paper, was carried out within the framework of R&D Project in support of PhD student (session 2019), contract № 192ПД0025-15.

REFERENCES

Analytics Insight. (2019, December 8). *AI and BI: Powering the Next-Generation of Analytics.* Retrieved from https://www.analyticsinsight.net/ai-and-bi-powering-the-next-generation-of-analytics/

Berntzen, L., & Krumova, M. (2017). Big Data from a Business Perspective. In M. Themistocleous & V. Morabito (Eds.), *Information Systems* (pp. 119–127). Springer. doi:10.1007/978-3-319-65930-5_10

BI-Survey. (2019). *Top Business Intelligence Trends 2020: What 2,865 BI Professionals Really Think.* BARC (Business Application Research Center). Retrieved from https://bi-survey.com/top-business-intelligence-trends

Buttle, F., & Maklan, S. (2019). *Customer Relationship Management: Concepts and Technologies* (4th ed.). Routledge. doi:10.4324/9781351016551

Cheng, C., Zhong, H., & Cao, L. (2020). Facilitating speed of internationalization: The roles of business intelligence and organizational agility. Retrieved from doi:10.1016/j.jbusres.2020.01.003

Conrad, A. (2019). *The Future of Business Intelligence (BI) in 2020* [Blog]. Retrieved from https://www.selecthub.com/business-intelligence/future-of-bi/

Countants. (2020, January 18). *10 Leading Trends in Business Intelligence in the Year 2020* [Blog]. Retrieved from https://www.countants.com/blogs/10-leading-trends-in-business-intelligence-in-the-year-2020/

de Souza, J. G. C. (2018). Generating E-Commerce Product Titles and Predicting their Quality. *Proceedings of the 11th International Natural Language Generation Conference*, 233–243. 10.18653/v1/W18-6530

Dedić, N., & Stanier, C. (2016). Measuring the Success of Changes to Existing Business Intelligence Solutions to Improve Business Intelligence Reporting. In A. Tjoa, L. Xu, M. Raffai, & N. Novak (Eds.), *Research and Practical Issues of Enterprise Information Systems. CONFENIS 2016. Lecture Notes in Business Information Processing* (Vol. 268). Springer., doi:10.1007/978-3-319-49944-4_17

Durcevic, S. (2019, November 28). *Top 10 Analytics and Business Intelligence Trends For 2020* [Blog]. Retrieved from https://www.datapine.com/blog/business-intelligence-trends/

E-commerce, customer relation management (CRM) and secure transactions. (n.d.). Retrieved March 9, 2020, from https://ec.europa.eu/eurostat/web/products-datasets/-/isoc_bde15dec

E-commerce purchases datasets. (n.d.). Retrieved March 9, 2020, from https://ec.europa.eu/eurostat/web/products-datasets/-/isoc_ec_ebuyn2

E-commerce sales datasets. (n.d.). Retrieved March 9, 2020, from https://ec.europa.eu/eurostat/web/products-datasets/-/isoc_ec_evaln2

Egetoft, K. (2019, January 29). *Data-Driven Analytics: Practical Use Cases for Financial Services.* Part 3 of the "Data Management for Financial Services" Series. Digitalist Magazine by SAP. Retrieved from https://www.digitalistmag.com/customer-experience/2019/01/29/data-driven-analytics-practical-use-cases-for-financial-services-06195123

EU Open Data Portal. (n.d.). Retrieved March 9, 2020, from https://data.europa.eu/euodp/en/data/

Gartner. (2019, October21). *Top 10 Strategic Technology Trends for 2020. A Gartner Special Report.* Retrieved fromhttps://emtemp.gcom.cloud/ngw/globalassets/en/doc/documents/432920-top-10-strategic-technology-trends-for-2020.pdf

GMDH Shell Software. (n.d.). Retrieved March 9, 2020, from https://gmdhsoftware.com/

Grosseck, G., Țîru, L. G., & Bran, R. A. (2019). Education for Sustainable Development: Evolution and Perspectives: A Bibliometric Review of Research, 1992–2018. *Sustainability*, *11*(21), 6136. doi:10.3390u11216136

Gupta, R., & Pathak, C. (2014). A Machine Learning Framework for Predicting Purchase by online customers based on Dynamic Pricing. *Procedia Computer Science*, *36*, 599–605. doi:10.1016/j.procs.2014.09.060

Harvard Business Review Analytic Services. (2019). *Machine Learning: The Next Generation of Customer Experience*. Harvard Business School Publishing. Retrieved March 9, 2020, from https://cdn2.hubspot.net/hubfs/1965778/HBR-AS_CIandT_Machine%20Learning_%20The%20Next%20Generation%20of%20Customer%20Experience.pdf

Henschen, D. (2018). *Embrace the Era of Smart Analytics*. Retrieved from https://www.constellationr.com/blog-news/embrace-era-smart-analytics

Huez, A. (2020). *5 Business Intelligence Trends for 2020*. Retrieved from https://toucantoco.com/blog/en/5-business-intelligence-trends-for-2020/

IDC and EMC, The Digital Universe in 2020: Big data, Bigger Digital Shadow, and Biggest Growth in the Far East, Big Data in 2020. (n.d.). Retrieved from https://www.emc.com/leadership/digital-universe/2012iview/big-data-2020.htm

inTelegy. (2018). *Service Offerings: Data Driven Management*. Retrieved from https://www.intelegy.com/data-driven-management

IQLECT. (2018). *The Importance of Predictive Analytics for E-commerce Stores*. Retrieved March 9, 2020, from https://medium.com/swlh/the-importance-of-predictive-analytics-for-e-commerce-stores-d7ef0ce2d32e

Kamthania, D., Pahwa, A., & Madhavan, S. S. (2018). Market Segmentation Analysis and Visualization Using K-Mode Clustering Algorithm for E-Commerce Business. *CIT. Journal of Computing and Information Technology*, 26(1), 57–68. doi:10.20532/cit.2018.1003863

Kimball, R., & Ross, M. (2013). *The Datawarehouse Tool Kit: The Definitive Guide to Dimensional Modeling* (3rd ed.). John Wiley & Sons, Inc.

Kissflow. (2020). *4 Trends That are Transforming BPM in 2020. Process automation bots to everything. What's been pinging BPM's radar this year.* Retrieved from https://kissflow.com/bpm/4-trends-revolutionizing-business-process-management/

Kopanakis, J. (2019, May 9). *How Artificial Intelligence Positively Influences Business Decision Making* [Blog]. Retrieved from https://www.mentionlytics.com/blog/how-artificial-intelligence-positively-influences-business-decision-making/

Korolov, M. (2018, Apr 18). *New AI tools make BI smarter — and more useful.* CIO. Retrieved from https://www.cio.com/article/3268965/new-ai-tools-make-bi-smarter-and-more-useful.html

Kutz, M. (2016). *Introduction to e-commerce: Combining business and information technology.* BookBoon.

Management Solutions. (2018). *Machine Learning, a key component in business model transformation.* Retrieved March 9, 2020, from https://www.managementsolutions.com/sites/default/files/publicaciones/eng/machine-learning.pdf

Microsoft Power, B. I. (2020). *Data Visualization.* Retrieved from https://powerbi.microsoft.com/en-us/

Morgan, L. (2019, January 22). *What You Need to Know about Augmented Analytics.* Retrieved from https://www.informationweek.com/big-data/big-data-analytics/what-you-need-to-know-about-augmented-analytics/a/d-id/1333696

Nagaty, K. A. (2010). *E-Commerce Business Models: Part 1. In Encyclopedia of E-Business Development and Management in the Global Economy.* IGI Global.

Oracle® Warehouse Builder User's Guide 10g Release 2 (10.2.0.2). (2009). *Understanding Data Quality Management.* Retrieved from https://docs.oracle.com/cd/B31080_01/doc/owb.102/b28223/concept_data_quality.htm

Rajarshi, D. (2019). *eCommerce Business Models that Work in 2019: A Brief Guide.* Retrieved March 9, 2020, from https://medium.com/pluginhive/types-of-ecommerce-business-models-271ea438f2aa

Roy, P. (2017). *The data-driven world.* Intergen. Retrieved from https://www.intergen.co.nz/blog/Priyanka-Roy/dates/2017/8/The-data-driven-world/

Rud, O. (2009). *Business Intelligence Success Factors: Tools for Aligning Your Business in the Global Economy.* Retrieved from https://www.amazon.com/Business-Intelligence-Success-Factors-Aligning/dp/0470392401

Sen, M. (2019). *Application of Artificial Intelligence in Business.* Retrieved from https://www.fastnewsfeed.com/technology/application-of-artificial-intelligence-in-business/

Srinivasan, S. (2019). *Data Driven Culture*. Retrieved from https://storybydata.com/datacated-challenge/data-driven-culture/

Statista, Top benefits that companies realize through the use of data and analytics worldwide as of 2019. (2020). Retrieved from https://www.statista.com/statistics/895263/worldwide-barriers-effective-data-analytics-use/

Stubseid, S., & Arandjelovic, O. (2018). Machine Learning Based Prediction of Consumer Purchasing Decisions: The Evidence and Its Significance. *Proceedings of AI and Marketing Science workshop at AAAI-2018*. Retrieved March 9, 2020, from https://core.ac.uk/download/pdf/158368656.pdf

Tech Wire Asia. (2019). *Augmented analytics to simplify acquiring business intelligence*. Retrieved from https://techwireasia.com/2019/02/augmented-analytics-to-simplify-acquiring-business-intelligence/

Uphindia Ind. (2019). *Augmented analytics will be next big disruptor: Gartner*. Retrieved from https://uphindia.com/2019/03/24/augmented-analytics-will-be-next-big-disruptor-gartner/

ADDITIONAL READING

Elgendy, N., & Elragal, A. (2016). Big Data Analytics in Support of the Decision Making Process. *Procedia Computer Science*, *100*, 1071–1084. doi:10.1016/j.procs.2016.09.251

Hall, P., Phan, W., & Whitson, K. (2016). *The Evolution of Analytics Opportunities and Challenges for Machine Learning in Business*. Retrieved from https://www.sas.com/content/dam/SAS/en_us/doc/whitepaper2/evolution-of-analytics-108240.pdf

Khan, W. A., Chung, S. H., Awan, M. U., & Wen, X. (2019). Machine learning facilitated business intelligence (Part I): Neural networks learning algorithms and applications. *Industrial Management & Data Systems*, *120*(1), 164–195. doi:10.1108/IMDS-07-2019-0361

Koehler, J. (2018). Business Process Innovation with Artificial Intelligence: Levering Benefits and Controlling Operational Risks. *European Business&Management*, *4*(2), 55–66. doi:10.11648/j.ebm.20180402.12

Kościelniak, H., & Puto, A. (2015). BIG DATA in decision making processes of enterprises. *Procedia Computer Science*, *65*, 1052–1058. doi:10.1016/j.procs.2015.09.053

Kraus, M., Feuerriegel, S., & Oztekin, A. (2020). Deep learning in business analytics and operations research: Models, applications and managerial implications. *European Journal of Operational Research*, *281*(3), 628–641. doi:10.1016/j.ejor.2019.09.018

Rouhani, S., Ashrafi, A., Zare Ravasan, A., & Afshari, S. (2016). The impact model of business intelligence on decision support and organizational benefits. *Journal of Enterprise Information Management*, *29*(1), 19–50. doi:10.1108/JEIM-12-2014-0126

KEY TERMS AND DEFINITIONS

Adaptive Case Management (ACM): It is an approach to case management that helps knowledge workers who need the most flexibility when handling their cases.

Artificial Intelligence: It is a scientific area related to development and application of methods and algorithms for knowledge learning, perception, representation, reasoning, planning, etc. of a system that characterizes with flexible adaptation for achieving specific goals and solving problems with different level of complexity.

Big Data: It is a research field studying methods and algorithms for too large and complex data sets extraction, processing, and analysis.

Business Analytics: It deals with technologies, techniques and methods for investigation, exploration and analysis of past business events and processes.

Business Intelligence: It includes technologies, techniques and methods for data analysis and knowledge presentation for facilitation the business decision making process.

Business Process Management (BPM): It is a discipline in operations management in which people use various methods to discover, model, analyze, measure, improve, optimize, and automate business processes.

Decision Making: It is a process for alternatives recognition based on custom preferences and specific goals with aim an appropriate solution to be chosen.

E-Commerce: It is related to buying and selling goods and services via Internet where business transactions between businesses, business and customers, customers and customers, customers and businesses occur.

Machine Learning: It is research field part of artificial intelligence that provides a system opportunity to automatically learn from data with aim predictive, classification and clustering tasks to be solved.

Predictive Modelling: It is a process related to models creation concerning data usage and processing with aim business items, events and processes to be predicted.

Robotic Process Automation (RPA): It is a form of business process automation technology based on metaphorical software robots (bots) or on artificial intelligence (AI)/digital workers.

Self-Service: It is possibility of business users to create their reports and to analyze within an approved and predefined data model in analytics platform without involving the organization's BI and IT teams.

Star Schema Modeling: It is a process for entity-relationship diagram development based on data processing about facts and dimensions.

Chapter 7
Causal Feature Selection

Walisson Ferreira Carvalho
Centro Universitario Una, Brazil

Luis Zarate
Pontificia Universidade Catolica de Minas Gerais, Brazil

ABSTRACT

Feature selection is a process of the data preprocessing task in business intelligence (BI), analytics, and data mining that urges for new methods that can handle with high dimensionality. One alternative that have been researched to deal with the curse of dimensionality is causal feature selection. Causal feature selection is not based on correlation, but the causality relationship among variables. The main goal of this chapter is to present, based on the issues identified on other methods, a new strategy that considers attributes beyond those that compounds the Markov blanket of a node and calculate the causal effect to ensure the causality relationship.

INTRODUCTION

Year after year, the volume of data has proliferated at remarkable speed. However, large volumes and variety of data do not necessarily translate into quality and, due to this exponential growth, researchers are dealing with new challenges on the process of discovering knowledge. These challenges involve: the comprehension and modeling of the problem being considered, that quality of data, and identifying relevant data. One well-known problem is the Curse of Dimensionality. The Curse of Dimensionality is a term presented by Bellman in 1957 to describe a problem caused by an exponential increase in volume, especially complications when it comes to analyzing and organizing data in high-dimensional spaces (Keogh & Mueen, 2017).

The more data is available, the greater the need to analyze it in order transform it into knowledge, and then convert knowledge into information. Three areas of knowledge are currently dealing with this very subject: Business Intelligence (BI), Analytics, and Data Mining.

Business Intelligence can be defined as the process of transforming data into information and, consequently, into knowledge. Analytics can be defined as the process of transforming data into insights.

DOI: 10.4018/978-1-7998-5781-5.ch007

Whereas Data Mining is the process of discovering potentially useful and unknown information from a collection of data. All three processes have the same input: data. Their shared aim to produce information and knowledge to support decisions' makers.

Despite their minor differences, all three processes are dependent of the quality of data, not only on the volume that enters the pipeline. Therefore, quality data is a critical factor of success. This quality of data can be understood from the concept of Smart Data, which refers to the process of transforming raw data into quality data. The process of discovering smart data is defined by the Gartner Group as "a next-generation data discovery capability that provides business users or citizen data scientists with insights from advanced analytics."

It is well known that the pipeline for transforming raw data into knowledge and, consequently, in information (or insights) includes the preprocessing stage. According to Garcıa et al. (2015) preprocessing is the most important stage in data mining and is affected by the volume of data as well. In the event raw data is not ready to be analyzed, it is necessary to prepare it before being processed by learner's model algorithm. The preprocessing phase is responsible for transforming data and includes data cleaning, integration, normalization, and dealing with missing data.

One strategy used during the preprocessing stage is dimensionality reduction, a technique that can be feature extraction, feature selection, or instance selection. Feature extraction is associated with constructing new features as functions of existing ones. Transformation, discretization, and Principal Components Analysis (PCA) are techniques of feature extraction. Meanwhile, feature selection aims to reduce the number of features by selecting the more representative subset of variables in a given problem.

The reduction of dimensionality can also consider attributes and samples in a process known as hybrid partitioning. In other words, the data set can be reduced in terms of column (attributes) or rows (samples). The reduction of sample is known as Instance Selection and is a technique used to select the best subset of examples and naturally improves the performance of the learning's algorithm, but the focus of this chapter is on feature selection because it facilitates the learning task and aims to select the optimal subset of features that best represents a problem.

Triguero et al. (2019) emphasized that data preprocessing is one of the most important stages in the process of transforming data into information and Feature Selection is a data preprocessing strategy that should be applied to mitigate problems in the data pipeline.

Take, for instance, the Analytics' process that, despite of its growth, is still prone to some challenges such as how to handle the amount of data, the lack of quality in data, computational resources, and high dimensionality. Analytics can be classified as Descriptive, Predictive, and Prescriptive. Descriptive is related to historical data. In this preliminary stage, the question to be answered is "What is happening?". Predictive is related to the future, using data from the past to predict the future to answer such questions as "What will happen in the future?". Prescriptive is dedicated to trying to answer the question "What should be done?". In general, applying a satisfactory Analytics process requires having smart data that can answer these questions.

Besides mitigating computational complexity, feature selection results in predictive models that are easier to understand due to the reduced number of attributes. According to Garcıa et al. (2015) feature selection is a family of methods with that have the following immediate positive effects on the data analysis:

1. Improve data quality;
2. Increases performance of Data Mining Algorithms;
3. Makes the results easier to understand.

Since 1997, when a special issue of the journal Artificial Intelligence was dedicated to relevance, the definition of relevance and the process of feature selection was a concern for researchers. In their paper Kohavi & John (1997) presented a taxonomy where the attributes of a data set were divided into three categories: strong relevant, weak relevant, and irrelevant.

Bolon-Canedo et al. (2015) define feature selection as the process of selecting relevant features and discarding those variables that are redundant or irrelevant. It is important to stress that, in mid-1990s, data sets had fewer attributes than they do nowadays; currently, some data sets are massive, and they asserted that feature selection is an issue that cries out for a solution.

Throughout the history of Machine Learning, correlation exerts a strong influence mostly on learning algorithms and over the definition of attribute relevance. However, correlation does not always imply causation. Moreover, coincidental correlations, also known as spurious correlations, can occur.

Therefore, if in one hand feature selection is essential for the quality of Business Intelligence (BI), Analytics, and Data Mining. On the other hand, it is crucial the research for new methods that search for relationship among variables far beyond the simple correlation.

Since the mid-1990s, many techniques had been developed for feature selection. Paul (2017) stress that it is a challenge to identify features that are not just correlated with the target, but that it is associated with the target in a meaningful way. One strategy that has been gaining strength is the selection of features through the causality relationship among variables.

Causality is an area of research that has been very much evident over the last few decades, especially after the conquest of the Alan Turing prize by Judea Pearl in 2011. Since then, many researches involving causal inference have been taken in different fields of knowledges such as application of causality, missing data, feature selection and other.

One of the most common representations of the causality relationship is the Bayesian Network (BN). BN is a probabilistic graphical model that represents a set of variables and its probability distribution. It is represented by a Directed Acyclic Graph (DAG) in which each node represents a random variable and each arc linking two nodes is interpreted as a direct influence from one node to another. Causal feature selection has been studied by many researchers such as Borboudakis & Tsamardinos (2019), (Tsamardinos et al., 2018), (Yang et al., 2019) and others.

Predominantly these studies use the concept of Markov Blanket (MB) to select the relevant attributes for a target (T) feature in a data set. The set of nodes that compounds the Markov Blanket of target, MB(T) in a BN consists of parents, children, and spouses of T. The parents of a target are the direct causes, children of the target are direct effects, and spouses represent direct causes of direct effects. In a BN, all other variables are conditionally independent on T given MB(T).

In this sense, based on issues identified after a review of the methods that has been proposed to select relevant features based on causality, this chapter presents a new strategy that consider not only the Markov Blanket, but also potential indirect causes, grandparents, and direct effects of the causes, siblings, of one target. Besides growing the selection of features, this strategy also consists in computing the causal effect between variables to ensure the causal relationship.

BACKGROUND

Before going deeply into the causal theory, it is necessary to present some statistical concepts such as joint distribution, marginal and conditional probability distribution. These concepts will be introduced using Table 1, which contains data on hospital surgeries.

Table 1. Data on hospital surgeries

	Death		Total
Local Infection	No	Yes	
No	4704	506	5210
Yes	208	58	266
Total	4912	564	5476

Joint distribution is the probability distribution. Consider, for instance, the data presented in Table 1. the joint distribution of death (YES) over local infection (YES) is 1.1% (58/5476) as shown in Table 2. Marginal distribution is the sum of the joint probabilities over one variable. According to the data in Table 1 and the joint distribution in Table 2, the marginal distribution of death equal YES is 9.2% + 1.1% = 10.3% and the marginal distribution of local infection (NO) is 95.1%, resulting in 85.9%+9.2%

Table 2. Joint distribution

	Death		Total
Local Infection	No	Yes	
No	85.9%	9.2%	95.1%
Yes	3.8%	1.1%	4.9%
Total	89.7%	10.3%	100.0%

Another concept that must be highlighted is the concept of independence among events. Two events are independents when the knowledge about one event does not give any information about the other. Formally speaking, two events are independents when $P(A|B) = P(A)$. In the example of Table 2, death and local infection are not independent because the probability of death increases from 10.3% to 21.8%. The number of deaths (58) by the number of local infections equals yes (266) when it is known that local infection had occurred.

This definition of independence can be expanded to a set of variables V. Let P be a joint distribution over a set of variables V and X, then let Y and Z be three variables (or subset of variables) of V. Variables X and Y are conditionally independent given Z, if $P(x, y|z) = P(x|z)$. This means that once Z is known, learning Y does not improve the knowledge of X. To denote the conditional independence of X and Y given Z uses the following representation: IND(X, Y|Z).

Pearl & Mackenzie (2018) presented a hierarchy of knowledge that they called Ladder of Causation. This hierarchy is composed of three levels: Seeing, Doing, and Imagining, with each level of the ladder aiming to answer a different kind of question.

According to Pearl & Mackenzie (2018) at the first level, Seeing, we are just observing data, meaning data are being related with each other. At the second level, Doing, variables are being manipulated to check what would happen if it were different. The higher level, Imagining, is related to the ability to comprehend the reason.

According to Pearl (2009) a Causal Model is pair $M = < D, \theta_D >$, with D representing a causal structure and θ_D a set of parameters. The causal structure, D, is Directed Acyclic Graph (DAG) and the set of parameters, θ_D, of the Causal Model M. θ_D assigns functions $x_i = f_i\left(pa_i, u_i\right), i = 1, 2, 3, ..., n$. where pa_i stands for the set of variables that renders x_i and u_i represents disturbances or unobserved variables. The set of equations in this form and in which each variable has its own equation and appears at the left-hand side (dependent variable) of the equation is called Structured Causal Model (SCM) or, simply, Causal Model.

As previously stated, Bayesian Networks are frequently used to represent the causality relationship among variables. Bayesian Network, a term coined by Pearl in 1985, is a pair B = (G,P), in which G represents a DAG, G(V,E), and P is the joint probability distribution over the variables. As such, Bayesian Network is a graphical representation of the joint distribution of a set of random variables.

In a DAG G(V,E), the set of vertices V represents the features of a data set and the set of edges E represents the relationship between two vertices (variables). In a causal interpretation of BN, Causal Bayesian Network, each directed edge of the BN is interpreted as a direct causal influence between variables, in which the arrow pointing from a node to another reflects the direction of the causality. Consider, for instance. Figure 1, where node A represents a direct cause of node C and C is a direct effect of node A.

It is important to underscore other concepts that are in a DAG, such as those shown in Figure 1, and kinship terms, such as parents, children, and spouses, are used to denote various relationships in a DAG. In a relationship between two nodes X and Y with a single arrowhead pointing from X to Y, X is called parent of Y, Y is child of X. Considering variable E in Figure 1, B is a parent of E; G and T are children of E; and, F is spouse of E given that F is also parent of T.

Considering the equation $x_i = f_i\left(pa_i, u_i\right)$. which is part of the causal model and Figure 1, the target node (T) is rendered by nodes E and F. Therefore, replacing the variables in the equation, results in the following causal relationship: $t_i = f_t\left(e, f, u_t\right)$.. This relationship of a variable is known as Markovian Parents, which is defined as: "a set of variables PAi is said to be Markovian Parents of Xi if PAj is a minimal set of predecessors of Xj that renders Xj independent of all its other predecessors." (Pearl, 2009, p. 14). Therefore, nodes E and F of Figure 1 are the Markovian Parents of T.

Using this definition, it is possible to conclude that the set of parents, PA_j, of variable X_i is enough to determine the probability of X_i. In other words, knowing the values of other variables that are not in PA set is redundant since the Markovian Parents is known.

Some other functions that can be extracted from Figure 1 are:

1. $a_1 = u_1$
2. $b_1 = u_2$
3. $c_1 = f(a_1, b_1, u_3)$

Figure 1. Bayesian Network.

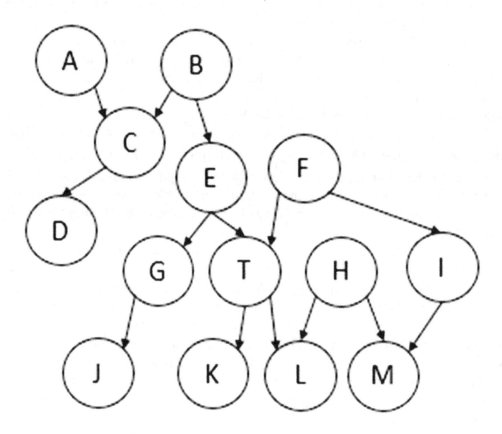

4. $d_1 = f(c_1, u_4)$

In addition to the kinship terminology presented above and in light of the definition of Markovian Parents, another important concept that must be introduced is that of d−separation. In a graph, a set of nodes C is said to d-separate two sets A from B if C blocks the path between A and B. Path is a sequence of consecutive edges (of any directionality) in the graph and blocking is the interruption of the flow between the nodes that are connected by the path. A set of nodes D blocks the path (p) between A and B if:

- **Rule 1**: p contains a chain A ® C ® B or a fork A ¬ C ® B such that C is a node in the subset D;
- **Rule 2**: p contains a collider A ® C ¬ B and C is not in D nor is descendant of C in D.

Statically speaking, d-separation means that A and B are conditionally independent given C. Put differently, two variables A and B are d-separated by C in a DAG if IND(A,B|C) is in the joint distribution. In Figure 1, according to Rule 1, node E blocks the path from B to T. In this case, variables B and T were dependents and became independents given E. Conversely, node C does not block the path from A to B, Rule 2; initially variables A and B were independent and become dependent once C is known.

Most Bayesian Network learning algorithms are based on score-search methods or constraint-based methods. Bayesian learning algorithms based on constraint methods used to analyze the dependence (or independence) relationship among variables to construct the Bayesian Network. These kinds of algorithms are also known as algorithms based on independence tests. This group of algorithms has two premises that are important to stress:

- **Markov Condition:** every variable is independent of any subset of its non-descendant variables conditioned on its parents;
- **Faithfulness Condition:** A BN(G,P) G and P are faithful, if, and only if, every conditional independence entailed by the G and the Markov Condition is also present in P. If P and G are faithful to each other, then G is a perfect map, P-map for short, of P.

These two assumptions, Markov and Faithfulness, ensure that conditional and unconditional distribution probability is represented by d-separation relationship in the causal graph.

Constraint-based algorithms is one of the most frequently used approaches for learning Bayesian Network, especially those based on conditional independence, and one of the most frequently used algorithms is PC, which stands for the initials of its inventors (Spirtes et al., 2000). PC is a refinement of Inductive Causation (IC), (Pearl, 2009).

The main steps of PC are:

Step 1:   Construct the complete graph;
Step 2:   Remove edges according to condition independence information;
Step 3:   Orient the v-structure;
Step 4:   Orient the remaining edges;

In the first step, a complete undirected graph is created. During the second step, edges between nodes, variables, are removed based on the conditional independence test given a threshold. The skeleton of the graph is obtained at the end of the second step.

In the third step, PC initiates the orientation of the edges between nodes. The rule used to direct an edge is that given a triple of vertices X, Y, Z such that the pairs X, Y and Y, Z are adjacent in G but the nodes X and Z are not adjacent, and if Y is not d-separated by X given Z, orient X - Y - Z as X -> Y <- Z. The structure presented is known as a v-structure. At this step, the algorithm has created a partially directed acyclic graph (PDAG).

In the fourth and last step, the remaining edges are oriented according to the following rules proposed by Meek (1995):

- If A -> B, B and C are adjacent, A and C are not adjacent, and if there is no arrowhead at B, then orient B - C as B -> C.
- If there is a directed path from A to B, and an edge between A and B, then orient A - B as A -> B.
- If A -> B <- C, A - D - C, A and C are not adjacent, and D - B, then orient D - B as D -> B.

PC algorithm has as its output a set of DAGs that are Markov equivalent, known as Completed Partially Directed Acyclic Graph (CPDAG). Two DAGs are Markov equivalent, if the elements of the set represent the same joint probability distribution, meaning the true causal graph is unknown.

PC is a global leaner whose main drawback is its computational cost. It is considered a global learner because it seeks out causal relationships among all features of the data set. According to Aliferis et al. (2010), PC cannot handle more than one hundred variables because in a worst-case scenario, PC is exponential. Gao et al. (2017) states that the usage of global learners, such as PC, is limited when dataset have large number of features.

One way of reducing the computational cost of learning the causal relationship is searching locally, given that global learning may be wasteful. This means that instead of constructing the whole graph, the causal relationship among features could be identified based on a local-to-global approach. Aliferis et al. (2010) pointed out that one way to address the problem of methods is learning the local neighborhood of a specific target variable directly, and primarily algorithms that use the Markov Blanket concept.

Markov Blanket is another important set of nodes in a BN. Graphically speaking, the Markov Blanket of a variable target T, MB(T), is the set of parents, children, and spouses of a variable T. Considering Figure 1, the Markov Blanket of the node T is composed by nodes E and F, parents of T; nodes K and L, children of T and node H, spouse of T.

According to the Markov Blanket concept and the definition of d-separate, Markov Blanket d-separates a target node from the other nodes that are not in the Markov Blanket. In a faithful BN, the Markov Blanket of a variable is unique.

Statistically speaking, the Markov Blanket of T is the minimal set conditioned on which all other nodes are independent of T (Pearl, 2009). A subset of variable M of V is the Markov Blanket of T Î V if and only if any subset S of V is independent of V\M given M, i.e. IND(T, S\M|M).

As previously mentioned, Causal Bayesian Network's learners' algorithms do not construct the true graph, but rather a set of DAGs that are Markov Equivalent. One mechanism that can be used to identify the true graph is through interventions, an intervention being a modification in one function of the SCM while the other functions remain intact. Local learning has been used as a more efficient alternative to constructing the Causal Bayesian Network whereas Markov Blanket has been used as the starting point for local learners' algorithm.

One important aspect in feature selection is defining the concept of relevance or a relevant attribute. There are many definitions of relevance in the literature. For the purpose of this work, the definitions of strong and weak relevance presented in (Kohavi and John, 1997) will be used. According to (Kohavi and John, 1997) a feature Xi is strongly relevant to a target (T) variable if and only if there exists some values xi, t and vi with $P\left(X_i = x_i, V^{\setminus X_i} = v_i\right) > 0$. such that: $P(T = t \mid X_i = x_i, V^{\setminus X_i} = v_i) \neq P(T = t \mid X^{\setminus i} = v_i)$.

A feature X_i is weakly relevant to T if and only if it is not relevant and there is a set of attributes V and x_i, t and v_i with $P\left(X_i = x_i, V^{\setminus X_i} = v_i\right) > 0$. such that: $P(T = t \mid X_i = x_i, V^{\setminus X_i} = v_i) \neq P(T = t \mid V^{\setminus i} = v_i)$.

A feature is relevant if it is either weakly or strongly relevant; otherwise, it is irrelevant. It is also important to emphasize that the relevance of an attribute depends on the objective being pursued. A feature that is irrelevant for classification may be relevant for predicting the class conditional probabilities.

Apart from the possibility that an attribute's relevance (or irrelevance) is dependent on the objective that is being pursued, it is worth underscoring the importance of a multivariate analysis instead of a univariate one. In a univariate analysis, the relevance (or irrelevance) is determined by the dependencies between the target and each variable individually. If Xi is independent of the target (T), Xi is irrelevant to T. As previously stated, this kind of analysis can lead to falsely irrelevant or falsely relevant variables. In a multivariate analysis, the concept of relevance of a variable Xi considers the context of the other variables X\i of the data set.

In 1996, Koller & Sahami (1996) demonstrated that the Markov Blanket (MB) of variable is expected to be an optimal set of attributes aimed at predicting a target (T) variable. As such, MB(T) represents the most relevant variables. As stated earlier, Markov Blanket and relevance, are straight related.

Tsamardinos & Aliferis (2002) made the association between Causal Bayesian Network and the concepts of relevance introduced by Kohavi & John (1997). According to Tsamardinos & Aliferis (2002), considering a faithful BN and based on the definitions of relevance presented by Kohavi & John (1997), a set of features (S) is strongly relevant if and only if each attribute of S $\hat{I}$ MB(T). Features that are not in the MB(T), having a connecting path to T, are considered weakly relevant to T and a feature is considered irrelevant to T if it is disconnected from T in the graph.

Considering the example of Markov Blanket presented in Figure 1, features E, F, K, L, and H are strongly relevant to the target considering that those features compound the Markov Blanket of T.

In Aliferis et al. (2010), causal feature selection algorithms are defined as those methods that induce the causal structure to solve the feature selection problem. Guyon & Elisseeff (2008) compared the goals of Feature Selection and causal discovery to establish their relationship and concluded that the application of causal discovery in the process of selecting features improves comprehension of the data and makes prediction possible under manipulations and changes.

Since the paper by Koller & Sahami (1996), many studies on Markov Blanket learning have been made and numerous ways to apply its theory to select the best subset of features based on this approach have been proposed, such as Grow-Shrink (GS), Iterative Associative Markov Blanket (IAMB), Max-Min Parents and Children / Max Min Markov Blanket (MMPC/MMMB), HITONPC/MB, Causal Markov Blanket (CMB), Forward-Backward Selection with Early Dropping (FBED), Parallel, Forward–Backward with Pruning (PFBP), Efficient Local Causal Discovery (ELCD), and EOMB.

Gao & Ji (2015) divide the Markov Blanket learners' algorithm into two different approaches: non-topology-based and topology-based. The non-topology-based approach applies the concept of Markov Blanket directly by testing the conditional independence between each variable and the target. Contrarily, topology-based methods begin by identifying the set of parents and children of a given target T and then seek the spouses in order to complete the MB.

One of the first algorithms that used the Markov Blanket concept was Grow-Shrink (GS) (Margaritis & Thrun, 1999). This algorithm is divided in two stages: Grow and Shrink. First, it grows quickly then shrinks, removing false positives. Its main goal is to construct the Bayesian Network by identifying the nodes of the Markov Blanket.

Like Grow-Shrink, IAMB (Iterative Associative Markov Blanket) presented by Tsamardinos et al. (2003) is structured in two phases, grow and shrink, and the main difference in this algorithm is during the growing stage. While in GS, the potential features of the MB are ordered according their degree of association with any given empty set of attributes. IAMB reorders the sample each time a new feature is included into the Markov Blanket.

Max-Min Parents and Children / Max Min Markov Blanket (MMPC/MMMB), introduced by Tsamardinos et al. (2006), is also divided into two stages. Actually, it can be considered two separated algorithms, with the first one identifying the parents and children of a target variable (T), PC(T), through Max-Min Parents and Children (MMPC). Afterwards, the search for the spouses of T, common parents of the children of T, is performed.

HITON/PC and MMPC/MMMB are similar in their main steps and both were considered by Aliferis et al. (2010) as being the first Markov Blanket learning algorithm. HITON/PC was presented by Aliferis et al. (2003b) and, as a topology-based, it first identifies the set of Parents and Children (PC) of a target and, in sequence, the Parents of Children of the Parents and Children of T, resulting in a superset of the Markov Blanket of T. After that, false positive variables of this superset are removed based on statistical tests.

Causal Markov Blanket (CMB) is topology-based algorithm for discovering Markov Blanket divided into three steps (Gao & Ji, 2015). During the first step, the independence relationship changes among a target's Parent and Child (PC) conditioning on the target node. The second step is a repetition of the first one, but the independence tests are conditioned on one PC node's MB set. In the third step, steps 1 and 2 are repeated aiming to identify neighboring nodes as new targets to identify more direct causes and effects of the original target (Gao & Ji, 2015).

Forward-Backward Selection with Early Dropping (FBED) presented by Borboudakis & Tsamardinos (2019) is a forward-backward method based on the theory of maximal ancestral graphs. This algorithm is called Early Dropping because during the forward stage, at each iteration, it removes those attributes that are conditionally independent of the target T, given the set of currently selected features S.

Forward–Backward with Pruning (PFBP) selects rows as well as columns (attributes and samples) based on conditional independence tests and meta-analysis techniques. This algorithm uses three heuristics to make earlier decisions, Early Dropping, Early Stopping, and Early Return. The first heuristic, Early Dropping, has already been presented. Early Stopping is a heuristic that considers the current iteration to decide whether to drop or include a feature in the selected set of variables. The Early Returning returns the current best selection of features. This algorithm makes use of p-values and log-likehoods to evaluate its earlier decisions (Tsamardinos et al., 2018).

EOMB, Efficient Oriented Markov Blanket, is a constraint-based discovery algorithm with four main steps. The Parents and Children of T are identified in the first step, which is a topology-based algorithm. The search for spouses of the target is performed during the second step, using conditional independent's tests. The relationship of potential descendants is checked in the third step, given the superset of parents. Finally, the direct effects (children) are discovered through a triangular structure between a target variable and its child variables in the fourth step. (Yang et al., 2019)

Efficient Local Causal Discovery (ELCD) is a local causal discovery algorithm that was developed from the EOMB. ELCD involves two steps: the Markov Blanket of target is learned by using EOMB and then the MB of nodes, variables, adjacent to the MB of T are discovered (Yang et al., 2019).

Table 3 presents related works based on Markov Blanket's concept to select features. These learning algorithms are presented in chronological order.

Issues, Controversies, Problems

As presented in the previous section, mostly causal feature selection algorithms are based on the Markov Blanket concept. Even though learning Markov Blanket mitigates the problem of constructing the complete Bayesian Network, there are two issues that need to be pointed out.

The first one is related to the causality relationship among the variables of the Markov Blanket of a given target. The relationship between the concept of relevance of attributes proposed by Kohavi & John (1997) and the concept of Markov Blanket is not necessarily a relation of causality, particularly if it was learned based only on the conditional distribution among variables. Considering the ladder of knowledge presented by Pearl & Mackenzie (2018) it would be the first level, in other words, level Association in which the main activity is Seeing. At this level is answered questions such as "how would seeing X change my belief in Y".

Table 3. Markov Blanket learners' algorithm

Algorithm	Summary	Authors
Grow-Shrink (GS)	This algorithm is divided into two steps: Grow and Shrink. First, it grows quickly and then shrinks and removes false positives.	(Margaritis & Thrun, 1999)
Iterative Associative Markov Blanket (IAMB)	Similar to GS, but during the growing stage, IAMB reorders the candidates' features of the MB based on updated CI testing results every time a new feature is inserted in MB.	(Tsamardinos et al., 2003)
HITONPC/MB	HITONPC is an algorithm that first discovers the parents and children (direct causes and effects) of T and parents and children and then the parents and children of direct causes and effects. Afterwards, it removes false positive features.	(Aliferis et al., 2003)
Max-Min Parents and Children/ Max Min Markov Blanket (MMPC/ MMMB)	This algorithm first searches for parents and children of T and then searches for the spouses of T in order to learn the Markov Blanket of T.	(Tsamardinos et al., 2006)
Causal Markov Blanket (CMB)	This is a local learner algorithm that identifies direct effects and causes of a target variable T based on discovering the Markov Blanket.	(Gao & Ji, 2015)
Forward-Backward Selection with Early Dropping (FBED)	This algorithm uses the forward-backward approach for selecting features. It is called Early Dropping because candidates' attributes are discarded during the forward stage at each iteration.	(Borboudakis & Tsamardinos, 2019)
Forward–Backward with Pruning (PFBP)	This algorithm uses three heuristics to make earlier decisions: Early Dropping, Early Stopping and Early Return. P-values and log-likelihoods are used to evaluate the quality of those decisions.	(Tsamardinos et al., 2018)
Efficient Oriented Markov Blanket (EOMB)	This method starts by discovering the parents and children of a target. The search for the spouses is carried out in sequence and, at the end, potential new direct effects are tested.	(Yang et al., 2019)
Efficient Local Causal Discovery (ELCD)	This is a local learner algorithm based on EOMB. This algorithm recursively learns the Markov Blanket until the Bayesian Network has been discovered in its entirety.	(Yang et al., 2019)

There is a mantra that states that there is "no causation without manipulation" (Holland, 1986 p.51). To put another way, to ensure that there is a causal relationship between two events, it is necessary to make interventions, but interventions are not normally viable due to ethics, cost, and time constraints.

The second issue is related to discarding relevant attributes. Once that grandparents (indirect causes) and siblings (consequences of causes) are not considered in the Markov Blanket. According to the concept of relevance, these features can only be weakly relevant, so they are discarded. Besides that, due to Markov Equivalence, there is a potential confusion between sibling or grandparents and parents because different types of graph's structure may satisfy the same set of dependencies and independencies. Take for instance, the conditional distribution IND(A,B|C) can result in a chain A ® C ® B or a fork A ¬ C ® B. Notice that A can be sibling or grand-parent of B.

Another misleading scenario that may lead to discard relevant variables may occur due to Simpson's paradox. Take for instance one distribution that satisfy two independence relationship, X1 DEP Y and

IND(Y,X1|X2) . In this case, the dependency relationship between X1 and Y becomes an independence relationship given a new variable, X2. The reason why the dependency relationship is vanished is the Simpson's Paradox, that states that two variables that are dependents may become independent given a third one.

Those ambiguities reported in the two last paragraphs do not allow to determine whether is a fork or chain, in other words, it is not possible to distinguish if a variable is sibling or grandparent of the target. If it is not possible to distinguish between sibling and grandparent, sibling can be, falsely, interpreted as cause. This issue of ambiguity between forks and chains (sibling and grandparent) may lead to confusion of correlation versus causation.

Another issue is that a parent may become grandparent if another variable is observed. For example, the classical example of smoking and lung cancer. If only these two variables are considered, "smoking" is a direct cause of "cancer", figure 2a. Nonetheless if a new variable "tar in lungs" is observed, smoking becomes an indirect cause of cancer as presented in figure 2b. If only Markov Blanket was taken in account, variable smoking would be considered weakly relevant and discarded.

Figure 2. Example of indirect effect

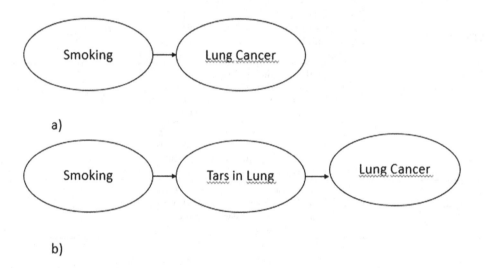

a)

b)

SOLUTIONS AND RECOMMENDATIONS

Considering the issue of discarding relevant attributes, a possible solution is not only selecting Markov Blanket of target, but also the neighbors of the direct parents and children of the target. So, in figure 2, for example, would be selected, besides the MB(T), variables B, grand parent of T, and G, sibling of T.

After selecting the subset of variables, it is necessary to discovery the true graph, the real direction of edges between nodes, and resolve the ambiguity between forks or chains, grand parents or siblings. When the true causal relationship cannot be learned only from properties of distribution, one alternative is manipulation. This manipulation can be done using do-calculus proposed by Pearl (2009) that computes the causal effect of a variable in another. Based on this causal effect, it is possible to determine the true direction of the edges between two nodes. The application of do-calculus in all variables of a dataset may have a high computational cost, but it is feasible in small subsets.

Another alternative of interventions is to compute the direct effect of a variable in another. Direct effect identifies how much one variable is sensible to changes in another one when all other features are fixed. In other words, the effect that is not mediated by other variables of the model. The direct effect can be calculated using partial correlation between features. Partial correlation of X and Y given Z, ρ_{XY-Z}. Z is a subset with all variables except X and Y, is the residual correlation of the least squares predictor of X and Y to Z. If $\rho_{XY-Z} = 0$ .implies that X and Y are independent given the subset Z. Therefore, according to the value of the partial correlation, direct effect, is possible to analyze if a relationship between two features is a causality relationship or a spurious correlation.

Applying these two solutions, increasing the number of selected features and computing the causal, or direct, effect, tends to resolve the problems highlighted in the previous section. First, because potentially relevant attributes such as indirect causes, grandparent, effects of the causes, siblings, are being be considered. Second, once that the effect of a variable in another is being computed, it is expected to disambiguate causal relationship between features.

FUTURE RESEARCH DIRECTIONS

Nowadays feature selection is a challenge for Analytics. Using causality relationship among features instead of computing pairwise correlation seems a fertile field to be researched, but there are many open problems to be addressed.

The first open problem has to do with performance. Feature selection as well as causal leaners' algorithms have high computational complexity, research that improves the performance of these methods and make them scalable are welcomed.

Another prominent area in relation to attribute selection is Online Streaming Feature Selection (OSFS). OSFS consist of selecting group of relevant features from streaming data and still have open problems such as not knowing the features in advance or streaming features in which candidate features are generated dynamically. (Xuegang et al., 2017)

Lastly, recommendations presented in the preceding section should be implemented and applied in real data and results compared with other solutions of feature selection based on the theory of causality. Carvalho & Zarate (2019) applied some those recommendations, but did not compare results.

CONCLUSION

This chapter discussed a twofold theory. First, feature selection. In order to find relevant features in a huge volume data, feature selection is an imperative preprocessing task that cannot be neglected, especially in this scenario of big dimensionality. Second, causality. Researchers have dedicated their efforts to causality and the cause and effect relationship among features. In this sense, causal feature selection can be further explored by researchers, especially because, more than just simply correlating features, it tries to explain the reasons that lead a sample to a classification.

Another point that should be highlighted is that the causality theory is aligned with data analytics. The pyramid of knowledge of causal theory (Seeing, Doing, and Imagining) can be applied to the three types of analytics: Descriptive, Predictive, and Prescriptive. Descriptive and Seeing are interrelated and represent the historical data that have been observed.

Predictive task is used to answer questions such as "what will happen in the future?" and is related to the do calculus of causal inference. Do calculus leads to interventions to make predictions from previous interventions. Prescriptive is related to the counterfactual, meaning the behavior of the model if it were made differently.

Besides that, as stated before, feature selection is a process in the preprocessing task that is critical to Business Intelligence (BI), Analytics, and Data Mining. Methods of feature selection that go beyond the simple correlation among features to identify the relevance of an attribute to target, may lead to better results in data analysis. Therefore, it may be concluded that the causal feature selection has significant contributions to make to data analysis and the preprocessing task of feature selection. It is expected that, by using causal relationship among features, the most relevant variables to a target will be discovered.

REFERENCES

Aliferis, C., Tsamardinos, I., & Statnikov, A. (2003). Hiton: A novel markov blanket algorithm for optimal variable selection. *AMIA ... Annual Symposium proceedings / AMIA Symposium. AMIA Symposium*, 21–5.

Aliferis, C. F., Statnikov, A., Tsamardinos, I., Mani, S., & Koutsoukos, X. D. (2010). Local causal and markov blanket induction for causal discovery and feature selection for classification part i: Algorithms and empirical evaluation. *Journal of Machine Learning Research*, *11*, 171–234.

Bol'on-Canedo, V., S'anchez-Maron~o, N., & Alonso-Betanzos, A. (2015). Recent advances and emerging challenges of feature selection in the context of big data. *Knowledge-Based Systems*, *86*, 33–45. doi:10.1016/j.knosys.2015.05.014

Borboudakis, G., & Tsamardinos, I. (2019). Forward-backward selection with early dropping. *Journal of Machine Learning Research*, *20*(1), 276–314.

de Carvalho, W. F., & Zarate, L. E. (2019). Causality relationship among attributes applied in an educational data set. In *Proceedings of the 34th ACM/SIGAPP Symposium on Applied Computing, SAC '19* (pp. 1271–1277). New York, NY: Association for Computing Machinery. 10.1145/3297280.3297406

Gao, T., Fadnis, K., & Campbell, M. (2017). Local-to-global Bayesian net-work structure learning. In D. Precup & Y. W. Teh (Eds.), *Proceedings of the 34th International Conference on Machine Learning*, volume 70 *of Proceedings of Machine Learning Research* (pp. 1193–1202). Sydney, Australia: PMLR.

Gao, T., & Ji, Q. (2015). Local causal discovery of direct causes and effects. In C. Cortes, N. D. Lawrence, D. D. Lee, M. Sugiyama, & R. Garnett (Eds.), Advances in Neural Information Processing Systems (Vol. 28, pp. 2512–2520). Curran Associates, Inc.

Guyon, I., & Elisseeff, A. (2008). *An Introduction to Feature Extraction*. Academic Press.

Holland, P. W., Glymour, C., & Granger, C. (1985). Statistics and causal inference. *ETS Research Report Series*, *1985*(2), i–72. doi:10.1002/j.2330-8516.1985.tb00125.x

Keogh, E., & Mueen, A. (2017). *Curse of Dimensionality*. Springer US. doi:10.1007/978-1-4899-7687-1_192

Kohavi, R., & John, G. H. (1997). Wrappers for feature subset selection. *Artificial Intelligence*, *97*(1–2), 273–324. doi:10.1016/S0004-3702(97)00043-X

Koller, D., & Sahami, M. (1996). Toward optimal feature selection. In *Proceedings of the Thirteenth International Conference on International Conference on Machine Learning, ICML'96* (pp. 284–292). San Francisco, CA: Morgan Kaufmann Publishers Inc.

Margaritis, D., & Thrun, S. (1999). Bayesian network induction via local neighborhoods. In *Proceedings of the 12th International Conference on Neural Information Processing Systems, NIPS'99* (pp. 505–511). Cambridge, MA: MIT Press.

Meek, C. (1995). Causal inference and causal explanation with background knowledge. In *Proceedings of the Eleventh Conference on Uncertainty in Artificial Intelligence, UAI'95* (pp. 403–410). San Francisco, CA: Morgan Kaufmann Publishers Inc.

Paul, M. J. (2017). Feature selection as causal inference: Experiments with text classification. In *Proceedings of the 21st Conference on Computa- tional Natural Language Learning (CoNLL 2017)* (pp. 163–172). Vancouver, Canada: Association for Computational Linguistics. 10.18653/v1/K17-1018

Pearl, J. (2009). Causality: Models, Reasoning and Inference. Cambridge University Press. doi:10.1017/CBO9780511803161

Pearl, J., & Mackenzie, D. (2018). *The Book of Why: The New Science of Cause and Effect* (1st ed.). Basic Books, Inc.

Spirtes, P., Glymour, C., & Scheines, R. (2000). *Causation* (2nd ed.). Prediction, and Search.

Triguero, I., Garcıa-Gil, D., Maillo, J., Luengo, J., Garc'ıa, S., & Herrera, F. (2019). Transforming big data into smart data: An insight on the use of the k-nearest neighbors algorithm to obtain quality data. *Wiley Interdisciplinary Reviews. Data Mining and Knowledge Discovery*, *9*(2), 9. doi:10.1002/widm.1289

Tsamardinos, I., & Aliferis, C. (2002). Towards principled feature selection: Relevancy, filters and wrappers. *Proceedings of the Ninth International Workshop on Artificial Intelligence and Statistics.*

Tsamardinos, I., Aliferis, C. F., & Statnikov, A. (2003). Time and sample efficient discovery of markov blankets and direct causal relations. *Proceedings of the Ninth ACM SIGKDD International Conference on Knowl- edge Discovery and Data Mining*, *3*, 673–678.

Tsamardinos, I., Borboudakis, G., Katsogridakis, P., Pratikakis, P., & Christophides, V. (2018). A greedy feature selection algorithm for big data of high dimensionality. *Machine Learning*, *108*. PMID:30906113

Tsamardinos, I., Brown, L., & Aliferis, C. (2006). The max-min hill-climbing bayesian network structure learning algorithm. *Machine Learning*, *65*(1), 31–78. doi:10.100710994-006-6889-7

Xuegang, H., Zhou, P., Li, P., Wang, J., & Wu, X. (2017). A survey on online feature selection with streaming features. *Frontiers of Computer Science*, 1–15.

Yang, S., Wang, H., & Hu, X. (2019). *Efficient local causal discovery based on Markov blanket*. Academic Press.

ADDITIONAL READING

Glymour, C., Zhang, K., & Spirtes, P. (2019). Review of causal discovery methods based on graphical models. *Frontiers in Genetics*, *10*, 524. doi:10.3389/fgene.2019.00524 PMID:31214249

Sun, Y., Todorovic, S., & Goodison, S. (2010). Local-learning-based feature selection for high-dimensional data analysis. *IEEE Transactions on Pattern Analysis and Machine Intelligence*, *32*(9), 1610–1626. doi:10.1109/TPAMI.2009.190 PMID:20634556

Talvitie, T., Eggeling, R., & Koivisto, M. (2019). Learning bayesian net- works with local structure, mixed variables, and exact algorithms. *International Journal of Approximate Reasoning*, *115*, 69–95. doi:10.1016/j.ijar.2019.09.002

Tsagris, M., & Tsamardinos, I. (2019). Feature selection with the r package mxm. *F1000 Research*, *7*, 1505. doi:10.12688/f1000research.16216.2 PMID:31656581

Yang, J., Li, L., & Wang, A. (2011). A partial correlation-based bayesian network structure learning algorithm under linear sem. *Knowledge-Based Systems*, *24*(7), 963–976. doi:10.1016/j.knosys.2011.04.005

KEY TERMS AND DEFINITIONS

Causal Effect: Given two variables X and Y, causal effect of X on Y can be summarized as a function from X to the probability distribution of Y.

Curse of Dimensionality: Refers to the problem when analyzing data in high dimensional space that does not occur in low dimensional.

Direct Effect: Given two variables X and Y, direct effect measures how sensible Y is in relation to X when other variables of the model are fixed.

Feature Selection: A task in the preprocessing stage that aims to select the most relevant subset of features given a target.

Global Learning: It is an approach that learn Bayesian Network searching the whole DAG space, using all variables.

Local Learning: It is an approach that learn Bayesian Network limiting the DAG space to some variables that are potential candidates for local structures such as Markov Blanket or Parents and Children of a given target.

Markov Blanket: In a graph, Markov Blanket is a subset of features that includes parents, children and spouses of a specific node.

Markovian Parents: In a graph, given a variable X represented by a node, Markovian Parents is a subset of predecessor's variables, nodes, that renders X.

Neighborhood: In graph theory, the neighborhood of a vertex V is the subgraph composed of all vertices adjacent to V.

Chapter 8
K–Nearest Neighbors Algorithm (KNN):
An Approach to Detect Illicit Transaction in the Bitcoin Network

Abdelaziz Elbaghdadi
Abdelmalek Essaadi University, Morocco

Soufiane Mezroui
Abdelmalek Essaadi University, Morocco

Ahmed El Oualkadi
iD https://orcid.org/0000-0002-4953-1000
Abdelmalek Essaadi University, Morocco

ABSTRACT

The cryptocurrency is the first implementation of blockchain technology. This technology provides a set of tracks and innovation in scientific research, such as use of data either to detect anomalies either to predict price in the Bitcoin and the Ethereum. Furthermore, the blockchain technology provide a set of technique to automate the business process. This chapter presents a review of some research works related to cryptocurrency. A model with a KNN algorithm is proposed to detect illicit transaction. The proposed model uses both the elliptic dataset and KNN algorithm to detect illicit transaction. Furthermore, the elliptic dataset contains 203,769 nodes and 234,355 edges; it allows to classify the data into three classes: illicit, licit, or unknown. Each node has associated 166 features. The first 94 features represent local information about the transaction. The remaining 72 features are called aggregated features. The accuracy exceeded 90% with k=2 and k=4, the recall reaches 56% with k=3, and the precision reaches 78% with k=4.

DOI: 10.4018/978-1-7998-5781-5.ch008

I. INTRODUCTION

New Technologies are created to spur financial innovation and improve the financial inclusion. These technologies deviate to their main goals and give a new opportunity for criminals and terrorists to launder their proceeds or their illicit activities. The Financial Action Task Force international standards combating money laundering and the financing of terrorism members in 2012 adopted their standards to monitor the risks relating to new technology. In 2014, the Financial Action Task Force (FATF) published virtual currency key definitions and potential AML /CFT Risks regarding the revolution of the cryptocurrency and their mechanisms associated with payment for giving a new method for transmitting values over the internet.

The FATF defines cryptocurrency as a decentralized convertible virtual currency protected by cryptography. The FATF discover and analyze the concrete action taken by criminals to launder incriminated funds through cryptocurrencies, they offer recommendations for compliance officers and companies that deal with cryptocurrencies.

Today, data analysis can be used to detect the anomalies or predict the future results with the help of data in the different fields. Furthermore, others issues should be solved with data analysis in the cryptocurrencies such as the influence of the distance used in the performance of k-Nearest Neighbors (KNN) model and how to use deep learning methods to evaluate precision, recall, F1 and accuracy for this task. The aim of this study is the detection of illicit transaction with KNN algorithm using Elliptic dataset. Furthermore, the blockchain technology uses it for a set field such as Business Intelligence, this technology gives a set technique such as smart contract to automate the processes in the enterprise without a central authority.

The rest of this chapter is organized as follows. The related works in cryptocurrency are presented in section II. In the third section, the Bitcoin and Ethereum network overview are described. In the fourth section, the machine learning technique is described. The fifth section presents the proposed methodology in this study. In the sixth section, the obtained results are discussed. Finally, the conclusion is given.

II. RELATED WORKS

The blockchain technology creates potential innovations in the processing of the business activities in various sectors, which makes this technology face to a set of attacks and illicit activity. This section reviews some related work which target cryptocurrency, such as anomaly detection, data analysis and business intelligence

1. Detection of Fraud and Anomalies in Cryptocurrency

The openness is one of the main characteristics of the Bitcoin network. This technology is open to public at any time. In addition, the public key of the bitcoin is a 160 bits hash generated by the secp256k1 curve (Antonopoulos M. Andreas, 2014) (Joppe W. Bos and al, 2014).This address can change often (Antonopoulos M. Andreas, 2014), and this propriety removes the possibility to identify the Bitcoin users via the public key. This still removes the possibility of tracking identity by analyzing the use of public keys on the network. However the address bitcoin is the main identifier to make a transaction and any one can stipulate that if two addresses (public key) are used as entries in the same transaction, then the same user controls these public keys (Sarah Meiklejohn and al. 2013), For that reason the structure, form a Directed Acyclic Graph (DAG) can be used as technical analysis of transactions. Reid and Harrigan propose a method for breaking the bitcoin system in to DAGs, as part of their research on Bitcoin anonymity, they first developed a user graph that represents the flow of Bitcoin between users over time ((Reid and Harrigan 2013). Furthermore, K-means and Role Extraction are used to identify users who make the transactions typically associated with money laundering. Fifteen features are extracted using all transactions having a minimum of 650 transactions in the network. (Reid Fergal, and Martin Harrigan, 2012).

The researchers and the blockchain enthusiasts notice that, since their launch, blockchain has been implemented in the different fields such as cryptocurrency, IOT (Internet of things) and finance. The utility of this technology can be deviate to the original goal such as money laundering and illicit activity. That is why many of research papers target this technology such frauds and anomalies detection and identification of Bitcoin users etc. Zambre and al attempted to distinguish between normal users and malicious users based on real reported cases (Zambre, Deepak, and Ajey Shah 2013). Monamo and al use trimmed k-means clustering for anomaly detection (Monamo, Patrick, Vukosi Marivate, and Bheki Twala, 2016). To analyze the behavior patterns of user and transactions Pham and al use two types of graphs. Consequently, they detected three of the 30 known cases (Pham Thai, and Steven Lee, 2016). In addition, these authors have obtained similar results using k-means clustering Local Outlier Factor and power degree and densification in their subsequent study (Pham Thai, and Steven Lee, 2016). Yining Hu and al have created a transaction graph using data differentiate between laundering and regular transaction lies in their output value and neighborhood information (Yining Hu and al, 2019). Furthermore, Mark Weber and al use the elliptic data set to classify illicit and licit transaction (M. Weber and al, 2019). They used the variations of Logistic Regression (LR), Random Forest, Multilayer perceptron, and Graph convolutional networks (GCN) which is an emerging new method of capture relational information. Mark Weber and al share experimental results using a set of methods, from standard classification techniques (Logistic Regression, Random Forest, and Multilayer Perceptron) to the more sophisticated Graph Convolutional Networks. Important conclusions can be drawn from this work, including that: the Random Forest is figured as the best classification model for this problem. In addition, GCN are not the best performing models but is an interesting finding.

Moreover, a lot of the research works have been done based on others cryptocurrency such as Ethereum and Monero etc. A deep learning approach is proposed to detect DDos (Distributed Denial of Service) attack in the Bitcoin ecosystem (Ui-Jun Baek and al, 2019). In 2020, Abdelaziz and al have discussed the untraceability and unlinkability and describe how this cryptocurrency works and have presented some attacks against this technology (Abdelaziz, Soufiane, and Ahmed, 2020). Furthermore, the illicit activity has targeted as well the Ethereum blockchain, through the identification of Ponzi schemas deployed as a smart contract. In 2019, Chen and al classify the account with the help of the operation code using unsupervised learning, the interesting finding is the Random Forest has possibility to classify 305 out of 394 identified smart-Ponzi schemes (Chen Weili and al, 2019). To detect illicit the fraudulent activity on the blockchain Ethereum network. OKane examines the transactions enacted by scams available on Etherscamdb database along with token and exchange addresses using a set of algorithms as the following: principal component analysis, random forest and K-means (O'Kane 2018). Steven Farrugia and al propose an approach to identify the illicit accounts on the Ethereum blockchain, this study uses an XGBoost classifier which 42 features as input, which XGBoost is an open source software allowing to implement Gradient boosting methods in both R and Python programming languages (Farrugia, Steven,

Joshua Ellul, and George Azzopardi, 2020. The XGBoost was attained a mean accuracy of 0.963 ($\pm$ 0.006) with a mean AUC (Area Under the ROC curve) of 0.994 ($\pm$ 0.0007).

2. Data Analysis in Cryptoccurency and Business Intelligence Using Blockchain

Several related work uses the data either to predict the price or to trade digital currencies. A supervise learning algorithms such as logistic regression, Naive Bayes Theory and SVM have used to identify cryptocurrency market (Colianni Stuart, Stephanie Rosales, and Michael Signorotti, 2015). A linear model and sentiment analysis have been used to predict price both in the Ethereum and bitcoin cryptocurrencies (Abraham, Jethin; Higdon, Daniel; Nelson, John; and Ibarra, Juan 2018). Israa and al have analyzed the evolution of the entire bitcoin transaction graph with the help of data analysis (Israa Alqassem, Iyad Rahwan, and Davor Svetinovic, December 2018). Jingming and al. have achieved a study using data of Monero cryptocurrency and discussed the potentials of the blockchain in the energy industry. The obtained result of this study have shown the electricity consumption of the Monero mining (Jingming Li Nianping Li Jinqing Peng Haijiao Cui Zhibin Wu November, 2018). Salim Lahmiri and al have used deep learning algorithm to predict the price of bitcoin, Digital cash and Ripple cryptocurrencies (Salim Lahmiri, Stelios Bekiros, 2019).

In 2016, Ingo Weber and al have developed a technique to integrate blockchain into the choreography of processes without central authority (Ingo Weber, Xiwei Xu, Régis Riveret, Guido Governatori, Alexander Ponomarev, Jan Mendling, 2016). A block chain-based framework is proposed as well as the use of smart contract to derive the possible advantage of the supply chain process design. The authors have provided a workable use case for business process disintermediation (Shuchih Ernest Chang, Yi-Chian Chen, and Ming-Fang Lu, 2018). Melanie Swan have discussed Blockchain distributed ledgers in the context of public and private Blockchains (Melanie Swan, 2018). Daniel E and O'Leary have investigated some of the implications and strategies that include the use of that open information. (Daniel E. O'Leary, 2018).

3. Summary

The blockchain technology offers a set of tracks in the scientific research as mentioned previously. The table 1 shows a review of some related work which target this topic.

III. THE BITCOIN AND ETHEREUM NETWORK OVERVIEW

The Merkle Trees was incorporated into the design of the concept of the cryptography to verify the integrity of a set of data without necessarily having all of them at the time (Vujičić, Jagodić, and Randjić 2018). Furthermore, a system to secure the chain of blocks with the help of the cryptography technique that signify time-stamp a digital document are developed (Bralić, Stančić, and Stengard, 2020). The Proof of Work (PoW) has been proposed as a prototype for digital cash to solve the double-spending problem (A. Meneghetti, M. Sala, D Taufer, 2020). Moreover, in 2008 Satoshi Nakamoto conceptualized the theory of distributed blockchains, he has developed a design in a unique way to add blocks to the initial chain without requiring them to be signed by trusted parties(S. Nakamoto, 2008). The Bitcoin

Table 1. A review of some related works.

Cryptocurencies		
Bitcoin	**Monero**	**Ethereum**
✓ DDos attack detection in bitcoin Ecosystem with help of data analysis ✓ Anomalies Detection (Identify the bitcoin users, Illicit Transaction detection in the bitcoin Network, Money laundering etc.) ✓ Predict the Price of the Bitcoin cryptoccurency with help of data and sentiment analysis	✓ Untraceability and linkability in Monero Cryptocurrency using Data analysis ✓ Electricity consumption of the Monero mining	✓ Detection illicit Activity in the blockchain Ethereum ✓ Predict the Price of the Ethereum ✓ Trading in the cryptocurrency ✓ identify cryptocurrency market
Business intelligence using the Blockchain		
✓ use the blockchain Technology for business process (smart contract as example)		

is a set of the concept and technologies forms the base of the digital currency ecosystem, it is used to retain and transmit value between the participants in the Bitcoin network (Reid and Harrigan, 2013).

The Bitcoin network users communicate between each other using the Bitcoin protocol mainly via the internet. The Bitcoin users can transfer the Bitcoin in the network to do everything that can be done with traditional currency, buy or sell goods and services, send money to individuals or organization, or provide credit. To ensure the security in the network, the Bitcoin technologies includes functionalities that are based on encryption and digital signatures. The Bitcoins can be bought, sold and exchanged for other currencies on specialized exchanges. The Bitcoin is in a sense the perfect form of currency for the internet as it is fast, secure (Antonopoulos M. Andreas, 2014).

Contrary to traditional currencies, the Bitcoins are virtual. There is no physical coin or even a digital coin. The coins are included in the transactions transmitting the value from sender to receiver. The Bitcoin users have keys that prove ownership of transactions on the Bitcoin network and unlock the value to spend and transfer it to another recipient. These keys are often stored in a digital wallet on each user's computer. The possession of a key to unlock a transaction is the only prerequisite for spending Bitcoins, so this system gives users complete control. The Bitcoin is a fully distributed pair-to-pair system. Then, there is no server or point of control. The Bitcoins are created through a process called "mining", which involves finding the solution to a problem that is difficult to solve. Any participant in the Bitcoin network (i.e., any computer operating the complete Bitcoin stack) can act as a minor, using the computing power it has at its disposal to solve the problem. Every 10 minutes on average, a new solution is found by someone who is then able to validate the transactions in the last 10 minutes. In summary, the Bitcoin mining decentralizes the issuance of money and reconciliation procedures, making the intervention of an agency similar to central banks unnecessary. The Bitcoin protocol includes predefined algorithms that regulate the mining function on the network. The difficulty of the miner's task execution to record a block of transaction on the Bitcoin network is adjusted so that on average someone gets there every 10 minutes, regardless of the number of miners (and CPUs) working on this task at time t. The protocol halves the number of Bitcoins created every four years and limits the total number of Bitcoins issued to a total of 21 million pieces. Seen as its speed of issuance declines, over the long term, the Bitcoin currency is deflationary. The Bitcoin cannot be artificially inflated by generating money beyond the rate of emission expected. The Bitcoin is also the name of a protocol, a network, and an innovation in distributed computing. Bitcoin as a currency is really only the first application of this invention (Antonopoulos M. Andreas, 2014) (Du Mingxiao, Ma Xiaofeng, Zhang Zhe, Wang Xiangwei, Chen Qijun, 2017).

Figure 1. The 51% attack scheme

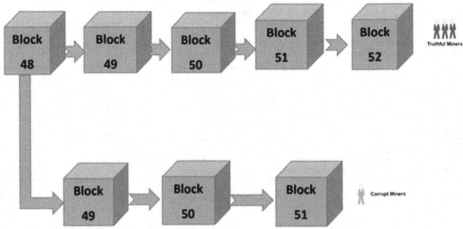

As mentioned previously, the Bitcoin has been invented in 2008 with the publication entitled "Bitcoin: A peer to peer electronic cash system" written under the pseudonym Satochi Nakamato which has combined a set of previous inventions such as b-money and hashcash system. To create a cryptocurrency not relying to any central authority for the transmission of money or the regulation. Furthermore, the main innovation has been the use of a distributed computing system (called algorithm « Proof of work ») realizing "election" every 10 minutes, allowing the decentralized network to arrive at a consensus on the status of transactions, that solves the problem of double spending or a unit of currency cannot be spent twice. Previously, the problem of double spending was a weakness of digital currency and was resolved by having all transactions verified by a clearing organization (Antonopoulos M. Andreas, 2014).

The Bitcoin network started in 2009 based on the paper published by Satochi Nakamato. The distributed computing which provides the security and resistance to Bitcoin has grown exponentially. The identity of the person or group of people behind the creation of Bitcoin is not known to this day. However, either Satoshi Nakamoto or anyone else has any control over the Bitcoin system, which operates only according to fully transparent mathematical principles (Antonopoulos M. Andreas, 2014) (Eyal and Sirer, 2014). In the literature, a set of attack target the blockchain technology has been proposed. The 51% or double spending attack is one of the famous attacks in the Bitcoin network. The miner or a group of the miner testing to spend their transactions on the blockchain twice. In this scenario of attack, the attacker can prevent new transactions from taking place or being confirmed. The attacker has the possibility to block a new transaction from taking place or to be confirmed. Furthermore the attacker able to reverse the transactions that have already validated (Martijn Bastiaan, 2015). When anyone (miner) valid a block of the transactions, the block will broadcast to anther miner on the network. The block can only be accepted if all transaction in the block are valid based on the available recording on a blockchain. However, the attacker with more than 50 Percent of a network's hash rate does not broadcast solutions to the rest of the network. The first version of the block is the public version of the blockchain which is being followed by legal miners. The second is used by the attacker who are not broadcasting it to the rest of the network. Figure 1 shows the 51% attack operation. The 51 Percent attack is one of theory attack because the attacker needs more than 50 percent of the computing power of the entire network.

A Sybil attack occurs when a large number of nodes on a network belonging to the same party try to cause disruption to the business (Eyal and Sirer 2014) . In order to be able to create major disruptions, they will, for example, try to create a large number of fake transactions or simply manipulate the relay handling the real transactions. This type of attack occurs mainly in reputation systems. It generally disrupts them by creating false identities. This most often happens in a P2P type computer network. The Sybil attack targets the peer-to-peer network (Eyal and Sirer 2014). A hacker wants to make this attack on the Bitcoin network. In this case, the several identities at the same time and undermines the authority of the reputation system are exploited in the network by a node. Its primary objective is to obtain the majority of the influence in the network to carry out illegal actions in the system. Furthermore, the Sybil attack is not easy to detect and prevent, but the following measures may be helpful:

- Increasing the cost of creating a new identity.
- Joining the network requires validation of identities or trust.
- Making different power to different members.

The second famous blockchain is Ethereum which are invented by Vitalik Buterin in 2014, this cryptocurrency described as "the world computer". Moreover, Ethereum is an open source, decentralized computing infrastructure that executes programs called smart contracts. A blockchain is used to synchronize and store the system state changes, as well as a cryptocurrency called "ether" to measure and limit the cost of execution resources (Wood Gavin, 2014).

The Ethereum platform allows developers to build strong decentralized applications with integrated economic functions. This Technology provides high availability, transparency, auditability and neutrality. Furthermore, it reduces or eliminates supervision and minimizes certain counterparty risks. The Ethereum has a lot of common features with other blockchains such as:

- A peer-to-peer network between the participants.
- To synchronization of state updates a Byzantine fault–tolerant consensus algorithm is used.
- The cryptographic primitives such as digital signatures and hashes, and a digital currency are used

The blockchain Ethereum uses the proof of stake (PoS) to validate each block, however, the Bitcoin uses the PoW. These two methods allow the creation of new blocks of a blockchain. These blocks contain the transactions performed. There are many differences between PoS and PoW. The PoS is a method that allows to record, validate transactions in blocks. For this, a person must have a certain number of tokens of a crypto-money. This method also allows the creation of new blocks but in a different way. To do this, users will make available the computing power of their machines. The latter will have to solve

Table 2. Different features between PoW and PoS

Type of methods	Use of resources	Degree of decentralization	Speed of transactions	Transaction fees
PoW	Very strong	low	slow	Quite high
PoS	Low	High Fairly	high	Low

more and more difficult mathematical calculations (Antonopoulos M. Andreas and Gavin Wood, 2018). Table 2 shows the difference between Ethereum and blockchain.

Both methods allow the same thing, i.e. the creation and validation of blocks in a blockchain. Each method has advantages and drawbacks. One of the big advantages of PoS is the energy gain. There is no need to spend astronomical amounts of electricity to validate transactions and enter them into the block chain. One of the big advantages of PoW is the security of the transactions as they all have to be validated by the miners.

The disadvantages of PoW are as the following:

- Requires very powerful equipment that is only owned by a minority of companies, which favours centralization
- Huge energy costs
- High transaction costs if the network begins to saturate

The disadvantages of PoS are as the follows (Saleh Fahad, 2020):

- Less secure than PoW
- Early investors have a big advantage
- Little use of token

IV. MACHINE LEARNING TECHNIQUE

Machine learning is a field of the artificial intelligence which is based on mathematical and statistical approaches to give computers the ability to "learn" from the data, i.e. to improve their performance in solving tasks without being explicitly programmed for each one. The machine learning algorithms can be categorized according to the learning mode used. The first category if the classes are predetermined and the examples are labelled, the system learns to classify according to a classification or grading model; this is called supervised learning (Mohamed Alloghani and al. 2020). However, when the system or operator has only sampled, but no label, and the number of classes and their nature has not been predetermined, this is called unsupervised learning or clustering. No experts are required. The algorithm must discover by itself the more or less hidden structure of the data. Data clustering is an unsupervised learning algorithm (Mohamed Alloghani and al, 2020). The Semi-supervised learning is a class of machine learning techniques that uses a set of labelled and unlabelled data. It is thus situated between supervised learning, which uses only labelled data, and unsupervised learning, which uses only unlabelled data. The use of untagged data, in combination with tagged data, has been shown to significantly improve the quality of learning (V. Engelen, E. Jesper, and H. Hoos, 2020). Furthermore, Machine learning solves two problems such as regression problem or classification problem which the first is used in order to predict a value and the second is used in order to predict a class(Mohamed Alloghani and al. 2020).

In the literature, a set of algorithms used to solve the different problems of machine learning has been proposed (J Qiu, Q Wu, G Ding, Y Xu, S Feng. 2016). The K-means is an algorithm for clustering the data. Furthermore, this algorithm belongs to unsupervised learning. This clustering algorithm is used to identify groups of observations with similar characteristics. Mathematically, given a set of points $(x_1,\ldots,x_n)$, one must try to divide the n points into k sets such as:

$$S = (S_1,\ldots,S_k)(\text{k} \leq \text{n}) \tag{1}$$

by minimizing the distance between the points and the center of the group or class, $\arg_s \min \sum_{i=1}^{k} \sum_{x_j \in S_i} \| x_j - \mu_i \|^2$ where μ_i is the centroid of the points in S_i and x_j is a point in S_i (Liu, Zhiguo, Changqing Ren, and Wenzhu Cai, 2020).

The Random Forest is a classification algorithm that reduces the variance of forecasts in a decision tree alone, thereby improving performance. It does this by combining multiple decision trees in a bagging approach. The random forest algorithm is proposed by L. Breiman. In its most classical formula, it performs parallel learning on multiple randomly constructed decision trees trained on different subsets of data. The ideal number of trees, which can be several hundred or more, is an important parameter: it is highly variable and depends on the problem(M. Schonlau, and R. Yuyan Zou, 2020). Logistic regression is a predictive technique. It aims to build a model to predict/explain the values taken by a qualitative target variable (most often binary, this is called binary logistic regression; if it has more than two modalities, it is called polytomous logistic regression) from a set of quantitative or qualitative explanatory variables (coding is necessary in this case) (Kuha Jouni, and Colin Mills, 2020). In machine learning, a convolutional neural network (CNN) is a type of acyclic artificial neural network, in which the connection pattern between neurons is inspired by the visual cortex of animals. The neurons in this region of the brain are arranged so that they correspond to overlapping regions when the visual field is paved. Their functioning is inspired by biological processes, they consist of a multi-layered stack of perceptrons, the purpose of which is to pre-process small amounts of information (Irfan Aziz, 2020). Furthermore, one of the machine learning technique for regression and classification problems is Gradient boosting which is used to calculate the weights of individuals when the construction of each new model. The gradient boosting can be considered as an optimization algorithm (Haihao Lu, Sai Praneeth Karimireddy, Natalia Ponomareva and Vahab Mirrokni, 2020).

A set of technique and metrics are used to evaluate the quality of prediction model (Qiu et al. 2016). Confusion matrix or contingency table is used to evaluate the quality of a classification. It is obtained by comparing the classified data with reference data, which must be different from those used for classification. This matrix is used to calculate a set of metrics such as precision, Recall and accuracy. To evaluate the proposed model, four evaluation metrics are used: Precision, Recall, accuracy and F1 Score. To see if the predictions are right or wrong the metrics using are defined in terms of true and false positives. These metrics are defined by:

- TN / True Negative: The case was negative but predicted negative.
- TP / True Positive: The case was positive but predicted positive.
- FN / False Negative: The case was positive and predicted negative.
- FP / False Positive: The case was negative and predicted positive.

Various metrics are used for this evaluation test. The first metric is precision which is defined as the report of correctly predicted positive observations to the total predicted positive observations. This metric is calculated by

$$\Pr ecision = \frac{TP}{TP+FP} \tag{2}$$

The second metric is Recall which is defined as the report gives the proportion of positive identifications was corrected and calculated by

$$\text{Re} \, call = \frac{TP}{TP+TN} \tag{3}$$

The third metric is the F-score which is defined as a compromise of accuracy and recall giving the performance of the system. This compromise is given in a simple way by the harmonic mean of accuracy and recall. The formula is calculated by

$$F1 = \frac{2 * precision * \text{Re} \, call}{precision + \text{Re} \, call} \tag{4}$$

The accuracy is the fourth metric which is defined as one of the criteria for evaluating classification models. Informally, the accuracy refers to the proportion of correct predictions made up by the model. Formally, accuracy is defined by

$$Accuracy = \frac{TP+TN}{TP+FN+TN+FP} \tag{5}$$

V. METHODOLOGY

The proposed approach uses both the Elliptic dataset and the KNN algorithm to detect illicit transaction. In this study, a model is developed by using the KNN algorithm and implemented in python. The dataset Elliptic is used to test the proposed model as shown in figure 2.

To test the performance of the proposed model, 25% of data is used and 75% for the training module. The Elliptic dataset contains 203,769 nodes and 234,355 edges as detailed in the next section. The feature scaling phase is used to normalize the range of independent variables or features of data.

Figure 2. Detection Model using KNN algorithm and Elliptic dataset.

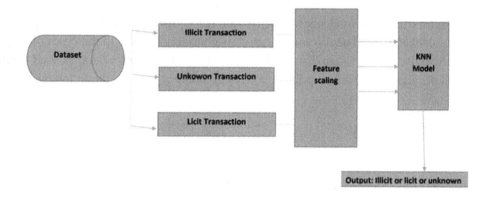

VI. ELLIPTIC DATASET OVERVIEW

The Elliptic dataset is a sup-graph of the Bitcoin data that contains 203.769 nodes and 234.355 edges, their use is to classify the data into three classes: illicit, licit or unknown .The transaction is licit if has been created by one entity belongs to exchanges, wallet providers, miners, financial service providers, etc. However, the transaction is illicit if has been created by one of the entities belong to scams, malware, terrorist organizations, ransom ware, Ponzi schemes, etc. No indication is provided on the other nodes which are classified as "unknown". Each node has associated to 166 features including number of inputs, number of the outputs, transaction fee, average number of incoming transactions etc. The first 94 features represent local information about the transaction The remaining 72 features, called aggregated features, are obtained by aggregating transaction (Mark Weber and al, 2019). In this study 165 features are used (time step feature is excluded)

Figure 3. Distance between two points

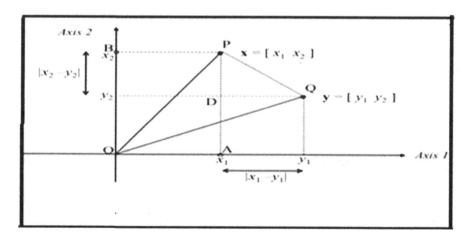

1. Euclidian Distance

Several functions are used to distance calculation such as Manhattan distance, Minkowski distance, Jaccard distance, Hamming distance, etc. The distance function is chosen according to the types of data being manipulated. In this study, the Euclidian distance between two points or two vectors is used (Figure 3).

To calculate the distance between two points P=(x1, x2) and Q= (y1, y2), the following equation is used:

$$d(Q,\mathrm{P}) = \sqrt{(x_1 - y_1)^2 + (x_1 - y_1)^2} \qquad (6)$$

For n-dimensional space, the distance Euclidian is calculated by:

$$d(Q,\mathrm{P}) = \sqrt{\sum_{i=1}^{n}(\mathrm{x}_i - y_i)^2} \qquad (7)$$

Such that P and Q has n input (parameters).

2. Principle of KNN Algorithm

The KNN algorithm is a supervised learning method which can be used in the regression and classification problems. These operations can be likened to the following analogy "tell me who your neighbors are, I'll tell you who you are". Therefore, to make a prediction, the KNN algorithm will base itself on the entire dataset. Indeed, for an observation, which is not part of the dataset that we want to predict, the algorithm will look for the K instances of the dataset closest to our observation. Then for these K neighbors, the algorithm will use their output variable y. Then, for K neighbors, the algorithm will use their output to calculate the value of the variable y of the observation you wish to predict. In addition, if KNN is used for the regression, it is the mean (or median) of the y variables of the K closest observations that will be used for the prediction. However, if KNN is used for classification, the mode of the variables y of the closest K observations will be used for prediction.

The steps of the KNN algorithm are described in Figure 4. This algorithm has a data set D, a distance function d, and an integer K (Number of neighbors) as an input. For a new observation X and to predict the output variable y, the algorithm should follow steps in the figure 4.

In relation to illicit transaction in the Bitcoin network problem, a transaction is considered as a vector with n parameters. Furthermore, each transaction is characterized by 165 features such that $T = (x_1,\ldots,x_{165})$, and the main aim is to predict to which class the transaction belongs: Illicit or licit or unknown.

VII. RESULTS AND DISCUSSION

As mentioned previously, a confusion matrix is used to test the performance of the classification model. Table 3 shows a confusion matrix for various values of k (k=2, k=3, K=4, K=5, and K=20).

Figure 4. Steps of KNN algorithm

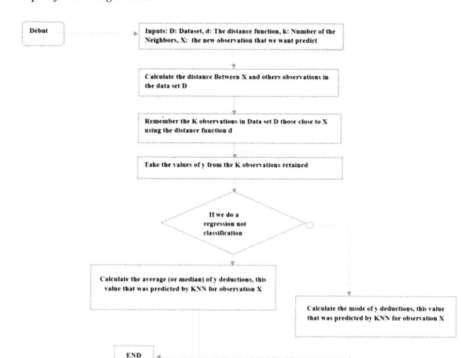

For k=2, 573 cases belong to illicit class and predict as unknown class, 546 cases belong to illicit and predict by the KNN model as illicit transaction and 21 case belong to illicit but predict as licit transaction. For k=3, 455 cases belong to illicit class and predict as unknown class, 645 cases belong to illicit and predict by the KNN model as illicit transaction and 40 case belong to illicit but predict as licit transaction. For k=4, 542 cases belong to illicit class and predict as unknown class, 564 cases belong to illicit and predict by the KNN model as illicit transaction and 34 case belong to illicit but predict as licit transaction. For k=5, 469 cases belong to illicit class and predict as unknown class, 631 cases belong to illicit and predict by the KNN model as illicit transaction and 40 case belong to illicit but predict as licit transaction. For k=20, 583 cases belong to illicit class and predict as unknown class, 524 cases belong to illicit and predict by the KNN model as illicit transaction and 33 case belong to illicit but predict as licit transaction.

In order to evaluate the proposed model and to find the best k value for the proposed system prediction, various k (k=2, k=3, K=4, K=5, and K=20) are used to calculate some metrics for each case. Table 4 shows the obtained results for various values of K and Euclidean distances.

The precision measures the percentage of the transaction identified as illicit that have been classified correctly. The precision reaches (74%, 29%, 78%, 71%, and 70%) with various k (k=2, k=3, k=4, k=5, k=20) respectively. The recall measures the percentage of actual illicit transactions that were classified correctly. The recall reaches (48%, 56%, 49%, 55%, and 46%) with various k (k=2, k=3, k=4, k=5, k=20) respectively. The accuracy is one of the criteria for evaluating classification models. The accuracy refers to the proportion of correct predictions made by the model. The accuracy measure reaches (89.62%, 89.91%, 90.08%, 90.09%, and 89.38%) with various k (k=2, k=3, k=4, k=5, k=20) respectively.

Table 3. Confusion matrix for each case

K=2			
	Unknown	**Illicit**	**Licit**
Unknown	38471	136	622
Illicit	573	546	21
Licit	3874	58	6642
	K=3		
	Unknown	Illicit	Licit
Unknown	37710	257	1262
Illicit	455	645	40
Licit	3104	18	7452
	K=4		
	Unknown	Illicit	Licit
Unknown	38395	154	680
Illicit	542	564	34
Licit	3619	24	6931
	K=5		
	Unknown	Illicit	Licit
Unknown	37981	240	1008
Illicit	469	631	40
Licit	3272	18	7284
	K=20		
	Unknown	Illicit	Licit
Unknown	38330	212	687
Illicit	583	524	33
Licit	3901	8	6665

Table 4. Obtained results for various k and Euclidean distances.

Metrics Value of K	Recall	Precision	F1	Accuracy
K=2	0.48	0.74	0.58	0.8962
K=3	0.56	0.29	0.38	0.8991
K=4	0.49	0.78	0.6	0.9008
K=5	0.55	0.71	0.62	0.9009
K=20	0.46	0.7	0.55	0.8938

VIII. CONCLUSION

Data analysis is important for detecting and predicting outcomes, for example, it can be used to detect anomalies or predict the future prices of cryptocurrencies such as Bitcoin, Ethereum, etc. This chapter reviews some issues in the cryptocurrency such as data analysis and business intelligence in the blockchain technology and proposes some solutions related to these issues. Moreover, the chapter proposes a model to detect an illicit transaction in Bitcoin cryptocurrency. This detection model uses Elliptic Dataset as reference and dives this dataset to both test and training models. The model is tested with same random value of neighbored and Euclidian distance. The evaluation of the proposed model is based on calculation of some metrics to evaluate KNN model such as precision, recall and F1 score.

The obtained results are very interesting. The accuracy exceeded the 90% with k=2 and k=4, the recall reaches 56% with k=3 and the precision reaches the 78% with k=4. In the next work, others issues should be solved such as: the influence of the distance used in the performance of KNN model and the comparison of this KNN approach with machine learning algorithms (SVM, Logistic Regression, Linear regression, Random Forest…) to shows how to use deep learning methods to evaluate precision, recall, F1 and accuracy for this task.

REFERENCES

Abdelaziz, E., Soufiane, M., & Ahmed, E. (2020). Survey of Monero Security. Dynamical and Control Systems, 12, 88-93.

Alloghani, M., Al-Jumeily, D., Mustafina, J., Hussain, A., & Aljaaf, A. J. (2020). A Systematic Review on Supervised and Unsupervised Machine Learning Algorithms for Data Science. In Supervised and Unsupervised Learning for Data Science. Springer. doi:10.1007/978-3-030-22475-2_1

Andreas, A. M. (2014). *Mastering Bitcoin: Unlocking Digital Cryptocurrencies*. O'Reilly Media, Inc.

Andreas, A. M., & Wood, G. (2018). *Mastering Ethereum: Building Smart Contracts and Dapps*. O'reilly Media.

Aziz, I. (2020). *Deep Learning: An Overview of Convolutional Neural Network*. CNN.

Baek, U.-J., Ji, S.-H., Park, J. T., Lee, M.-S., Park, J.-S., & Kim, M.-S. (2019). *DDoS Attack Detection on Bitcoin Ecosystem Using Deep-Learning*. IEEE Conference Publication. https://ieeexplore.ieee.org/abstract/document/8892837

Bastiaan, M. (2015). *Preventing the 51%-Attack: A Stochastic Analysis of Two Phase Proof of Work in Bitcoin*. Http://Referaat. Cs. Utwente. Nl/Conference/22/Paper/7473/Preventingthe-51-Attack-a-Stochasticanalysis-Oftwo-Phase-Proof-of-Work-in-Bitcoin.Pdf

Bos, Halderman, Heninger, Moore, Naehrig, & Wustrow. (2014). Elliptic Curve Cryptography in Practice. In *International Conference on Financial Cryptography and Data Security*. Springer.

Bralić, V., Stančić, H., & Stengard, M. (2020). A Blockchain Approach to Digital Archiving: Digital Signature Certification Chain Preservation. *Records Management Journal*, *ahead-of-print*(ahead-of-print). Advance online publication. doi:10.1108/RMJ-08-2019-0043

Chang, S. E., Chen, Y. C., & Lu, M. F. (2019). Supply Chain Re-Engineering Using Blockchain Technology: A Case of Smart Contract Based Tracking Process. *Technological Forecasting and Social Change*, *144*, 1–11. doi:10.1016/j.techfore.2019.03.015

Chen, W., Zheng, Z., Ngai, E. C.-H., Zheng, P., & Zhou, Y. (2019). Exploiting Blockchain Data to Detect Smart Ponzi Schemes on Ethereum. *IEEE Access: Practical Innovations, Open Solutions*, *7*, 37575–37586. doi:10.1109/ACCESS.2019.2905769

Deng, Z., Zhu, X., Cheng, D., Zong, M., & Zhang, S. (2016). Efficient KNN Classification Algorithm for Big Data. *Neurocomputing*, *195*, 143–148. doi:10.1016/j.neucom.2015.08.112

Documents - Financial Action Task Force (FATF). (2020). http://www.fatf-gafi.org/publications/financialinclusion/documents/bcbs-meeting-2-october-2014.html

Du Mingxiao, M. X., Zhe, Z., Wang, X., & Chen, Q. (2017). A Review on Consensus Algorithm of Blockchain. In *2017 IEEE International Conference on Systems, Man, and Cybernetics (SMC)*. IEEE. 10.1109/SMC.2017.8123011

Fahad. (2020). *Blockchain without Waste: Proof-of-Stake*. Academic Press.

Farrugia, S., Ellul, J., & Azzopardi, G. (2020, April 13). Detection of Illicit Accounts over the Ethereum Blockchain. *Expert Systems with Applications*, *150*, 113318. doi:10.1016/j.eswa.2020.113318

Fergal, R., & Harrigan, M. (2013). An Analysis of Anonymity in the Bitcoin System. In *Security and Privacy in Social Networks* (pp. 197–223). Springer. doi:10.1007/978-1-4614-4139-7_10

Gavin. (2014). *Ethereum: A Secure Decentralised Generalised Transaction Ledger*. Ethereum project yellow paper 151(2014): 1–32.

Henderson. (2012). Rolx: Structural Role Extraction & Mining in Large Graphs. *Proceedings of the 18th ACM SIGKDD International Conference on Knowledge Discovery and Data Mining*, 1231–1239.

Hu, Y., Seneviratne, S., Thilakarathna, K., Fukuda, K., & Seneviratne, A. (2019). *Characterizing and Detecting Money Laundering Activities on the Bitcoin Network*. arXiv preprint arXiv:1912.12060

Israa, A., Rahwan, I., & Svetinovic, D. (2018). The Anti-Social System Properties: Bitcoin Network Data Analysis. *IEEE Transactions on Systems, Man, and Cybernetics. Systems*.

Ittay, E., & Sirer, E. G. (2014). Majority Is Not Enough: Bitcoin Mining Is Vulnerable. In *International Conference on Financial Cryptography and Data Security*. Springer.

Jethin, A., Higdon, D., Nelson, J., & Ibarra, J. (2018). *Cryptocurrency Price Prediction Using Tweet Volumes and Sentiment Analysis*. SMU Data Science Review.

Jouni, K., & Mills, C. (2020). On Group Comparisons with Logistic Regression Models. *Sociological Methods & Research*, *49*(2), 498–525. doi:10.1177/0049124117747306

Lahmiri, S., & Bekiros, S. (2019). Cryptocurrency Forecasting with Deep Learning Chaotic Neural Networks. *Chaos, Solitons, and Fractals*, *118*, 35–40. doi:10.1016/j.chaos.2018.11.014

Li, J., Li, N., Peng, J., Cui, H., & Wu, Z. (2019). Energy Consumption of Cryptocurrency Mining: A Study of Electricity Consumption in Mining Cryptocurrencies. *Energy, 168*, 160–168. doi:10.1016/j.energy.2018.11.046

Liu, Z., Ren, C., & Cai, W. (2020). Overview of Clustering Analysis Algorithms in Unknown Protocol Recognition. In *MATEC Web of Conferences*. EDP Sciences. 10.1051/matecconf/202030903008

Lu, H., Karimireddy, S. P., Ponomareva, N., & Mirrokni, V. (2020). Accelerating Gradient Boosting Machines. *International Conference on Artificial Intelligence and Statistics*, 516–526.

Meiklejohn, S., Pomarole, M., Jordan, G., Levchenko, K., McCoy, D., & Voelker, G. M. (2013). A Fistful of Bitcoins: Characterizing Payments among Men with No Names. *Proceedings of the 2013 Conference on Internet Measurement Conference*, 127–140. 10.1145/2504730.2504747

Meneghetti, Sala, & Taufer. (2020). A Survey on PoW-Based Consensus. *Annals of Emerging Technologies in Computing*.

Monamo, P., Marivate, V., & Twala, B. (2016). Unsupervised Learning for Robust Bitcoin Fraud Detection. 2016 Information Security for South Africa (ISSA), 129–134. doi:10.1109/ISSA.2016.7802939

Nakamoto, S., & Bitcoin, A. (2008). *A Peer-to-Peer Electronic Cash System*. https://bitcoin.org/bitcoin.pdf

O'Kane, E. (2018). *Detecting Patterns in the Ethereum Transactional Data Using Unsupervised Learning*. Academic Press.

O'Leary, D. E. (2018). Open Information Enterprise Transactions: Business Intelligence and Wash and Spoof Transactions in Blockchain and Social Commerce. *Intelligent Systems in Accounting, Finance & Management, 25*(3), 148–158. doi:10.1002/isaf.1438

Qiu, J., Wu, Q., Ding, G., Xu, Y., & Feng, S. (2016). A Survey of Machine Learning for Big Data Processing. *EURASIP Journal on Advances in Signal Processing, 2016*(1), 67. doi:10.118613634-016-0355-x

Schonlau, M., & Yuyan Zou, R. (2020). The Random Forest Algorithm for Statistical Learning. *The Stata Journal, 20*(1), 3–29. doi:10.1177/1536867X20909688

Stuart, Rosales, & Signorotti. (2015). Algorithmic Trading of Cryptocurrency Based on Twitter Sentiment Analysis. *CS229 Project*, 1–5.

Swan, M. Chapter Five - Blockchain for Business: Next-Generation Enterprise Artificial Intelligence Systems. In P. Raj & G. C. Deka (Eds.), *Advances in Computers, Blockchain Technology: Platforms, Tools and Use Cases* (pp. 121–162). Elsevier. https://www.sciencedirect.com/science/article/pii/S0065245818300287.2018

Thai, P., & Lee, S. (2016). *Anomaly Detection in the Bitcoin System-a Network Perspective*. arXiv preprint arXiv:1611.03942

Van Engelen, J. E., & Hoos, H. H. (2020). A Survey on Semi-Supervised Learning. *Machine Learning, 109*(2), 373–440. doi:10.100710994-019-05855-6

Vujičić, D., Jagodić, D., & Randjić, S. (2018). Blockchain Technology, Bitcoin, and Ethereum: A Brief Overview. In *2018 17th International Symposium Infoteh-Jahorina (Infoteh)*. IEEE. 10.1109/INFOTEH.2018.8345547

Weber, I., Xu, X., Riveret, R., Governatori, G., Ponomarev, A., & Mendling, J. (2016). Untrusted Business Process Monitoring and Execution Using Blockchain. In M. La Rosa, P. Loos, & O. Pastor (Eds.), *Business Process Management* (pp. 329–347). Lecture Notes in Computer Science. Springer International Publishing. doi:10.1007/978-3-319-45348-4_19

Weber, M., Domeniconi, G., Chen, J., Weidele, D. K. I., Bellei, C., Robinson, T., & Leiserson, C. E. (2019). *Anti-Money Laundering in Bitcoin: Experimenting with Graph Convolutional Networks for Financial Forensics*. KDD '19 Workshop on Anomaly Detection in Finance, Anchorage, AK.

Zambre, D., & Shah, A. (2013). *Analysis of Bitcoin Network Dataset for Fraud*. Unpublished Report 27.

ADDITIONAL READING

Alexander, C., & Dakos, M. (2020). A Critical Investigation of Cryptocurrency Data and Analysis. *Quantitative Finance*, *20*(2), 173–188. doi:10.1080/14697688.2019.1641347

Patel, M. M., Tanwar, S., Gupta, R., & Kumar, N. (2020). A Deep Learning-Based Cryptocurrency Price Prediction Scheme for Financial Institutions. *Journal of Information Security and Applications*, *55*, 102583. doi:10.1016/j.jisa.2020.102583

KEY TERMS AND DEFINITIONS

AML/CFT: Anti-money laundering and countering the financing of terrorism.

Blockchain: Is a technology for the storage and transmission of information, transparent, secure, and operating without a central control body.

Business Intelligence: Business intelligence, or BI, is a tool that allows the generation of reports in an automated way and in real time. This methodology is based on professional software solutions. The collection of data and their aggregation in readable documents give the management and operational functions the keys to guide the company's strategy.

Cryptoccurency: Is a currency issued on a peer-to-peer basis, without the need for a central bank, that can be used by means of a decentralized computer network.

Data Analysis: Is a family of statistical methods whose main characteristics are that they are multidimensional and descriptive.

FATF: Financial Action Task Force is an intergovernmental organism for the fight against money laundering and the financing terrorist.

Money Laundering: Money laundering is the action of concealing the origin of money acquired in illegal ways (illegal speculation, mafia activities, drug and arms trafficking, extortion, corruption, tax evasion, etc.) by reinvesting it in legal activities (trade, real estate construction, casinos, etc.).

Section 4
Software and Security

Chapter 9
A Framework to Evaluate Big Data Fabric Tools

Ângela Alpoim
University of Minho, Portugal

João Lopes
University of Minho, Portugal

Tiago Guimarães
University of Minho, Portugal

Carlos Filipe Portela
University of Minho, Portugal

Manuel Filipe Santos
University of Minho, Portugal

ABSTRACT

A huge growth in data and information needs has led organizations to search for the most appropriate data integration tools for different types of business. The management of a large dataset requires the exploitation of appropriate resources, new methods, as well as the possession of powerful technologies. That led the surge of numerous ideas, technologies, and tools offered by different suppliers. For this reason, it is important to understand the key factors that determine the need to invest in a big data project and then categorize these technologies to simplify the choice that best fits the context of their problem. The objective of this study is to create a model that will serve as a basis for evaluating the different alternatives and solutions capable of overcoming the major challenges of data integration. Finally, a brief analysis of three major data fabric solutions available on the market is also carried out, including Talend Data Fabric, IBM Infosphere, and Informatica Platform.

DOI: 10.4018/978-1-7998-5781-5.ch009

1 INTRODUCTION

Today, it is essential for the success of organisations to "be smart". It can translate into quick and agile decisions, turning information into knowledge that can help make the best decisions (Zikopoulos and Eaton 2011). Data are generated, analysed and used on an unprecedented scale, and decision-making is being applied to all aspects of society (Srivastava 2013). Never have so many records been generated about what people do, think, feel or desire as they do today. Therefore, people's daily interactions with widespread systems create traces that capture various aspects of human behaviour, allowing different machine learning algorithms to extract valuable information about users and their actions.

The management and analysis of this huge amount of data, through the analysis of banking transactions, online surveys, access to websites or even with the appearance of connected devices such as smartphones or smartwatches, can be seen, simultaneously, as one of the most significant benefits and challenges of organizations. It is as important to obtain and generate information as being able to process it quickly (Volpato et al. 2014). And this is one of the greatest challenges: organising and modelling the data to facilitate the process of linking, transforming, processing and analysing the data collected in order to make the best decisions promptly (Cassavia et al., 2014). This case requires the exploitation of adequate resources, new methods, as well as the ownership of the appropriate technology (Oussous et al. 2017). The truth is that the process of selecting appropriate integration tools for different types of businesses is crucial, given the growing demand and need from data and information companies. However, it is important to realize two important factors before moving to a major data project and implementing a major data integration solution. According to a framework developed in a previous study (Portela et al. 2016), one of the most important aspects in this process is to frame the existing problem with two important questions:

1. Is it really a big data problem?
2. Is it really necessary to have large data tools to solve the problem in question?

These questions need to be assessed before choosing and investing in a large data solution, because even this investment can be seen as being at risk for many companies.

In this sense, after the correct framing of the project in its real dimension, and if it assumes the structure of a large data project, it is possible to implement the structure of BigDAF by introducing a tool analysis component, namely the Evaluation Model, which was developed to guide the decision and classification of tools taking into account the different requirements, needs and evaluation criteria of the different users, in order to select the best data integration solution, according to the needs of each company.

This research is therefore directed in the context of identifying and analysing some of the solutions existing in the market, adopting an Evaluation Model that can support the assessments developed, with the main objective of recommending the best option according to previously defined criteria, representing the most important decisions to be taken into account within the existing problem. In fact, this paper extends a study performed about Big Data Integration Tools (Alpoim et. all 2019).

This document is structured in seven sections. The first section provides a brief introduction to contextualize this study. The second section describes and characterises the concept of large data, presenting the data tools as well as the BigDAF structure concept. Section three represents the solution for evaluating large data integration tools, describing the main criteria that can be used to make this evaluation. Section four describes the results of this study and an example of the application of the evaluation model is presented; the next section introduces the discussion to the subject, finalising the research with the main conclusions concerning this chapter.

2 BACKGROUND

2.1 Big Data

Innovation and technological development combined with increased accessibility to digital devices have led to the emergence of what is considered by many to be the era of great data. As a result of this impact that the role of technologies is now assuming on people and their lives, there is an 'explosion' in the quantity, diversity and availability of digital data in real time (Pulse 2012). According to (Gupta & Chaudari, 2017), large data can be defined as "high volume information assets that require profitable and innovative ways of processing information for better perception and decision making". A complements of this definition is refered in (Hashem et al, 2014), associating large data as "a set of techniques and technologies that require new forms of integration to discover large values hidden from large data sets that are diverse, complex, and of a massive scale".

Smart reading of this information is essential because, according to some studies, the proper use of large data can play a very useful economic role for organisations, promoting innovation, competitiveness and productivity in all segments (Lima & Calazans, 2013). The benefits and values that organisations expect to create from the use of these technologies will also depend on the strategies adopted and the objectives they intend to achieve (Günther et al., 2017).

2.2 Big Data Fabric

The "data fabric" concept emerged as an approach to help organizations cope better with the rapid growth of data. This term refers to the technology that creates a convergent platform that supports the storage, processing, analysis and management of the enormous diversity of data that exists today, such as text, images or sensor data (Izzi et al., 2016). According to the Forrester study (Hoberman et al., 2018), this concept can be defined as: "Bringing together large disparate data sources automatically, intelligently and securely, and processing them into one large data platform technology, such as Hadoop and Apache Spark, to provide a unified, reliable and comprehensive view of customer and business data" (Izzi et al., 2016). The large data fabric helps companies in this processing process to quickly transform, integrate and secure large amounts of data into large data platforms to support a strong view of the customer and business [7, 2].

2.3 Examples of Big Data Fabric Tools

According to Forrester studies [10,7], most companies that have a large data tissue platform have been integrating various open source technologies such as Apache Flume, Spark, Hadoop, and have supported the platform with commercial products for data integration, security, governance, machine learning and data preparation technologies. However, organisations have realised that customising a large data fabric in this way to meet all business requirements requires significant time and effort. Thus, in order to sustain and exemplify the implemented evaluation model, research will focus on solutions such as *Talend, IBM and Informatica,* from which they were developed as a goal to integrate all layers of the architecture of the large data fabric (Beyer et al., 2018).

Talend Data Fabric is a complete solution that provides all the integration needs in a single platform. It allows users to access, transform, move and synchronize large data, taking advantage of Apache Hadoop. With this solution, it is possible to work with large volumes of data at high speed, performing real-time integrations and sharing information in an organized way (Talend Data Fabric 2020).

IBM's InfoSphere Information Server Enterprise Edition is a data integration platform that includes a family of products that allow users to understand, monitor, clean, transform and deliver data. It provides the capabilities of a highly scalable and flexible integration platform that handles all volumes of data (IBM InfoSphere, 2020).

Informatica Platform collects any type of data (structured, semi-structured and unstructured), through any integration pattern (real-time or streaming, for example), from any source (database, data warehouses, large data, social networks) and from any location (local data, cloud, hybrids). It has the ability to transform this data into reliable, secure, accessible, timely and actionable intelligence (Informatica Intelligent Data Platform, 2020).

2.4 Big Data Complexity Framework – BigDAF

One of the biggest mistakes an organisation can make when implementing a major data project is not understanding what the current needs of its business are. There are organizations that want to implement a large data project only in the desire to follow a trend without the real need to introduce such technology into the organization. In this context, in order to answer this question, it was developed a study (Portela et al. 2016), called BigDAF, capable of measuring a technological/business problem. The main objective of Table 1 is to support organisations to understand the significance of the big data issue and the key factors that determine the real need to invest in such a project. Introducing the "Big Data Complexity Framework", it aims at framing the dimension of the existing problem in the three main concepts associated with the Big Data theme, the 3 V's: Volume, Variety, Speed. According to the authors, this Framework provides four different evaluation results:

1. **Traditional BI issue:** The company is facing a problem that could be solved with a relative investment on storage capability and/or simple text processing tools. The period of data refresh and process is not a threat;
2. **BI Issue near Big Data challenge:** Defines a problem that might evolve to a big data issue. It could be solved through some advanced analytics tools and a system capable of scheduling tasks. Problems that fit in this class must complement its analysis with expected evaluation and consider the need to advance from the beginning to a big data project;
3. **Big Data Issue:** Need for investment in big data architecture, through a comfortable process skill. Once we reach a big data problem, its characteristics (volume, velocity and variety) are not a big issue because big data tools are prepared for these conditions;
4. **Complex Big Data Issue:** In this case, it is even more urgent to invest in a big data project. There is no possibility for the BI to be enough to support such a huge and instantaneous data flow with this complexity. Even the big data suppliers have to prove that they are capable of dealing with this problem because not all offers presented on the market will fully serve the customer's needs.

Table 1. Big Data Complexity Framework. Withdrawn from (Portela et al. 2016)

Dimension / CL	CLI	CL2	CL3	CL4	CL5
Volume	<1000GB	5TB – 50TB	50TB – 500TB	500TB – 2000TB	>2PT
Velocity	Batch	Intra-day	Hourly-refresh	Real-time	Streaming
Variety	Structured Data	Docs; XML; TXT; JSON	Web-log; sensors and device events	Image; social graph feeds; Geospatial information	Video; Voice

As mentioned above, the Framework addressed is essential to assess the needs of organisations and to understand whether these needs are met with large data resources and whether these organisations really need to make large investments in data (Portela et al. 2016). This initial approach can be adapted to detect whether a project involves large data and then introduce the model and structure proposed in this research to assess the large data integration tools available on the market. The practical application of these structures could simplify and support organisations in their decision-making processes by initially identifying exactly the type of data project according to the BigDAF structure. Then, the evaluation process of the available tools starts with the definition and prioritisation of key requirements and criteria. There will be a set of variables that need to be framed in the different business contexts and the needs of the organisations, such as the different types of data that are needed for the processing of results. For this reason, it is vital that this same assessment is weighted, with well-defined criteria, mainly to understand whether the solution offers what the organisation needs, whether it meets the business requirements and its integration needs for differentiated results.

The evaluation process of the data integration product begins with the definition and prioritization of critical requirements and criteria. The characteristics assessed are categorised into four main groups: **Ease of Integration and Implementation**, assessing the implementation capacity and security, as well as the adaptation to different contexts; **Quality of Service and Support**, framing the assessment of this tool with the existing documentation; **Usability** of tool; Finally, **Costs**, assessing the free version of the tool, as well as the price adjustment to the tool capacity. The criteria defined were based on the bibliographic review of studies such as (Marakas and O'Brien 2013), (Lněnička, 2015) and (Altalhi et al., 2017), in addition to (Hoberman et al., 2018) and (Beyer et al., 2018) reports. It has also been possible to combine information from other sources, including the G2 Crowd and Gartner websites, contributing to the perception of the most important criteria. The evaluation of each of the parameters can be performed using a scale from 1 to 10, where 1 represents the lowest possible score and 10 the highest. Two important factors should be considered before assigning the weights to the criteria:

1. **The Analytic Hierarchy Process method (AHP)** is the method used to organise and analyse complex decisions. It was developed by Thomas L. Saaty in the 1970s and has been improved ever since. It contains three parts: the final objective/problem in question, the possible solutions called alternatives, and the criteria by which it will judge the alternatives. The AHP method provides a framework for a necessary decision, quantifying its criteria by relating these elements to the overall objective. At the final stage of the process, numerical priorities are calculated for each of the alternative options (Saaty 2008) (Lněnička, 2015).

2. The sensitivity analysis, in order to support the decision-making process. After scoring all the criteria, the percentages relative to the weights are applied, and the total evaluation is presented at the end.

This process will be carried out for all the alternatives that the user wishes to compare.

Briefly, the process of determining and choosing the proper big data fabric solution should go through the following steps, according to Figure 1:

1. **Identify the Problem:** Understand the business case with clearly defined goals that generate business value for the company's business.
2. **Assess Type:** Use of the BigDAF framework, which serves as a guide to identify project type that best fits the context of the problem.
3. **Analyse Data Fabric Solutions:** The process of finding and selecting the best Data Fabric solutions available in the market.
4. **Evaluate the Solutions:** Use the "Evaluation Model" framework in order to evaluate the set of data fabric tools chosen in the previous step. The evaluation process begins with the definition and prioritisation of critical requirements and criteria and then apply the weights.
5. **Take a Decision:** Based on the scores obtained in step 4, choose the data fabric solution that had the highest score.

3 RESULTS

3.1 Applicability of the Framework

In the context of the above points, the applicability of evaluation models is already a recurrent practice in the technological environment. Forrester and Gartner are two of the most influential research and consulting firms in the world. Both are market research companies that provide their analysis on the potential of technologies in various areas. The June and July 2018 reports [7, 2] respectively of these two major benchmarks were considered for this study, in relation to the analysis of the best data integration tools currently on the market. Analysing the two reports, it can be concluded that the results are different. While, for example, in the evaluation of the Gartner Magic Quadrant, Informatica is considered a market leading solution, Forrester's Wave believes that this solution is still in a state that needs further growth and expansion of its functionality. The differences in evaluations and the choice of the best solutions are justified by the weight given to each of the evaluation categories and the criteria selected to conduct the evaluation, as well as the conclusions and opinions of the different analysts from both companies.

Reports such as Gartner's Magic Quadrant and Forrester's Wave are often the first source consulted in the evaluation of IT tools and solutions. These reports can be a great tool for finding the best options in a given market, but they end up providing only an overall picture, paying little attention to how these solutions work in different industries and in different cases of use.

In order to continue this research, an evaluation of three major tools is carried out: Talend Data Fabric, IBM Infosphere and the Informatica Platform. This evaluation led to the conclusion that, given the weights assigned and the evaluation given to the different criteria, Talend is the solution with the best

Table 2. Evaluation Model for Big Data Integration Solutions

Metrics	Features	Description	Weight	Alternatives		
				1	2	3
Ease of Integration and Implementation	Connecting to data sources and destination support	Ability to interact with a variety of different types of data structures, including relational and non-relational databases, XML, different data types and multiple file formats.				
	Data security and privacy	Whether the solution can overcome the challenges of privacy and data security effectively.				
	Simple and complex transformations	Integrated capabilities for achieving data transformation operations, including fundamental transformations (such as data type conversions, string manipulations and simple calculations) and complex transformations (such as sophisticated large-scale analysis operations).				
	Ease of implementation and integration	A width of support for hardware and operating systems on which data integration processes can be implemented. Also, it is essential to have a set of features in this type of solution to facilitate the integration process, such as diversity of pre-built connectors and to guarantee portability of the solution.				
	Scalability and adaptability	Whether the solution can quickly expand to meet business needs.				
Usability	Ability to use the tool	The ease of use of the tool, associated with the fact that it is intuitive, easy to handle and easy to learn. This perspective will vary according to the skills of the professionals involved.				
Quality of Service and Support	Quality of technical support and documentation available	The existence of efficient and timely technical support with high availability as well as adequate and quality documentation that responds promptly and effectively to the technical obstacles that may arise to users during the exploration of the tool. A wide range of options regarding customer support programs is also considered a key factor.				
Costs	Free trial	If the solution presents a free trial, in order to understand if it meets the needs of the business.				
	Professionals with the right skills	The existence in the organization of experts in data integration or have enough budget to hire professionals who have experience and knowledge in handling the chosen integration tool.				
	Price flexibility	The licensing and pricing methods are easy to understand, and the costs are attractive.				
	Return on investment	If the solution has a significant impact on the business about the investments that were made.				
Evaluation			100%			

score. The evaluation of the measurements was based on reports and opinions from professional experts in the field, and the calculations of the weights were introduced using the AHP method.

While there is no doubt that such a report can be very useful, it is also necessary to obtain more practical information in order to support the results obtained with a critical opinion of equal value. Thus, the use of white papers, reports by experts in the field and professional opinions are the best sources to support the right conclusions. In this sense, there are websites like G2 Crowd and Gartner peer insights, where IT professionals give opinions on product reviews and their experiences as users. For this

Figure 1. Process of choosing a big data fabric solution

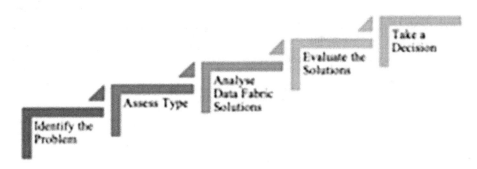

reason, and because their suitability for this study has been recognised, reviews of the above-mentioned websites are also considered to evaluate the three solutions, resulting in the final assessment presented in Table 2. In order to assign weights in the evaluation of large solutions, the ExpertChoice® tool was used, which is a software that performs analyses with several criteria, using the AHP method. Table 2 shows the Matrix performed, based on the Saaty scale.

Table 3. Comparison Matrix

	Ease of Integration and Implementation	Usability	Quality of Service and Support	Costs
Ease of Integration and Implementation		5.0	4.0	5.0
Usability			3.0	2.0
Quality of Service and Support				2.0
Costs	Incon: 0.08			

In the AHP method, the consistency ratio needs to be below 0.1 to be acceptable, as the above values indicate that there was inconsistency in the assessments. As it is possible to see, in Table 4, through the ExpertChoice tool, **the calculations are performed in order to choose the best solution, assigning weights for each one of the criteria.** The level of inconsistency is below the maximum value, which in this case is 0.08, revealing that the evaluations were consistent.

In Table 5, the evaluation of this solution is based on the different sources mentioned above. In order to illustrate the method applied for the evaluation of the solutions, a real example of application is given.

Using the usability criteria of the Talend Data Fabric solution, three assessments were calculated based on different sources, namely G2 Crowd, Gartner peer insights and Forrester's Wave. The evaluation resulted in 7.6 G2 Crowd, 8 Gartner peer insights and 8.7 Forrester's Wave. The average of the assessments was 8.1 and the weight of 19% was applied in this example. The same method was applied to the other criteria and led to their final evaluation. For this reason, this procedure was applied to the other solutions in order to verify and compare the final results.

Table 4. Attribution of the weights following the AHP

Ease of Integration and Implementation	0.599
Usability	0.194
Quality of Service and Support	0.086
Costs	0.121
Inconsistency = 0.08 **With 0 missing judgments**	

Table 5. Evaluation of three big data fabric solutions

			Solutions		
Metrics	**Features**	**Weight**	**Talend**	**IBM**	**Informatica**
Ease of Integration and Implementation	Connecting to data sources and destination support	60%	8,2	7,7	7,5
	Data security and privacy				
	Simple and complex transformations				
	Ease of implementation and integration				
Usability	Ability to use the tool	19%	8,1	7,3	5,9
Quality of Service and Support	Quality of technical support and documentation available	9%	8,2	8,2	7,2
Costs	Free Trial	0%	10	10	10
	Return on investment and price flexibility.	12%	7,6	6,8	5,3
Evaluation		**100%**	**8,1**	**7,6**	**6,9**

4 DISCUSSION

This research aims to provide a holistic view of what are considered to be the main requirements to be taken into account when choosing one of the many solutions available on the market. The model produced in this study can be seen as something that aims to simplify the way users should make final decisions, taking into account the different requirements and needs of the various areas. This framework aims to convey the idea that before evaluating and selecting a data integration solution, it is essential to assess what are the primary and "mandatory" features and functionalities for the business. After identifying the essential criteria and characteristics, it is necessary to carry out a weighting, in order to verify which solutions in the market are best suited to the company's needs and can effectively satisfy them. It is important to realise that different organisations in different areas represent a wide variety of needs. Thus, the criteria described in this model are broad and could, in fact, be adapted to any industry. Organisations should indeed understand the different use cases and then adapt this model, accordingly, based on the strengths and weaknesses of the solutions being assessed. In order to conclude the case study reported in the previous points, Talend had the highest score followed by IBM and finally Informatica.

Sensitivity analysis gives an idea of how classifications respond to changes in weights, a useful way of seeing which aspects need to be taken into account the most and which are important. As can be seen in Figure 2, the vertical line "At" represents the current weight, and the lines cross when there is a change in weight of the criteria, causing a change in classification. It can be concluded that in this case the assigned weights are evenly distributed, as the "At" line is far from the crossing of the three lines.

Figure 2. Weight sensitivity analysis

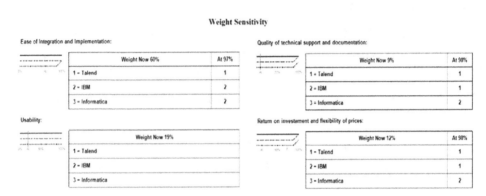

5 CONCLUSIONS AND FUTURE WORK

It is not new that today there is a wide variety of data solutions available on the market for efficient data management, storage and analysis. Thus, the need arises to introduce a model that could help in the choice of it, suitable for each context. The huge failure rate in recent years in implementing large data projects suggests that the best strategy for success may be to start more simply and gradually build the solution according to business needs.

With the development of this research, it is clear to underline that the choice of a large data integration solution is not simple. Organizations should not look for solutions that have the greatest number of features and functionalities, but rather, acquire the data integration tool that best suits their needs. It is necessary to understand that the wrong choice of these technologies can essentially lead to two problems: the unnecessary spending of funds, due to a poor framework between the problem and the solution, and also obtaining solutions that have a complex usability, without even being able to solve the existing problem in the same organisation. Thus, the main contribution concerning the work is, fundamentally, in the way that different organisational perspectives are framed in the most evident needs, at the moment of obtaining a tool that can offer the desired solutions. The application of BigDAF structures and the Evaluation Model adapt the different requirements and evaluation criteria of the different users to select the data integration solution that best suits the needs of each organisation.

It is also possible to frame this work in some future investigations in order to make it even more complete, as well as to offer a broader set of recommendations to all areas concerned. Above all, a clarification of how the needs of the organisation in question are determined is needed, as these tend to be the most critical factors in the survey of solutions that respond to them. Not least, a greater clarification of how the different solutions are classified, so as to make this stage more rigorous and less dependent on second opinions. The use of considerably current bibliographic references proves the relevance of this study, which can be widely adapted in various sectors.

REFERENCES

Altalhi, A. H., Luna, J. M., Vallejo, M. A., & Ventura, S. (2017). Evaluation and comparison of open source software suites for data mining and knowledge discovery. *Wiley Interdisciplinary Reviews. Data Mining and Knowledge Discovery, 7*(3), e1204. doi:10.1002/widm.1204

Alpoim, Â., Guimarães, T., Portela, F., & Santos, M. F. Evaluation Model for Big Data Integration Tools. Advances in Intelligent Systems and Computing (WorldCist 2019 - PIS Workshop). Volume 932, 2019, pp. 601-610. ISBN: 978-3-319-77699-6. Springer. (2019). DOI:10.1007/978-3-030-16187-3_58

Beyer, M., Thoo, E., & Zaidi, E. (2018). *Gartner Magic Quadrant for Data Integration Tools*. Academic Press.

Cassavia, N., Dicosta, P., Masciari, E., & Saccà, D. (2014). Data preparation for tourist data big data warehousing. In *Proceedings of 3rd International Conference on Data Management Technologies and Applications* (pp. 419-426). 10.5220/0005144004190426

Günther, W. A., Mehrizi, M. H. R., Huysman, M., & Feldberg, F. (2017). Debating big data: A literature review on realizing value from big data. *The Journal of Strategic Information Systems, 26*(3), 191–209. doi:10.1016/j.jsis.2017.07.003

Gupta, S., & Chaudari, M. S. (2015). Big Data issues and challenges. *International Journal on Recent and Innovation Trends in Computing and Communication, 3*(2), 62-66.

Hashem, I. A. T., Yaqoob, I., Anuar, N. B., Mokhtar, S., Gani, A., & Khan, S. U. (2015). The rise of "big data" on cloud computing: Review and open research issues. *Information Systems, 47*, 98–115. doi:10.1016/j.is.2014.07.006

Hoberman, E., Leganza, G., & Yuhanna, N. (2018). The Forrester Wave™. *Big Data Fabric, Q2*, 2018.

IBM InfoSphere. (2020, August 20). https://www.ibm.com/analytics/information-server

Informatica Intelligent Data Platform. (2020, August 20). www.informatica.com/nl/products/informatica-platform.html

Izzi, M., Warrier, S., Leganza, G., & Yuhanna, N. (2016). Big Data Fabric Drives Innovation And Growth. *Next-Generation Big Data Management Enables Self-Service And Agility*.

Lima, C. A. R., & Calazans, J. D. H. C. (2013). Pegadas Digitais: "Big Data" E Informação Estratégica Sobre O Consumidor. *NT – Sociabilidade, novas tecnologias, consumo e estratégias de mercado do SIMSOCIAL, 2013*.

Lněnička, M. (2015). Ahp model for the big data analytics platform selection. *Acta Informatica Pragensia*, *4*(2), 108–121. doi:10.18267/j.aip.64

Marakas, G. M., & O'Brien, J. A. (2013). *Introduction to Information Systems*. McGraw-Hill/Irwin.

Oussous, A., Benjelloun, F. Z., Lahcen, A. A., & Belfkih, S. (2017). Big Data technologies: A survey. *Journal of King Saud University-Computer and Information Sciences*.

Portela, F., Lima, L., & Santos, M. F. (2016). Why Big Data? Towards a project assessment framework. *Procedia Computer Science*, *98*, 604–609. doi:10.1016/j.procs.2016.09.094

Pulse, U. G. (2012). *Big data for development: Challenges & opportunities*. Naciones Unidas.

Saaty, T. L. (2008). Decision making with the analytic hierarchy process. *International Journal of Services Sciences*, *1*(1), 83–98. doi:10.1504/IJSSCI.2008.017590

Srivastava, D. (2013, December). Big data integration. In *Proceedings of the 19th International Conference on Management of Data* (pp. 3-3). Computer Society of India.

Talend Data Fabric. (2020, August 22). *A single, unified platform for modern data integration and management*. https://www.talend.com/products/data-fabric/

Volpato, T., Rufino, R. R., & Dias, J. W. (2014). *Big Data – Transformando Dados em Decisões*. University of Paranaense.

Zikopoulos, P., & Eaton, C. (2011). *Understanding big data: Analytics for enterprise class hadoop and streaming data*. McGraw-Hill Osborne Media.

192

Chapter 10
A Novel Approach Using Steganography and Cryptography in Business Intelligence

Sabyasachi Pramanik
https://orcid.org/0000-0002-9431-8751
Haldia Institute of Technology, India

Ramkrishna Ghosh
Haldia Institute of Technology, India

Mangesh M. Ghonge
https://orcid.org/0000-0003-0140-4827
Sandip Institute of Technology and Research Centre, India

Vipul Narayan
https://orcid.org/0000-0003-4248-5782

MMM Collage, Gorakhpur, India

Mudita Sinha
CHRIST University (Deemed), India

Digvijay Pandey
https://orcid.org/0000-0003-0353-174X
Department of Technical Education, India & IET, India

Debabrata Samanta
https://orcid.org/0000-0003-4118-2480
CHRIST University (Deemed), India

ABSTRACT

In the information technology community, communication is a vital issue. And image transfer creates a major role in the communication of data through various insecure channels. Security concerns may forestall the direct sharing of information and how these different gatherings cooperatively direct data mining without penetrating information security presents a challenge. Cryptography includes changing over a message text into an unintelligible figure and steganography inserts message into a spread media and shroud its reality. Both these plans are successfully actualized in images. To facilitate a safer transfer of image, many cryptosystems have been proposed for the image encryption scheme. This chapter proposes an innovative image encryption method that is quicker than the current researches. The secret key is encrypted using an asymmetric cryptographic algorithm and it is embedded in the ciphered image using the LSB technique. Statistical analysis of the proposed approach shows that the researcher's approach is faster and has optimal accuracy.

DOI: 10.4018/978-1-7998-5781-5.ch010

1. INTRODUCTION

The work in the business world has changed immensely in the past years. Computers and the internet is an essential tool in all business organizations. Clients can buy products over the internet. Meetings, Ticket bookings, hotel reservation, checking of stock prices, gaming, social networking and many other activities can be performed by using a Smartphone. Computers, information systems and telecommunications are the building blocks and facilities needed for these business models. But data plays a vital role to boost the usage of information systems, computers and communication. Organizations need an analysis of these data in their repositories to have an in-depth study on their business environment and competitiveness competence. The act of understanding precious intuition related to business data is called business intelligence. Personnel engaged in creating these insights are the function of a business analytic. This article utilizes the idea of business intelligence and how they bolster the utilization of business insights in security of e-business models (Aithal, P. S., 2016). Information created in online client transactions, be it deals, questions, criticism, look, or just perusing give the associations a likely abundance of data that could help fortify steadfastness for existing clients or make open doors for new leads. Information produced in inner databases kept up by associations could likewise be a wellspring of pertinent data to help associations in improving business activities and upgrade capacities and capabilities. Subsequently, in the time of the data age, organizations need to see their gathered information as a wellspring of serious advantage. Data mining (Gupta, M.K., Chandra, P., 2020) and text mining (Ritala, P. et al., 2020) are promising strategies to tackle the likely estimation of information found in organizations. The utilization of information mining and other information examination apparatuses produces helpful data or social capacities that encourage directors to settle on keen choices. The huge amount of confidential data has been transferred on the Internet. Information security turns out to be progressively significant for some applications, for instance, private transmission, video reconnaissance, military and clinical applications. Lately, there has been a ton of enthusiasm for steganography and steganalysis. Steganography is the craft of stowing away and sending information through evidently harmless transporters with an end goal to cover the presence of the information. The advanced picture information, for example, BMP, JPEG, and GIF are generally utilized as a transporter for steganography. Here the mystery message is implanted into a picture (or any media) called spread picture, and afterward sent to the collector who separates the mystery message from the spread message. In the wake of installing the mystery message, the spread picture is known as a stego picture. This picture ought not be recognizable from the spread picture, with the goal that the assailant can't find any inserted message. The reliability due to the change of shrouded information can be gotten by two different ways: encryption and steganography (Pramanik, S. et al, 2019, Pramanik, S. also, Raja, S. S., 2017). A blend of the two strategies can be utilized to build the information security. In encryption, the message is altered in a convincing manner so no information can be uncovered on the off chance that it is gotten by an assailant. While in steganography, the mystery message is inserted into a picture, frequently called spread picture, and afterward sent to the collector who removes the mystery message from the spread message. At the point when the mystery message is implanted into spread picture then it is known as a stego-picture. The perceivability of this picture ought not be recognizable from the spread picture, with the goal that it nearly gets outlandish for the aggressor to find any installed message. There are numerous methods for scrambling information, which fluctuate in their security, strength, execution, etc. Likewise, there are numerous ways for implanting a message into another. We use steganography to shroud information; cryptography is utilized to encode information. Steganography, can likewise be utilized with cryptography and the scrambled information is covered up into spread picture creating a stego picture. At getting end, from stego picture, information is recovered utilizing appropriate key. At the point when records are made there are normally a few bytes in the document that aren't generally required, or possibly aren't unreasonably significant. These territories of the document can be supplanted with the data that will be covered up, without fundamentally adjusting the record or harming it. This permits an individual to conceal data in the record and ensure that no human could recognize the adjustment in the document. The LSB (Pramanik, S., Bandyopadhyay, S. K., 2013) technique works best in picture records that have a high goal and utilize various hues, and with sound documents that have a wide range of sounds and that are of a high piece rate. The LSB strategy normally doesn't build the record size, yet relying upon the size of the data that will be covered up inside the document, the record can turn out to be recognizably mutilated. The creators wish to apply an imaginative calculation that will assist with acquiring adjustment as less as conceivable transporter record so the first picture become least affected while target of disguising the data can be satisfied effectively. The calculation will support to forestall figment with respect to the concealed information inside the first picture.

As a matter of fact the analyst's goal is to mix the two methodology steganography and cryptography to accomplish a more tied down way to deal with send information. Along these lines, rather than sending genuine information – it is scrambled utilizing an encryption key and afterward that encoded form is sent by means of a secured medium. At getting end, information is extricated first; this information is again in encoded structure which is decoded utilizing unscrambling key that is known to recipient as it were. A two layered assurance is given to give a made sure about transmission. Picture data is shrouded utilizing RSA calculation created private key. At that point that encoded information is covered up into a spread picture record and afterward stego picture is gotten. From it, the encoded information is recovered at recipient's end and afterward utilizing the public key the first data would be acquired by the collector. At accepting end, in the wake of recovering unique data, signature picture is drawn which is counted with the first one. Consequently, message confirmation cycle can be allowed. There are various applications to protect privacy by mining distributed data. The applications will enforce many restrictions, including how the data is distributed. Data mining worked on a data warehousing model to collect all data into a central location, and then run an algorithm against that data. Steganography is a hidden technique. Some other data contain hidden information without leaving any obvious signs of data alteration. This chapter ensures a novel concept related to the blending of steganography and cryptography technique in the challenges of business intelligence.

2. MAIN RELATED TOPICS

2.1 Security Goals:

Steganography has some security objectives like confidentiality, integrity, availability and reliability. They are appeared in fig 1. Confidentiality (Pramanik, S. et al., 2020) is likely the most well-known part of data security. There is a need to ensure the classified data. An association needs to prepare for those noxious activities that imperil the secrecy of its data. Data should be changed continually. Honesty (Hambouz, An., et al. 2019) implies that changes should be done distinctly by approved substances and through approved components. The data made and put away by an association should be accessible to approved substances. Data should be continually changed, which implies it must be open to approved substances. Honesty estimates shield information from unapproved adjustment. These measures give affirmation in the precision and finish of data. The need to guarantee information joins the two data that is taken care of on systems and data that is sent between structures, for instance, email. In taking care of respectability, it isn't only imperative to control access at the system level, in any case, to furthermore ensure that structure customers are simply prepared to adjust information that they are truly endorsed to change. Availability (Duan, X. et al, 2020) is one of the three essential elements of security that is available in all frameworks. Availability is the declaration that a PC framework is accessible or available by an approved client at whatever point it is required. Frameworks have a high request for accessibility to guarantees that the framework works true to form when required. Reliability (Mukherjee S. and Sanyal G., 2020) quality is a property of any security system that reliably performs as indicated by its determinations. In principle, a solid item is thoroughly liberated from specialized blunders; by and by, notwithstanding, merchants regularly express an item's unwavering quality remainder as a rate. Transformative items (those that have advanced through various variants over a critical timeframe) are normally considered to turn out to be progressively solid since it is expected that bugs have been wiped out before discharges.

Figure 1. Security Goals

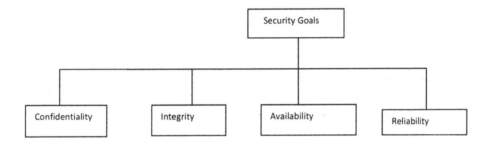

2.2 Security Attacks:

Different sorts of security assaults are found in steganography. They are appeared in fig 2. Some of them are Snooping, Denial of Service, Modification, Replaying, Repudiation, DoS and so forth. Assaults Threatening Confidentiality are Snooping and Traffic Analysis. Sneaking around (Chaharlang, J., Mosleh, M. and Rasouli-Heikalabad, S, 2020) alludes to unapproved admittance to or capture of information. Traffic investigation (Wang, M., Gu, W., and Ma, C. 2020) alludes to acquiring some other kind of data by observing on the web traffic. Assaults Threatening Integrity are Modification, Masquerading, Replaying and Repudiation. Change (Eyssa, A.A., Abdelsamie, F.E. and Abdelnaiem, 2020) implies that the assailant blocks the message and changes it. Disguising (Mahato, S., Khan, D. A. also, Yadav, D. K, 2020) or ridiculing happens when the aggressor imitates another person. Replaying implies the assailant gets a duplicate of a message sent by a client and later attempts to replay it. Disavowal implies that the sender of the message may later reject that she has sent the message; the recipient of the message may later reject that he has gotten the message. Assaults Threatening Availability is Denial of administration (DoS) (Handoko, W. T. et al, 2020). DoS are an extremely normal assault. It might back off or absolutely intrude on the administration of a framework. Figure 2 below shows the various types of security attacks found in steganography.

2.3 Information Hiding Techniques

Figure 2. Types of Security Attacks (A revoir)

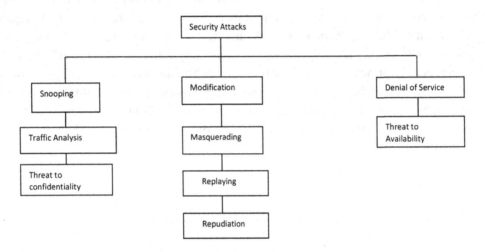

Data concealing procedures can be sorted into four fundamental sorts as appeared in figure 3 underneath. A portion of the procedures are clarified here. Steganography involves techniques which shroud a mystery data in the principle data (Kumar, S., Singh, A. what's more, Kumar, M., 2019).

Steganography Vs Cryptography: To have a superior comprehension of the terms, a correlation of "steganography" with "cryptography" is required. The term steganography signifies "spread composition" while cryptography signifies "mystery stating" (Rashid, A. what's more, Rahim M. K., 2016). Cryptography is the investigation of strategies for sending messages in unmistakable structure with the goal that lone the expected beneficiaries can eliminate the mask and read the message. The message we need to send is called plain content and camouflaged message is called figure text. The way toward changing over a plain book to a ciphertext is called enciphering or encryption, and the converse cycle is called translating or unscrambling (Taha, M. S., Rahim, M. S. M., Lafta, S. A., Hashim, M. A. furthermore, Alzuabidi, H. M., 2019) Encryption secures substance during the communication of the information from the communicator to collector. Notwithstanding, after reception and resulting unscrambling, the information is not, at this point ensured and is the unmistakable. Steganography conceals messages on display as opposed to scrambling the message; it is installed in the information (that must be secured) and doesn't need mystery transmission. The message is conveyed inside information. Steganography is accordingly more extensive than cryptography (Antonio, H., Prasad, P. W. C. what's more, Alsadoon, A., 2019)

Fingerprinting and Labeling: Fingerprints are additionally called marks by certain creators. Computerized watermarking (Embaby, A. A., Mohamed A., Shalaby, W. also, Elsayed, K. M., 2020) contrasts from "computerized fingerprinting". Fingerprinting are the qualities of an article that will in general recognize it from other comparable items. Fingerprinting (Douglas, M., Bailey, K., Leeney, M. et al.)

is the way toward adding fingerprints to an article and recording them, or distinguishing and recording fingerprints that are now natural for the item. Computerized fingerprinting produces a metafile that depict the substance of the source document.

Advanced Signature and Digital Watermark: There are clashing perspective focuses about the "computerized signature". A few creators utilize computerized signature (Zenati, An., Ouarda, W. also, Alimi, A. M., 2019) and computerized watermark equivalently, though a few creators recognize the advanced signature and computerized watermark. A computerized mark depends on the possibility of public key scrambling. A private key is utilized to scramble a hashed form of the picture. This scrambled document at that point frames an interesting "signature" for the picture since just the element marking the picture knows about the private key utilized. A related public key can be utilized to unscramble the mark. The picture under inquiry can be hashed utilizing the equivalent hashing capacity as utilized initially. In the event that these hashes coordinate, at that point the picture is real. Advanced mark can be utilized for something other than picture confirmation. Specifically, when joined with secure timestamp, an advanced mark can be utilized as evidence of first creation. A watermark, then again, is a code covertly inserted into the picture. The watermark takes into account confirmation of the beginning of a picture. Nonetheless, a watermark alone isn't sufficient to demonstrate first creation, since a picture could be set apart with different watermarks. It has additionally been brought up that computerized watermarks are not appropriate to ensure the credibility of a picture. The expression "installed signature" has been utilized as opposed to "watermarking" Because it possibly prompts disarray with cryptographic "advanced marks", it isn't utilized any longer.

2.4 Cryptography

Cryptography is about protecting the content of messages. Figure 4 below shows the generalized cryptographic system. The blocks in figure 4 are explained below.

Figure 3. Information Hiding Techniques

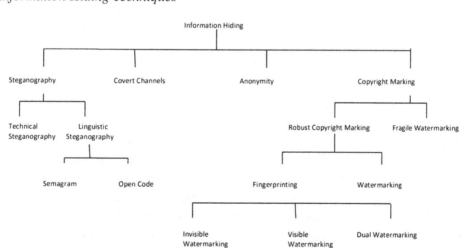

Figure 4. Cryptography System

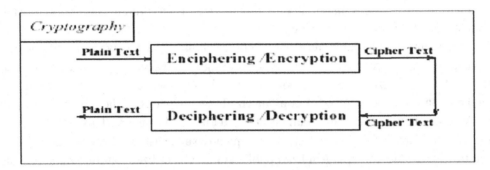

Plaintext & Cipher Text

Data encryption and cryptology, is the science of secrecy. Its purpose is to keep information in the hand of those who should have it and out of the hands of those who should not. Cipher text is encrypted text. Plaintext is what you have before encryption, and cipher text is the encrypted result.

CRYPTOLOGY

Cryptology = Cryptanalysis + Cryptography

Cryptography comes from the Greek word for "secret writing". Experts make a qualification among "Codes" and "Codes". Cryptography (from Greek kryptós, "covered up", and gráphein, "to compose") is, customarily, the investigation of methods for changing over data from its ordinary, understandable structure into a vast arrangement, delivering it disjointed without mystery information — the specialty of encryption.

Code: It is a character-for-character or bit-for-bit change, regardless of the etymological structure of the message.

Code: Code replaces single word with another word or image. It is almost old.

Cryptography: It is the whole process where a plain text and a special key are feed as input to an algorithm and the output is a cipher text that is totally different from the plain text and unreadable by the intruder.

Cryptanalysis: It is the art of analyzing the cipher text and breaking it.

The objective of cryptanalysis is to discover some shortcoming or instability in a cryptographic plan, along these lines allowing its disruption or avoidance. Cryptanalysis may be embraced by a vindictive assailant, endeavoring to undercut a framework, or by the framework's planner (or others) endeavoring to assess whether a framework has weaknesses, thus it isn't naturally an antagonistic demonstration. In present day practice, in any case, cryptographic calculations and conventions must be deliberately inspected and tried to offer any affirmation of the framework's security.

There is a wide assortment of cryptanalytic assaults, and they can be ordered in any of a few different ways. A typical differentiation turns on what an aggressor knows and what abilities are accessible. In a code text just assault, the cryptanalyst approaches just to the code text (great present day cryptosystems are typically adequately invulnerable to encode text just assaults). In a known-plaintext assault, the cryptanalyst approaches a code text and its comparing plaintext (or an excessive number of such matches). In a picked plaintext assault, the cryptanalyst may pick a plaintext and become familiar with its relating figure text (maybe ordinarily); at long last, in a picked figure text assault, the cryptanalyst may pick figure message and gain proficiency with their comparing plaintexts. Cryptanalysis of symmetric-key codes normally includes searching for assaults against the square codes or stream figures that are more proficient than any assault that could be against an ideal code. Public-key calculations depend on the computational trouble of different issues.

6.1. How Does Cryptography Work?

Encryptions are performed with the assistance of a key. A key is fundamentally a flood of irregular pieces made by a Key Generator. Key goes about as a contribution to the Encryption Algorithm. A key might be private or public. A cryptographic estimation or figure is a mathematical limit used in the encryption and unscrambling measure. A cryptographic computation works in blend in with a key – a word, number, or articulation – to encode the plaintext. The equal plaintext scrambles to different figure text with different keys. The security of encoded data is absolutely dependent on two things: the nature of the cryptographic count and the riddle of the key. A cryptographic estimation, notwithstanding every potential key and all the shows that make it work to incorporate a cryptosystem. Symmetric key cryptography alludes to encryption schemes in which a similar key is exchanged by both the sender and the receiver (or, less generally, in which their keys are separate but effectively calculable). Symmetric-key cryptosystems often use a similar key for encryption and unscrambling, but compared to other individuals, this message or message set may have an unexpected key. The key management required to use them safely is a vital burden of symmetric codes. In an ideal world, every unique pair of conveying parties would share an alternate key, and maybe every code text exchanged as well. The amount of keys needed increases as the square of the number of individuals in the company, which quickly requires complicated key administration plans to keep them all straight and mysterious. Its models are RC4 (Setyono, A. furthermore, Setiadi, D. R. I. M, 2019), AES, DES, 3DES and so on. Unbalanced key cryptography is the cryptography where two extraordinary yet numerically related keys are utilized — a public key and a private key. A public-key system is constructed to the extent that, despite the fact that they are fundamentally connected, estimating one key (the 'private key') is computationally infeasible from the other (the 'public key'). Rather, the two keys, as an interrelated pair, are covertly formed. Out in the open key cryptosystems, the public key might be unreservedly appropriated, while its matched private key must stay mystery. The public key is ordinarily utilized for encryption, while the private or mystery key is utilized for decoding. Models are RSA and Diffie-Hellman calculations (Gowda, S. N., 2016).

This chapter proposes a strategy dependent on AES (Bandekar, P. P. and Suguna, G. C., 2018), RSA (Damrudi, M. and Aval, K. J. 2019) and LSB strategy. The authors encode the image utilizing AES, the mystery key is scrambled utilizing RSA and it is covered up in the ciphered image utilizing LSB strategy. The significant points of interest of the methodology are dispensed with the issue of key transmission. Introduced approach is increasingly effective as far as calculation cost contrasted and plots that utilization topsy-turvy encryption. The anticipated methodology is progressively reliable for the quality of AES, RSA and LSB techniques.

2.5 Encryption Technique for Data Mining: Advanced Encryption Standard (AES)

This calculation has been made by two Belgian researchers, Joan Daemen and Vincent Rijmen to displace the DES and the 3DES (Ozighor, E. R. furthermore, Izegbu, I., 2a020) counts. The AES calculation is simpler to actualize, possesses lesser memory and utilizations key size of 128, 192 and 256 pieces. Table 1 shows the qualities of AES-128, AES-192 and AES-256 identified with the key length, block size and number of rounds of handling the key lengths.

Table 1. Number of rounds depends on the key length.

	Key Length (words)	Block Size (words)	Number of rounds
AES-128	4	4	10
AES-192	6	4	12
AES-256	8	4	14

Except for the last round for every circumstance, each and every other round is undefined. One single-byte-based substitution step, a line sharp change step, a fragment smart mixing step, and the creation of the round key are fused in each round. For encryption and unscrambling, the solicitation under which these four steps are performed is unmistakable. It is ideal to consider a 128-piece frustrate as containing a 4 X 4-byte display, sorted out as follows, to invite the ready advances used in a singular round:

Byte 0 Byte 4 Byte 8 Byte 12

Byte 1 Byte 5 Byte 9 Byte 13

Byte 2 Byte 6 Byte 10 Byte 14

Byte 3 Byte 7 Byte 11 Byte 15

The underlying four bytes of a 128-piece input square include the chief portion in the 4×4 group of bytes. The accompanying four bytes include the ensuing portion and from now on.

2.6 RSA Algorithm

One of the most famous key encryption calculations is the RSA calculation. RSA calculation is named after Ron Rivest, Adi Shamir and Len Adleman, who imagined it in 1977. The essential strategy was first found in 1973 by Clifford Cocks however this was a mystery until 1977(Rivest, R. L., Shamir, A. what's more, Adleman, L., 1977). The RSA calculation can be utilized for both encryption and decoding. Figure 5 underneath shows the schematic portrayal of RSA calculation. It utilizes a couple of keys-public and private key. Its security depends on the trouble of considering huge numbers. There are three stages included:

1. Key production:

Here, in this Key age measure, from the start, two prime numbers, p and q are created arbitrarily. At that point compute n=p*q and m = (p-1)X(q-1). The private key is (p, q). The public key is (n, e), e is co-prime to m. In the event that M is the plaintext and C is the code text, at that point

2. Encryption, C= Me mod [n].
3. Decoding, M=Cd modulus[n], where e, d=1 modulus [(p-1) (q-1)]

RSA Algorithm

1. Start.
2. m = the ASCII code of the message.
3. c = the ASCII code of the code text.
4. Create two gigantic prime numbers p and q (+100 integers).
5. Cycle ϕ (n) = (p − 1) (q − 1).
6. Cycle n = p*q
7. Pick any integer 1 < e < ϕ (n) which is co-prime to ϕ(n).
8. Cycle the assessment of d with the ultimate objective that (d X e) modulus ϕ(n) = 1.
9. Public key = (e, n).
10. Private key = (d, n).
11. The encryption of m is c = me modulus n.
12. The decoding of c is m = compact disc modulus n.
13. End.

The schematic representation of RSA Algorithm is shown in Fig. 5

The estimations of p, q and ϕ ought to likewise be left well enough alone. n is called as the modulus. e is known as the public type or encryption example. d is called the mystery example or unscrambling type.

Figure 5. Schematic representation of RSA Algorithm

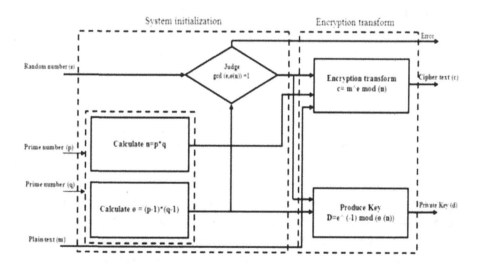

2.7 Substitution - Altering/Replacing the LSB

At the point when documents are made there are generally a few bytes in the record that aren't generally required, or if nothing else aren't unreasonably significant. These zones of the record can be supplanted with the data that will be covered up, without altogether adjusting the document or harming it. This permits an individual to conceal data in the record and ensure that no human could recognize the adjustment in the document. The LSB (Pramanik, S. et al. 2020) technique works best in Picture documents that have a high goal and utilize a wide range of hues, and with Audio records that have various sounds and that are of a high piece rate. The LSB strategy generally doesn't expand the record size, yet relying upon the size of the data that will be covered up inside the document, the document can turn out to be perceptibly twisted.

2.8 Data Mining:

Information mining (Sah H. R. what's more, Gunasekaran, G., 2015) uses strategies to mine monstrous educational lists so as to perceive designs in the enlightening file that may be utilized to develop noteworthy information that help relationship to fight even more effectively in the serious world. By uncovering models in the enlightening assortment, data mining can foresee and accomplice, things, or customers in an undeniably incredible route with the objective that the affiliation could give better things or organizations to the customers or improve the profitability of their exercises. To depict the power of information mining, we ought to use an essential comparability. These days, we have astonishing information base programming that can help us in doing a variety of information questions. These information inquiries grant us to isolate information from monster information bases. Nevertheless, in order to play out the data questions, we ought to at first know and express the request to be answered before the information base programming can help us with playing out the specific request.

3. SOME RELATED WORKS

In Lanza et al. suggested a multidimensional formalism in 2018 (Lanza, C. I., 2018) to discuss and test social pointers actually from fact sources derived from casual association data in this way. This formalism relies on two key perspectives: the semantic depiction through Connected Open Data of real factors and the assistance of multidimensional evaluation models similar to OLAP. Contrary to standard BI formalisms, according to the association's main objectives, we start the system by showing the fundamental social markers. All the essential streams of truth are shown and passed on from these subtleties to follow the pointers. The basic significance of on-demand social markers and the treatment of shifting estimates and estimates by spilling real factors are the key purposes of this method. By adding a true customer situation in the car division segment, we demonstrate the inspiration.

The researches of 2018 (Panwar, S. et al, 2018) examines the idea of stowing away the secret information in a picture which is called Image Steganography. Likewise, it utilizes a strategy known as Cryptography to improve the quality of security. Steganography shrouds the information and makes it hard to comprehend whether it really exists or not. Picture Steganography explicitly alludes to concealing the information inside a spread picture. Picture Steganography is accomplished utilizing Modified LSB. Adjusted LSB utilizes a specific condition to supplant the bits of the secret information in any event huge piece position of the pixels in the picture. Cryptography is accomplished by utilizing AES. Propelled Encryption Standard AES is utilized to encode the mystery information. Along these lines, Steganography and Cryptography when utilized together guarantee improved security of computerized messages.

The 2013 examination (Padmavathi, B. furthermore, Kumari, R. 2013) shows that the data which is to be communicated from sender to recipient in the framework must be encoded using the mixed estimation in cryptography. Also, the scrambled information must be covered up in an image or then again video or an audio document with the assistance of a steganographic calculation. Thirdly by utilizing an unscrambling procedure the recipient can see the first information from the concealed image or video or audio document. Transmitting information or archives should be possible through these ways will be made sure about. In this paper we actualized three scramble methods like DES, AES and RSA calculation alongside steganographic calculation like LSB replacement procedure and thought about their exhibition of scrambling strategies dependent on the investigation of its animating time at the hour of encryption and unscrambling process and furthermore its support size tentatively.

LSB, DWT and RSA count are the product of the 2019 analysis (Bhargava, S. and Mukhija, M. 2019) safe with the picture by the encryption strategy. Furthermore, this paper proposes fresh frameworks in which cryptography and steganography are combined to scramble the data and to cover the pieces of information by picture preparation in some other medium. By means of using LSB bits, DWT philosophies, the mixed image can be hidden in any other image with the objective that the message of the secret remains. The recipient can use his or her private key by applying the RSA calculation as the riddle data has been encoded by the public key of the recipient. Conceal the mixed DWT picture. Concentrate the encoded image from the distributed image and use DWT to decode text. In MATLAB, the proposed strategy is implemented.

4. THE PROPOSED METHODOLOGY

The examination approach utilizes the AES, RSA and LSB method. The innovative methodology is shown in fig 8. The plain text content is encoded utilizing AES calculation. A mystery key k is produced haphazardly. The key k is scrambled by the RSA algorithm. The figure key k' is inserted in the code text picture using the LSB approach. Encryption of the plain picture is finished by using AES and the riddle key is enciphered by RSA awry calculation. The nature of the methodology depends on the consolidated methodologies of RSA and AES. For tremendous information it isn't attainable to use RSA as DES is 1500 time faster than RSA. Fig 6 below shows how the image is stored in the database and then encrypted to form the stego-image. It shows the privacy protection of images. Fig 7 shows how the stego-image is decrypted to obtain the decrypted-image.

The proposed technique consists of encrypting the cover image with the AES technique and the secret key is encrypted using the RSA algorithm.

The proposed encryption algorithm is shown below

Proposed Algorithm for Encryption

1. Required: AES cryptographic calculation. RSA calculation, LSB approach
2. Info: Original picture I.
3. Yield: Stego-figured picture I2.
4. Produce subjectively secret key "k".

Figure 6. Privacy protection of images

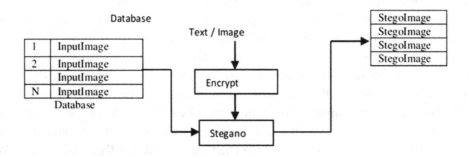

5. Encode the image I using AES count and the secret key "k".
6. Encode puzzle key "k" using RSA calculation.
7. Disguise the figured key "k0" using LSB computation in the encoded picture I1.
8. Return the stego-encoded picture I2.

The proposed decryption technique is as follows:
Proposed Algorithm for Decryption

1. Required: AES cryptographic calculation. RSA calculation, LSB approach

Figure 7. Extracted images matched with given query

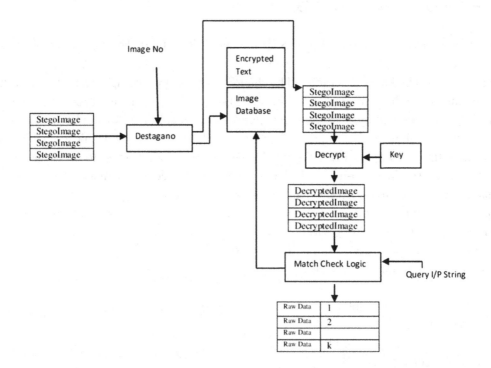

Figure 8. Proposed Methodology

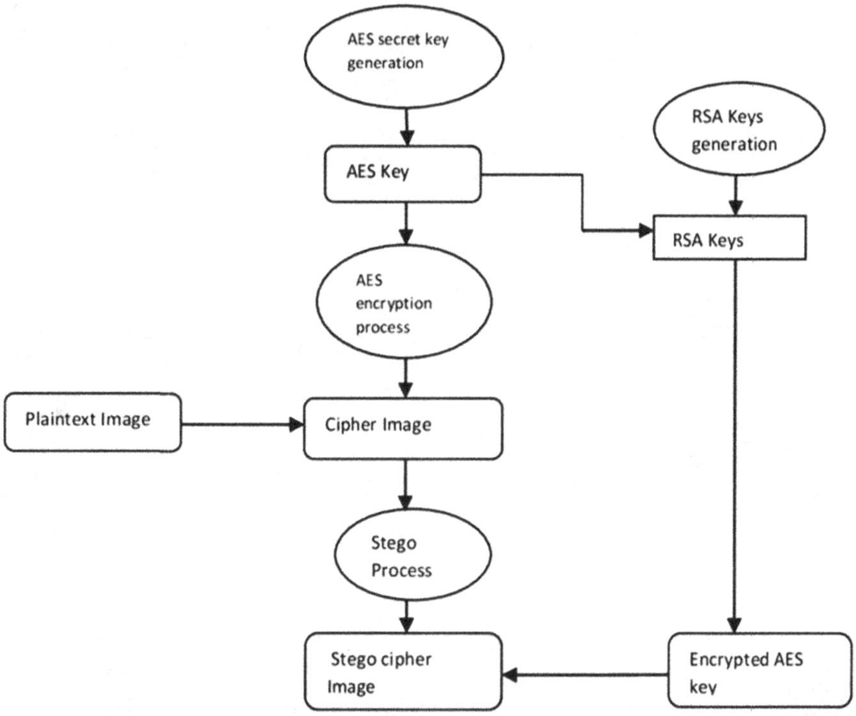

2. Info: Stego-encoded picture I2.
3. Yield: Decrypted picture I.
4. Remove using LSB strategy the encoded riddle key "k0" from the spread picture I2.
5. Unravel using RSA estimation the puzzle key "k0".
6. Unravel the image I1 by AES calculation and the riddle key "k".
7. Return the decoded picture I.

5. RESULTS:

Analysis of the proposed algorithm is made on four gray scale cover images lena.jpg and barbara.jpg, each of size 256 X 256, and baboon.jpg and cameraman.jpg each of size 512 X 512.

The encryption was performed by stream cipher by AES algorithm with a 128 bit key length. The key k has been scrambled with the RSA calculation. Fig 9a, 10a, 11a and 12a shows the cover images taken. By utilizing the LSB strategy, the key k' is embedded in the ciphered picture (Fig 9b, 10b, 11b, 12b). In the wake of extracting the mystery key and decryption (Fig 9c, 10c, 11c, 12c) we get the decrypted picture (Fig 9d, 10d, 11d, 12d).

Figure 9.

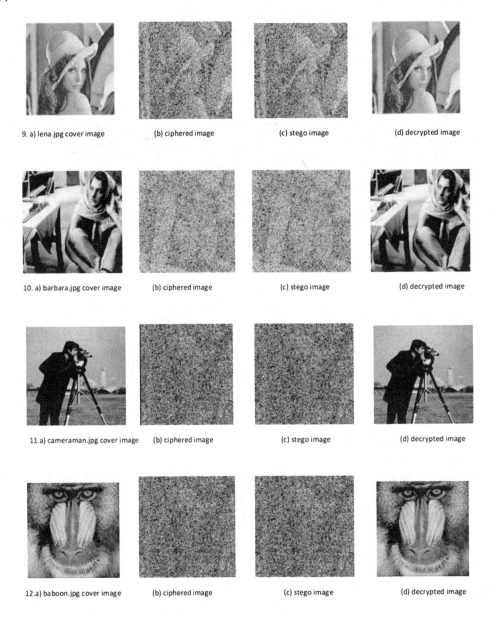

9. a) lena.jpg cover image (b) ciphered image (c) stego image (d) decrypted image

10. a) barbara.jpg cover image (b) ciphered image (c) stego image (d) decrypted image

11.a) cameraman.jpg cover image (b) ciphered image (c) stego image (d) decrypted image

12.a) baboon.jpg cover image (b) ciphered image (c) stego image (d) decrypted image

5.1 Noise Effects in the Images

A wide range of computerized information including images contains noise. On the off chance if the unscrambled image is like the cover image, at that point the encryption system has withheld the noise factor. Subsequent to decoding the scrambled stego-picture the quality of the final picture is acceptable (PSNR > 50 dB) with certifications that propose calculation is resistant against noise. Outputs are shown in Table 2.

Table 2. Resistance for noises

Images image (dB)	image size	PSNR of decrypted
Lena	256 x 256	54.57
Barbara	256 x 256	53.82
Cameraman	512 x 512	54.63
Baboon	512 x 512	56.24

PSNR (Pramanik, S and Singh, R. P. 2017) is the magnitude between a sign's best possible force and the influence of corrupt clamor that affects its depiction's degree of accuracy. The sign here is the spread picture, and the commotion is the blunder in the stego picture achieved by the shrouded pieces. If the evaluation of PSNR is strong, the definition of the stego image will be satisfactory by then. Let the pixels of the spread image be taken as C (I, j) and the pixels of the stego image as S (I, j) for the M x N fixed image dimension. The following condition decides the PSNR appreciation

$$PSNR = 10 \log_{10} \frac{255 \, X \, 255 \, X \, M \, X \, N}{\sum_{i=1}^{M} \sum_{j=1}^{N} (S_{ij} - C_{ij})^2}.$$

5.2 The Correlation Scrutiny:

The scientists attempted to discover the connection between's the abutting pixels in the plaintext picture and code picture and got an irrelevant relationship, so it's tedious to break the proposed approach using connection assaults. The outcomes are shown in Tables 3, 4, 5 and 6.

The correlation coefficient (Banik, B. G. and Banik, A. 2020) (CC) is evaluated by the following formula

Table 3. Lena: Correlation scrutiny of two adjacent pixels.

	Cover image	Coded image	Stego-coded
Row-wise Pixels	0.9335	0.0234	0.0332
Vertical Pixels	0.9284	0.0512	0.0047
Diagonal Pixels	0.9635	0.0231	0.0221

Table 4. Barbara: Correlation scrutiny of two adjacent pixels.

	Cover image	Coded image	Stego-coded
Row-wise Pixels	0.9572	0.0314	0.0028
Vertical Pixels	0.9259	0.0258	0.0037
Diagonal Pixels	0.9327	0.0612	0.0217

$$CC = \frac{cov(x, y)}{\sigma_x \sigma_y} = \frac{\sum_{n=1}^{N} (x_i - E(x))(y_i - E(y))}{\sqrt{\sum_{n=1}^{N} (x_i - E(x))^2} \sqrt{\sum_{n=1}^{N} (y_i - E(y))^2}} \text{ .where,}$$

and x, y are the pixel estimations of any area in the spread picture and encoded picture individually. If the value of CC is nearer to 1, it means that the cover image can be easily obtained from the encrypted image.

5.3 Entropy Evaluation:

Entropy (Kui, X. S. and Wu, J. 2018) analysis E(s) is a crucial technique to find the robustness of an encryption scheme. It is defined by the formula as

Table 5. Cameraman: Correlation scrutiny of two adjacent pixels.

	Cover image	Coded image	Stego-coded
Row-wise Pixels	0.9412	0.0065	0.0256
Vertical Pixels	0.9334	0.0238	0.0038
Diagonal Pixels	0.9542	0.0234	0.0126

$$E(s) = \sum_{i=0}^{2^N - 1} P(m_i) \log_2 \frac{1}{P(m_i)} \text{ .where, P}(m_i) \text{ is the probability of symbol } m_i.$$

In a grayscale image the value of N=8, as $(2^8-1) = 255$ for grayscale image. For grayscale image the optimized entropy value is 8. For an immune cryptosystem, the entropy must be nearer to the optimized value. The proposed methodology has a nearing value of 8 in each case of the test images as shown in Table 7.

Table 8 shows the comparison technique of the proposed technique with AES algorithms (Kalubandi, V. K. P. et al.)

The values in Table 8 show that the proposed technique is superior to the existing technique (Kalubandi, V. K. P. et al.).

Table 6. Baboon: Correlation scrutiny of two adjacent pixels.

	Cover image	Coded image	Stego-coded
Row-wise Pixels	0.9359	0.0249	0.0012
Vertical Pixels	0.9541	0.0542	0.0038
Diagonal Pixels	0.9327	0.0230	0.0254

Table 7. Entropy value of: Cover image, Encrypted image and Stego-ciphered image

Image	Cover image	Coded image	Stego-coded
Lena	7.5201	7.2843	7.3275
Barbara	7.8322	7.6573	7.7820
Cameraman	7.6214	6.8741	7.2471
Baboon	7.5287	7.1279	7.3347

6. DISCUSSIONS

6.1 An Example of RSA Encryption

6.1.1 Key Generation

a.   Create two enormous prime numbers p and q: To make the model simple to tail he researchers will utilize little numbers, however this isn't secure. To discover arbitrary primes, start at an irregular number and go up in a climbing request. Take numbers until a prime number is gotten. How about we take

p=7

q=19

b.   Let n=p*q

n=7*19=133

c.   Let m = (p-1)*(q-1)

Table 8. CC and Entropy value of Proposed Technique (lena.jpg) and AES algorithm (Kalubandi, V. K. P. et al.)

Statistical Image Analysis	Proposed Approach (lena.jpg)		AES Technique (Kalubandi, V. K. P. et al.)			
	Cover Image	Enciphered Image	Cover Image		Enciphered Image	
Row-wise Correlation	0.9578		0.0652	0.9342	0.0251	
Upright Correlation	0.9231		0.0574	0.9174	-0.0384	
Diagonal Correlation	0.9592		0.0312	0.9226	-0.0127	
Entropy Measure			7.7943		7.6721	
Statistical Image Analysis	Proposed Approach (baboon.jpg)		AES Technique (Kalubandi, V. K. P. et al.)			
	Cover Image	Enciphered Image	Cover Image		Enciphered Image	
Row-wise Correlation	0.9337		0.0689	0.9441	- 0.0462	
Upright Correlation	0.9783		0.0527	0.9510	0.0421	
Diagonal Correlation	0.9657		0.0581	0.9278	- 0.0256	
Entropy Measure			7.6642		7.3614	

$$m = (7-1)*(19-1)$$
$$=6*18=108$$

d. Pick a little prime e, co-prime to m. This implies the biggest number that can precisely isolate both e and m (their most prominent regular divisor, or gcd) is 1.

$$e=2=>gcd(e,108)=2(FALSE)$$
$$e=3=>gcd(e,108)=3(FALSE)$$
$$e=4=>gcd(e,108)=4(FALSE)$$
$$e=5=>gcd(e,108)=1(TRUE)$$

e. Discover d, with the end goal that d*e %m=1: This condition is proportionate to discovering d which fulfills de=1+nm where n is any whole number. Reworking this as $d = (1+nm)/e$. Presently check through the estimations of n until a number answer for e is found.

$$n=0=>d=1/5(FALSE)$$
$$n=1=>d=109/5(FALSE)$$
$$n=2=>d=217/5(FALSE)$$
$$n=3=>d=325/5=65(TRUE)$$

PUBLIC KEY SECRET KEY

n=133 n=133

e=5 d=65

6.1.2 Encryption

The message must be a number not exactly the littler of p and q.

$$C=Pe \%n$$

$$=65\% \ 133$$

$$=7776\% \ 133$$

$$=62$$

Both encryption and decoding in RSA include raising and whole number to a number force, mod n. In the event that the exponentiation is done over the whole numbers and, at that point diminished module n, the middle qualities would be enormous. Luckily, as the first, model shows, there can be utilization of a property of particular number-crunching:

[(a mod n) * (b mod n)] mod n = (a*b) mod n

Along these lines there can be a decrease in the middle of the road results modulo n. This makes the estimation down to earth. Another thought is the proficiency of exponentiation, in light of the fact that with RSA there are dealings with possibly enormous exponentiations. To perceive how effectiveness may be expanded, and on the off chance that there is a desire to register x16, at that point a direct methodology requires 15 augmentations:

$$x16=x*x*x*x*x*x*x*x*x*x*x*x*x*x*x*x$$

Be that as it may, a similar conclusive outcome can be accomplished with just four duplications if consistently taken the square of every halfway outcome, progressively framing x2, x4, x8, and x16.

Key length:

The key length for a protected RSA transmission is ordinarily 1024 pieces. 512 pieces is currently not, at this point thought about secure. For greater security or on the off chance that you are suspicious, utilize 2048 or even 4096 pieces. With the quicker PCs accessible today, the time taken to scramble and unscramble even with a 4096-piece modulus truly isn't an issue any longer. By and by, it is still adequately incomprehensible for you or an interloper to split a message with a 512-piece key. An association like NSA who has the most recent supercomputers can presumably split it by beast power in a sensible time, on the off chance that they decide to give their assets something to do on it.

6.1.3 Decryption

This works very much like encryption.

$P=C^d \% n$

$=62^{65\%}$ 133

Network data security has become one of the most important fields in Information technology. That is because web technology is being used everywhere and security has been a big concern. In this regard RSA algorithm is not very much secured because RSA is a public key cryptography. If plain text input message is beyond 11 character (letter or number) the software can't encrypt this message.

6.2 Attacks on RSA Algorithm

The following are three possible ways of dealing with the attack on the RSA calculation:

Brute Force: The most basic assault technique for any code is savage control, which involves trying all imaginable private keys. The length of the key here specifies the number of possible keys.

Numerical assaults: There are a few methodologies, all comparable as a result to figuring the result of two primes.

Timing assaults: These rely upon the running season of the unscrambling calculation. The protection against the savage power approach is the equivalent for RSA (Pramanik, S. et al. 2014) concerning different cryptosystems, in particular, utilize an enormous key space. Subsequently, the bigger the quantity of pieces in e and d, the better it is. Be that as it may, on the grounds that the counts in question, both in key age and in encryption/decoding, are perplexing, the bigger the size of the key, the more slow the framework will run. Timing assaults is disturbing for two reasons. It originates from a totally surprising course and it is a code text just assault. Timing assault can be clarified utilizing the measured exponentiation calculation, yet this assault can be received to work with any execution that doesn't run in fixed time. In this calculation, measured exponentiation is practiced a tiny bit at a time, with one secluded increase acted in each cycle and an extra particular duplication performed for every one of 1 piece. The assault is least complex to comprehend in an extraordinary case. Assume the objective framework utilizes a secluded increase work that is exceptionally quick in practically all case however in a couple of cases takes substantially more time than a whole normal particular exponentiation. The assault continues a little bit at a time beginning with the furthest left piece bk. Assume that the main j pieces are known (to acquire the guaranteeing example, start with j=0 and rehash the assault until the whole type is known). For a given code text, the aggressor can finish the main j cycles of the 'for' circle. The activity of the resulting step relies upon the obscure example bit. In the event that the bit is set d<-(d*a) mod n will be executed. For a couple of estimations of an and d, the measured augmentation will be incredibly moderate, and the assailant knows which these are. Hence, if the watched chance to execute the unscrambling calculation is in every case moderate when this specific cycle is delayed with a 1 piece, at that point this bit is thought to be 1. On the off chance that various watched execution times for the whole calculation are quick, at that point this bit is thought to be 0. By and by, secluded exponentiation usage don't have outrageous planning varieties, in which the execution season of a solitary emphasis can surpass the mean execution season of the whole calculation.

Since it is seen that RSA algorithm has a major security problem so to look for better and more secure data encryption and decryption techniques there is a need to go for Cellular Automata (CA). Fundamentally Cellular Automata (Azza, A.A., Lian, S. 2020) is an equal framework that comprises of an ordinarily huge number of limited automata (limited state machines) as rudimentary cells. The phones are privately associated, as it were, the worldwide organization underpins just nearby associations. The framework develops through nearby changes: all phones are refreshed simultaneously, contingent upon their present status and on the conditions of the neighboring cells on the organization. Cell Automata is utilized as arbitrary grouping generator. The inalienable parallelism of CA cells with their effortlessness and nearby cooperations makes it especially reasonable for planning an ease crypto-equipment.

6.3 The Factoring Problem

Distinguishing proof of three methodologies of RSA should be possible numerically:

Calculate n its two prime components. This empowers estimation of m = (p-1) x (q-1), which, thusly, empowers assurance of d=e-1(mod (n)). Decide (n) legitimately, without first deciding p and q. Once more, this empowers assurance of d=e-1 (mod (n)). Decide d legitimately, without first deciding mod (n).

Cryptanalysis of RSA has zeroed in on the undertaking of calculating n into its prime elements. Deciding mod (n) given n is proportional to figuring n. With by and by known calculations, deciding d given e and n seems, by all accounts, to be at any rate as tedious as the considering issue. Consequently, we can utilize calculating execution as benchmark against which to assess the security of RSA. For a huge n with enormous prime variables, calculating is a difficult issue. Accordingly, we should be cautious in picking a key size for RSA. Notwithstanding determining the size of n, various different requirements have been recommended. To evade estimations of n that might be calculated all the more effectively, the calculation puts the accompanying imperatives on p and q.

1. p and q ought to contrast long by just a couple of pieces.
2. Both (p-1) and (q-1) ought to contain an enormous prime factor.
3. gcd (p-1,q-1) ought to be little.
4. Furthermore on the off chance that e<n and d<n1/4, at that point d can be effortlessly decided.

6.4 Different Levels of Security of Cellular Automata (CA) Cryptosystems:

Huge Key Space: The quantity of conceivable key is huge (2128) and all key are equiprobable to happen. This arbitrariness in key age gives irregular likelihood dissemination in key space. Since we can change the size of the minor and significant CA (Debnath, B., Das, J. C. what's more, De, D., 2018) the key size can likewise fluctuate. So we can have a variable key space of any subjective size.

Security Level 1-Linear Transformation: Each byte of token T is exposed to an arbitrary revolution chose by Minor CA state. Since Minor CA is a magnificent pseudo-arbitrary generator, this turn of token acquaints a level of arbitrariness with the info token.

Security Level 2-Affine Transformation and On-line Synthesis of Major CA: The state progress of a Major CA which is added substance produces a relative change (Ramalingam, M., Isa, N. A. M. furthermore, Puviarasi, R. 2020). On the fly age of significant CA diminishes the memory prerequisite by a huge sum and just as improves the security. The quantity of all conceivable CA having the cycle structure of Major CA is higher than 2128. Subsequently, each seed (SN) produces distinctive Major CA furnishing us with the enormous chance of 2128 diverse Major CA. This guarantees that each key worth (K) will scramble distinctively and no key will be unnecessary. Accordingly the CAC fulfills one of the significant models of a safe cryptosystem.

Security Level 3-Non-relative Transformation: This is a non-relative reversible CA change, which empowers CAC to produce a non-relative gathering, which is the substituting gathering. The relative gathering is a little subgroup of the rotating gathering. In this manner CAC, having the option to create the substituting gathering, which is a lot bigger than the relative gathering, fulfills another significant rule of a safe cryptosystem, which says that capacity to produce the exchanging bunch on the message space is one of the most grounded security conditions.

Security Level 4-Key-blending: The halfway token is next XORed with the state SN of the minor CA. This is straightforward and takes just a solitary clock cycle. In any case, it makes the scrambled token (Tencr) absolutely capricious. The best way to return back to the first string is to arbitrarily attempt with 128 pieces, which will cost O (2128) tasks, for each token.

Security Level 5: In request to additionally build the degree of security, our Scheme can be utilized in bricklaying mode, which will utilize staggered encryption. This should be possible with a minor addition of the expense while utilizing a similar essential structure.

Now looking at the above-mentioned reasons it can be said that Cellular Automata Cryptosystem (CAC) (Achkoun, K., Hanin, C. & Omary, F. 2019) is always best, but the acceptance of any cryptosystem depends on its sustainability against various cryptanalysis attacks. And it has been proved that if differential cryptanalysis is performed with 50 different files having 11 different sizes, then also CA is significantly better than that of DES and RSA. Tests with some more cases like Shannon's Security Quotient proves that CAC is better than others.

7. CONCLUSION

Expanding data assets are required to drive development in the business analysis and data mining. Organizations are starting to understand that the utilization of data mining and text mining gives them a serious edge. With data expanding in an exponential way, the capacity to utilize data mining to filter through a gigantic measures of data and recognize important examples will turn into a key device in improving key territories of the business, for example, clients, activities and the supply chain. Thus, the privacy and security of data needs to be improvised in any organization. This article enhances the security mechanism of data using various encryption and steganographic algorithms in the sphere of business intelligence of an organization.

FUTURE RESEARCH DIRECTIONS

In this rapidly changing world buyers are directly mentioning snappier progressively capable help from associations. To stay genuine, associations must meet or outperform the wants for clients. Associations ought to depend all the more seriously on their business insight structures to stay in front of different contenders and future events. Business understanding customers are beginning to demand Real time Business Intelligence or near continuous examinations relating to their business, particularly in bleeding edge exercises. They will by and large expect up until this point in time and new information along these lines as they screen stock articulations on the web. Month to month examination or even step by step examination won't work. In the not far-removed future associations will transform into dependent on consistent business information in much a comparative style as people for the most part hope to get information on the web in just a couple of snap of a mouse. Moreover, soon business information will turn out to be more democratized where end customers from all through the association will have the choice to see information on their particular bit to see how it's performing. Along these lines, later on, the capacity requirements of business information will augment similarly the purchaser desires increment. It is in this way basic that associations adjust to a fast movement to stay genuine.

REFERENCES

Achkoun, K., Hanin, C. & Omary, F. (2019). SPF-CA: A new cellular automata based block cipher using key-dependent S-boxes. *Journal of Discrete Mathematical Sciences and Cryptography*. Doi:10.10 80/09720529.2019.1649031

Aithal, P. S. (2016). A Review on Various E-Business and M-Business Models & Research Opportunities. *International Journal of Management, IT and Engineering, 6*(1), 275-298. Available at SSRN: https://ssrn.com/abstract=2779175

Antonio, H., Prasad, P. W. C., & Alsadoon, A. (2019). Implementation of Cryptography in Steganography for Enhanced Security. *Multimedia Tools and Applications, 78*(23), 32721–32734. doi:10.100711042-019-7559-7

Azza, A. A., & Lian, S. (2020). *Multi-secret image sharing based on elementary cellular automata with steganography*. Multimed Tools Appl. doi:10.100711042-020-08823-8

Bandekar, P. P., & Suguna, G. C. (2018). LSB Based Text and Image Steganography Using AES Algorithm. *3rd International Conference on Communication and Electronics Systems (ICCES)*, 782-788. 10.1109/CESYS.2018.8724069

Banik, B. G., & Banik, A. (2020). Robust, Imperceptible and Blind Video Steganography using RGB Secret, Maximum Likelihood Estimation and Fibonacci Encryption. *International Journal of Electronic Security and Digital Forensics*, *12*(2), 174–199. doi:10.1504/IJESDF.2020.106310

Bhargava, S., & Mukkhija, M. (2019). Hide Image and Text using LSB, DWT and RSA based on Image Steganography. *ICTACT Journal on Image and Video Processing*, *9*(3), 1940–1946. doi:10.21917/ijivp.2019.0275

Chaharlang, J., Mosleh, M., & Rasouli-Heikalabad, S. (2020). A novel quantum steganography-Steganalysis system for audio signals. *Multimedia Tools and Applications*, *79*(25-26), 17551–17577. doi:10.100711042-020-08694-z

Damrudi, M., & Aval, K. J. (2019). Image Steganography using LSB and Encrypted Message with AES, RSA, DES, 3DES and Blowfish. *International Journal of Engineering and Advanced Technology*, *8*(63), 204–208.

Debnath, B., Das, J. C., & De, D. (2018). Design of Image Steganographic Architecture using Quantum-Dot Cellular Automata for Secure Nanocommunication Networks. *Nano Communication Networks*, *15*, 41–58. doi:10.1016/j.nancom.2017.11.001

Douglas, M., Bailey, K., Leeney, M., & Curran, K. (2018). An overview of steganography techniques applied to the protection of biometric data. *Multimedia Tools and Applications*, *77*(13), 17333–17373. doi:10.100711042-017-5308-3

Duan, X., Guo, D., Liu, N., Li, B., Gou, M., & Qin, C. (2020). A New High Capacity Image SteganographyMethod Combined with Image Elliptic Curve Cryptography and Deep Neural Network. *IEEE Access: Practical Innovations, Open Solutions*, *8*, 25777–25788. doi:10.1109/ACCESS.2020.2971528

Embaby, A. A., Mohamed, A., Shalaby, W., & Elsayed, K. M. (2020). Digital Watermarking Properties, Classification and Techniques. *International Journal of Engineering and Advanced Technology*, *9*(3), 2742–2750. doi:10.35940/ijeat.C5773.029320

Eyssa, A. A., Abdelsamie, F. E., & Abdelnaiem, A. E. (2020). An Efficient Image Steganography Approach over Wireless Communication System. *Wireless Personal Communications*, *110*(1), 321–337. doi:10.100711277-019-06730-2

Gowda, S. N. (2016). An advanced Diffie-Hellman approach to image steganography. *2016 IEEE International Conference on Advanced Networks and Telecommunications Systems (ANTS)*, 1-4. 10.1109/ANTS.2016.7947849

Gupta, M.K., & Chandra, P. (2020). A comprehensive survey of data mining. *Int. J. Inf. Tecnol.* doi:10.100741870-020-00427-7

Hambouz, A., Shaheen, Y., Manna, A., Al-Fayoumi, M., & Tedmori, S. S. (2019). Achieving Data Integrity and Confidentiality Using Image Steganography and Hashing Techniques. *2nd International Conference on new Trends in Computing Sciences (ICTCS)*, 1-6. doi: 10.1109/ICTCS.2019.8923060

Kalubandi, V. K. P., Vaddi, H., Ramineni, V., & Agilandeeswari Loganathan, A. (2016). A Novel Image Encryption Algorithm using AES and Visual Cryptography. *Proceedings of NGCT 2016*. 10.1109/NGCT.2016.7877521

Kui, X. S., & Wu, J. (2018). A Modification Free Steganography Method Based on Image Information Entropy. *Security and Communication Networks*, 1–8. doi:10.1155/2018/6256872

Kumar, S., Singh, A., & Kumar, M. (2019). *Information Hiding with Adaptive Steganography based on Novel Fuzzy Edge Identification*. Defence Technology. doi:10.1016/j.dt.2018.08.003

Lanza-Cruz, I., Berlanga, R., & Aramburu, M. J. (2018). Modelling Analytical Streams for Social Business Intelligence. *Informatica (Vilnius)*, *5*(3), 33. doi:10.3390/informatics5030033

Mahato, S., Khan, D. A., & Yadav, D. K. (2020). A Modified Approach to Data Hiding in Microsoft Word Documents by Change-Tracking Technique. *Journal of King Saud University-Computer and Information Sciences*, *32*(2), 216–224. doi:10.1016/j.jksuci.2017.08.004

Mukherjee, S., Roy, S., & Sanyal, G. (2018). Image Steganography using Mid Position Value Technique. *Procedia Computer Science*, *132*, 461–468. doi:10.1016/j.procs.2018.05.160

Ozighor, E. R., & Izegbu, I. (2020). Information Protection against Security Threats in an Insecure Environment using Cryptography and Steganography. *Computing in Science & Engineering*, *8*(5), 1671–1692.

Padmavathi, B., & Kumari, R. (2013). A Survey on Performance Analysis of DES, AES and RSA Algorithm alongwith LSB Substitution Technique. *International Journal of Scientific Research (Ahmedabad, India)*, *2*(4), 170–174.

Panwar, S., Damani, S., & Kumar, M. (2018). Digital Image Steganography using Modified LSB and AES Cryptography. *International Journal of Recent Engineering Research and Development*, *3*(6), 18–27.

Pradhan, A., Sekhar, K. R., & Swain, G. (2018). Digital Image Steganography Using LSB Substitution, PVD and EMD, Mathematical Problems in Engineering. *Article ID*, *1804953*. Advance online publication. doi:10.1155/2018/1804953

Pramanik, S., Bandyopadhyay, S. K., & Ghosh, R. (2020). Signature Image Hiding in Color Image using Steganography and Cryptography based on Digital Signature Concepts. *2020 2nd International Conference on Innovative Mechanisms for Industry Applications (ICIMIA)*, 665-669.

Pramanik, S., & Bandyopadhyay, S. (2013). Application of Steganography in Symmetric Key Cryptography with Genetic Algorithm. *International Journal of Computers and Technology*, *10*(7).

Pramanik, S., & Raja, S. S. (2019). Analytical Study on Security Issues in Steganography. *Think India Journal*, *22*(3), 106–114.

Pramanik, S., & Raja, S. S. (2020). A Secured Image Steganography using Genetic Algorithm, Advances in Mathemetics. *Scientific Journal*, *9*(7), 4533–4541. doi:10.37418/amsj.9

Pramanik, S., & Samir Kumar Bandyopadhyay, S. K. (2014). Hiding Secret Message in an Image, International Journal of Innovative Science. *Engineering & Technology*, *1*(3), 553–559.

Pramanik, S., & Singh, R. P. (2017). Role of Steganography in Security Issues. *International Conference on Advance Studies in Engineering and Science*, 1225-1230.

Pramanik, S., Singh, R.P., & Ghosh, R. (2019). A New Encrypted Method in Image Steganography. *Indonesian Journal of Electrical Engineering and Computer Science, 14*(3), 1412–1419. .v13.i3.pp1412-1419 doi:10.11591/ijeecs

Pramanik, S., Singh, R. P., & Ghosh, R. (2020). *Application of bi-orthogonal wavelet transform and genetic algorithm in image steganography*. Multimed Tools Appl. doi:10.100711042-020-08676-1

Ramalingam, M., Isa, N. A. M., & Puviarasi, R. (2020). A Secured Data Hiding using Affline Transformation in Video Steganography. *Procedia Computer Science, 171*, 1147–1156. doi:10.1016/j.procs.2020.04.123

Rashid, A., & Rahim, M. K. (2016). Critical Analysis of Steganography "An Art of Hidden Writing". *International Journal of Security and Applications, 10*(1), 259–282. doi:10.14257/ijsia.2016.10.3.24

Ritala, P., Schneider, S., & Michailova, S. (2020). Innovation management research methods: embracing rigor and diversity. *R&D Management*. doi:10.1111/radm.12414

Rivest, R. L., Shamir, A., & Adleman, L. (1977). *A Method for Obtaining Digital Signatures and Public-Key Cryptosystems*. htts://people.csail.mit.edu/rivest/Rsapaper.pdf

Sah, H. R., & Gunasekaran, G. (2015). Privacy preserving data mining using visual steganography and encryption. *10th International Conference on Computer Science & Education (ICCSE)*, 154-158. 10.1109/ICCSE.2015.7250234

Setyono, A., & Setiadi, D. R. I. M. (2019). Securing and Hiding Secret Message in Image using XOR Transposition Encryption and LSB Method. *Journal of Physics: Conference Series, 1196*, 012039. doi:10.1088/1742-6596/1196/1/012039

Swain, G. (2018). *High Capacity Image Steganography Using Modified LSB Substitution and PVD against Pixel Difference Histogram Analysis*. Security and Computer Networks. doi:10.1155/2018/1505896

Taha, M. S., Rahim, M. S. M., Lafta, S. A., Hashim, M. A., & Alzuabidi, H. M. (2019). Combination of Steganography and Cryptography: A Short Survey. *ICSET, 2019*, 052003. Advance online publication. doi:10.1088/1757-899X/518/5/052003

Von Leipzig, T., Gamp, M., Manz, D., Schöttle, K., Ohlhausen, P., Oosthuizen, G., Palm, D., & von Leipzig, K. (2017). Initialising customer-orientated digital transformation in enterprises. *Procedia Manufacturing, 8*, 517–524. doi:10.1016/j.promfg.2017.02.066

Wang, M., Gu, W., & Ma, C. (2020). A Multimode Network Steganography for Covert Wireless Communication based on BitTorrent. *Security and Communication Networks*. Advance online publication. doi:10.1155/2020/8848315

Zenati, A., Ouarda, W., & Alimi, A. M. (2019). SSDIS-BEM: A New Signature Steganography Document Image System based on Beta Elliptic Modeling. *Engineering Science and Technology, an International Journal, 23*(3), 470-482.

Compilation of References

Abdelaziz, E., Soufiane, M., & Ahmed, E. (2020). Survey of Monero Security. Dynamical and Control Systems, 12, 88-93.

Acharjya, D.P. (2016). A Survey on Big Data Analytics: Challenges, Open Research Issues and Tools. *International Journal of Advanced Computer Science and Applications, 7*(2).

Achkoun, K., Hanin, C. & Omary, F. (2019). SPF-CA: A new cellular automata based block cipher using key-dependent S-boxes. *Journal of Discrete Mathematical Sciences and Cryptography*. Doi:10.1080/09720529.2019.1649031

Afzali, G. A., & Mohammadi, S. (2017). Privacy preserving big data mining: Association rule hiding using fuzzy logic approach. *IET Information Security, 12*(1), 15–24. doi:10.1049/iet-ifs.2015.0545

Aithal, P. S. (2016). A Review on Various E-Business and M-Business Models & Research Opportunities. *International Journal of Management, IT and Engineering, 6*(1), 275-298. Available at SSRN: https://ssrn.com/abstract=2779175

Aliferis, C., Tsamardinos, I., & Statnikov, A. (2003). Hiton: A novel markov blanket algorithm for optimal variable selection. *AMIA ... Annual Symposium proceedings / AMIA Symposium. AMIA Symposium*, 21–5.

Aliferis, C. F., Statnikov, A., Tsamardinos, I., Mani, S., & Koutsoukos, X. D. (2010). Local causal and markov blanket induction for causal discovery and feature selection for classification part i: Algorithms and empirical evaluation. *Journal of Machine Learning Research, 11*, 171–234.

Alkharboush, N., & Li, Y. (2010). A decision rule method for data quality assessment. *Proceedings of the 15th International Conference on Information Quality*.

Alloghani, M., Al-Jumeily, D., Mustafina, J., Hussain, A., & Aljaaf, A. J. (2020). A Systematic Review on Supervised and Unsupervised Machine Learning Algorithms for Data Science. In Supervised and Unsupervised Learning for Data Science. Springer. doi:10.1007/978-3-030-22475-2_1

Alnoukari, M., Alhawasli, H., Alnafea, H. A., & Zamreek, A. (2012). Business Intelligence: Body of Knowledge. In Business Intelligence and Agile Methodologies for Knowledge-Based Organizations: Cross-Disciplinary Applications (pp. 1-13). IGI Global.

Alnoukari, M. (2009). Using Business Intelligence Solutions for Achieving Organization's Strategy: Arab International University Case Study. *Internetworking Indonesia Journal, 1*(2), 11–15.

Alnoukari, M., & Hanano, A. (2017). Integration of business intelligence with corporate strategic management. *Journal of Intelligence Studies in Business, 7*(2), 5–16. doi:10.37380/jisib.v7i2.235

Alpoim, Â., Guimarães, T., Portela, F., & Santos, M. F. Evaluation Model for Big Data Integration Tools. Advances in Intelligent Systems and Computing (WorldCist 2019 - PIS Workshop). Volume 932, 2019, pp. 601-610. ISBN: 978-3-319-77699-6. Springer. (2019). DOI:10.1007/978-3-030-16187-3_58

Al-Qirim, N., Rouibah, K., Serhani, M. A., Tarhini, A., Khalil, A., Maqableh, M., & Gergely, M. (2019). The Strategic Adoption of Big Data in Organizations. In Z. Sun (Ed.), *Managerial Perspectives on Intelligent Big Data Analytics* (pp. 43–54). IGI Global. doi:10.4018/978-1-5225-7277-0.ch003

Alserafi, A., Abell'o, A., Romero, O., & Calders, T. (2016). *Towards information profiling: data lake content metadata management.* Paper presented at the IEEE 16th International Conference on Data Mining Workshops (ICDMW), Barcelona, Spain. 10.1109/ICDMW.2016.0033

Altalhi, A. H., Luna, J. M., Vallejo, M. A., & Ventura, S. (2017). Evaluation and comparison of open source software suites for data mining and knowledge discovery. *Wiley Interdisciplinary Reviews. Data Mining and Knowledge Discovery*, *7*(3), e1204. doi:10.1002/widm.1204

Amooee, G., Bidgoli, B., & Dehnavi, M. (2011). A Comparison Between Data Mining Prediction Algorithms for Fault Detection. *International Journal of Computer Science Issues*, *8*(6), 425–431.

Analytics Insight. (2019, December 8). *AI and BI: Powering the Next-Generation of Analytics.* Retrieved from https://www.analyticsinsight.net/ai-and-bi-powering-the-next-generation-of-analytics/

Andreas, A. M. (2014). *Mastering Bitcoin: Unlocking Digital Cryptocurrencies.* O'Reilly Media, Inc.

Andreas, A. M., & Wood, G. (2018). *Mastering Ethereum: Building Smart Contracts and Dapps.* O'reilly Media.

Antonio, H., Prasad, P. W. C., & Alsadoon, A. (2019). Implementation of Cryptography in Steganography for Enhanced Security. *Multimedia Tools and Applications*, *78*(23), 32721–32734. doi:10.100711042-019-7559-7

Apgar, D. (2015). The False Promise of Big Data: Can Data Mining Replace Hypothesis-Driven Learning in the Identification of Predictive Performance Metrics? *Systems Research and Behavioral Science*, *32*(1), 28–49. doi:10.1002res.2219

Aria, M., & Cuccurullo, C. (2017). bibliometrix: An R-tool for comprehensive science mapping analysis. *Journal of Informetrics*, *11*(4), 959–975. doi:10.1016/j.joi.2017.08.007

Azevedo, A. (2012). *Data Mining Languages for Business Intelligence* (Doctoral Thesis). Retrieved from RepositoriUM: http://hdl.handle.net/1822/22892

Azevedo, A. I. R. L., & Santos, M. F. (2009). An architecture for an effective usage of data mining in business intelligence systems. *Knowledge Management and Innovation in Advancing Economies: Analyses & Solutions*, 1319-1325.

Azevedo, A., & Santos, M. F. (2012). Closing the Gap between Data Mining and Business Users of Business Intelligence Systems: A Design Science Approach. *International Journal of Business Intelligence Research*, *3*(4), 14–53. doi:10.4018/jbir.2012100102

Aziz, I. (2020). *Deep Learning: An Overview of Convolutional Neural Network.* CNN.

Azza, A. A., & Lian, S. (2020). *Multi-secret image sharing based on elementary cellular automata with steganography.* Multimed Tools Appl. doi:10.100711042-020-08823-8

Bae, D. H., Kim, J. H., Kim, S. W., Oh, H., & Park, C. (2013) Intelligent SSD: a turbo for big data mining. *Proceedings of the 22nd ACM international conference on Information & Knowledge Management*, 1573-1576. 10.1145/2505515.2507847

Baek, U.-J., Ji, S.-H., Park, J. T., Lee, M.-S., Park, J.-S., & Kim, M.-S. (2019). *DDoS Attack Detection on Bitcoin Ecosystem Using Deep-Learning.* IEEE Conference Publication. https://ieeexplore.ieee.org/abstract/document/8892837

Baldi, P., Brunak, S., Chauvin, Y., Andersen, C., & Nielsen, H. (2000). Assessing the accuracy of prediction algorithms for classification: An overview. *Bioinformatics (Oxford, England)*, *16*(5), 412–424. doi:10.1093/bioinformatics/16.5.412 PMID:10871264

Bandekar, P. P., & Suguna, G. C. (2018). LSB Based Text and Image Steganography Using AES Algorithm. *3rd International Conference on Communication and Electronics Systems (ICCES)*, 782-788. 10.1109/CESYS.2018.8724069

Banik, B. G., & Banik, A. (2020). Robust, Imperceptible and Blind Video Steganography using RGB Secret, Maximum Likelihood Estimation and Fibonacci Encryption. *International Journal of Electronic Security and Digital Forensics*, *12*(2), 174–199. doi:10.1504/IJESDF.2020.106310

Bastiaan, M. (2015). *Preventing the 51%-Attack: A Stochastic Analysis of Two Phase Proof of Work in Bitcoin.* Http:// Referaat. Cs. Utwente. Nl/Conference/22/Paper/7473/Preventingthe-51-Attack-a-Stochasticanalysis-Oftwo-Phase-Proof-of-Work-in-Bitcoin.Pdf

Batini, C., & Scannapieco, M. (2006). *Data Quality. Concepts, Methodologies and Techniques* (1st ed.). Springer-Verlag.

Batran, M., Mejia, M. G., Kanasugi, H., Sekimoto, Y., & Shibasaki, R. (2018). Inferencing human spatiotemporal mobility in greater Maputo via mobile phone big data mining. *ISPRS International Journal of Geo-Information*, *7*(7), 259. doi:10.3390/ijgi7070259

Beheshti, A., Benatallah, B., Sheng, Q., & Schiliro, F. (2020). Intelligent Knowledge Lakes: The Age of Artificial Intelligence and Big Data. In U. Leong, J. Yang, Y. Cai, K. Karlapalem, A. Liu, & X. Huang (Eds.), *Web Information Systems Engineering. WISE 2020. Communications in Computer and Information Science* (Vol. 1155). Springer. doi:10.1007/978-981-15-3281-8_3

Berntzen, L., & Krumova, M. (2017). Big Data from a Business Perspective. In M. Themistocleous & V. Morabito (Eds.), *Information Systems* (pp. 119–127). Springer. doi:10.1007/978-3-319-65930-5_10

Beyer, M., Thoo, E., & Zaidi, E. (2018). *Gartner Magic Quadrant for Data Integration Tools.* Academic Press.

Bhargava, S., & Mukkhija, M. (2019). Hide Image and Text using LSB, DWT and RSA based on Image Steganography. *ICTACT Journal on Image and Video Processing*, *9*(3), 1940–1946. doi:10.21917/ijivp.2019.0275

Bischof, C., Gabriel, M., Rabel, B., & Wilfinger, D. (2016). Strategic Implications of BIG DATA – A Comprehensive View. *Proceedings of the Management International Conference (MIC 2016)*, 143–160.

BI-Survey. (2019). *Top Business Intelligence Trends 2020: What 2,865 BI Professionals Really Think.* BARC (Business Application Research Center). Retrieved from https://bi-survey.com/top-business-intelligence-trends

Blake, R., & Mangiameli, P. (2008). The effects and interactions of data quality and problem complexity on Data Mining. *Proceedings of the 13th International Conference on Information Quality*, 160—175

Bol'on-Canedo, V., S'anchez-Maron~o, N., & Alonso-Betanzos, A. (2015). Recent advances and emerging challenges of feature selection in the context of big data. *Knowledge-Based Systems*, *86*, 33–45. doi:10.1016/j.knosys.2015.05.014

Borboudakis, G., & Tsamardinos, I. (2019). Forward-backward selection with early dropping. *Journal of Machine Learning Research*, *20*(1), 276–314.

Borek, A., Parlikad, A., Webb, J., & Woodall, P. (2014). *Total Information Risk Management.* Morgan Kaufmann.

Bos, Halderman, Heninger, Moore, Naehrig, & Wustrow. (2014). Elliptic Curve Cryptography in Practice. In *International Conference on Financial Cryptography and Data Security.* Springer.

Bouaziz, S., Nabli, A., & Gargouri, F. (2019). Design a Data Warehouse Schema from Document-Oriented database. *Procedia Computer Science*, *159*(1), 221–230. doi:10.1016/j.procs.2019.09.177

Braganza, A., Brooks, L., Nepelski, D., Ali, M., & Moro, R. (2017). Resource management in big data initiatives: Processes and dynamic capabilities. *Journal of Business Research*, *70*, 328–337. doi:10.1016/j.jbusres.2016.08.006

Bralić, V., Stančić, H., & Stengard, M. (2020). A Blockchain Approach to Digital Archiving: Digital Signature Certification Chain Preservation. *Records Management Journal, ahead-of-print*(ahead-of-print). Advance online publication. doi:10.1108/RMJ-08-2019-0043

Brock, V., & Khan, H. U. (2017). Big data analytics: Does organizational factor matters impact technology acceptance? *Journal of Big Data*, *4*(21), 1–28. doi:10.118640537-017-0081-8

Buhl, H. U., Röglinger, M., Moser, F., & Heidemann, J. (2013). Big data. *Business & Information Systems Engineering*, *5*(2), 65–69. doi:10.100712599-013-0249-5

Buttle, F., & Maklan, S. (2019). *Customer Relationship Management: Concepts and Technologies* (4th ed.). Routledge. doi:10.4324/9781351016551

Cai, C. H., Fu, A. W., Cheng, C. H., & Kwong, W. W. (1998). Mining association rules with weighted items. *Proceedings of the International Database Engineering and Applications Symposium*, 68–77. 10.1109/IDEAS.1998.694360

Cai, L., & Zhu, Y. (2015). The Challenges of Data Quality and Data Quality Assessment in the Big Data Era. *Data Science Journal*, *14*(0), 2. doi:10.5334/dsj-2015-002

Campbell, C. (2015). *Top five differences between data lakes and data warehouses*. Retrieved 07 May, 2020, from https://www.blue-granite.com/blog/bid/402596/top-five-differencesbetween-data-lakes-and-data-warehouses

Căpuşneanu, S., Topor, D., Constantin, D., & Marin-Pantelescu, A. (2020). Management Accounting in the Digital Economy: Evolution and Perspectives. In I. Oncioiu (Ed.), Improving Business Performance Through Innovation in the Digital Economy (pp. 156-176). Hershey, PA: IGI Global.

Carter, C. L., Hamilton, H. J., & Cercone, N. (1997). Share-Based measures for itemsets. In *Proceedings of the Ist European Symposium on Principles of Data Mining and Knowledge Discovery*. Springer-Verlag. 10.1007/3-540-63223-9_102

Cassavia, N., Dicosta, P., Masciari, E., & Saccà, D. (2014). Data preparation for tourist data big data warehousing. In *Proceedings of 3rd International Conference on Data Management Technologies and Applications* (pp. 419-426). 10.5220/0005144004190426

Chaharlang, J., Mosleh, M., & Rasouli-Heikalabad, S. (2020). A novel quantum steganography-Steganalysis system for audio signals. *Multimedia Tools and Applications*, *79*(25-26), 17551–17577. doi:10.100711042-020-08694-z

Chandra, P., & Gupta, M. K. (2018). Comprehensive survey on data warehousing research. *International Journal of Information Technology*, *10*(2), 217–224. doi:10.100741870-017-0067-y

Chang, B. J. (2018). Agile Business Intelligence: Combining Big Data and Business Intelligence to Responsive Decision Model. *Journal of Internet Technology*, *19*(6), 1699–1706.

Chang, S. E., Chen, Y. C., & Lu, M. F. (2019). Supply Chain Re-Engineering Using Blockchain Technology: A Case of Smart Contract Based Tracking Process. *Technological Forecasting and Social Change*, *144*, 1–11. doi:10.1016/j.techfore.2019.03.015

Che, D., Safran, M., & Peng, Z. (2013). *From Big Data to Big Data Mining: Challenges, Issues, and Opportunities*. Proceedings of the 18th International conference Database Systems for Advanced Applications workshop. 10.1007/978-3-642-40270-8_1

Cheng, C., Zhong, H., & Cao, L. (2020). Facilitating speed of internationalization: The roles of business intelligence and organizational agility. Retrieved from doi:10.1016/j.jbusres.2020.01.003

Chen, H., Chiang, R. H., & Storey, V. C. (2012). Business intelligence and analytics: From big data to big impact. *Management Information Systems Quarterly*, *36*(4), 1165–1188. doi:10.2307/41703503

Chen, J., Li, K., Rong, H., Bilal, K., Yang, N., & Li, K. (2018). A disease diagnosis and treatment recommendation system based on big data mining and cloud computing. *Information Sciences*, *435*, 124–149. doi:10.1016/j.ins.2018.01.001

Chen, M., Mao, S., & Liu, Y. (2014). Big data: A survey. *Mobile Networks and Applications*, *19*(2), 171–209. doi:10.100711036-013-0489-0

Chen, W., Zheng, Z., Ngai, E. C.-H., Zheng, P., & Zhou, Y. (2019). Exploiting Blockchain Data to Detect Smart Ponzi Schemes on Ethereum. *IEEE Access: Practical Innovations, Open Solutions*, *7*, 37575–37586. doi:10.1109/AC-CESS.2019.2905769

Chen, Y., Zhu, F., & Lee, J. (2013). Data quality evaluation and improvement for prognostic modeling using visual assessment based data partitioning method. *Journal of Computers in Industry*, *64*(3), 214–225. doi:10.1016/j.compind.2012.10.005

Cheung, C. F., & Li, F. L. (2012). A Quantitative Correlation Coefficient Mining Method for Business Intelligence in Small and Medium Enterprises of Trading Business. *Expert Systems with Applications*, *39*(7), 6279–6291. doi:10.1016/j.eswa.2011.10.021

Chongwatpol, J. (2016). Managing big data in coal-fired power plants: A business intelligence framework. *Industrial Management & Data Systems*, *116*(8), 1779–1799. doi:10.1108/IMDS-11-2015-0473

Chow-White, P. A., & Green, S. Jr. (2013). Data Mining Difference in the Age of Big Data: Communication and the social shaping of genome technologies from 1998 to 2007. *International Journal of Communication*, *7*, 28.

Cios, K., Pedrycz, W., Swiniarski, R., & Kurgan, L. (2007). *Data Mining: A Knowledge Discovery Approach*. Springer-Verlag.

Cody, W. F., Kreulen, J. T. V., Krishna, V., & Spangler, W. S. (2002). The integration of business intelligence and knowledge management. *IBM Systems Journal*, *41*(4), 697–713. doi:10.1147j.414.0697

Columbus, L. (2019). *The Global State of Enterprise Analytics, 2020*. Retrieved May 9, 2020 from: https://www.forbes.com/sites/louiscolumbus/2019/10/21/the-global-state-of-enterprise-analytics-2020/#4966b9ba562d

Conrad, A. (2019). *The Future of Business Intelligence (BI) in 2020* [Blog]. Retrieved from https://www.selecthub.com/business-intelligence/future-of-bi/

Countants. (2020, January 18). *10 Leading Trends in Business Intelligence in the Year 2020* [Blog]. Retrieved from https://www.countants.com/blogs/10-leading-trends-in-business-intelligence-in-the-year-2020/

D'Alconzo, A., Barlet-Ros, P., Fukuda, K., & Choffnes, D. R. (2016). Machine learning, data mining and Big Data frameworks for network monitoring and troubleshooting. *Computer Networks*, *107*(1), 1–4. doi:10.1016/j.comnet.2016.06.031

Damrudi, M., & Aval, K. J. (2019). Image Steganography using LSB and Encrypted Message with AES, RSA, DES, 3DES and Blowfish. *International Journal of Engineering and Advanced Technology*, *8*(63), 204–208.

Das, D., Sadiq, A. S., Ahmad, N. B., & Lloret, J. (2017). Stock Market Prediction with Big Data through Hybridization of Data Mining and Optimized Neural Network Techniques. *Multiple-Valued Logic and Soft Computing*, *29*(1-2), 157–181.

Davenport, T. H. (2014). How strategists use 'big data' to support internal business decisions, discovery and production. *Strategy and Leadership*, *42*(4), 45–50. doi:10.1108/SL-05-2014-0034

Davidson, I., Grover, A., Satyanarayana, A., & Tayi, G. (2004). *A General Approach to Incorporate Data Quality Matrices into Data Mining Algorithms*. Proceedings of the *10th ACM SIGKDD International Conference on Knowledge Discovery and Data Mining*. 10.1145/1014052.1016916

de Carvalho, W. F., & Zarate, L. E. (2019). Causality relationship among attributes applied in an educational data set. In *Proceedings of the 34th ACM/SIGAPP Symposium on Applied Computing, SAC '19* (pp. 1271–1277). New York, NY: Association for Computing Machinery. 10.1145/3297280.3297406

de Souza, J. G. C. (2018). Generating E-Commerce Product Titles and Predicting their Quality. *Proceedings of the 11th International Natural Language Generation Conference*, 233–243. 10.18653/v1/W18-6530

Debnath, B., Das, J. C., & De, D. (2018). Design of Image Steganographic Architecture using Quantum-Dot Cellular Automata for Secure Nanocommunication Networks. *Nano Communication Networks*, *15*, 41–58. doi:10.1016/j.nancom.2017.11.001

Debortoli, S., Müller, O., & vom Brocke, J. (2014). Comparing business intelligence and big data skills. *Business & Information Systems Engineering*, *6*(5), 289–300. doi:10.100712599-014-0344-2

Decker, K. M., & Focardi, S. (1995). *Technology overview: A report on Data Mining. Technical Report*. Swiss Scientific Computing Center.

Dedić, N., & Stanier, C. (2016). Measuring the Success of Changes to Existing Business Intelligence Solutions to Improve Business Intelligence Reporting. In A. Tjoa, L. Xu, M. Raffai, & N. Novak (Eds.), *Research and Practical Issues of Enterprise Information Systems. CONFENIS 2016. Lecture Notes in Business Information Processing* (Vol. 268). Springer., doi:10.1007/978-3-319-49944-4_17

Deng, Z., Zhu, X., Cheng, D., Zong, M., & Zhang, S. (2016). Efficient KNN Classification Algorithm for Big Data. *Neurocomputing*, *195*, 143–148. doi:10.1016/j.neucom.2015.08.112

Depeige, A., & Doyencourt, D. (2015). Actionable Knowledge As A Service (AKAAS): Leveraging big data analytics in cloud computing environments. *Journal of Big Data*, *2*(1), 12. doi:10.118640537-015-0023-2

Dixon, J. (2010). *Pentaho, Hadoop, and data lakes*. Retrieved 07 May, 2020, from https://jamesdixon.wordpress.com/2010/10/14/pentaho-hadoop-and-data-lakes/

Documents - Financial Action Task Force (FATF). (2020). http://www.fatf-gafi.org/publications/financialinclusion/documents/bcbs-meeting-2-october-2014.html

Douglas, M., Bailey, K., Leeney, M., & Curran, K. (2018). An overview of steganography techniques applied to the protection of biometric data. *Multimedia Tools and Applications*, *77*(13), 17333–17373. doi:10.100711042-017-5308-3

Du Mingxiao, M. X., Zhe, Z., Wang, X., & Chen, Q. (2017). A Review on Consensus Algorithm of Blockchain. In *2017 IEEE International Conference on Systems, Man, and Cybernetics (SMC)*. IEEE. 10.1109/SMC.2017.8123011

Duan, X., Guo, D., Liu, N., Li, B., Gou, M., & Qin, C. (2020). A New High Capacity Image SteganographyMethod Combined with Image Elliptic Curve Cryptography and Deep Neural Network. *IEEE Access: Practical Innovations, Open Solutions*, *8*, 25777–25788. doi:10.1109/ACCESS.2020.2971528

Dubey, R., Gunasekaran, A., & Childe, S. J. (2018). *Big data analytics capability in supply chain agility: the moderating effect of organizational flexibility. In Management Decision*. Emerald. doi:10.1108/MD-01-2018-0119

Du, H. S., Ke, X., Chu, S. K. W., & Chan, L. T. (2017). A bibliometric analysis of emergency management using information systems (2000-2016). *Online Information Review*, *41*(4), 454–470. doi:10.1108/OIR-05-2017-0142

Durcevic, S. (2019, November 28). *Top 10 Analytics and Business Intelligence Trends For 2020* [Blog]. Retrieved from https://www.datapine.com/blog/business-intelligence-trends/

E-commerce purchases datasets. (n.d.). Retrieved March 9, 2020, from https://ec.europa.eu/eurostat/web/products-datasets/-/isoc_ec_ebuyn2

E-commerce sales datasets. (n.d.). Retrieved March 9, 2020, from https://ec.europa.eu/eurostat/web/products-datasets/-/isoc_ec_evaln2

E-commerce, customer relation management (CRM) and secure transactions. (n.d.). Retrieved March 9, 2020, from https://ec.europa.eu/eurostat/web/products-datasets/-/isoc_bde15dec

Egetoft, K. (2019, January 29). *Data-Driven Analytics: Practical Use Cases for Financial Services.* Part 3 of the "Data Management for Financial Services" Series. Digitalist Magazine by SAP. Retrieved from https://www.digitalistmag.com/customer-experience/2019/01/29/data-driven-analytics-practical-use-cases-for-financial-services-06195123

El-Darwiche, B., Koch, V., Meer, D., Shehadi, R., & Tohme, W. (2014). *Big data maturity: An action plan for policymakers and executives.* Accessed April 25, 2020, https://www.strategyand.pwc.com/media/file/Strategyand_Big-data-maturity.pdf

Embaby, A. A., Mohamed, A., Shalaby, W., & Elsayed, K. M. (2020). Digital Watermarking Properties, Classification and Techniques. *International Journal of Engineering and Advanced Technology, 9*(3), 2742–2750. doi:10.35940/ijeat.C5773.029320

English, L. (2011). *Information Quality Applied: Best Practices for Improving Business Information Processes and Systems.* Wiley Publishing.

Erevelles, S., Fukawa, N., & Swayne, L. (2016). Big Data consumer analytics and the transformation of marketing. *Journal of Business Research, 69,* 897-904.

Espinosa, R., & Zubcoff, J. (2011). A set of experiments to consider data quality criteria in classification techniques for Data Mining. *Proceedings of the International Conference on Computational science and its applications.* 10.1007/978-3-642-21887-3_51

EU Open Data Portal. (n.d.). Retrieved March 9, 2020, from https://data.europa.eu/euodp/en/data/

Even, A., & Shankaranarayanan, G. (2007). Utility-Driven assessment of data quality. *The Data Base for Advances in Information Systems, 38*(2), 75–93. doi:10.1145/1240616.1240623

Eyssa, A. A., Abdelsamie, F. E., & Abdelnaiem, A. E. (2020). An Efficient Image Steganography Approach over Wireless Communication System. *Wireless Personal Communications, 110*(1), 321–337. doi:10.100711277-019-06730-2

Fahad. (2020). *Blockchain without Waste: Proof-of-Stake.* Academic Press.

Fahimnia, B., Sarkis, J., & Davarzani, H. (2015). Green supply chain management: A review and bibliometric analysis. *International Journal of Production Economics, 162,* 101–114. doi:10.1016/j.ijpe.2015.01.003

Fang, H. (2015, 8-12 June). *Managing data lakes in big data era: what's a data lake and why has it became popular in data management ecosystem.* Paper presented at the 2015 IEEE International Conference on Cyber Technology in Automation, Control, and Intelligent Systems (CYBER), Shenyang, China. 10.1109/CYBER.2015.7288049

Fan, S., Lau, R., & Zhao, J. A. (2015). Demystifying Big Data Analytics for Business Intelligence Through the Lens of Marketing Mix. *Big Data Research, 2*(1), 28–32. doi:10.1016/j.bdr.2015.02.006

Fan, W., & Bifet, A. (2013). Mining Big Data: Current Status, and Forecast to the Future. *SIGKDD Explorations, 14*(2), 1–5. doi:10.1145/2481244.2481246

Farid, M., Roatis, A., Ilyas, I., Hoffman, H., & Chu, X. (2016). *CLAMS: bringing quality to Data Lakes.* Paper presented at the International Conference on Management of Data (SIGMOD/PODS'16), San Francisco, CA.

Faroukhi, A. Z., El Alaoui, I., Gahi, Y., & Amine, A. (2020). Big data monetization throughout Big Data Value Chain: A comprehensive review. *Journal of Big Data*, *7*(1), 3. doi:10.118640537-019-0281-5

Farrugia, S., Ellul, J., & Azzopardi, G. (2020, April 13). Detection of Illicit Accounts over the Ethereum Blockchain. *Expert Systems with Applications*, *150*, 113318. doi:10.1016/j.eswa.2020.113318

Fayyad, U. M., Piatetski-Shapiro, G., & Smyth, P. (1996). From Data Mining to Knowledge Discovery: An Overview. In *Advances in Knowledge Discovery and Data Mining* (pp. 1–34). AAAI Press/The MIT Press.

Fehrenbacher, D., & Helfert, M. (2012). Contextual Factors Influencing Perceived Importance and Trade-offs of Information Quality. *Communications of the Association for Information Systems*, *30*(8), 111–126. doi:10.17705/1CAIS.03008

Fergal, R., & Harrigan, M. (2013). An Analysis of Anonymity in the Bitcoin System. In *Security and Privacy in Social Networks* (pp. 197–223). Springer. doi:10.1007/978-1-4614-4139-7_10

Fodor, I. K. (2002). *A survey of dimension reduction techniques.* LLNL Technical Report.

Fosso Wamba, S., Akter, S., Edwards, A., Chopin, G., & Gnanzou, D. (2015). How 'big data' can make big impact: Findings from a systematic review and a longitudinal case study. *International Journal of Production Economics*, *165*, 234–246. Advance online publication. doi:10.1016/j.ijpe.2014.12.031

Fosso Wamba, S., Gunasekaran, A., Akter, S., & Ren, S. (2017). Big data analytics and firm performance: Effects of dynamic capabilities. *Journal of Business Research*, *70*, 356–365. doi:10.1016/j.jbusres.2016.08.009

Freitas, A. (2002). *Data Mining and Knowledge Discovery with Evolutionary Algorithms.* Springer-Verlag. doi:10.1007/978-3-662-04923-5

Fu, J., Chen, Z., Wang, J., He, M., & Wang, J. (2012). Distributed storage system big data mining based on HPC application-A solar photovoltaic forecasting system practice. International Information Institute (Tokyo) Information.

Gallinucci, E., Golfarelli, M., & Rizzi, S. (2018). Schema profiling of document-oriented databases. *Information Systems*, *75*(1), 13–25. doi:10.1016/j.is.2018.02.007

Gandomi, A. H., Sajedi, S., Kiani, B., & Huang, Q. (2016). Genetic programming for experimental big data mining: A case study on concrete creep formulation. *Automation in Construction*, *70*, 89–97. doi:10.1016/j.autcon.2016.06.010

Gao, T., Fadnis, K., & Campbell, M. (2017). Local-to-global Bayesian net-work structure learning. In D. Precup & Y. W. Teh (Eds.), *Proceedings of the 34th International Conference on Machine Learning*, volume 70 *of Proceedings of Machine Learning Research* (pp. 1193–1202). Sydney, Australia: PMLR.

Gao, T., & Ji, Q. (2015). Local causal discovery of direct causes and effects. In C. Cortes, N. D. Lawrence, D. D. Lee, M. Sugiyama, & R. Garnett (Eds.), Advances in Neural Information Processing Systems (Vol. 28, pp. 2512–2520). Curran Associates, Inc.

Gartner. (2019, October21). *Top 10 Strategic Technology Trends for 2020. A Gartner Special Report.* Retrieved from https://emtemp.gcom.cloud/ngw/globalassets/en/doc/documents/432920-top-10-strategic-technology-trends-for-2020.pdf

Gavin. (2014). *Ethereum: A Secure Decentralised Generalised Transaction Ledger.* Ethereum project yellow paper 151(2014): 1–32.

Ge, M., Helfert, M., & Jannach, D. (2011). Information quality assessment: validating measurement dimensions and processes. *Proceedings of the 19th European Conference on Information Systems.*

Geng, L., & Hamilton, H. (2006). Interestingness measure for Data Mining: A survey. *ACM Computing Surveys, 38*(3), 9. doi:10.1145/1132960.1132963

Gibson, N. (2010). *Improving information products for System 2 Design Support* (Ph.D. Thesis). University of Arkansas.

Giebler, C., Stach, C., Schwarz, H., & Mitschang, B. (2018). *BRAID - a hybrid processing architecture for big data.* Paper presented at the 7th International Conference on Data Science, Technology and Applications (DATA) (2018), Porto, Portugal.

Giebler, C., Gröger, C., Hoos, E., Schwarz, H., & Mitschang, B. (2019). Modeling Data Lakes with Data Vault: Practical Experiences, Assessment, and Lessons Learned. In A. Laender, B. Pernici, E. Lim, & J. de Oliveira (Eds.), Lecture Notes in Computer Science: Vol. 11788. *Conceptual Modeling. ER 2019.* Springer. doi:10.1007/978-3-030-33223-5_7

Giudice, P., Musarella, L., Sofo, G., & Ursino, D. (2019). An approach to extracting complex knowledge patterns among concepts belonging to structured, semi-structured and unstructured sources in a data lake. *Information Sciences, 478*(1), 606–626. doi:10.1016/j.ins.2018.11.052

GMDH Shell Software. (n.d.). Retrieved March 9, 2020, from https://gmdhsoftware.com/

Gorelik, A. (2019). *The Enterprise Big Data Lake: Delivering the Promise of Big Data and Data Science.* O'Reilly Media, Inc.

Goti-Elordi, A., de-la-Calle-Vicente, A., Gil-Larrea, M. J., Errasti-Opakua, A., & Uradnicek, J. (2017). Application of a business intelligence tool within the context of big data in a food industry company. *Dyna (Bilbao), 92*(3), 347–353.

Gowda, S. N. (2016). An advanced Diffie-Hellman approach to image steganography. *2016 IEEE International Conference on Advanced Networks and Telecommunications Systems (ANTS)*, 1-4. 10.1109/ANTS.2016.7947849

Grosseck, G., Țîru, L. G., & Bran, R. A. (2019). Education for Sustainable Development: Evolution and Perspectives: A Bibliometric Review of Research, 1992–2018. *Sustainability, 11*(21), 6136. doi:10.3390u11216136

Grossman, R. (2019). Data Lakes, Clouds, and Commons: A Review of Platforms for Analyzing and Sharing Genomic Data. *Trends in Genetics, 35*(3), 223–234. doi:10.1016/j.tig.2018.12.006 PMID:30691868

Gryncewicz, W., Sitarska-Buba, M., & Zygała, R. (2020). Agile Approach to Develop Data Lake Based Systems. In M. Hernes, A. Rot, & D. Jelonek (Eds.), *Towards Industry 4.0 — Current Challenges in Information Systems. Studies in Computational Intelligence* (Vol. 887, pp. 201–216). Springer. doi:10.1007/978-3-030-40417-8_12

Guillet, F., & Howard, J. (2007). *Quality Measures in Data Mining.* Springer-Verlag. doi:10.1007/978-3-540-44918-8

Günther, W. A., Mehrizi, M. H. R., Huysman, M., & Feldberg, F. (2017). Debating big data: A literature review on realizing value from big data. *The Journal of Strategic Information Systems, 26*(3), 191–209. doi:10.1016/j.jsis.2017.07.003

Gupta, M., & George, J. F. (2016). Toward the development of a big data analytics capability. *Information & Management, 53*, 1049-1064.

Gupta, M.K., & Chandra, P. (2020). A comprehensive survey of data mining. *Int. J. Inf. Tecnol.* doi:10.100741870-020-00427-7

Gupta, S., & Chaudari, M. S. (2015). Big Data issues and challenges. *International Journal on Recent and Innovation Trends in Computing and Communication, 3*(2), 62-66.

Gupta, R., & Pathak, C. (2014). A Machine Learning Framework for Predicting Purchase by online customers based on Dynamic Pricing. *Procedia Computer Science, 36*, 599–605. doi:10.1016/j.procs.2014.09.060

Gustafsson, P., Lindström, Å., Jägerlind, C., & Tsoi, J. (2006). A Framework for Assessing Data Quality – from a Business Perspective. *Software Engineering Research and Practice*, 1009-1015.

Guyon, I., & Elisseeff, A. (2008). *An Introduction to Feature Extraction*. Academic Press.

Hai, R., Geisler, S., & Quix, C. (2016). *Constance: An Intelligent Data Lake System*. Paper presented at the 2016 International Conference on Management of Data, San Francisco, CA. 10.1145/2882903.2899389

Halevy, A., Korn, F., Noy, N., Olston, C., Polyzotis, N., Roy, S., & Whang, S. (2016). Managing Google's data lake: An overview of the Goods system. *A Quarterly Bulletin of the Computer Society of the IEEE Technical Committee on Data Engineering*, *39*(3), 5–14.

Hambouz, A., Shaheen, Y., Manna, A., Al-Fayoumi, M., & Tedmori, S. S. (2019). Achieving Data Integrity and Confidentiality Using Image Steganography and Hashing Techniques. *2nd International Conference on new Trends in Computing Sciences (ICTCS)*, 1-6. doi: 10.1109/ICTCS.2019.8923060

Hang, Y., & Fong, S. (2009). A Framework of Business Intelligence-driven Data Mining for e-Business. In *Proceedings of the 2009 Fifth International Joint Conference on INC, IMS and IDC* (pp. 1964-1970). IEEE Computer Society. 10.1109/NCM.2009.403

Harvard Business Review Analytic Services. (2019). *Machine Learning: The Next Generation of Customer Experience*. Harvard Business School Publishing. Retrieved March 9, 2020, from https://cdn2.hubspot.net/hubfs/1965778/HBR-AS_CIandT_Machine%20Learning_%20The%20Next%20Generation%20of%20Customer%20Experience.pdf

Hashem, I. A. T., Yaqoob, I., Anuar, N. B., Mokhtar, S., Gani, A., & Khan, S. U. (2015). The rise of "big data" on cloud computing: Review and open research issues. *Information Systems*, *47*, 98–115. doi:10.1016/j.is.2014.07.006

Häubscher, R., Puntambekar, S., & Nye, A (2007). Domain specific interactive Data Mining. *Proceedings of the 11th International Conference User Model. Workshop Data Mining User Model*, 81-90.

Heinrich, B., Kaiser, M., & Klier, M. (2008). Does the EU insurance mediation directive help to improve data quality? – A metric-based analysis. *Proceedings of the 16th European Conference on Information Systems*.

Heinrich, B., Kaiser, M., & Kier, M. (2009). A Procedure to Develop Metrics for Currency and its Application in CRM. *ACM Journal of Data and Information Quality*, *1*(1), 1–28. doi:10.1145/1515693.1515697

Heinrich, B., Kaiser, M., & Klier, M. (2007). How to measure Data Quality? – A metrics based approach. *28th International Conference on Information Systems*.

Heinrich, B., & Klier, M. (2009). A novel data quality metric for timeliness Considering supplemental data. *Proceedings of the 17th European Conference on Information Systems*, 2701-2713.

Helfert, M., & Foley, O. (2009). *A Context Aware Information Quality Framework*. Paper presented at Fourth International Conference on Cooperation and Promotion of Information Resources in Science and Technology, Beijing, China.

Helfert, M., Foley, O., Ge, M., & Cappiello, C. (2009). Limitations of Weighted Sum Measures for Information Quality. *Proceedings of Americas Conference on Information Systems*.

Henderson. (2012). Rolx: Structural Role Extraction & Mining in Large Graphs. *Proceedings of the 18th ACM SIGKDD International Conference on Knowledge Discovery and Data Mining*, 1231–1239.

Henschen, D. (2018). *Embrace the Era of Smart Analytics*. Retrieved from https://www.constellationr.com/blog-news/embrace-era-smart-analytics

Hoberman, E., Leganza, G., & Yuhanna, N. (2018). The Forrester Wave™. *Big Data Fabric, Q2*, 2018.

Holland, P. W., Glymour, C., & Granger, C. (1985). Statistics and causal inference. *ETS Research Report Series*, *1985*(2), i–72. doi:10.1002/j.2330-8516.1985.tb00125.x

Holmlund, M., Van Vaerenbergh, Y., Ciuchita, R., Ravald, A., Sarantopoulos, P., Villarroel-Ordenes, F., & Zaki, M. (2020). Customer Experience Management in the Age of Big Data Analytics: A Strategic Framework. *Journal of Business Research*, *116*, 356–365. doi:10.1016/j.jbusres.2020.01.022

Hu, Y., Seneviratne, S., Thilakarathna, K., Fukuda, K., & Seneviratne, A. (2019). *Characterizing and Detecting Money Laundering Activities on the Bitcoin Network*. arXiv preprint arXiv:1912.12060

Huang, S. C., McIntosh, S., Sobolevsky, S., & Hung, P. C. (2017). Big data analytics and business intelligence in industry. *Information Systems Frontiers*, *19*(6), 1229–1232. doi:10.100710796-017-9804-9

Huez, A. (2020). *5 Business Intelligence Trends for 2020*. Retrieved from https://toucantoco.com/blog/en/5-business-intelligence-trends-for-2020/

Hu, X., & Cercone, N. (2004). A Data Warehouse/Online Analytic Processing Framework for Web Usage Mining and Business Intelligence Reporting. *International Journal of Intelligent Systems*, *19*(7), 585–606. doi:10.1002/int.20012

IBM InfoSphere. (2020, August 20). https://www.ibm.com/analytics/information-server

IDC and EMC, The Digital Universe in 2020: Big data, Bigger Digital Shadow, and Biggest Growth in the Far East, Big Data in 2020. (n.d.). Retrieved from https://www.emc.com/leadership/digital-universe/2012iview/big-data-2020.htm

Informatica Intelligent Data Platform. (2020, August 20). www.informatica.com/nl/products/informatica-platform.html

Inmon, B. (2016). *Data Lake Architecture: Designing the Data Lake and Avoiding the Garbage Dump*. Technics Publications.

inTelegy. (2018). *Service Offerings: Data Driven Management*. Retrieved from https://www.intelegy.com/data-driven-management

IQLECT. (2018). *The Importance of Predictive Analytics for E-commerce Stores*. Retrieved March 9, 2020, from https://medium.com/swlh/the-importance-of-predictive-analytics-for-e-commerce-stores-d7ef0ce2d32e

Israa, A., Rahwan, I., & Svetinovic, D. (2018). The Anti-Social System Properties: Bitcoin Network Data Analysis. *IEEE Transactions on Systems, Man, and Cybernetics. Systems*.

Ittay, E., & Sirer, E. G. (2014). Majority Is Not Enough: Bitcoin Mining Is Vulnerable. In *International Conference on Financial Cryptography and Data Security*. Springer.

Izzi, M., Warrier, S., Leganza, G., & Yuhanna, N. (2016). Big Data Fabric Drives Innovation And Growth. *Next-Generation Big Data Management Enables Self-Service And Agility*.

Janecek, A. (2009). *Efficient feature reduction and classification methods* (Ph.D. Thesis). University of Vienna.

Jethin, A., Higdon, D., Nelson, J., & Ibarra, J. (2018). *Cryptocurrency Price Prediction Using Tweet Volumes and Sentiment Analysis*. SMU Data Science Review.

Jiang, P., & Liu, X. S. (2015). Big data mining yields novel insights on cancer. *Nature Genetics*, *47*(2), 103–104. doi:10.1038/ng.3205 PMID:25627899

Jin, D. H., & Kim, H. J. (2018). Integrated Understanding of Big Data, Big Data Analysis, and Business Intelligence: A Case Study of Logistics. *Sustainability*, *10*(10), 3778. doi:10.3390u10103778

Jouni, K., & Mills, C. (2020). On Group Comparisons with Logistic Regression Models. *Sociological Methods & Research, 49*(2), 498–525. doi:10.1177/0049124117747306

Jourdan, Z., Rainer, R. K., & Marshall, T. E. (2008). Business Intelligence: An Analysis of the Literature. *Information Systems Management, 25*(2), 121–131. doi:10.1080/10580530801941512

Jovanovic, P., Nadal, S., Romero, O., Abelló, A., & Bilalli, B. (2020). Quarry: A User-centered Big Data Integration Platform. *Information Systems Frontiers, 22*(2), 1–25.

Jurgelevičius, A., & Sakalauskas, L. (2018). Big data mining using public distributed computing. *Information Technology and Control, 47*(2), 236–248. doi:10.5755/j01.itc.47.2.19738

Kaiser, M. (2010). A conceptional approach to unify completeness, Consistency, and accuracy as quality dimensions of data values. *European and Mediterranean Conference on Information Systems.*

Kalubandi, V. K. P., Vaddi, H., Ramineni, V., & Agilandeeswari Loganathan, A. (2016). A Novel Image Encryption Algorithm using AES and Visual Cryptography. *Proceedings of NGCT 2016.* 10.1109/NGCT.2016.7877521

Kamthania, D., Pahwa, A., & Madhavan, S. S. (2018). Market Segmentation Analysis and Visualization Using K-Mode Clustering Algorithm for E-Commerce Business. *CIT. Journal of Computing and Information Technology, 26*(1), 57–68. doi:10.20532/cit.2018.1003863

Keeton, K., Mehra, P., & Wilkes, J. (2010). Do you know your IQ? A research agenda for information quality in systems. *Performance Evaluation Review, 37*(3), 26–31. doi:10.1145/1710115.1710121

Keogh, E., & Mueen, A. (2017). *Curse of Dimensionality.* Springer US. doi:10.1007/978-1-4899-7687-1_192

Khine, P., & Wang, Z. (2019). A Review of Polyglot Persistence in the Big Data World. *Information, 10*(4), 141–165. doi:10.3390/info10040141

Kimball, R., & Ross, M. (2013). *The Datawarehouse Tool Kit: The Definitive Guide to Dimensional Modeling* (3rd ed.). John Wiley & Sons, Inc.

Kimble, C., & Milolidakis, G. (2015). Big Data and Business Intelligence: Debunking the Myths. *Global Business and Organizational Excellence, 35*(1), 23–34. doi:10.1002/joe.21642

Kim, K. Y. (2014). Business Intelligence and Marketing Insights in an Era of Big Data: The Q-sorting Approach. *Transactions on Internet and Information Systems (Seoul), 8*(2).

Kim, Y., & Gao, J. (2006). Unsupervised gene selection for high dimensional data. *Proceedings of IEEE Symposium of Bioinformatics and Bioengineering*, 227-232. 10.1109/BIBE.2006.253339

Kissflow. (2020). *4 Trends That are Transforming BPM in 2020. Process automation bots to everything. What's been pinging BPM's radar this year.* Retrieved from https://kissflow.com/bpm/4-trends-revolutionizing-business-process-management/

Knight, S. (2011). The combined conceptual life-cycle model of information quality: Part 1, an investigative framework. *International Journal of Information Quality., 2*(3), 205–230. doi:10.1504/IJIQ.2011.040669

Kohavi, R., & John, G. H. (1997). Wrappers for feature subset selection. *Artificial Intelligence, 97*(1–2), 273–324. doi:10.1016/S0004-3702(97)00043-X

Koller, D., & Sahami, M. (1996). Toward optimal feature selection. In *Proceedings of the Thirteenth International Conference on International Conference on Machine Learning, ICML'96* (pp. 284–292). San Francisco, CA: Morgan Kaufmann Publishers Inc.

Kolle, S. R., & Thyavanahalli, S. H. (2016). Global research on air pollution between 2005 and 2014: A bibliometric study. *Collection Building*, *35*(3), 84–92. doi:10.1108/CB-05-2016-0008

Kolle, S., Vijayashree, M., & Shankarappa, T. (2017). Highly cited articles in maleria research: A bibliometric analysis. *Collection Building*, *36*(2), 1–12. doi:10.1108/CB-10-2016-0028

Kopanakis, J. (2019, May 9). *How Artificial Intelligence Positively Influences Business Decision Making* [Blog]. Retrieved from https://www.mentionlytics.com/blog/how-artificial-intelligence-positively-influences-business-decision-making/

Korolov, M. (2018, Apr 18). *New AI tools make BI smarter — and more useful.* CIO. Retrieved fromhttps://www.cio.com/article/3268965/new-ai-tools-make-bi-smarter-and-more-useful.html

Kranjc, J., Orač, R., Podpečan, V., Lavrač, N., & Robnik-Šikonja, M. (2017). ClowdFlows: Online workflows for distributed big data mining. *Future Generation Computer Systems*, *68*, 38–58. doi:10.1016/j.future.2016.07.018

Kriegel, H.-P., Borgwardt, K., Kröger, P., Pryakhin, A., Schubert, M., & Zimek, A. (2007). Future trends in data mining. *Data Mining and Knowledge Discovery*, *15*(1), 87–97. doi:10.100710618-007-0067-9

Kui, X. S., & Wu, J. (2018). A Modification Free Steganography Method Based on Image Information Entropy. *Security and Communication Networks*, 1–8. doi:10.1155/2018/6256872

Kulakli, A., & Shubina, I. (2020). A bibliometric study on Mobile Applications for PTSD treatment: The period of 2010-2019. *Proceedings of 6th International Conference on Information Management*, 319-323.

Kulakli, A., & Osmanaj, V. (2020). Global research on big data in relation with artificial intelligence (A bibliometric study: 2008-2019). *International Journal of Online and Biomedical Engineering*, *16*(2), 31–46. doi:10.3991/ijoe.v16i02.12617

Kumar, S., Singh, A., & Kumar, M. (2019). *Information Hiding with Adaptive Steganography based on Novel Fuzzy Edge Identification.* Defence Technology. doi:10.1016/j.dt.2018.08.003

Kuo, C. F. J., Lin, C. H., & Lee, M. H. (2018). Analyze the energy consumption characteristics and affecting factors of Taiwan's convenience stores-using the big data mining approach. *Energy and Building*, *168*, 120–136. doi:10.1016/j.enbuild.2018.03.021

Kutz, M. (2016). *Introduction to e-commerce: Combining business and information technology.* BookBoon.

Lahmiri, S., & Bekiros, S. (2019). Cryptocurrency Forecasting with Deep Learning Chaotic Neural Networks. *Chaos, Solitons, and Fractals*, *118*, 35–40. doi:10.1016/j.chaos.2018.11.014

Lanza-Cruz, I., Berlanga, R., & Aramburu, M. J. (2018). Modelling Analytical Streams for Social Business Intelligence. *Informatica (Vilnius)*, *5*(3), 33. doi:10.3390/informatics5030033

Larson, D., & Chang, V. (2016). A review and future direction of agile, business intelligence, analytics and data science. *International Journal of Information Management*, *36*(5), 700–710. doi:10.1016/j.ijinfomgt.2016.04.013

Laurent, A., Laurent, D., & Madera, C. (2020). *Data Lakes* (Vol. 2). John Wiley & Sons. doi:10.1002/9781119720430

Lenca, P., Meyer, P., Vaillant, B., & Lallich, S. (2004). *A multicriteria decision aid for interestingness measure selection.* Technical Report LUSSI-TR-2004-01-EN, LUSSI Department, GET/ENST, Bretagne, France.

Liang, T. P., & Liu, Y. H. (2018). Research landscape of business intelligence and big data analytics: A bibliometric study. *Expert Systems with Applications*, *111*, 2–10. doi:10.1016/j.eswa.2018.05.018

Li, J., Li, N., Peng, J., Cui, H., & Wu, Z. (2019). Energy Consumption of Cryptocurrency Mining: A Study of Electricity Consumption in Mining Cryptocurrencies. *Energy*, *168*, 160–168. doi:10.1016/j.energy.2018.11.046

Lima, C. A. R., & Calazans, J. D. H. C. (2013). Pegadas Digitais: "Big Data" E Informação Estratégica Sobre O Consumidor. *NT – Sociabilidade, novas tecnologias, consumo e estratégias de mercado do SIMSOCIAL, 2013.*

Lin, C., & Kunnathur, A. (2019). Strategic orientations, developmental culture, and big data capability. *Journal of Business Research, 105*, 49–60. doi:10.1016/j.jbusres.2019.07.016

Lin, H. Y., & Yang, S. Y. (2019). A cloud-based energy data mining information agent system based on big data analysis technology. *Microelectronics and Reliability, 97*, 66–78. doi:10.1016/j.microrel.2019.03.010

Linoff, G. S. (2008). Survival Data Mining Using Relational Databases. *Business Intelligence Journal, 13*(3), 20–30.

Linstedt, D., & Olschimke, M. (2016). Intermediate Data Vault Modeling. In D. Linstedt & M. Olschimke (Eds.), *Building a Scalable Data Warehouse with Data Vault 2.0* (pp. 123–150). Morgan Kaufmann.

Li, Q., Li, S., Zhang, S., Hu, J., & Hu, J. (2019). A Review of Text Corpus-Based Tourism Big Data Mining. *Applied Sciences (Basel, Switzerland), 9*(16), 3300. doi:10.3390/app9163300

Liu, Z., Ren, C., & Cai, W. (2020). Overview of Clustering Analysis Algorithms in Unknown Protocol Recognition. In *MATEC Web of Conferences.* EDP Sciences. 10.1051/matecconf/202030903008

Liu, B., Fu, Z., Wang, P., Liu, L., Gao, M., & Liu, J. (2018). Big-data-mining-based improved k-means algorithm for energy use analysis of coal-fired power plant units: A case study. *Entropy (Basel, Switzerland), 20*(9), 702. doi:10.3390/e20090702

Liu, B., Hsu, W., & Chen, S. (1997). Using general impressions to analyze discovered classification rules. *Proceedings of the 3rd International Conference on Knowledge Discovery and Data Mining*, 31–36.

Li, X. T., & Feng, F. (2018). Enterprise Customer Relationship Management Based On Big Data Mining. Latin American Applied Research-. *International Journal (Toronto, Ont.), 48*(3), 163–168.

Llave, M. R. (2018). Data lakes in business intelligence: Reporting from the trenches. *Procedia Computer Science, 138*, 516–524. doi:10.1016/j.procs.2018.10.071

Lněnička, M. (2015). Ahp model for the big data analytics platform selection. *Acta Informatica Pragensia, 4*(2), 108–121. doi:10.18267/j.aip.64

Lněnička, M., & Komárková, J. (2015). The Impact of Cloud Computing and Open (Big) Data on the Enterprise Architecture Framework. *Proceedings of the 26th International Business Information Management Association Conference*, 1679-1683.

Lu, H., Karimireddy, S. P., Ponomareva, N., & Mirrokni, V. (2020). Accelerating Gradient Boosting Machines. *International Conference on Artificial Intelligence and Statistics*, 516–526.

Lunh, H. P. (1958). A Business Intelligence System. *IBM Journal of Research and Development, 2*(4), 314–319. doi:10.1147/rd.24.0314

Lu, S., Hu, H., & Li, F. (2001). Mining weighted association rules. *Intelligent Data Analysis, 5*(3), 211–225. doi:10.3233/IDA-2001-5303

Lv, S., Kim, H., Zheng, B., & Jin, H. (2018). A review of data mining with big data towards its applications in the electronics industry. *Applied Sciences (Basel, Switzerland), 8*(4), 582. doi:10.3390/app8040582

Maccioni, A., & Torlone, R. (2017). Crossing the finish line faster when paddling the data lake with KAYAK. *Proceedings of the VLDB Endowment International Conference on Very Large Data Bases, 10*(12), 1853–1856. doi:10.14778/3137765.3137792

Mahato, S., Khan, D. A., & Yadav, D. K. (2020). A Modified Approach to Data Hiding in Microsoft Word Documents by Change-Tracking Technique. *Journal of King Saud University-Computer and Information Sciences, 32*(2), 216–224. doi:10.1016/j.jksuci.2017.08.004

Maimon, O., & Rokach, L. (2010). *Data mining and knowledge discovery handbook.* Springer-Verlag. doi:10.1007/978-0-387-09823-4

Malysiak-Mrozek, B., Stabla, M., & Mrozek, D. (2018). Soft and declarative fishing of information in Big Data Lake. *IEEE Transactions on Fuzzy Systems, 26*(5), 2732–2747. doi:10.1109/TFUZZ.2018.2812157

Management Solutions. (2018). *Machine Learning, a key component in business model transformation.* Retrieved March 9, 2020, from https://www.managementsolutions.com/sites/default/files/publicaciones/eng/machine-learning.pdf

Mansur, M., & Noor, M. (2005). *Outlier Detection Technique in Data Mining: A Research Perspective.* Postgraduate Annual Research Seminar 2005, Universiti Teknologi Malaysia.

Marakas, G. M., & O'Brien, J. A. (2013). *Introduction to Information Systems.* McGraw-Hill/Irwin.

Margaritis, D., & Thrun, S. (1999). Bayesian network induction via local neighborhoods. In *Proceedings of the 12th International Conference on Neural Information Processing Systems, NIPS'99* (pp. 505–511). Cambridge, MA: MIT Press.

Margolies, L. R., Pandey, G., Horowitz, E. R., & Mendelson, D. S. (2016). Breast imaging in the era of big data: Structured reporting and data mining. *AJR. American Journal of Roentgenology, 206*(2), 259–264. doi:10.2214/AJR.15.15396 PMID:26587797

Mariani, M., Baggio, R., Fuchs, M., & Höepken, W. (2018). Business intelligence and big data in hospitality and tourism: A systematic literature review. *International Journal of Contemporary Hospitality Management, 30*(12), 3514–3554. doi:10.1108/IJCHM-07-2017-0461

Marín-Ortega, P. M., Dmitriyevb, V., Abilovb, M., & Gómezb, J. M. (2014). ELTA: New Approach in Designing Business Intelligence Solutions in Era of Big Data. *Procedia Technology, 16,* 667–674. doi:10.1016/j.protcy.2014.10.015

Marz, N., & Warren, J. (2015). *Big Data: Principles and best practices of scalable real-time data systems.* Manning Publications Co.

Massaro, A., Contuzzi, N., & Galiano, A. (2020). Intelligent Processes in Automated Production Involving Industry 4.0 Technologies and Artificial Intelligence. In M. Habib (Ed.), *Advanced Robotics and Intelligent Automation in Manufacturing* (pp. 97–122). IGI Global. doi:10.4018/978-1-7998-1382-8.ch004

Maté, A., Llorens, H., de Gregorio, E., Tardío, R., Gil, D., Munoz-Terol, R., & Trujillo, J. (2015). A novel multidimensional approach to integrate big data in business intelligence. *Journal of Database Management, 26*(2), 14–31. doi:10.4018/JDM.2015040102

Mazón, J., Jacobo, J., Garrigós, I., & Espinosa, R. (2012). Open Business Intelligence: on the importance of data quality awareness in user-friendly Data Mining. *Proceedings of the Joint EDBT/ICDT Workshops.* 10.1145/2320765.2320812

Mazzei, M. J., & Noble, D. (2017). Big data dreams: A framework for corporate strategy. BUSHOR-1369. *ScienceDirect.* Elsevier.

Mazzei, M. J., & Noble, D. (2020). Big Data and Strategy: Theoretical Foundations and New Opportunities. In *Strategy and Behaviors in the Digital Economy.* IntechOpen. https://www.intechopen.com/books/strategy-and-behaviors-in-the-digital-economy/big-data-and-strategy-theoretical-foundations-and-new-opportunities

Meek, C. (1995). Causal inference and causal explanation with background knowledge. In *Proceedings of the Eleventh Conference on Uncertainty in Artificial Intelligence, UAI'95* (pp. 403–410). San Francisco, CA: Morgan Kaufmann Publishers Inc.

Mehmood, H., Gilman, E., Cortes, M., Kostakos, P., Byrne, A., Valta, K., . . . Riekki, J. (2019, 8-12 April 2019). *Implementing Big Data Lake for Heterogeneous Data Sources*. Paper presented at the 35th International Conference on Data Engineering Workshops (ICDEW), Macao, Macao.

Mehta, N., & Pandit, A. (2018). Concurrence of big data analytics and healthcare: A systematic review. *International Journal of Medical Informatics, Elsevier, 114*, 57–65. doi:10.1016/j.ijmedinf.2018.03.013 PMID:29673604

Meiklejohn, S., Pomarole, M., Jordan, G., Levchenko, K., McCoy, D., & Voelker, G. M. (2013). A Fistful of Bitcoins: Characterizing Payments among Men with No Names. *Proceedings of the 2013 Conference on Internet Measurement Conference*, 127–140. 10.1145/2504730.2504747

Mellor, J. C., Stone, M. A., & Keane, J. (2018). Application of data mining to "big data" acquired in audiology: Principles and potential. *Trends in Hearing, 22*, 1–10. doi:10.1177/2331216518776817 PMID:29848183

Meneghetti, Sala, & Taufer. (2020). A Survey on PoW-Based Consensus. *Annals of Emerging Technologies in Computing*.

Michalewicz, Z., Schmidt, M., Michalewicz, M., & Chiriac, C. (2007). *Adaptive Business Intelligence*. Springer-Verlag.

Microsoft Power, B. I. (2020). *Data Visualization*. Retrieved from https://powerbi.microsoft.com/en-us/

Mikalef, P., Pappas, O. I., Giannakos, N. M., Krogstie, J., & Lekakos, G. (2016). Big Data and Strategy: A Research Framework. *Tenth Mediterranean Conference on Information Systems (MCIS)*, 1-9.

Miloslavskaya, N., & Tolstoy, A. (2016). Big Data, Fast Data and Data Lake Concepts. *Procedia Computer Science, 88*, 300–305. doi:10.1016/j.procs.2016.07.439

Mirzaie, M. (2019). *Big Data Quality: A systematic literature review and future research directions*. Cornell University.

Monamo, P., Marivate, V., & Twala, B. (2016). Unsupervised Learning for Robust Bitcoin Fraud Detection. 2016 Information Security for South Africa (ISSA), 129–134. doi:10.1109/ISSA.2016.7802939

Morgan, L. (2019, January 22). *What You Need to Know about Augmented Analytics*. Retrieved from https://www.informationweek.com/big-data/big-data-analytics/what-you-need-to-know-about-augmented-analytics/a/d-id/1333696

Morota, G., Ventura, R. V., Silva, F. F., Koyama, M., & Fernando, S. C. (2018). Machine learning and data mining advance predictive big data analysis in precision animal agriculture. *Journal of Animal Science, 96*(4), 1540–1550. doi:10.1093/jasky014 PMID:29385611

Moss, L. T., & Shaku, A. (2003). *Business Intelligence Roadmap: The Complete Project Lifecycle for Decision-Support Applications*. Pearson Education.

Mukherjee, S., Roy, S., & Sanyal, G. (2018). Image Steganography using Mid Position Value Technique. *Procedia Computer Science, 132*, 461–468. doi:10.1016/j.procs.2018.05.160

Munshi, A., & Mohamed, Y. (2018). Data Lake Lambda Architecture for Smart Grids Big Data Analytics. *IEEE Access: Practical Innovations, Open Solutions, 6*(1), 40463–40471. doi:10.1109/ACCESS.2018.2858256

Nadal, S., Herrero, V., Romero, O., Abell, A., Franch, X., Vansummeren, S., & Valerio, D. (2017). A Software Reference Architecture for Semantic-Aware Big Data Systems. *Information and Software Technology, 90*(1), 75–92. doi:10.1016/j.infsof.2017.06.001

Nagaty, K. A. (2010). *E-Commerce Business Models: Part 1. In Encyclopedia of E-Business Development and Management in the Global Economy.* IGI Global.

Nakamoto, S., & Bitcoin, A. (2008). *A Peer-to-Peer Electronic Cash System.* https://bitcoin. org/bitcoin. pdf

Nargesian, F., Zhu, E., Miller, R., Pu, K., & Arocena, P. (2019). Data lake management: Challenges and opportunities. *Proceedings of the VLDB Endowment International Conference on Very Large Data Bases, 12*(12), 1986–1989. doi:10.14778/3352063.3352116

Naumann, F., & Rolker, C. (2000), Assessment methods for Information Quality criteria. *Proceedings of the 14th International Conference on Information Quality*, 148-162.

Nelson, R., Todd, P. A., & Wixom, B. H. (2005). Antecedents of Information and System Quality: An Empirical Examination Within the Context of Data Warehousing. *Journal of Management Information Systems, 21*(4), 199–235. doi:10.1080/07421222.2005.11045823

Njah, H., Jamoussi, S., & Mahdi, W. (2019). Deep Bayesian network architecture for Big Data mining. *Concurrency and Computation, 31*(2), e4418. doi:10.1002/cpe.4418

Nocker, M., & Sena, V. (2019). Big Data and Human Resources Management: The Rise of Talent Analytics. *Social Sciences, 8*(10), 273. doi:10.3390ocsci8100273

Nogueira, I., Romdhane, M., & Darmont, J. (2018). *Modeling Data Lake Metadata with a Data Vault.* Paper presented at the the 22nd International Database Engineering & Applications Symposium, Villa San Giovanni, Italy. 10.1145/3216122.3216130

O'Dowd, E. (2018). *Unstructured Healthcare Data Needs Advanced Machine Learning Tools.* HIT Infrastructure.

O'Halloran, K. L., Tan, S., Pham, D. S., Bateman, J., & Vande Moere, A. (2018). A digital mixed methods research design: Integrating multimodal analysis with data mining and information visualization for big data analytics. *Journal of Mixed Methods Research, 12*(1), 11–30. doi:10.1177/1558689816651015

O'Kane, E. (2018). *Detecting Patterns in the Ethereum Transactional Data Using Unsupervised Learning.* Academic Press.

O'Leary, D. E. (2018). Open Information Enterprise Transactions: Business Intelligence and Wash and Spoof Transactions in Blockchain and Social Commerce. *Intelligent Systems in Accounting, Finance & Management, 25*(3), 148–158. doi:10.1002/isaf.1438

Ohsaki, M., Kitaguchi, S., Okamoto, K., Yokoi, H., & Yamaguchi, T. (2004). Evaluation of rule interestingness measures with a clinical dataset on hepatitis. *Proceedings of the 8th European Conference on Principles of Data Mining and Knowledge Discovery*, 362–373. 10.1007/978-3-540-30116-5_34

Oliveria, U., Espindola, L., & Marins, F. (2017). Analysis of supply chain risk management research. *Gestão & Produção, 25*(4).

Oracle® Warehouse Builder User's Guide 10g Release 2 (10.2.0.2). (2009). *Understanding Data Quality Management.* Retrieved from https://docs.oracle.com/cd/B31080_01/doc/owb.102/b28223/concept_data_quality.htm

Oussous, A., Benjelloun, F. Z., Lahcen, A. A., & Belfkih, S. (2017). Big Data technologies: A survey. *Journal of King Saud University-Computer and Information Sciences.*

Ozighor, E. R., & Izegbu, I. (2020). Information Protection against Security Threats in an Insecure Environment using Cryptography and Steganography. *Computing in Science & Engineering, 8*(5), 1671–1692.

Padmavathi, B., & Kumari, R. (2013). A Survey on Performance Analysis of DES, AES and RSA Algorithm alongwith LSB Substitution Technique. *International Journal of Scientific Research (Ahmedabad, India), 2*(4), 170–174.

Palem, G. (2014). Formulating an Executive Strategy for Big Data Analytics. *Technology Innovation Management Review, 4*(3), 25–34. doi:10.22215/timreview/773

Panwar, S., Damani, S., & Kumar, M. (2018). Digital Image Steganography using Modified LSB and AES Cryptography. *International Journal of Recent Engineering Research and Development, 3*(6), 18–27.

Passlick, J., Lebek, B., & Breitner, M. H. (2017). A Self-Service Supporting Business Intelligence and Big Data Analytics Architecture. In J. M. Leimeister & W. Brenner (Eds.), Proceedings der 13. Internationalen Tagung Wirtschaftsinformatik (WI 2017) (pp. 1126–1140). Academic Press.

Paul, M. J. (2017). Feature selection as causal inference: Experiments with text classification. In *Proceedings of the 21st Conference on Computa- tional Natural Language Learning (CoNLL 2017)* (pp. 163–172). Vancouver, Canada: Association for Computational Linguistics. 10.18653/v1/K17-1018

Pearl, J. (2009). Causality: Models, Reasoning and Inference. Cambridge University Press. doi:10.1017/CBO9780511803161

Pearl, J., & Mackenzie, D. (2018). *The Book of Why: The New Science of Cause and Effect* (1st ed.). Basic Books, Inc.

Phan, D. D., & Vogel, D. R. (2010). A Model of Customer Relationship Management and Business Intelligence Systems for Catalogue and Online Retailers. *Information & Management, 47*(2), 69–77. doi:10.1016/j.im.2009.09.001

Piatetsky-Shapiro, G. (2007). Data mining and knowledge discovery 1996 to 2005: Overcoming the hype and moving from "university" to "business" and "analytics". *Data Mining and Knowledge Discovery, 15*(1), 99–105. doi:10.100710618-006-0058-2

Piltaver, R. (2011). *Constructing understandable and accurate classifiers using Data Mining algorithms.* Jožef Stefan International Postgraduate School.

Pipino, L., Lee, Y., & Wang, R. Y. (2002). Data quality assessment. *Communications of the ACM, 45*(4), 211–218. doi:10.1145/505248.506010

Polese, F., Troisi, O., Grimaldi, M., & Romeo, E. (2019). A Big Data-Oriented Approach to Decision-Making: A Systematic Literature Review. *22nd International Conference Proceedings*, 472-496.

Popovič, A., Coelho, P. S., & Jaklič, J. (2009). The Impact of Business Intelligence System Maturity on Information Quality. *Information Research, 14*(4).

Portela, F., Lima, L., & Santos, M. F. (2016). Why Big Data? Towards a project assessment framework. *Procedia Computer Science, 98*, 604–609. doi:10.1016/j.procs.2016.09.094

Power, D. J. (2007). *A Brief History of Decision Support Systems, Version 4.0.* Retrieved March 10, 2010, from DSS-Resources.com: http://dssresources.com/history/dsshistory.html

Pradhan, A., Sekhar, K. R., & Swain, G. (2018). Digital Image Steganography Using LSB Substitution, PVD and EMD, Mathematical Problems in Engineering. *Article ID, 1804953*. Advance online publication. doi:10.1155/2018/1804953

Pramanik, S., Bandyopadhyay, S. K., & Ghosh, R. (2020). Signature Image Hiding in Color Image using Steganography and Cryptography based on Digital Signature Concepts. *2020 2nd International Conference on Innovative Mechanisms for Industry Applications (ICIMIA)*, 665-669.

Pramanik, S., Singh, R.P., & Ghosh, R. (2019). A New Encrypted Method in Image Steganography. *Indonesian Journal of Electrical Engineering and Computer Science, 14*(3), 1412–1419. .v13.i3.pp1412-1419 doi:10.11591/ijeecs

Pramanik, S., & Bandyopadhyay, S. (2013). Application of Steganography in Symmetric Key Cryptography with Genetic Algorithm. *International Journal of Computers and Technology*, *10*(7).

Pramanik, S., & Raja, S. S. (2019). Analytical Study on Security Issues in Steganography. *Think India Journal*, *22*(3), 106–114.

Pramanik, S., & Raja, S. S. (2020). A Secured Image Steganography using Genetic Algorithm, Advances in Mathematics. *Scientific Journal*, *9*(7), 4533–4541. doi:10.37418/amsj.9

Pramanik, S., & Samir Kumar Bandyopadhyay, S. K. (2014). Hiding Secret Message in an Image, International Journal of Innovative Science. *Engineering & Technology*, *1*(3), 553–559.

Pramanik, S., & Singh, R. P. (2017). Role of Steganography in Security Issues. *International Conference on Advance Studies in Engineering and Science*, 1225-1230.

Pramanik, S., Singh, R. P., & Ghosh, R. (2020). *Application of bi-orthogonal wavelet transform and genetic algorithm in image steganography*. Multimed Tools Appl. doi:10.100711042-020-08676-1

Prat, N., & Madnick, S. (2008). Measuring Data Believability: a Provenance Approach. *Proceedings of the 41st Hawaii International Conference on System Sciences*. 10.1109/HICSS.2008.243

Pulse, U. G. (2012). *Big data for development: Challenges & opportunities*. Naciones Unidas.

Puonti, M., Raitalaakso, T., Aho, T., & Mikkonen, T. (2017). Automating Transformations in Data Vault Data Warehouse Loads. *Frontiers in Artificial Intelligence and Applications*, *292*(1), 215–230. doi:10.3233/978-1-61499-720-7-215

Qi, E., Yang, X., & Wang, Z. (2019). Data mining and visualization of data-driven news in the era of big data. *Cluster Computing*, *22*(4), 10333–10346. doi:10.100710586-017-1348-8

Qiu, J., Wu, Q., Ding, G., Xu, Y., & Feng, S. (2016). A Survey of Machine Learning for Big Data Processing. *EURASIP Journal on Advances in Signal Processing*, *2016*(1), 67. doi:10.118613634-016-0355-x

Quix, C., & Hai, R. (2018). Data Lake. In S. Sakr & A. Zomaya (Eds.), *Encyclopedia of Big Data Technologies* (pp. 1–8). Springer International Publishing. doi:10.1007/978-3-319-63962-8_7-1

Quix, C., Hai, R., & Vatov, I. (2016). *Metadata Extraction and Management in Data Lakes With GEMMS Complex Systems. Informatics and Modeling Quarterly*, *9*(9), 67–83.

Rajarshi, D. (2019). *eCommerce Business Models that Work in 2019: A Brief Guide*. Retrieved March 9, 2020, from https://medium.com/pluginhive/types-of-ecommerce-business-models-271ea438f2aa

Ramalingam, M., Isa, N. A. M., & Puviarasi, R. (2020). A Secured Data Hiding using Affline Transformation in Video Steganography. *Procedia Computer Science*, *171*, 1147–1156. doi:10.1016/j.procs.2020.04.123

Ram, J., Zhang, C., & Koronios, A. (2016). The implications of Big Data analytics on Business Intelligence: A qualitative study in China. *Procedia Computer Science*, *87*, 221–226. doi:10.1016/j.procs.2016.05.152

Rashid, A., & Rahim, M. K. (2016). Critical Analysis of Steganography "An Art of Hidden Writing". *International Journal of Security and Applications*, *10*(1), 259–282. doi:10.14257/ijsia.2016.10.3.24

Ravat, F., & Zhao, Y. (2019). Data Lakes: Trends and Perspectives. In S. Hartmann, J. Küng, S. Chakravarthy, G. Anderst-Kotsis, A. Tjoa, & I. Khalil (Eds.), Lecture Notes in Computer Science: Vol. 11706. *Database and Expert Systems Applications. DEXA 2019* (pp. 304–313). Springer. doi:10.1007/978-3-030-27615-7_23

Ritala, P., Schneider, S., & Michailova, S. (2020). Innovation management research methods: embracing rigor and diversity. *R&D Management*. doi:10.1111/radm.12414

Rivest, R. L., Shamir, A., & Adleman, L. (1977). *A Method for Obtaining Digital Signatures and Public-Key Cryptosystems*. htts://people.csail.mit.edu/rivest/Rsapaper.pdf

Rodríguez, N., & Casanovas, J. (2010). A structural model of information system quality: an empirical research. *Proceedings of the Americas Conference on Information Systems*.

Roh, Y., Heo, G., & Whang, S. (2019). A Survey on Data Collection for Machine Learning: A Big Data - AI Integration Perspective. *IEEE Transactions on Knowledge and Data Engineering, 31*(2), 99–112. doi:10.1109/TKDE.2019.2946162

Roy, P. (2017). *The data-driven world*. Intergen. Retrieved from https://www.intergen.co.nz/blog/Priyanka-Roy/dates/2017/8/The-data-driven-world/

Rud, O. (2009). *Business Intelligence Success Factors: Tools for Aligning Your Business in the Global Economy*. Retrieved from https://www.amazon.com/Business-Intelligence-Success-Factors-Aligning/dp/0470392401

Saaty, T. L. (2008). Decision making with the analytic hierarchy process. *International Journal of Services Sciences, 1*(1), 83–98. doi:10.1504/IJSSCI.2008.017590

Sadovskyi, O., Engel, T., Heininger, R., Böhm, M., & Krcmar, H. (2014). Analysis of Big Data enabled Business Models using a Value Chain Perspective. Proceedings of Multikonferenz Wirtschaftsinformatik (MKWI 2014), 1127–1137.

Sah, H. R., & Gunasekaran, G. (2015). Privacy preserving data mining using visual steganography and encryption. *10th International Conference on Computer Science & Education (ICCSE)*, 154-158. 10.1109/ICCSE.2015.7250234

Saidali, J., Rahich, H., Tabaa, Y., & Medouri, A. (2019). The combination between Big Data and Marketing Strategies to gain valuable Business Insights for better Production Success. *Procedia Manufacturing, 32*, 1017–1023. doi:10.1016/j.promfg.2019.02.316

Sang, J., Gao, Y., Bao, B. K., Snoek, C., & Dai, Q. (2016). Recent advances in social multimedia big data mining and applications. *Multimedia Systems, 22*(1), 1-3.

Satish, L., & Yusof, N. (2017). A Review: Big Data Analytics for enhanced Customer Experiences with Crowd Sourcing. *Procedia Computer Science, 116*, 274–283. doi:10.1016/j.procs.2017.10.058

Sawadogo, P., Kibata, T., & Darmont, J. (2019). *Metadata management for textual documents in data lakes*. Paper presented at the 21st International Conference on Enterprise Information Systems (ICEIS 2019), Heraklion, Greece. 10.5220/0007706300720083

Sawadogo, P., Scholly, É., Favre, C., Ferey, É., Loudcher, S., & Darmont, J. (2019). Metadata Systems for Data Lakes: Models and Features. In T. Welzer, J. Eder, V. Podgorelec, R. Wrembel, M. Ivanović, J. Gamper, M. Morzy, T. Tzouramanis, J. Darmont, & A. Latifić (Eds.), *New Trends in Databases and Information Systems. ADBIS 2019. Communications in Computer and Information Science* (Vol. 1064, pp. 440–451). Springer. doi:10.1007/978-3-030-30278-8_43

Schäffer, T., & Leyh, C. (2017). Master Data Quality in the Era of Digitization - Toward Inter-organizational Master Data Quality in Value Networks: A Problem Identification. In F. Piazolo, V. Geist, L. Brehm, & R. Schmidt (Eds.), *Innovations in Enterprise Information Systems Management and Engineering. ERP Future 2016. Lecture Notes in Business Information Processing* (Vol. 285, pp. 99–113). Springer. doi:10.1007/978-3-319-58801-8_9

Schonlau, M., & Yuyan Zou, R. (2020). The Random Forest Algorithm for Statistical Learning. *The Stata Journal, 20*(1), 3–29. doi:10.1177/1536867X20909688

Sen, M. (2019). *Application of Artificial Intelligence in Business*. Retrieved from https://www.fastnewsfeed.com/technology/application-of-artificial-intelligence-in-business/

Şen, E., Körük, E., Serper, N., & Çalış Uslu, B. (2019). Big Data Analytics and Simulation for Better Strategic Management. *Journal of Current Research on Engineering. Science and Technology*, *5*(2), 1–12.

Setyono, A., & Setiadi, D. R. I. M. (2019). Securing and Hiding Secret Message in Image using XOR Transposition Encryption and LSB Method. *Journal of Physics: Conference Series*, *1196*, 012039. doi:10.1088/1742-6596/1196/1/012039

Shadroo, S., & Rahmani, A. M. (2018). Systematic survey of big data and data mining in internet of things. *Computer Networks*, *139*, 19–47. doi:10.1016/j.comnet.2018.04.001

Shams, S., & Solima, L. (2019). Big data management: Implications of dynamic capabilities and data incubator. *Management Decision*, *57*(8), 2113–2123. doi:10.1108/MD-07-2018-0846

Shankaranarayanan, G. (2005). Towards implementing total data quality management in a datawarehouse. *Journal of Information Technology Management*, *16*(1), 21–30.

Shankaranarayanan, G., & Cai, Y. (2006). Supporting data quality management in decision-making. *Decision Support Systems*, *42*(1), 302–317. doi:10.1016/j.dss.2004.12.006

Sharda, R., Delen, D., & Turban, E. (2018). *Business Intelligence, Analytics, and Data Science: a Managerial Perspective* (4th ed.). Upper Saddle River, NJ: Pearson Education, Inc.

Shengdong, M., Zhengxian, X., & Yixiang, T. (2019). Intelligent Traffic Control System Based on Cloud Computing and Big Data Mining. *IEEE Transactions on Industrial Informatics*, *15*(12), 6583–6592. doi:10.1109/TII.2019.2929060

Shen, Y. D., Zhang, Z., & Yang, Q. (2002). Objective-Oriented utility-based association mining. *Proceedings of the IEEE International Conference on Data Mining*, 426–433.

Shuai, H., MingChao, L., QiuBing, R., & ChengZhao, L. (2018). Intelligent determination and data mining for tectonic settings of basalts based on big data methods. *Yanshi Xuebao*, *34*(11), 3207–3216.

Singh, S., & Yassine, A. (2018). Big data mining of energy time series for behavioral analytics and energy consumption forecasting. *Energies*, *11*(2), 452.

Sitarska-Buba, M., & Zygala, R. (2020). Data lake: Strategic challenges for small and medium sized enterprises. In M. Hernes, A. Rot, & D. Jelonek (Eds.), *Towards Industry 4.0-current challenges in information systems. Lecture Notes in Computational Intelligence* (Vol. 887, pp. 183–200). Springer. doi:10.1007/978-3-030-40417-8_11

Song, C. W., Jung, H., & Chung, K. (2019). Development of a medical big-data mining process using topic modeling. *Cluster Computing*, *22*(1), 1949–1958. doi:10.100710586-017-0942-0

Song, G. Y., Cheon, Y., Lee, K., Park, K. M., & Rim, H. C. (2014). Inter-category Map: Building Cognition Network of General Customers through Big Data Mining. *Transactions on Internet and Information Systems (Seoul)*, *8*(2).

Spirtes, P., Glymour, C., & Scheines, R. (2000). *Causation* (2nd ed.). Prediction, and Search.

Srinivasan, S. (2019). *Data Driven Culture*. Retrieved from https://storybydata.com/datacated-challenge/data-driven-culture/

Srivastava, D. (2013, December). Big data integration. In *Proceedings of the 19th International Conference on Management of Data* (pp. 3-3). Computer Society of India.

Stang, J., Hartvigsen, T., & Reitan, J. (2010). The Effect of Data Quality on Data Mining – Improving Prediction Accuracy by Generic Data Cleansing. *Proceedings of the 2010 International Conference on Information Quality.*

Statista, Top benefits that companies realize through the use of data and analytics worldwide as of 2019. (2020). Retrieved from https://www.statista.com/statistics/895263/worldwide-barriers-effective-data-analytics-use/

Statistica. (2020). Retrieved May 9, 2020 from: https://www.statista.com/statistics/871513/worldwide-data-created/#statisticContainer

Strohmeier, S., & Piazza, F. (2013). Domain driven Data Mining in human resource management: A review of current research. *Journal of Expert Systems with Applications, 40*(7), 2410–2420. doi:10.1016/j.eswa.2012.10.059

Štrukelj, T., Mulej, M., & Zabukovšek, S. (2020). Socially Responsible Culture and Personal Values as Organizational Competitiveness Factors. In Z. Nedelko & M. Brzozowski (Eds.), *Recent Advances in the Roles of Cultural and Personal Values in Organizational Behavior* (pp. 81–101). IGI Global. doi:10.4018/978-1-7998-1013-1.ch005

Stuart, Rosales, & Signorotti. (2015). Algorithmic Trading of Cryptocurrency Based on Twitter Sentiment Analysis. *CS229 Project*, 1–5.

Stubseid, S., & Arandjelovic, O. (2018). Machine Learning Based Prediction of Consumer Purchasing Decisions: The Evidence and Its Significance. *Proceedings of AI and Marketing Science workshop at AAAI-2018.* Retrieved March 9, 2020, from https://core.ac.uk/download/pdf/158368656.pdf

Sundararaman, A. (2012). *Information Quality Strategy - an Empirical Investigation of the Relationship Between Information Quality Improvements and Organizational Outcomes* (Unpublished Ph.D. Thesis). Birla Institute of Technology and Science, India.

Sundararaman, A. Kandasamy, P., & Raji, D. (2018). Data Science Techniques To Improve accuracy of Provider Network Directory. *IEEE 25th International Conference on High Performance Computing Workshops (HiPCW)*, 119-128

Sundararaman, A. (2011.) A framework for linking Data Quality to business objectives in decision support systems. *3rd International Conference on Trendz in Information Sciences and Computing*, 177-181. 10.1109/TISC.2011.6169110

Sun, Z., Sun, L., & Strang, K. (2018). Big data analytics services for enhancing business intelligence. *Journal of Computer Information Systems, 58*(2), 162–169. doi:10.1080/08874417.2016.1220239

Sun, Z., Zou, H., & Strang, K. (2015). Big Data Analytics as a Service for Business Intelligence. *14th Conference on e-Business, e-Services and e-Society (I3E)*, 200-211. 10.1007/978-3-319-25013-7_16

Suoniemi, S., Meyer-Waarden, L., & Munzel, A. (2017). Big Data Resources, Marketing Capabilities, and Firm Performance. In *2017 Winter AMA Conference*. American Marketing Association.

Suriarachchi, I., & Plale, B. (2016). *Crossing Analytics Systems: A Case for Integrated Provenance in Data Lakes.* Paper presented at the 12th International Conference on e-Science (e-Science), Baltimore, MD.

Swain, G. (2018). *High Capacity Image Steganography Using Modified LSB Substitution and PVD against Pixel Difference Histogram Analysis.* Security and Computer Networks. doi:10.1155/2018/1505896

Swan, M. Chapter Five - Blockchain for Business: Next-Generation Enterprise Artificial Intelligence Systems. In P. Raj & G. C. Deka (Eds.), *Advances in Computers, Blockchain Technology: Platforms, Tools and Use Cases* (pp. 121–162). Elsevier. https://www.sciencedirect.com/science/article/pii/S0065245818300287.2018

Symeonidis, A., Athanasiadis, I. N., & Mitkas, P. A. (2007). A retraining methodology for enhancing agent intelligence. *Journal of Knowledge-Based Systems, 20*(4), 388–396. doi:10.1016/j.knosys.2006.06.003

Taha, M. S., Rahim, M. S. M., Lafta, S. A., Hashim, M. A., & Alzuabidi, H. M. (2019). Combination of Steganography and Cryptography: A Short Survey. *ICSET*, *2019*, 052003. Advance online publication. doi:10.1088/1757-899X/518/5/052003

Taleb, M. A. S., & Dssouli, R. (2018). Big Data Quality: A Survey. *2018 IEEE International Congress on Big Data (Big Data Congress)*, 166-173. 10.1109/BigDataCongress.2018.00029

Talend Data Fabric. (2020, August 22). *A single, unified platform for modern data integration and management.* https://www.talend.com/products/data-fabric/

Tan, P., Kumar, V., & Srivastava, J. (2002). Selecting the right interestingness measure for association patterns. *Proceedings of the 8th International Conference on Knowledge Discovery and Data Mining*, 32–41. 10.1145/775047.775053

Tech Wire Asia. (2019). *Augmented analytics to simplify acquiring business intelligence.* Retrieved from https://techwireasia.com/2019/02/augmented-analytics-to-simplify-acquiring-business-intelligence/

Teixeira de Azevedo, M., Martins, A. B., & Kofuji, S. T. (2019). Digital Transformation in the Utilities Industry: Industry 4.0 and the Smart Network Water. In L. Ferreira, N. Lopes, J. Silva, G. Putnik, M. Cruz-Cunha, & P. Ávila (Eds.), *Technological Developments in Industry 4.0 for Business Applications* (pp. 304–330). IGI Global. doi:10.4018/978-1-5225-4936-9.ch013

Terrizzano, I., Schwarz, P., Roth, M., & Colino, J. E. (2015). *Data Wrangling: The Challenging Yourney from the Wild to the Lake.* Paper presented at the 7th Biennial Conference on Innovative Data Systems Research (CIDR '15), Asilomar, CA.

Thai, P., & Lee, S. (2016). *Anomaly Detection in the Bitcoin System-a Network Perspective.* arXiv preprint arXiv:1611.03942

Thyssenkrupp Elevator, A. (2020). *MAX: the game changer.* Retrieved 04 May, 2020, from https://www.thyssenkrupp-elevator.com/en/max/

Tomcy, J., & Pankaj, M. (2017). *Data Lake for Enterprises.* Packt Publishing Ltd.

Triguero, I., Garcıa-Gil, D., Maillo, J., Luengo, J., Garc'ıa, S., & Herrera, F. (2019). Transforming big data into smart data: An insight on the use of the k-nearest neighbors algorithm to obtain quality data. *Wiley Interdisciplinary Reviews. Data Mining and Knowledge Discovery*, *9*(2), 9. doi:10.1002/widm.1289

Tsai, C. F., Lin, W. C., & Ke, S. W. (2016). Big data mining with parallel computing: A comparison of distributed and MapReduce methodologies. *Journal of Systems and Software*, *122*, 83–92. doi:10.1016/j.jss.2016.09.007

Tsamardinos, I., & Aliferis, C. (2002). Towards principled feature selection: Relevancy, filters and wrappers. *Proceedings of the Ninth International Workshop on Artificial Intelligence and Statistics.*

Tsamardinos, I., Aliferis, C. F., & Statnikov, A. (2003). Time and sample efficient discovery of markov blankets and direct causal relations. *Proceedings of the Ninth ACM SIGKDD International Conference on Knowl- edge Discovery and Data Mining*, *3*, 673–678.

Tsamardinos, I., Borboudakis, G., Katsogridakis, P., Pratikakis, P., & Christophides, V. (2018). A greedy feature selection algorithm for big data of high dimensionality. *Machine Learning*, 108. PMID:30906113

Tsamardinos, I., Brown, L., & Aliferis, C. (2006). The max-min hill-climbing bayesian network structure learning algorithm. *Machine Learning*, *65*(1), 31–78. doi:10.100710994-006-6889-7

Turban, E., Sharda, R., & Delen, D. (2011). *Decision support and Business Intelligence.* Pearson Education.

Uphindia Ind. (2019). *Augmented analytics will be next big disruptor: Gartner.* Retrieved from https://uphindia.com/2019/03/24/augmented-analytics-will-be-next-big-disruptor-gartner/

Van Engelen, J. E., & Hoos, H. H. (2020). A Survey on Semi-Supervised Learning. *Machine Learning, 109*(2), 373–440. doi:10.100710994-019-05855-6

Vercellis, C. (2009). *Business Intelligence: Data Mining and Optimization for Decision Making*. West Sussex, UK: John Wiley and Sons.

Volpato, T., Rufino, R. R., & Dias, J. W. (2014). *Big Data – Transformando Dados em Decisões*. University of Paranaense.

Von Leipzig, T., Gamp, M., Manz, D., Schöttle, K., Ohlhausen, P., Oosthuizen, G., Palm, D., & von Leipzig, K. (2017). Initialising customer-orientated digital transformation in enterprises. *Procedia Manufacturing, 8,* 517–524. doi:10.1016/j.promfg.2017.02.066

Vujičić, D., Jagodić, D., & Randjić, S. (2018). Blockchain Technology, Bitcoin, and Ethereum: A Brief Overview. In *2018 17th International Symposium Infoteh-Jahorina (Infoteh)*. IEEE. 10.1109/INFOTEH.2018.8345547

Walls, C., & Barnard, B. (2020). Success Factors of Big Data to Achieve Organisational Performance: Qualitative Research. *Expert Journal of Business and Management, 8*(1), 17–56.

Wang, H., & Wang, S. (2008). A Knowledge Management Approach to Data Mining Process for Business Intelligence. *Industrial Management & Data Systems, 108*(5), 622–634. doi:10.1108/02635570810876750

Wang, M., Gu, W., & Ma, C. (2020). A Multimode Network Steganography for Covert Wireless Communication based on BitTorrent. *Security and Communication Networks*. Advance online publication. doi:10.1155/2020/8848315

Wang, S., & Wang, H. (2011). *Mining data quality in completeness*. University of Massachusetts.

Wang, S., & Yuan, H. (2014). Spatial data mining: A perspective of big data. *International Journal of Data Warehousing and Mining, 10*(4), 50–70. doi:10.4018/ijdwm.2014100103

Wang, Y., Kung, L., & Byrd, T. A. (2018). Big data analytics: Understanding its capabilities and potential benefits for healthcare organizations. *Technological Forecasting and Social Change, 126*, 3–13. doi:10.1016/j.techfore.2015.12.019

Weber, M., Domeniconi, G., Chen, J., Weidele, D. K. I., Bellei, C., Robinson, T., & Leiserson, C. E. (2019). *Anti-Money Laundering in Bitcoin: Experimenting with Graph Convolutional Networks for Financial Forensics*. KDD '19 Workshop on Anomaly Detection in Finance, Anchorage, AK.

Weber, I., Xu, X., Riveret, R., Governatori, G., Ponomarev, A., & Mendling, J. (2016). Untrusted Business Process Monitoring and Execution Using Blockchain. In M. La Rosa, P. Loos, & O. Pastor (Eds.), *Business Process Management* (pp. 329–347). Lecture Notes in Computer Science. Springer International Publishing. doi:10.1007/978-3-319-45348-4_19

Wixon, B., & Watson, H. (2010). The BI-Based Organization. *International Journal of Business Intelligence Research, 1*(1), 13–28. doi:10.4018/jbir.2010071702

Woodall, P., & Parlikad, A. (2010). A hybrid approach to assessing data quality. *Proceedings of the 15th International Conference on Information Quality*.

Wu, X., Zhu, X., Wu, G. Q., & Ding, W. (2014). Data mining with big data. *IEEE Transactions on Knowledge and Data Engineering, 26*(1), 97–107. doi:10.1109/TKDE.2013.109

Xuegang, H., Zhou, P., Li, P., Wang, J., & Wu, X. (2017). A survey on online feature selection with streaming features. *Frontiers of Computer Science*, 1–15.

Xu, L., Jiang, C., Chen, Y., Wang, J., & Ren, Y. (2016). A framework for categorizing and applying privacy-preservation techniques in big data mining. *Computer, 49*(2), 54–62. doi:10.1109/MC.2016.43

Xu, L., Jiang, C., Wang, J., Yuan, J., & Ren, Y. (2014). Information security in big data: Privacy and data mining. *IEEE Access : Practical Innovations, Open Solutions, 2,* 1149–1176.

Xu, L., Jiang, C., Wang, J., Yuan, J., & Ren, Y. (2014). Information security in big data: Privacy and data mining. *IEEE Access: Practical Innovations, Open Solutions, 2,* 1149–1176. doi:10.1109/ACCESS.2014.2362522

Yang, S., Wang, H., & Hu, X. (2019). *Efficient local causal discovery based on Markov blanket.* Academic Press.

Yang, H., & Simon, F. (2009). A Framework of Business Intelligence-Driven Data Mining for E-business. *Fifth International Joint Conference on INC, IMS and IDC.*

Yang, Q., & Wu, X. (2006). 10 challenging problems in Data Mining research. *International Journal of Information Technology & Decision Making, 5*(4), 597–604. doi:10.1142/S0219622006002258

Yang, T., Xie, J., Li, G., Mou, N., Li, Z., Tian, C., & Zhao, J. (2019). Social Media Big Data Mining and Spatio-Temporal Analysis on Public Emotions for Disaster Mitigation. *ISPRS International Journal of Geo-Information, 8*(1), 29. doi:10.3390/ijgi8010029

Yermish, I., Miori, V., Yi, J., Malhotra, R., & Klimberg, R. (2010). Business Plus intelligence Plus technology equals Business intelligence. *International Journal of Business Intelligence Research, 1*(1), 48–63. doi:10.4018/jbir.2010071704

Yu, D., Xu, Z., & Wang, W. (2018). Bibliometric analysis of fuzzy theory research in China: A 30-year perspective. *Knowledge-Based Systems, 141,* 188–199. doi:10.1016/j.knosys.2017.11.018

Yu, W. (2017). Challenges and Reflections of Big Data Mining Based on Mobile Internet Customers. *Agro Food Industry Hi-Tech, 28*(1), 3221–3224.

Zambre, D., & Shah, A. (2013). *Analysis of Bitcoin Network Dataset for Fraud.* Unpublished Report 27.

Zeller, J. (2007, May 8). *Business Intelligence: The Chicken or the Egg.* Retrieved February 15, 2009, from BI Review magazine: https://www.information-management.com/bissues/20070601/2600340-1.html

Zenati, A., Ouarda, W., & Alimi, A. M. (2019). SSDIS-BEM: A New Signature Steganography Document Image System based on Beta Elliptic Modeling. *Engineering Science and Technology, an International Journal, 23*(3), 470-482.

Zhang, H., & Zhang, Z. (2019). Research on the Big Data Cloud Computing Based on the Network Data Mining. In Basic & Clinical Pharmacology & Toxicology (Vol. 124, pp. 150-151). Wiley.

Zhang, X., Jang-Jaccard, J., Qi, L., Bhuiyan, M. Z., & Liu, C. (2018). Privacy Issues in Big Data Mining Infrastructure, Platforms, and Applications. *Security and Communication Networks, 2018,* 1–3. doi:10.1155/2018/6238607

Zhang, Y. B. (2019). Application of the Data Mining Technology in the Financial Management of Colleges and Universities in the Age of the Big Data. *Basic & Clinical Pharmacology & Toxicology, 124*(3), 143–143.

Zhang, Y., Guo, S. L., Han, L. N., & Li, T. L. (2016). Application and exploration of big data mining in clinical medicine. *Chinese Medical Journal, 129*(6), 731–738. doi:10.4103/0366-6999.178019 PMID:26960378

Zhu, D. (2016). Big data-based multimedia transcoding method and its application in multimedia data mining-based smart transportation and telemedicine. *Multimedia Tools and Applications, 75*(24), 17647–17668. doi:10.100711042-016-3466-3

Zhu, J., Ge, Z., Song, Z., & Gao, F. (2018). Review and big data perspectives on robust data mining approaches for industrial process modeling with outliers and missing data. *Annual Reviews in Control, 46,* 107–133. doi:10.1016/j.arcontrol.2018.09.003

Zhu, L., Li, M., Zhang, Z., Du, X., & Guizani, M. (2018). Big data mining of users' energy consumption patterns in the wireless smart grid. *IEEE Wireless Communications*, 25(1), 84–89. doi:10.1109/MWC.2018.1700157

Zhu, X., & Davidson, I. (2007). *Knowledge Discovery and Data Mining: Challenges and Realities*. IGI Global. doi:10.4018/978-1-59904-252-7

Zikopoulos, P., & Eaton, C. (2011). *Understanding big data: Analytics for enterprise class hadoop and streaming data*. McGraw-Hill Osborne Media.

About the Contributors

Ana Azevedo is an Integrated member of CEOS.PP research center and was a member of its Directive Board. She is a senior lecture in the Information Systems Department, School of Business / Polytechnic of Porto, Porto, Portugal, teaching courses on E-Commerce, Decision Support Systems, Business Intelligence, and Research Methodologies. She holds a PhD in Information Systems and Technologies, University of Minho, Portugal. She is member of the Scientific Board of the Master in E-Business. She published several articles in journals, conferences, and book chapters. She is associate editor of the International Journal of Technology and Human Interaction (IJTHI). She is a member of the Editorial Review Board of the International Journal of Decision Support System Technology (IJDSST), of the International Journal of Business Intelligence Research (IJBIR), of the International Journal of Grid and Utility Computing (IJGUC), of the Electronic Journal of e-Learning (EJEL), and of the International Journal of Systems and Society (IJSS). She is chair of several conferences and special sessions in conferences. She served as editor for several books and special issues in journals. She regularly serves as member of the program committee for several conferences and also serves as a regular reviewer for several journals and conferences. She as several publications in Scientific Journals, Conferences and other. Her primary areas of research interests are Business Intelligence, Analytics, Decision Support Systems, Data mining, E-Business and Digital Transformation. Her research interests also include e assessment and gender issues in information systems research and STEM.

* * *

Walisson Carvalho graduated in Computer Science from the Pontifical Catholic University of Minas Gerais and a master's degree in Public Administration from the João Pinheiro Foundation. PhD student in course at the Pontifical Catholic University of Minas Gerais in the area of Machine Learning and Data Mining. Specialist in Training of Trainers and also in Teaching and Learning In Higher Education both from the University of Tampere (UTA) Tampere / Finland.

Mohammad Daradkeh is an Associate Professor of Business Analytics and Information Systems in the Faculty of Information Technology and computer Sciences, Yarmouk University. Before joining Yarmouk University, Dr. Daradkeh has been working as a Lecturer in the Department of Informatics and Enabling Technologies at Lincoln University, New Zealand for two years. He received his PhD in Software and Information Technology from Lincoln University, New Zealand, and MSc. and BSc. in Computer Science from Yarmouk University, Jordan. His research interests lie primarily in the areas of Business Intelligence and Analytics, Visual Analytics, Decision Support Systems, and Uncertainty and

Risk Management. He is currently teaching in undergraduate and graduate courses related to Decision Support systems, Business Intelligence and Analytics, Software Project Management, and Data Analytics. Dr. Daradkeh has published in Int. J. of Decision and Information Sciences, Int. J. of Business Information Systems, Int. J. of Decision Support Systems Technology, Journal of Organizational and End User Computing, Information Technology and People, and Int. J. of Information Systems in the Service Sector.

Ahmed El Oualkadi is a full professor at the department of information and communication systems at the National school of applied sciences of Tangier, Abdelmalek Essaadi University in Morocco. His research interests include electronics, wireless communications, embedded system applications and information theory.

Abdelaziz Elbaghdadi is a PhD student at the Laboratory of Information and Communication Technologies (LabTIC) at the National school of applied sciences of Tangier, Abdelmalek Essaadi University in Morocco. His research interests include mathematics, Data analysis and security.

Mangesh M. Ghonge is currently working as Assistant Professor at Sandip Institute of Technology and Research Centre, Nashik (MS), India. He received his BE, MTech degree in Computer Science & Engineering from SGBAU, Amravati and RTMNU, Nagpur respectively. He completed his PhD from SGBAU, Amravati on topic "Assignment based Selfish Node detection System in Mobile Ad hoc Networks". His more than 30 research papers published in various International journals including Scopus indexed journal. He has presented research paper in IEEE conferences at Singapore, Malaysia, also presented more than 10 papers in IEEE conferences. He has invited as resource person in many workshop/seminars/FDP. His 02 patent are published by Indian Patent office. He has also contributed in Board of Studies, Computer Science & Engineering of Sandip University, Nashik as a Member. His research interest includes security in wireless networks, Ad-Hoc networks, and network protocols. Also includes implementation of open source software. He acquired knowledge in sciences/skills that covers areas of Computer Science, Networking, Databases and Programming, and more. He is member of CSI, IACSIT, IAENG, IETE and CSTA.

Ramkrishna Ghosh is an Assistant Professor in Information Technology of Haldia Institute Of Technology and a Ph.D. Scholar in the School of Computer Engineering of KIIT Deemed to be University. He has 13 years of experience as an Assistant professor, Lecturer, Software Faculty as well as a Software Developer. He has published papers in 15 international Journals and 3 conferences. Apart from this has authored 6 engineering books. His research interests include Wireless Sensor Network, Cryptography, Soft Computing, Steganography, Image Processing etc. He has travelled all over India through his teaching only.

Roumiana Ilieva is Associate Professor in Automated Systems for Data Processing and Management, Dept. Management and Business Information Systems, Faculty of Management (FM), Technical University of Sofia MEng in Automation, MA in Economics: University of Delaware, USA, PhD in Engineering (Automation). Specializes and teaches in the fields of Business Intelligence (BI) & eGovernance at the Universities of Amsterdam and The Hague (2007), Lancaster (Infolab21, 2008, 2017), Southampton Solent (2010, 2013), Westminster and UCL, London (2009, 2011), Portsmouth (2016, 2018, 2019), UK; Otto-von-Guericke-Universität Magdeburg (2013); Universidad Publica de Navarra,

Pamplona, Spain (2015); eXchange Security, Donau-Universität Krems, Austria, (2011); Space Challenges, Association Tsiolkovsky (2010-2012), etc. Major areas of research and teaching: Heterogeneous Intelligent Systems (AI, ML, BI), Robotic Process Automation (RPA), etc. Author of over 100 scientific publications. Member of IEEE: Computer Society; Robotics and Automation Society; Systems, Man, and Cybernetics Society; SAP University Alliances; National Key Expert at the Scientific-Technical Union of Mechanical Engineering (STUME) in Automated Systems, IT & ERP; Computer Science Expert in Machine Building, Biomechanics and Robotics at Fidweb/SoCourt Ltd., Berlin /Innovative Products Development/; PC member of JeDEM and CeDEM & Asia '11-20, Austria, IEETeL'20, Italy, etc.

Malinka Ivanova is an Associate Professor in Communications and Computer Science, scientific specialty "Automation of engineering work and automated design systems". She specializes in computer science (Internet technology, applied computer graphics, multimedia, cryptographic methods and information protection, E-learning, Micro/Nanotechnologies) at the Tokyo Institute of Technology, Goethe University of Frankfurt am Main, Academy of Sciences of Slovakia, Technical University of Bratislava. She has received short-term trainings in the field of e-learning in Bled, Slovenia; Innsbruck, Austria, and Frejus, France. She is a member of the Union of Automation and Informatics and the Union of Electronics Electriotechnics and Communications.

Atik Kulakli is an Associate Professor of Management Information Systems at the American University of the Middle East, Kuwait. He received his bachelor's (BA) degree in management from Dokuz Eylul University. He had two master's degrees. MSc degree from the Management Engineering Department of Istanbul Technical University and an MA degree in Information Studies from University College London (UCL). He received a Ph.D. degree from Istanbul Technical University. His research interests include management information systems, technology management, internet-mobile technologies, supply chain-operations management, blockchain, educational technologies (e-learning, e-university), and its applications. He had a professional career in managing positions for industries such as Pharmaceutical, Telecommunication, Internet Service Provider, Contact, and Call Center, and he has consultancy experience in business management areas before joining academia. He has professional association memberships, conference and symposium organization committee responsibilities in editorial boards, scientific committees, and conference session chairs. He is a reviewer for leading scientific journals and book chapters, including Journal of Medical Internet Research, Online Information Review, Information Discovery and Delivery, IGI Global Book Project; various academic conferences including IEEE ICIM 2020, IEEE ICEMIS 2017, ISPR 2005 to 2020, ICBDB 2019-2020, MLMI 2019-2020, CLSB 2020.

Soufiane Mezroui is an Assistant professor at the department of information and communication systems at the National school of applied sciences of Tangier, Abdelmalek Essaadi University in Morocco. His research interests include Applied mathematics, computer science and information theory.

Vipul Narayan is currently working as a Research cum Teaching Fellow in the Department of Computer Science and Engineering, M.M.M. University of Technology, Gorakhpur and has three years of teaching experience. He has received his Master's Degree from M.M.M.U.T, Gorakhpur in 2016. He has received B.Tech degree from M.D.U. Rohtak in 2012. He has published 16 papers in National and International conferences. His research interests include Wireless Sensor Network protocols.

Yoto Nikolov is Director, Network and Information Security, Ministry of Finance. A result-driven, experienced system security architect. Proofed leadership management skills, currently responsible for the security operations of 8 000 users. Possesses a master's degree in E-Government and IT Security. PhD student in "Automated Systems for Data Processing and Management" at the PhD School at French Faculty of Electrical Engineering, Technical University of Sofia. His PhD research is focused on AI-based models and data automation for cybersecurity optimization. More than 4 years of executive leadership, system integration and risk management experience across both law enforcement and financial sectors. More than 7 years' experience in IT, network architecture, cryptography and classified security activities. Founder of ASRSolutions LTD for specialized security systems and cyber warfare.

Digvijay Pandey is a Lecturer in the Department of Technical Education, Research Scholar IET Lucknow, Dr A.P.J Abdul Kalam Technical University, India.

Tzvetilina Peycheva is Head of the Business Analytics Team, IBS Bulgaria. In-depth knowledge and experience in projects related to data analysis, business intelligence systems, data warehouse architectures, data integration, data manipulation and analysis. PhD student in "Automated Systems for Data Processing and Management" at the PhD School at French Faculty of Electrical Engineering, Technical University of Sofia.

Carlos Filipe Portela went to the University of Minho in Guimarães, where he studied information system and obtained his degree in 2007 (Lic), 2009 (MSc) and 2013 (PhD). He holds a PhD in Information Systems and Technologies. He belongs to the Research Centre ALGORITMI where he is developing his work in the topic "Pervasive Intelligent Decision Support Systems". His research was started in the INTCare R&D project being then extended to education and public administration areas. He already has relevant indexed publications in the main research topics: Intelligent Decision Support Systems, Intelligent Systems, Pervasive Data, Business Intelligence, Data Mining and Knowledge Discovery. He has also been co-organizer of several workshops and reviewer of many indexed journals and conferences in these topics. Currently he also is an Invited Assistant Professor of the Information Systems Department, School of Engineering, University of Minho, Portugal, where he has been supervising several master students in the areas above mentioned and a Guest Lecturer in Porto Polytechnic - ESEIG. He is always in a continuing looking for opportunities to research and innovation in the society.

Sabyasachi Pramanik is an Assistant Professor in the Department of Computer Science and Engineering, Haldia Institute of Technology, India. He has published various journals including SCI/Scopus. He is an active reviewer in many international journals of IEEE/Springer/Elsevier/Inderscience and IGI Global. He is a member of the editorial board in many journals. He is a professional member of various organizations. His research interests include Data Hiding, Network Security and Machine Learning.
Debabrata Samanta is a Professional IEEE Member, an Associate Life Member of Computer Society Of India (CSI), and a Life Member of the Indian Society for Technical Education (ISTE). He obtained his B.Sc. (Physics Honors), from Calcutta University; Kolkata, India. He obtained his MCA, from the Academy of Technology, under WBUT, West Bengal. He obtained his Ph.D. in Computer Science and Engg. from the National Institute of Technology, Durgapur, India, in the area of SAR Image Processing. His areas of interest are Artificial Intelligence, Natural Language Processing, and Image Processing. He is presently working as Assistant Professor, Department of Computer Science, CHRIST (Deemed to be

University), Bangalore, India. He is the owner of 16 Indian Patents. He has authored and coauthored over 129 papers in SCI / SCOPUS / SPRINGER / ELSEVIER Journals and IEEE / Springer /Elsevier Conference proceedings in areas of Artificial Intelligence, Natural Language Processing and Image Processing. He has authored in Springer Nature also. He has received the "Scholastic Award" at the 2nd International Conference on Computer Science and IT application, CSIT-2011, Delhi, India. He has published 9 books, available for sale on Amazon and Flipkart. He has edited 1 book available on the GOOGLE BOOK server. He has authored and coauthored 2 Elsevier and 5 Springer Book Chapter. He is a Convener, Keynote speaker, Technical Programme Committee (TPC) member in various conferences/ workshops, etc. He was an invited speaker at several Institutions.

Mudita Sinha is currently associated with Christ University as Faculty of Marketing. She has completed her PhD, Masters in Marketing Management and MBA. Dr Sinha is an experienced researcher, faculty and salesperson with proven abilities. She is a competent professional with over 12 years of combined experience in Industry, Business Education, Institutional Affairs & administrative functions. Dr Sinha has published several articles in various National and International Journals of repute in Marketing and General Management. To keep her knowledge updated and deliver best quality she participates and presents research articles in different National and International level conferences.

Luis E. Zárate received the M.S. and Dr. degrees from the Federal University of Minas Gerais, Brazil in 1992 and 1998, respectively. He received the B.S. degree in Electronics Engineering in 1981 from URP, Perú . Since 1992 he holds research and professor position at Pontifical Catholic University of Minas Gerais, Brazil. Professor Zárate has a research interest in Data Mining and Machine Learning, Formal Concept Analysis, Soft Computing. He is a scientific coordinator of the Applied Computational Intelligence Laboratory – LICAP and is responsible for several research projects supported by governmental organizations in Brazil.

Index

Ensure Quality Research is Introduced to the Academic Community

Become an IGI Global Reviewer for Authored Book Projects

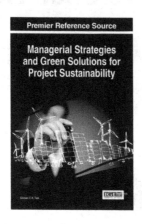

The overall success of an authored book project is dependent on quality and timely reviews.

In this competitive age of scholarly publishing, constructive and timely feedback significantly expedites the turnaround time of manuscripts from submission to acceptance, allowing the publication and discovery of forward-thinking research at a much more expeditious rate. Several IGI Global authored book projects are currently seeking highly-qualified experts in the field to fill vacancies on their respective editorial review boards:

Applications and Inquiries may be sent to:
development@igi-global.com

Applicants must have a doctorate (or an equivalent degree) as well as publishing and reviewing experience. Reviewers are asked to complete the open-ended evaluation questions with as much detail as possible in a timely, collegial, and constructive manner. All reviewers' tenures run for one-year terms on the editorial review boards and are expected to complete at least three reviews per term. Upon successful completion of this term, reviewers can be considered for an additional term.

If you have a colleague that may be interested in this opportunity,
we encourage you to share this information with them.

Printed in the United States
By Bookmasters